Towards participatory social policy

Peter Beresford

First published in Great Britain in 2016 by

Policy Press
University of Bristol
1-9 Old Park Hill
Bristol
BS2 8BB
UK
t: +44 (0)117 954 5940
pp-info@bristol.ac.uk
www.policypress.co.uk

North America office:
Policy Press
c/o The University of Chicago Press
1427 East 60th Street
Chicago, IL 60637, USA
t: +1 773 702 7700
f: +1 773-702-9756
sales@press.uchicago.edu
www.press.uchicago.edu

Contents

List of photographs and sources

Foreword

Yasmin Alibhai-Brown, journalist and author

Ours is an age of rage, miserliness, crudity and startling ignorance. Seventy years ago, although Britons were exhausted and depleted by barbarous world wars, they were generous, idealistic, hungry for education and collectivist. That past and our present didn't just happen. Politics, policies and national conversations make, change and manipulate public attitudes, sometimes to prepare the ground for major ideological or economic remodelling .

After the two world wars, the poor and working classes would, in time, have wearily returned to the old, unjust status quo. In 1945, before this fatalism set in, while the wounds and horrifying memories were still fresh, the Labour government tapped into and drew on the nation's anguish and insecurities as it embarked on reconstruction and radical change. The people were primed, made ready for the welfare state. It, was, in effect, a quiet, very British, revolution. Without the pain of war, without astute politicking there would have been no gain.

Margaret Thatcher's counter revolution aimed to incapacitate this welfare state. Men and women, she believed, had obligations only to their own families. She wanted this nation to be like the USA, ultra competitive, avaricious, selfishly Darwinist. It took longer than the Thatcherites imagined, to get the mind shift in Britain, partly because social democracy was well embedded and generations had got used to free healthcare, education, social care, state help from cradle to grave. But the seeds sowed by Thatcher in the late 1970s, diligently watered and fertilised over the years, finally bore fruit. A growing number of Britons now think the welfare state is a tax burden and a disincentive to those who are lazy, dependent scroungers. In the last election, in May 2015, we witnessed internecine feuds between those on benefits, between indigenous and migrant families living in social housing, between various groups of low paid workers, and growing ethnic mistrust. Millions voted for a party which promised to starve and weaken the welfare state, in my view, the one achievement that made Britain truly great.

Why and when did taking care of each other as humans become contentious? When the powerful decided that is how we should think and behave. In the past decade, inequality has not only become more acceptable, it is now a divisive policy tool: the poor, migrants, lone parents, disabled people, have been demonised and left utterly vulnerable by politicians and right-wing journalists. They are the 'collateral damage', those who were unfit for survival in the jungle that is Great Britain.

This is why *All our Welfare* matters so very much. And why the author, Peter Beresford, deserves huge respect for daring to stand up against the storms of misplaced disaffection. He combines sensitivity with hard facts, is passionate yet scrupulously exact and evidence based, brings together activist fervour, personal stories, political understanding and academic research. Every page is infused with a sense of urgency. On page 1 he quotes the motto of the old borough of Battersea: 'Not for me, not for you, but for us'. We once knew how important this simple truth was. Not any more.

Ill informed and easily roused citizens seem not to understand that the foundations of modern Britain are being destroyed. They will realise what happened one day, when the ground beneath their feet seems shaky, their lives vulnerable and unstable. Too late.

Beresford isn't simply being a romantic nostalgic about post-war institutions and policies. He knows some reforms are urgently needed, particularly in the NHS, and makes thoughtful and excellent recommendations. But none of that can happen because social engineering has prepared the ground for destruction of the welfare state. An alternative narrative might wake people up before the apocalypse arrives. Beresford gives us a true historical account, a persuasive counter-narrative and a visionary modernised system. I have not read a more compelling defence of our fragile and perishing social democracy.

This is a handbook for politicians who hitherto have felt helpless as the juggernauts of the right move in and demolish all that is truly great in Great Britain.

December 2016

Dedication

This book is dedicated first to all those people whose struggles and suffering gave us the UK welfare state and to the children that they hoped would never have to live again as they had done – in poverty, insecurity, ill-health, unhappiness, division and squalor. It is also dedicated to all those who have fought to defend and advance all that is best about the welfare state.

Second, I want to dedicate it to my parents and my partner Suzy's parents, clearly without whom it would never have happened. In loving memory of William and Ida Beresford and Joan and John Croft with all our love and thanks. They lived through many of the troubles of the twentieth century.

Finally I must dedicate this book to Suzy, my partner, without whom none of what I have done would have been possible – and to our children and grandchildren – in whom hope for the future lies.

Acknowledgements

It is difficult to do justice to all the people who have helped me writing this book. I owe some an obvious debt; notably members of my family who kindly contributed their thoughts about the welfare state. Thank you. Also thanks to Ruth Beresford for reading through a draft and for her helpful comments and Peter Taylor-Gooby for his helpful advice on 'public opinion' and welfare. Thanks too to the constructive comments of the three reviewers, Nick Ellison, Iain Ferguson and Guy Daly, who read the manuscript and helped identify improvements.

There are also more distant debts. I owe my mother all that I learned from her experience of growing up in poverty in the East End, the only child of Jewish immigrants who had fled persecution, and the problems that trying to escape poverty left her with.

I owe a massive debt to all the disabled people, mental health service users/survivors and other service users I have worked with, learned from and made friends with. They have offered me and the world, new ways of seeing and our debt to them, especially those no longer with us, is incalculable. Thanks, particularly to everyone in *Shaping Our Lives*.

I want specifically to thank Maggie H. – who exemplified all that is best in a mental health professional – and all the psychiatric hospital staff who helped me, particularly the physio who gave me confidence, the male nurse who just sat and talked to us and the chaplain who treated us with kindness and respect – also to Harry Secombe for the kind and supportive letter he wrote to us. I want to thank especially my fellow patients, notably Maria, Pat, 'Dot', Ginny, Maureen and Kaiser. I'll never forget you.

I would like to thank the late A.H. Halsey and Olive Stevenson, my original PhD supervisors for the lessons I learned from them. There are three other academics I particularly want to thank too. All were a formative influence on me. First, C. Wright-Mills, whose *Sociological Imagination* (1959) helped me to understand sociology and thereby gain a better understanding of myself and the world I live in. As Wright-Mills said, crucially sociology enables us to make the connections between history and biography – between our lives and the forces acting on them. For me this insight into the intersections between the two was a light-bulb moment.

Second, David Matza; his book, *Becoming Deviant* demands that 'attention must be paid to the meaning which the individual – whether deviant or not – gives to his (sic) situation and behaviour' (Taylor, 1970). We need to 'appreciate' or understand people's viewpoints and behaviour, rather than seek to impose our theories or meanings on them.

Finally, Gareth Stedman Jones; his *Outcast London*, first published in 1971 was an inspiration to me in my first research on vagrancy. His preface to his second edition of 1984 and third edition of 2013 not only trace his journey, but also have shown the continuing and increasing relevance of his study both for our times and my work (Stedman Jones, 1971, 1984 and 2013).

I would also like to thank my fellow strugglers who have worked to advance the knowledge, experience and narratives of people on the receiving end of social policy. There are too many to name and I hope they will forgive me that I can only mention a few, including Mo Stewart, Louise Pembroke, Colin Barnes, Kathy Boxall and Jasna Russo.

One last thing I ought to say. This book was largely written in my spare time, without any grant support or as part of my paid job. In an academic world dominated by the Thatcherite 'research excellence framework' (REF) which is preoccupied with 'grant capture' getting articles published in supposedly more elite (and unread) 'peer reviewed [mainly commercial] journals', there is little space for undertaking a labour-intensive long-term task like this. I wrote this book because I was puzzled by and concerned about the increasing marginalisation of social policy when it is desperately important for so many lives. How could there be such a weak response to the depradations of neoliberal social policy? Why weren't more cogent alternatives being offered? I also wrote the book without a publisher or contract because I felt it had to be written. Usually what we are meant to do is write the books that publishers think will have a ready market and which fit their expectations. So I must offer a massive thanks to Alison Shaw and the Policy Press team for taking this book forward and publishing it as they have. I must also thank Konstantin Shlykov, of the Press Office of the Russian Embassy in London for the enormous help he gave me in tracing the origins of the photograph of my grandfather wearing his private's uniform in the Imperial Russian Army (http://oldvladikavkaz.livejournal.com/68794.html).

Finally I want to thank Suzy Croft. None of my work would have been possible without her as a partner. Much of the work that this book is rooted in was work that I did jointly with her. As a social work practitioner, committed to the people with whom she works, like many others, she has never gained the formal recognition that she deserves in spades. At least here I can make clear how much I and the work on which this book is based owe her, so that her place in the pantheon of work on participation and participatory practice can be more adequately recognised. Thank you Suzy.

Introduction: Owning not othering our welfare

I keep my ideals, because in spite of everything I still believe
that people are really good at heart.
   (Anne Frank)

Not for me, not for you, but for us.
   (The Motto of the old Borough of Battersea)

Now men will go content with what we spoiled.
  Or, discontent, boil bloody, and be spilled.
  They will be swift with swiftness of the tigress,
  None will break ranks, though nations trek from progress.
  (From 'Strange Meeting', Wilfred Owen, 1918)

As I write the Queen is in her ninetieth year. For most of us in Britain, she is the last living link with a past we never knew. This is the past of the royal abdication, the great depression and the suffering of the Second World War – Dunkirk, the Blitz, the fall of Singapore, El Alamein, Normandy and the Holocaust. All of these foreshadowed the creation of the British welfare state, a transformative event in the history of social policy. All of these fundamentally altered the world's map. Now, that welfare state, which was for many of the Queen's contemporaries, both the product of and antidote to much of the suffering and loss that they knew when young, is subjected to constant questioning. There is enormous uncertainty about the welfare state and talk of its demise, with some powerful voices pressing for it.

Yet we live in an age that is increasingly reminiscent of the past that gave birth to the welfare state; a past of economic decline, unfettered market, social division, insecure and harsh employment, increasing inequality, poverty and suffering, xenophobia, external conflict and imperial ambitions. This doesn't just raise large questions about the welfare state but even bigger ones about where we might be heading instead – if it really has run its course. It is with the second of these questions that this book is primarily concerned, although to answer it, it is also important to try and re-examine the welfare state, and social policy more generally. As I have been writing this book, there has been an accelerating flow of headline grabbing books, surveys, inquiries and evidence-based research reports, highlighting that austerity politics were having a particularly damaging effect on the most vulnerable, impoverished and powerless people and groups in society (for example, Duffy, 2014; O'Hara, 2014a). Yet in May 2015 a Conservative government was elected that promised further massive and unprecedented cuts in welfare spending and local services – and that looks set to be our continuing direction of travel.

This is a book that takes the welfare state as a starting point and a case study for understanding social policy more generally. It starts with Britain, but certainly doesn't end there, since the issues with which it is concerned are truly international in scope as well as being increasingly affected by global factors. This is also a book about both looking after each other and the role each of us may play in doing that.

Thus this book is about welfare. While 'welfare' has in some mouths become a dirty word, it is essentially concerned with how we take care of each other as human beings. This distinguishes it from other public policies, like foreign policy – how we connect with other countries – and military or defence policy – how we keep ourselves secure when foreign relations end in conflict. Welfare has become one of the most contentious areas of government and public policy. It constantly makes headline news, is increasingly an election issue and generates strong, polarised and frequently ill-informed opinions. We might pause and ask ourselves why how we look after each other has ever become so contentious!

I have been a child of the welfare state. My life has run parallel to it. The welfare state was created between 1944 and 1948. I was born on 1 May 1945, a day after Hitler killed himself and a week before the Second World War in Europe ended. It was only when I came to write this that I realised how important and intimate a part the welfare state has played in my life. I have directly experienced many aspects of it over the course of my life; good and bad, routine and heavy end. Much of my working life has also been concerned with it. It has been a focus of my work as writer, researcher, educator and activist. It has constantly connected with my life. Much writing about social policy is by people with a vested interest in it as academics, researchers, policymakers and advisers. My starting point has been different since I have been actively involved in service user movements and campaigns which have sought to challenge the traditional social construction of social policy.

Voices of experience

My own links and engagements with the welfare state and the emphasis I have placed in my work on patient, public and service user involvement, have, not surprisingly, influenced why I have written this book and the way I have approached the task. Thus it is crucially concerned with the say that people have over their own welfare. It draws equally upon experiential and academic knowledge; lived experience as well as research findings. As well as the usual voices of politicians, policymakers and academic experts, the reader will encounter many people's direct experience of social policy and the welfare state here. There is also an emphasis here on diversity and inclusion, making it possible for the widest range of such voices to be recognised, valued and heard.

These voices include my own and my family's. You'll find the latter in the boxed comments that run through the book and you can check them out in the list of family members at the back of the book. The book is not restricted to these family viewpoints. It also draws on the experience and ideas of a very wide range of people as welfare service users, to ensure the inclusion of a diverse range of viewpoints and experience. I have, however, also come to realise that my family is surprisingly diverse in terms of class, culture, sexuality, ethnicity, age, disability and faith, as well of course as of gender. I hope the comments they offer will encourage the reader to think about their own life and that of their family in relation to social policy and the welfare state. There is a tendency for people only to associate social policy with other people's lives and then often in a negative way. An aim of this book is to try and reconnect social policy, both to the world in which it operates and to the reader. Then she or he may better be able to think of it in relation to themselves and, as a result, better understand it in relation to the lives of others.

The different sources employed here are offered to complement each other, without any assumptions that one is better or more valid than the other. Having close contact with the welfare state has not encouraged sentimentality, or seeing it through rose-tinted glasses. Instead it seems more likely to serve as a corrective to these.

The state of welfare

The creation of the welfare state represents for me one of those defining moments in history that mark the boundary between the modern age and the dark ages that went before. As such it feels no less significant than the renaissance or the industrial revolution. At the same time its creation seems to belong to a bygone era, a kinder, more corporate time when the nation had a clearer sense of moral purpose. The welfare state is at the very heart of what it means to be a British citizen. With no bills of rights defining citizenship, the welfare state is one of the few guaranteed rights that a Briton can point to. It represents belonging, being bound together with others in something we all own and can use.

The strength of the welfare state was that it was universal; everyone could be comfortable using it because using it was a positive thing. It was there to make all citizens healthier and more secure, to create a level playing field. It was accessible, free at the point of use. It represented security and prosperity. Now that is no longer the case. It feels that increasingly it is only for the very poor and provides only the lowest possible level of support. Access is made as difficult as possible. It looks more like poor relief. At best a safety net, at worst a stigma.

Charlie Croft
Brother-in-law

Much of my first-hand experience of the welfare state has been complicated and problematic. Yet in my work, I have argued and fought determinedly for the welfare state. What explains this apparent contradiction? First, while the welfare state has frequently fallen short in practice, I believe its key principles remain groundbreaking and illuminating. Second, the alternatives offered to it, have frequently seemed backward-looking, unfair and defective. The more I have found out about them, the more inadequate they have seemed to be. They have often just taken us back to the indignities and cruelties associated with the Poor Law of the past, instead of transcending the limitations of the welfare state.

The aim of this book is not just to try and make sense of past and present struggles over welfare, but more important, to explore a different vision for the future. It draws on personal and other experience, as well as academic evidence, both to explore the inconsistencies of the welfare state and to highlight the possibilities of new participatory ways forward already emerging, to secure our rights and needs as citizens and human beings. It starts from the belief that if we are to learn from the strengths and shortcomings of the original welfare state and what it has become since, then we need to have as good an understanding as possible of its origins and reality. Sadly, much current discussion about welfare is superficial, ahistorical and tendentious.

In 1945, the Crown Film Unit released the documentary, *A Diary for Timothy*. Made in 1944–45 by Humphrey Jennings, the groundbreaking documentarist, with a script written by the novelist, EM Forster, and read by the actor, Michael Redgrave, it told the story of the last year of the war and the prospects for the future, through the eyes of baby Timothy, born on 3 September 1944, five years after the war began (Jennings, 1945; Jennings, 1982). It was full of hope for a fairer peacetime. 'What's going to happen in 1945 and in the years to follow when we're not here and you are?', the narrator asks of Timothy:

> Are you going to have greed for money or power ousting decency from the world as they have in the past, or are you going to make the world a different place?

I am one such Timothy. Now I have reached pensioner status. There have since been different answers to the enormous question the film asked. For some right-wing commentators, we are 'the baby boomers' who have taken an unfair share of 'the houses, jobs and welfare' and who threaten to overburden the young and public finances more generally as more and more of us survive into old and very old age (Willetts, 2011). But others who share and celebrate the optimism and altruism of *A Diary for Timothy*, 'about building a better world, and not returning to the harsh and indifferent snob-ridden, class society of the inter-war years', take the opposite view. For example,

> I suspect its writer and director would have been immensely disappointed with how things have turned out almost seventy years later. Today, income inequality is as great as it was in the nineteenth century, and we live in a society in which the most plutocratic government in fifty years scapegoats the poorest for the failures of the wealthy. In spite of a massive increase in wealth since the 1940s, Britain is again a country that doesn't provide enough dwellings for its population, has a Right Wing government that blames mass unemployment on the unemployed and has abdicated all responsibility for maintaining full employment, while the Labour Party's level of ambition is pathetic and utterly inadequate to the situation. (French, 2013)

The parents of children like Timothy, who are still alive, are now very old. They were the group who lived through many of the horrors of the twentieth century. It was due to their influence and efforts that the welfare state reforms took place and they and their offspring were meant to be its beneficiaries. Now sadly they are the victims of an underfunded, insecure, unreliable and poor quality social care system.

Whichever of the views above we take, it seems that the hopes of a more caring and equal society embodied in wartime documentaries like *A Diary for Timothy*, have not been realised. Taking the British welfare state and subsequent developments as its focal point, the aim of this book will be to explore how we might get public policy closer to achieving those aspirations forged in the most widespread and terrible conflict and suffering that the world has even yet seen.

What's the welfare state?

My very first thought was I'm not entirely sure what 'The Welfare State' is, because it is, in my experience, perhaps a slightly antiquated term that I associate with Thatcherite Britain and people my parent's age getting het up about…In terms of what it stands for, let's start with the NHS. The NHS is amazing. It's what Britain, I think, can be proudest of. It's a wonderful, wonderful thing. It is not perfect of course but to take it for granted or to bad-mouth it is, I think, ungrateful or short-sighted as a Brit. I definitely think Danny Boyle got it right by giving it a showcase spot in the 2012 Olympic opening ceremony.

A lot of what comes under the banner of The Welfare State is so intrinsically linked to political machinations that I confess to being rather turned off by it. One party's policies on reform/housing/benefits/whatever – are prime punchbag material for another party to publicly decry how off-message/off-Britain/anti-the-people's-interests the other party are, and I find it distasteful really that the subject of human welfare and wellbeing and happiness and individual rights should be hashed out and contested in this way. This is a very naive view, I appreciate, as everything is political, but, for instance, the way the bedroom tax was used for political punchbagging for days and days was tedious and awful and neglected the heart of the matter – which was the welfare at the centre of it all.

It's said that our welfare system is 'soft' and easily abused, that immigrants come to the UK to make use of it, as do benefits scroungers, parents who have 11 babies etc, etc. My feeling is that a welfare state is of paramount importance, that its robustness is important too and that of course it's going to be fallible and abused, but better that it exists in the first place and that for the most part it exists to do good and is good. I dare say abuse of the system costs the taxpayer far less than most things on the national tax bill.

Freddie Hutchins
Nephew

Collective memory is short. Already much of the original welfare state has been lost. The local authorities that gave couples the keys to a council home when they got married; the social care that was part of the universalist National Health Service, rather than a residual local authority means-tested provision, are now long gone. There is no free milk for all at school to help children develop strong bones and fewer and fewer 'lollipop' people keeping children safe at crossings and supplementing their own pensions. Will those who never knew such opportunities find it hard to believe they ever existed? Will they think it unnecessary or even outlandish to have had them? Will a day come when there is the same inability in the UK to understand a free health service that exists in the United States?

The structure of the book

Using the creation of the UK welfare state as a case study of change, the book examines the past, present and future of social policy or 'public policy' as it is called in some countries. The first part of the book tries to make sense of existing social policy. The opening chapter considers mainstream discussions of welfare and the welfare state and then sets out the narrative approach adopted in this book. Chapter Two offers a history of social policy which explores the economics, politics and ideology, going back to both the old and the 'new' Poor Law, putting them in their broader historical context and helping us understand why they generated such popular fear and loathing. The third chapter looks at the twentieth-century origins of the welfare state; the pressures and changes in war and peace that help explain its creation; the Great War and the inter-war depressions. Chapter Four explores the more immediate origins of the welfare state rooted in the Second World War, leading to the publication of the Beveridge Report. Chapter Five examines the principles of the welfare state as they were embodied in the reforms of the wartime national and particularly the post-war Labour governments and how these principles were interpreted. The focus of Chapter Six is the so-called 'welfare consensus' that lasted through the 1950s and 1960s. While it has been suggested that over this period, the main political parties were essentially in agreement to support the principles of the welfare state, was there this same consensus among people on the receiving end? What do we know about their views? Were they mainly supportive of the welfare state and what was their experience of it like?

Chapter Seven focuses on the period from the late 1970s to the present when the welfare state came in for hostile criticism under changing economic, social, cultural, political and ideological circumstances. Have these developments dealt with the shortcomings of the welfare state, or indeed resulted in new or even old problems surfacing? This chapter examines the way in which through an alliance of powerful interests, the conjuring trick of presenting old problems as new solutions has been performed. Chapter Eight focuses on social policy as an analytical approach and academic discipline. It identifies longstanding themes in the social construction and epistemology of the discipline, particularly those of science and the 'expert' and questions how helpful they have been in the development and understanding of social policy. This is a central chapter since it links us with the problems of past and present social policy and takes us to the second part of the book which is concerned with future social policy.

The next seven chapters are concerned with alternative, more democratic approaches to conceiving of and rebuilding social policy and welfare. Chapter Nine highlights developments which gave a new priority to the first hand voices of people on the receiving end of traditional social policy. Chapter Ten identifies a series of principles for a new democratised and 'user-led' approach to welfare that can overcome the limitations of both the original welfare state and its market-driven successors. Chapter Eleven explores the knowledge base for such a different approach to social policy and welfare; one which values and draws upon the lived experience and research of people on the receiving end of welfare – service users. The latter has come to be called user-controlled research. Chapter Twelve opens up discussion to examine a wide range of developments, ideas and pressures that point to a truly new approach to social policy and also highlights two key issues neglected by the post-war welfare state: participation and diversity. Chapter Thirteen looks more closely at matters of policy and their implications for the future. Chapter Fourteen draws on prefiguring examples and experience to explore the kinds of services, support, practice, organisations and structures that are likely to be able to deliver such arrangements for welfare and well-being. Chapter Fifteen considers how we might move closer towards such a socially constructed and co-owned blueprint for advancing our wellbeing. A final chapter reflects on the journey that welfare and social policy have made and the issues that yet have to be faced, as well as considering some of the more personal and experiential issues raised in the book. Two appendices offer details of the family members who have contributed their views on the welfare state to this book and set out the key research projects I have undertaken which have informed the book.

This book is concerned with reconnecting social policy with first-hand experience and enabling people's greater involvement in such policy. The illustrations included reflect this, connecting the past, present and future of social policy and my own and my family's own first-hand experience of the welfare state. Social policy tends to be concerned with difference and social divisions, both reinforcing and challenging them and, as we have seen, often coming under attack when it seeks to address them. These illustrations highlight class, difference, status and migration, issues that continue to shape social policy and welfare state developments and discussions.

Conclusion

I have now reached that stage in my life when I can expect to make increasing calls on the welfare state, particularly its pension, health and social care services. The children for whom that wartime generation sought to make provision, like me, are now themselves the grandparents or even great grandparents who are likely to need more help themselves. Towards the end of the film, *A Diary for Timothy*, Goronwy, the Welsh coalminer who features in it, reflects:

> One afternoon, I was sitting thinking about the past, the last war, the unemployed, broken homes, scattered families and then, I thought, has all this really got to happen again?

This question is again raised for us today and it is raised no less for this book – as it was for Timothy, towards the film's end. Talking to the baby, the narrator asks:

> Well dear Tim ... up to now we've done the talking ... What are you going to say about it and what are you going to do?...You heard what Goronwy was thinking, unemployment after the war and then another war and then more unemployment. Will it be like that again? ... Or are you going to make the world a different place – you and the other babies? (Jennings, 1945)

The challenge for all of us now, including this author, is not just how well have we addressed that issue so far, but how well we can and will for the future. Like Anne Frank, whose quote begins this book, I believe that most of us – I am too old to say all of us – are 'good at heart' and want to care for each other. What we need are the structures and circumstances that support rather than discourage that.

PART ONE

The legacy of the past

Conventional accounts of social policy have tended to present it as a battle between welfare state past and a more pluralist present; between paternalistic central planning and a drive for personalised choice and control, or most baldly, between neoliberal market and old style 'statism'. The aim of the first part of the book is to try and get a better understanding of current trends in social policy and possible futures, by looking more carefully at their relationships with the past and with people on the receiving end. It also sets the scene for an exploration of how we look after each other, which places an emphasis on it as a participatory and democratic project.

ONE

Setting the scene for welfare and social policy

We have a system that increasingly taxes work and subsidizes nonwork.
(Milton Friedman)

… the welfare state has caused millions to live deprived and even depraved lives …
(James Bartholomew, 2013)

If you are not careful, the newspapers will have you hating the people who are being oppressed, and loving the people who are oppressing them.
(Malcolm X)

The bad-mouthing of welfare

The UK welfare state has long had a poor press, but this probably reached its nadir in 2013. It was then that it was accused of colluding in mass murder. Occupying the lofty moral high ground was the *Daily Mail*, the tabloid newspaper which has the second highest sales, as well as being one of the most influential political institutions in Britain. Its front page headline described Mick Philpott, who killed six of his children by starting a house fire, as the 'vile product of welfare UK' (Dolan and Bentley, 2013). This was then picked up by right-wing blogger Guido Fawkes, who called the welfare state 'Philpott's evil accomplice' (Guido Fawkes, 2013). We should remember that this is the same *Daily Mail* whose proprietor and editorials supported Adolf Hitler and Sir Oswald Mosley, leader of the British Union of Fascists before the war, and which more recently had to pay damages to a Tamil hunger striker for falsely claiming that he secretly ate burgers during his 23 days without food (Jones, 2010) and invaded a memorial service being held for the uncle of the then Leader of the Labour Party, Ed Miliband.

This certainly was not always the way the welfare state was presented in the press. In 1948, heralding the new social security system, the *Daily Mirror* proclaimed: 'We are leading the whole world in Social Security ... Our State belongs to the people – unlike so many countries where the people belong to the state – Social Security converts our democratic ideal into human reality.'

Less predictably perhaps, *The Times* asked whether the next generation would be able to 'reap the benefits of a social service State while avoiding the perils of a Santa Claus State', concluding that, 'it would be a grave mistake to overlook the deep feelings and sense of purpose and common humanity which all the new social services are trying, however imperfectly, to express' (cited in Kynaston, 2008, 285).

If the emergence of totalitarian ideology and mechanised mass slaughter were the negative inheritance of the twentieth century, then its great achievement was the introduction in Europe and beyond of new collective commitments to improve people's health and wellbeing. In the UK this culminated in the creation of the post-Second World War welfare state, which became an international beacon for achieving this ideal.

Yet the debate about welfare, framed in terms of 'welfare reform' has more recently become a very narrow one, particularly in England. Thus a development that was transformative in its political, historical, social, economic and cultural implications, affecting almost all, if not every life and every institution in the UK, the welfare state, has been reduced to an ideologised discussion framed in terms of restricting and cutting cash benefits paid to 'shirkers', immigrants and others who 'don't need them' (Maddox, 2013). The National Health Service has long been seen as the 'jewel in the crown' of the welfare state. Yet significantly discussions about it, both for and against, tend to have been separated from those about 'welfare reform'. Given the wide recognition that the NHS continues to command enormous public support, it is difficult to see what would justify this arbitrary separation of key pillars of the welfare state – health services and social security, other than a desire to isolate and attack those on the receiving end of benefits and welfare benefits themselves. This has also translated into public policy which has emphasised the 'ring-fencing' of funding for the NHS, with all major political parties claiming it is 'safe in their hands', while stressing the need to cut and cap welfare benefits spending. The inappropriateness of isolating different key arms of the welfare state was elegantly highlighted by Olive Stevenson, a major figure in the development of social work and also an adviser to the Supplementary Benefits Commission in the 1970s, the body which replaced the National Assistance Board set up under the post-war welfare state reforms. In her autobiography she reported the comments of her predecessor in the role, Eileen Younghusband:

> The comments which jumped out of the page concerned the difference which the National Health Service had made to poor people. She showed graphically how before 1947, the costs of illness weighed on people's lives, especially those of the elderly. Overnight it seemed, the creation of the NHS changed the main focus of benefit claims. I have never forgotten this and am reminded of it when I read of those in the United States who are trapped by uninsurable healthcare. (Stevenson, 2013, 54)

Perhaps there is little surprise then (if even less justification), for the way the critics of the welfare state cherry-pick what they now choose to associate with it, rather than addressing it in its entirety and judging it on its overall merit.

A particular focus in current welfare reform has also been on older and disabled people and how 'we' can reduce the increasing 'burden' 'they' represent. Ironically, the indications are that such 'welfare reform' is actually causing damage to the people welfare is meant to help (see, for example, Adams and Phillips, 2013). How and why have we got to this position and where do we need to be? In a world where demographics are massively changing and the numbers and proportions of older and disabled people are greatly increasing, it is unlikely to be enough to try to define the numbers down by increasingly harsh approaches to assessment or eligibility, as governments now seem to be doing, or simply to argue that people will have to work longer, or do much more to look after themselves. Each of these suggestions, as we will see, raises its own questions.

Yet academic social policy does not seem able to advance effective alternative discussions to challenge this situation. Instead it largely seems at best to be drowned out and at worst sucked into this ever narrowing debate. At a time when traditional understandings of social policy have come in for unprecedented attack, the discipline of social policy seems unable to offer a sustained counter-critique which carries conviction and has any wider resonance with the public. Instead we are onlookers as media, politicians and survey makers repeatedly ask 'the public' questions about welfare benefits and people receiving them and then feed back to us that these are major issues for the public. But they tend much less to ask them questions or press their views about the 'super rich', bankers getting big bonuses or multinationals paying minimum taxation, which provide more relevant targets for public anger and disquiet.

What most seems to be needed now is a return to the confidence and challenge that originally underpinned the welfare state. For all the talk about 'thinking outside the box', 'thinking the unthinkable' and challenging conventional wisdoms, much discussion about welfare seems unimaginative and backward looking – and this includes much academic or 'expert' discussion. What is needed instead is thinking that goes back to first principles and which takes full account of newer thinking; of environmentalism and sustainability; of diversity, inclusion and identity; of participation and empowerment. This book aims to be part of this move.

Revisiting 'social policy'

So a key aim of this book is to challenge the reductionism and narrowness of current political and public discussion about social policy and welfare and reopen discussion. To start that process, we need to begin to examine what in the UK has come to be called social policy and in the United States, public policy. In Chapter Eight we will look more closely at social policy as both a discipline and practical policy.

If economics was seen as the 'dismal science' by the Victorian historian Thomas Carlyle, judging by the lack of popular and even academic interest in it currently, social policy now appears to have taken over this unfortunate mantle. This highlights an outstanding contradiction. How can a subject – like social policy – which now routinely commands media headlines and sparks off the keenest controversy at all levels in society – seem to be of such limited interest as a subject of study to students and others? As social policy has increasingly become front page news, so academic courses have closed. The Social Policy Association (SPA), the professional body of social policy, for example, has only 500 members. Yet social policy is a subject which can also truly say, like the now deceased and disgraced *News of The World*, 'All human life is there'. Here is a field of study and practice concerned with all the complexities and intimacies of life, death, sex and violence and the public policy responses to them. It can have a powerful bearing on any of our lives. How can that not be interesting? What is happening – indeed, perhaps we should be asking, what is going wrong – that makes social policy such a minority interest?

I believe that key to the marginalisation of academic social policy is the nature of its relationship with 'us', its subjects and the subjects of practical social policy. It is my contention that the answer lies in the degree to which social policy as academic discipline (and indeed as a public policy) has distanced itself from most of us. This book seeks to challenge this problem by reconnecting it with its subjects in as much of their flesh and blood reality as possible. It seeks to do this in several ways:

1. by foregrounding social policy's day-to-day practice and reality, rather than keeping it at a safe distance;
2. by drawing on both first-hand life experience and an academic and scholarly approach;
3. perhaps most important, by drawing on and giving centre stage to the lived experience and experiential knowledge of those with the most intimate understandings of social policy – its face-to-face practitioners, service users and those who try and support them as family, friends and neighbours.

In his introductory social policy textbook for students, the mainstream social policy academic, Pete Alcock, draws a helpful distinction between social policy as an academic discipline and social policy as 'the focus of what is studied' (Alcock, 2008, 2). He goes on to describe social policy in the latter sense as: 'the term used to refer to the actions taken within society to develop and deliver services for people in order to meet their needs for welfare and wellbeing' (Alcock, 2008, 2).

Alcock is far from alone in offering such a non-problematic definition of social policy, which presents it as a kind of benign domain of collective action to improve people's lives and conditions. As Kevin Farnsworth, another social policy academic, has argued, most research carried out into welfare states: 'centres on a relatively narrow conception of welfare as social provision and the extent to which various collective interventions meet the needs of the individual' (Farnsworth, 2013, 4).

It is difficult to see how such an approach can be sustained given that social policies have also included the Nazi Aktion T4 or euthanasia programme, which resulted in the killing of more than 200,000 physically or mentally disabled people and the compulsory sterilisation policies for people with learning difficulties that operated in many countries as recently as the 1970s, including Sweden and the USA. Such policies clearly had far from benevolent intentions for the people they targeted. Since then it has frequently also been argued that the political New Right and then neoliberal social policies which were first associated with Thatcherism, have had highly damaging effects on many people affected by them.

Thus this book is concerned with building and renewing connections, both between social policy and those on the receiving end of it and between academic social policy and the policy world with which it is ostensibly concerned. But primarily it is a book that is concerned with breaking out of narrow academic and theoretical traditions and is concerned with *how we look after each other in society*. Its starting point is how people are treated in society and how they treat each other. It's also a book about how the state and other institutions within and beyond specific societies treat people. This includes the market, political parties, social movements and social organisations like charities. Thus it is a book that would probably be expected to fit into the space of social or public policy, even if it sometimes might be pulling in other directions.

Not one of us can truly expect to look after ourselves through the whole course of our life without help from others. Indeed it can be argued that we all need some help throughout our lives, although it may not be defined as such. This help may come in many ways and take many forms. That's why across time and cultures, almost invariably human societies, communities and groupings can be seen to make some kind of formal provision to respond to members needing help. But it should be remembered that this may be harsh, punitive and damaging, as well as supportive and humanistic. Nonetheless we can expect it to be an inescapable part of collective living in the past, present and future.

The book doesn't start from any conventional fixed ideological position, but rather the simple question, how do we feel people should behave towards each other especially at times in their lives when they are facing difficulties and disasters, personal and social – and may not have the wherewithal to deal with them on their own? Of course, the question is itself inherently ideological. But it is one that is primarily concerned with the achievement of our wellbeing, rather than being tied to a particular prescribed or imposed route to attaining it.

We may all have different answers to this question, but the real point is that it has to be addressed. We know this from our history books. We may want to think that it is a question that can be left to sort itself out. But that is an answer in itself – and not a very helpful one. It is important to remember that this is neither an abstract question, nor one that is only for people who feel a commitment to each other or shared allegiance and identity. Remember that even in war this issue has to be and is often faced. What is to be done to enemies who are wounded, killed, disabled, taken prisoner or whose land is occupied? Yes, they can just be slaughtered, raped or degraded and their communities razed to the ground and historically that has often been their fate – and still sometimes is. But for many years now, with the Geneva Convention and other legal frameworks, there has been a sense that more is needed and there have been commitments to much more. So these are not just issues that are posed within societies or in relation to those with whom we identify or have kinship. They are much bigger issues about our understandings of being human, humanity and our relations with each other. How do we see ourselves and how do we see other people?

We do really need to think from the beginning again. Of course the post-war welfare state did not represent a total break from a longer-term past (perhaps this is its key if unacknowledged problem and one to which we shall be drawn back). But it was, at the same time, in many ways ground-breaking. Before and since there has been help and support based on personal, familial, community, charitable, religious, municipal and of course purchase or exchange relationships. But it was only with the welfare state and its international equivalents that there has been help and assistance based on notions of public service, citizenship rights and social equality. This is a breath-taking shift. To receive help from the National Health Service routinely without direct payment simply on the basis of needing it, was a step change at the level of moving from Newtonian to atomic physics. No wonder that Americans only familiar with the US system have often found it difficult to comprehend this British institution. It is because so many of us in the UK have grown up with and taken this radical reform for granted, without really understanding it, that accelerating developments towards the privatisation and destruction of the NHS in recent years, have been able to advance without real public comprehension or explicit broad based resistance.

A different approach to social policy narrative

While, as I said earlier in the Introduction, I have always upheld and supported the key principles of the welfare state, my experience of it has often pointed in a different direction. It has always been at least ambiguous in its reality for me. This is perhaps not surprising, given that my direct experience on the receiving end of welfare has included its more controversial and heavy-end activities. This include living for a long time – eight years – on poverty level state benefits and being a long-term user of mental health services (over a period of 12 years). It has also meant difficult personal experiences of welfare state services like benefit appeal tribunals, milk tokens, unemployment and training schemes, rent tribunals and the working of environmental health services and repairs done by the local authority in default of the private landlord doing them. Few of these were experiences anyone would want to repeat.

Thus a major paradox has emerged for me as I have written this book. I remain committed to the values and principles underpinning the welfare state. I see it providing a basis for a society committed to its citizens' wellbeing for the future. Yet the evidence of my own experience might be seen to suggest something very different. My personal experience highlights shortcomings in the welfare state, frequent occasions where it seems incapable of acting according to its own principles and where it has actually caused harm and abuse, rather than safeguarding people's rights and meeting their needs. Isn't there a fundamental contradiction here? Am I and others who are supportive of it, barking up the wrong tree? I don't think so. I think there is another more subtle truth here, one which it may be difficult to uphold in the heavily politicised context of social policy. Of course the welfare state has fallen short in many ways. But it did also achieve many of its key commitments; reducing poverty and inequality, improving the health of the nation, increasing social mobility and so on. It also successfully took on reforms which challenged some of its earlier inherent weaknesses, for example, its failure to address difference and diversity.

In the welfare state's more recent years, particularly since the rise of Mrs Thatcher and the political New Right and increasing constraints on its budget, many of the failings of welfare services can be seen as the result of the efforts and impact of its critics and political opponents anxious to undermine such services. Much of the hostile reaction to the welfare state that has shaped the second half of its history has also been backward looking, harking back to pre-welfare state days, rather than offering real alternatives.

Certainly not all the problems of the welfare state can be laid at the door of its more recent ideological and political opponents, however. It has always seemed to me to have its own internal inadequacies. Thus in looking to the future, we need to look both beyond the welfare state and beyond its predecessors for insights and that is the aim here.

So, there has long been a massive and increasing contradiction for me; the gap between the principles of the welfare state, to which I and countless others have been committed and how it has actually worked and what experience of it has felt like. Why has there so often been this gap? Can we overcome it and if so how?

Of course there will always be a gap between human aspirations and our ability to realise them. That will be no less true of the welfare state than anything else. But it doesn't really seem to be that which we are discussing here. Too often, of course with some exceptions, the welfare state seems to have fallen short of what has been hoped of it. It seems important to try and explore the reasons for this and that is one of the objectives of this book. It's something we will be drawn back to in Chapter Six, where we look more closely at some of the experience of people on the receiving end of welfare state services during those times when there seemed to be strong cross-party support for the welfare state.

The book will draw particularly on the experience and understandings of people on the receiving end of welfare services to make sense of gaps between its aspirations and reality. The movements that have been developed by such groups, notably during the last quarter of the twentieth century; women's, black and civil rights movement, LGBTQ, disabled people's and survivors movements, all offer some of the most groundbreaking and revolutionary insights for the future of welfare. They have drawn on and developed the first-hand experience and knowledge of welfare state service users – a resource which significantly has been conspicuously neglected both by the traditional welfare state and its ideological opponents.

The importance of narrative

A key characteristic of much of the discussion and writing about welfare is that it has come from academic, political, ideological, professional and other 'expert' perspectives. We will examine this issue in more detail later. While we may all in some sense or other have experience of the welfare state on the receiving end, as a 'service user', the production of accounts, ideas and theories about welfare has tended to be narrowly based and associated with 'expert' status. It has reflected a 'them' and 'us' in the social construction of social policy as both discipline and practice, with limited overlaps between the producers of social policy and its recipients, particularly those on the end of the most difficult and devalued areas of provision.

A large and important problem emerged for me early on in my study of social policy was that prevailing academic discussions tended to isolate and separate people's actual experience of social policy from critiques and conclusions about it. The two were not connected, the former tended not to be present. Of course there were attitude and information surveys and data was collected about the operation of social policy. But people's actual experience of social policy, what it felt like, what they thought about it, how helpful or not they found it – their 'experiential knowledge' did not seem to be a priority for analysts and commentators. This went beyond even the lack of engagement of people on the receiving end of social policy and their experience in such discussions. It extended even to the exclusion of the experience of the commentators themselves.

Of course, it could be argued that this followed from their concern to avoid problems of personalisation and bias in their discussions. What I have found interesting, however, as someone coming from and keenly aware of a service user perspective, was how different to their expert analyses, the views of such commentators could be, if and when they were affected by those same issues that they researched and wrote about. Thus people who themselves or whose parents now needed social care support, who had been major commentators about it, would suddenly tell you how difficult the system was to negotiate. Or researchers who were international experts on healthcare management could be heard telling their pet personal story of the difficulties they encountered, for instance, going to A&E (accident and emergency), for which their working lives had clearly not prepared them.

This book seeks to move away from this distancing of social policy from its day-to-day reality in two ways. First it aims to ensure that the perspectives of people on the receiving end and the contributions they can and have made to social policy are placed centre stage. Second, it seeks to link broader discussion and theory with the day-to-day experience of welfare. Thus it seeks to learn from people's lived experience.

I share the view of Virginia Nicholson, writing about women's lives during the Second World War, when she said: 'My approach to historical research is, as far as possible, to merge it with biography and the telling of stories. I believe that the personal and idiosyncratic reveal more about the past than the generic and comprehensive' (Nicholson, 2012, xvi).

Education

I was a product of an environment as a child in which we really believed that education was the answer to all our problems. Because education, we believed, tackled ignorance and if we could get rid of ignorance, the world would be a better place. Now you know what a naïve view that is...It does seem to me, that we do operate generally on what has been called the Ozian principle of education. That's based of course on what the Wizard of Oz said when the straw man asks him for a brain. And, if you remember, the Wizard said, 'I can't give you a brain, but I can give you a diploma.' And of course he said, 'If you wear your diploma, everyone will think that you've got a brain…'. I don't know what true education is. But I do know there is not much new under the sun. And it was a sixteenth-century monk who said that 'True education is based on three methods of learning: authority – someone tells you that it is so; reason – and you use your mental faculties to work out if things are so; and finally – experience' and he added that 'only the last named, experience, is finally reliable'.

From his speech on retiring as Principal of Norwich City College, 1983
John Croft
Father-in-law

I would only differ in saying that I believe the two elements are of equal value, that they offer insights for the present, the past and the future and that I have adopted a different route to achieve the same approach.

A key way in which I will seek to do this is by offering a parallel narrative of my own experience of the welfare state through the course of my life. Partly the aim has been to offer a consistent flesh and blood thread of experience to relate to the broader more conventional discussion of welfare offered here. But equally important, as I have developed this idea, is that I have realised how helpful juxtaposing such experience can be in helping us understand both the complexities, realities and difficulties associated with welfare state history. Certainly, introducing personal experience makes for complication and contradiction. We can come to see that the broad-brush stories that are best remembered may only tell part of the story. We also see and, should perhaps not be surprised, that what has passed into folklore, may be the opposite of actual encounters and individual experience. Of course one personal history has limited usefulness and has no quantitative relevance. But it does help in giving indications of what the welfare state is actually like; what it may feel like on the receiving end, regardless of the aims and ambitions of its initiators and reformers. It helps exemplify policy and practice.

From housing solution to housing problem

I was a volunteer on the 'Notting Hill Summer Project' set up by the Notting Hill People's Association. We were making a survey of local housing as well as running play schemes. I joined as I didn't have a home to go to after finishing college. This was in 1967. I remember seeing Michael X, the Black Power activist (who formerly worked as an enforcer for the property owner Peter Rachman and was subsequently executed for murder in Port of Spain), standing in the street in Notting Hill, looking more saintly than anyone I have ever seen. What shocked me was seeing so much poverty next to plenty. We were interviewing local people about their housing situation. I remember going into one flat, where all that the black family living there had, as their water supply, was a standpipe. Nearby even then you'd see homes that were gentrified and comfortable. It was a time of transition and we know that the solution has largely been to make Notting Hill a ghetto of wealth. The Notting Hill Housing Trust was another organisation linked with the Project. Things have moved on since then, Now 'Notting Hill Housing' is a massive housing association with thousands of units. Its CEO, reported to be on a salary of £180,000, justifies developing property for 'wealthy individuals' to fund its 'social housing' for people on low income, although the housing it provides for the latter is diminishing as it increasingly becomes a developer of commercial housing (Fearn, 2014).

The author

In this book I have referred to my own identity in relation to narrative more and in different ways than I have done previously in other writings. On previous occasions I have discussed my experience as a mental health service user because of its central relevance to my own and indeed other people's understanding of mental health issues. But here I have also referred to my ethnic and class backgrounds. I have done this because in times of great xenophobia and increasing inequality, it has become clear to me in the writing of this book that these issues are as central to an understanding of social policy as are issues of direct experience on its receiving end. I have not explored my sexuality or gender position in any detail, although of course I am conscious of them. Instead I have sought to ensure that such issues are fully and properly considered as other key domains of difference, social division, equality and inequality.

Such first-hand knowledge has generally had little place in social policy writings and discussions. This might sometimes be because it was beyond the experience of commentators and policymakers and not readily available to draw upon. But perhaps more important, it has tended to be devalued and marginalised. Social policy has framed itself as either an administrative or scientific endeavour. From its origins in the nineteenth century, its emphasis has been on the 'objective'; particularly the definition and measurement of phenomena. The subjective, human experience and responses have had little or no place in this. Where they have featured it has largely only been as data reinterpreted and restructured by social policy analysts.

There is, however, increasing recognition in related disciplines of the useful role such narrative can play set alongside more traditional and conventional approaches to developing knowledge and understanding. Beginning on this journey I have come to realise how significant my involvement with the welfare state has been during the course of my life. Perhaps that is true for many of us, if we reflect on the issue. As well as personal, direct experience of a wide range of systems and services from an early age, I have also engaged with the welfare state as an activist, educator, researcher, writer, as a member of service user organisations and movements and even for a brief period as a 'welfare officer'.

My key criterion is that everything I have referred to, I actually had first-hand knowledge or experience of or I saw it happening to someone close to me. Second, as often as possible, there were corroborating sources, so that I haven't had just to rely on distant memory or vague recollections. I have sought to be rigorous in not including events or experiences which I do not recall clearly. Instead, generally where I do refer to experiences it is because they had a powerful impact on me, or I have been able to check them in one way or another.

My experience of the welfare state is far from unique. Equally it is not offered as typical or representative. The point is that all these things happened. This is what the welfare state over its years could be and feel like to those on the receiving end. I have tried not to distinguish between good and bad experiences. There have been both. What is perhaps unusual, particularly in relation to most authors of social policy texts, is that my experiences have included the heavy end of welfare as well as its more universalist services like education, health and other public provision. Social policy has been a focus of my life, in all aspects of my identity. In offering direct experiences, I have included but drawn distinctions between these experiences as:

- a citizen and service user
- a parent and family member
- a worker within the system
- an activist engaging with and often challenging it
- a researcher investigating and analysing it.

My experiential knowledge will be based on both individual and collective experience, for example as a member of groups and campaigns, as well as an unaffiliated service user. I will also draw on research findings which I have been involved in producing (as well as other research), focusing on service users' perspectives, user involvement and, increasingly, coming from a service user perspective. This last, user involvement and user-controlled research is gaining increasing importance as a research methodology in its own right (Beresford and Croft, 2012).

I will also draw upon experiences, in which I was involved, of people close to me. I have included insights from the experience of my extended family because they offer a much wider range of perspectives, in terms of age, gender and so on, that also connect directly with my life. This includes both my family of origin and the family that I have acquired in my life. I have sought from each family member directly related to me, their thoughts about the welfare state, past, present or future, trying not to influence either their focus or their opinion. They are not offered as 'representative' views. This is how the welfare state is for one family.

I have also offered many other accounts and discussions from people on the receiving end of social policy. All these sources offer different insights. All represent direct experiences. What I have most sought to do here is break down the longstanding division that there has been in social policy between policy development, analysis and critical comment and first-hand experience. In this book I have particularly tried to do this in relation to my own thinking. It is not just that our first-hand experience has insights to offer, but we need to set it against conventional thinking and theorising – from whatever political or ideological quarter. It seems very unlikely that it will be helpful for them to be separated. It is to be expected that new insights may be gained if they are reconnected with each other.

In this book, I have sought to include personal narrative drawing on direct experience. But the whole book also needs to be understood in terms of narrative. While I am seeking to offer a particular kind of narrative approach to social policy, it also needs to be recognised that all accounts of social policy, including mainstream accounts of the welfare state represent and offer some kind of narrative. What is perhaps interesting and complex is the relation between the more conventional academic narratives that are offered here and the more personal contributions which are included.

Clive Baldwin in his examination of 'social work narratives', comments that:

> of all the areas explored in this book, social policy...
> seems the least amenable to being understood as a
> narrative enterprise. After all, policy operates at a level of

abstraction far from individual narratives or concerns and policy documents do not always have an obvious narrative structure. (Baldwin, 2013, 73)

Baldwin still believes, however, that such documents and social policy more generally can be understood 'narratively' and highlights the existence of social policy narratives, even though as he says, 'narrative policy analysis is also less well developed than narrative approaches to other areas' (Baldwin, 2013, 73). Social policy can be understood in narrative terms, indeed it is often presented as grand narratives, but it is not usually discussed in these terms, but presented rather as objective, neutral and scientific in its basis.

A frequent problem in social policy therefore, has not just been that one group has offered its prescriptions for another group, thus leading to an essential 'them' and 'us' in the development of social policy, but also that this separation also seems significantly to have gone on within us as people concerned with the development of social policy. Thus there has been an attempt to separate 'ourselves' from the focus of our study. While this may have been underpinned by what was seen as a virtuous ambitious of avoiding the contamination of personal bias, it has, I would suggest, actually more often been unhelpful. It has encouraged people prescribing and conceptualising social policy to ignore what it might feel like either to them or other people to have this happen to them. Earlier in my work, I often encountered problems of understanding from other social policy commentators who seemed to feel that my emphasis on user involvement, and on listening to the viewpoints of people on the receiving end, weakened the rigour and integrity of the subject. Yet interestingly, as I have said, I have subsequently frequently noted their own shock, surprise and sometimes pain, when they have had to deal with the social policy system, for example, on behalf of a parent needing support and then have discovered just what the system that they have been party to developing is actually like and how it feels in reality.

Perhaps the lesson of history from Mrs Thatcher's reforms onwards and adopting an international perspective which takes account of other approaches to social and public policy, is that the post-second world war welfare state offered a more promising way forward to meeting the rights and needs of its people than any of the alternatives that have since emerged. What of course continues to be needed is a real determination to improve it. In this it reflects an earlier observation about the golden age of UK television, that it represented 'the least worst television in the world' (Shulman, 1973). The principles of the

British welfare state may similarly have offered the potential to secure the 'least worst social policy' in the world. The responsibility lies with us to make sure that this potential can be examined and understood to its fullest possible extent, alongside more recent thinking to chart our way to a welfare state or wellbeing society fit for the twenty-first century.

I need to make one additional point. This book challenges social policy schools of thought and advances another approach. In so doing, it is necessarily critical of some social policy discussions and developments. But it is not intended as any kind of personal attack on the people involved in these. I hope I have succeeded in making this distinction adequately and apologise in advance if I have in any case failed. I have received much help both specifically in writing this book and also over the course of my professional life from other social policy academics, including key figures in the field and acknowledge my debt to them, as well as many service users and others. I hope that this book will encourage discussion within and about social policy. It is certainly not intended to close it off.

The welfare state has been a focus of my working life. But the book actually grew out of two broader concerns; one personal, the other political and social. First was my feeling, as I come to the end of my formal working life, that I needed to make better sense of all that I have learned and seen happen in social policy. Second, that we appear to have moved into a period when more and more people seem to face more and more difficulties living their lives and this actually seems to be part of the culture and atmosphere of the times. What's urgently needed is a different way of coming at social policy and welfare and the aim here is to help make that possible.

TWO

The past

Caring for the feeble, and allowing them to breed, would lead to the degeneration of humanity.

(Charles Darwin, *Descent of Man*, cited in Wise, 2009, 216)

Laws provide, as much as is possible, that the Goods and Health of Subjects be not injured by the Fraud and Violence of others; they do not guard them from the Negligence or Ill-husbandry of the Possessors themselves.

(John Locke)

The legacy of the Poor Law

The long-term history of UK social policy is the history of the Poor Law. The two are inextricably linked. It is difficult to understand the creation of the welfare state and its subsequent development without recognising this. Nearly three quarters of a century after its demise, the Poor Law still intimidates. Only very old people can have any direct experience or real remembrance of it. But its shadow still looms over us. It has long been the symbol of all that is awful about needing official help. We can still get some sense of its brutality from Dickens' *Oliver Twist* or David Lean's film version of the novel. We can get an echo of the cruelty of its ideology from the thinking and behaviour of Scrooge in Dickens' *A Christmas Carol*. He is much better seen as a symbol of Poor Law philosophy, than the miser we have largely come to understand him to be (Spufford, 2014). But the Poor Law is more than an anachronistic folk memory. It was the basis for collective intervention where people couldn't maintain themselves for perhaps a millennium. Its origins are most often associated with the great Elizabethan Acts of 1597 and 1601. But these were the culmination of more than a hundred years of earlier legislation. Indeed as unwritten law, the Poor Law can be traced back to Anglo-Saxon times.

The Poor Law may now be lost in the past and a distant and uncertain memory, but it still offers an enormous window for understanding social policy and our attitudes to it. It provides insights on almost every issue that still concerns us: political, social, personal, ethical, moral, emotional, cultural and ideological. It also has a power that continues to be inadequately recognised. This is the power to provide us with key warnings from history.

This Poor Law had several key abiding principles. It drew a distinction between those who it was felt could and could not support themselves – those who could and could not work, long known as the 'potent' and the 'impotent' poor. Under successive Acts, those who it was thought could work would be made to work, or punished if they failed to. Those judged as unable to work: children, old, sick, impaired, distressed or mad people, could be given some support. Because life was locally based and the Poor Law was long paid for at parish level, a distinction was also drawn between an area's or a town's own poor – and outsiders. This rapidly translated into categorising the latter as 'vagrants' and outcasts, to be branded, punished and moved on. Over time this label was attached to many groups officially distrusted, including wandering musicians, actors, labourers, beggars, migrants and fugitives. The walls that are now a tourist attraction in some long-established towns and cities, were part of the process of policing the essentially local nature of the Poor Law.

The Poor Law was always a barometer of major social and economic change. As feudalism broke down in the middle ages and lords no longer maintained their social responsibilities to their serfs, so it changed. Under the mercantilism of the Tudors and after, with land enclosure taking away the livelihood of many ordinary people, it underwent massive reform. With the onset of capitalism, with an increasingly urbanised population dependent on the vagaries of the market as wage-earners, it underwent further major change. However, we must also remember that the apparatus of local and central government was never the only supplier of collective welfare. Until the reformation, the church and monasteries played an important part. Afterwards secular and religious charities were significant. Nonetheless the Poor Law had a central role, especially at times of difficulty and major transition. Also, however grudgingly, in reality there always had to be some practical acknowledgement, particularly in the harshest times, that people often weren't working not because they refused to, but because social and economic conditions did not necessarily make it possible.

The principles of the Poor Law

It is the New Poor Law of 1834 that occupies the most important place in modern memory. This is perhaps because there are still people alive who may have first-hand experience of its last leavings, or heard about it directly from others who did. But perhaps more to the point this was the latest and most developed and perhaps feared version of Poor Law philosophy. As Sarah Wise the social historian has observed:

> The year 1834 marked the triumph of those who believed that poverty was caused by moral failure – that the system of parish assistance dating back to the reign of Elizabeth I had encouraged dependency and had caused a population explosion among the very class of people least able to afford to care for their children. (Wise, 2009, 76)

Clearly all policy systems are ultimately value-based, however thought-through or not this is. But the New Poor Law was the result of the most determined efforts to produce a rational and coherent policy system. What made possible such a systematic and unprecedented approach was that it was inextricably ideological in its origins. This was not, as was the old Poor Law, a system that had grown out of the chances and changes of many years of experience, implementation and changing conditions. Here was a Poor Law intended to be comprehensive, based on thinking that was most concerned with achieving a kind of scientific effectiveness. The New Poor Law grew out of the ideology developed by Jeremy Bentham and John Stuart Mill, known as utilitarianism. It was also associated with the widely believed principle of Thomas Malthus that population increased faster than resources, unless checked by discouraging the poor from having children and Ricardo's 'iron law of wages', which was based on the belief that subsidising the wages of poor workers (as the old Poor Law had often done under the so-called Speenhamland system) undermined the wages of all workers (Spicker, 2011). These philosophies were also closely inter-linked with laissez-faire or 'let it be' economics, where the aim is for private parties and the market to be as free as possible from government restrictions. The economist and philosopher, Adam Smith, viewed the economy as a natural system and the market as an organic part it, with laissez-faire as a moral programme and the market its instrument to ensure 'men' (sic) the rights of natural law (Smith, 2009).

According to Baldock, all industrial societies developed a version of the Victorian Poor Law in the nineteenth century (Baldock, 2012, 23). England's New Poor Law was most closely associated with two fundamental principles; those of 'less eligibility' and 'deterrence' (Fraser, 2010). *Less eligibility* meant that the conditions that applied to someone who turned to the Poor Law would be worse than what they could expect outside it, if they supported or looked after themselves. Given the harshness of life for 'the lower classes' in nineteenth-century UK industrialised society, it is clear that the bar could be expected to be set disturbingly low. Second, and closely associated with this, *deterrence* meant that the regime of the Poor Law would be such that it would strongly discourage anyone from wanting to turn to it for assistance unless they absolutely had to, because it would be so unpleasant.

What particularly distinguished the New Poor Law from its predecessors was how it sought to impose these principles. This was through what was known as the 'workhouse test'. By this only those who were 'genuinely destitute', that is to say lacking any material possession except the clothes they stood up in, would be able to apply for poor relief. Or put another way, anyone else, drawing on anything they still had to pawn, sell or exchange, could be expected to try to avoid the Poor Law at all costs. There had long been workhouses. This was nothing new. In the past help or as it was known, 'poor relief' might be provided as indoor or outdoor relief. That is to say that someone who needed medical or other help might be admitted to the workhouse or its infirmary. Others might receive outdoor relief in the form of a cash payment, either to maintain them, if they were out of work, or to supplement wages, if these were insufficient to support them. What was different now was the principle that support of *any* kind, for *any* reason, would only be provided inside a 'well-regulated workhouse'. If you wanted help, the plan was that this would only be possible to get by submitting yourself to the rigorous regime of the workhouse. Those people who were capable of supporting themselves outside the workhouse would prefer to do so (Harris, 2012, 113).

As Sarah Wise suggested in her study of a slum area in Bethnal Green in the late nineteenth century, most poor people had little direct experience of the Poor Law because they strove so desperately to keep away from it (Wise, 2009). Thus the New Poor Law was really only narrowly concerned with those who had absolutely nothing. As Harris has highlighted, it was not concerned with the relief of poverty, but only with responding to the extremes of destitution (Harris, 2004, 46–7). What was also new about it was that it sought to introduce a centralised system of control, in contrast to the localism of its predecessors. A central body, the Poor Law Commission (replaced in 1847 by the Poor Law Board) regulated local parishes now combined into Poor Law Unions. If the essential aim of the New Poor Law was to prevent the able-bodied securing poor relief, its harsh regime spread to all the groups with whom it directly dealt, from unmarried and deserted mothers, to the aged poor, from chronically sick and disabled people, to those at the end of life. Elderly husbands and wives, after a lifetime of toil and struggle together, were routinely subjected to enforced separation. Pauper children would be put up for adoption or harsh enslaving apprenticeships (Longmate, 1974; May, 1999; Anstruther, 1984). We can only imagine what levels of cruelty, abuse, sexual and other violence took place in workhouses which were both unaccountable and despising of their charges. As Sarah Wise wrote in her local study:

> Fatal falls down stairs, mysterious defenestrations in the Imbeciles Ward, louse infestations a certainty for anyone passing through the reception rooms, physical assaults upon lunatics, children dying in fires because they had been locked into their dormitory – it all helped the Bethnal Green very-poor, of whom there were an estimated 25,000, to make the decision to chance their luck elsewhere. (Wise, 2009, 82)

Despite massively high levels of poverty, throughout the 1880s, for example, official statistics showed that only an average 3 per cent of the population of England and Wales were reliant on parish poor relief (Wise, 2009, 82).

The unit costs of the workhouse system were high, but the system was based on the premise, which seemed to work, that this would ultimately save money because the harshness of the regime would discourage so many from seeking support. Three groups can be seen to be directly or indirectly affected by the New Poor Law. These were:

1. those who were destitute who turned to it for help and became its inmates and were included as paupers';
2. those who were destitute but used every device (including crime, suicide and starvation) and with the help of family and friends desperately tried to keep from it;
3. an even wider pool of people at risk of destitution at any time because of the extreme insecurities of minimally regulated capitalist economies.

Together, these must have accounted for a very large number of people and significant proportion of the population. This would help explain why the Poor Law exerted such a baleful influence for so long over the 'working classes'. At the same time the actual number entering the workhouse, as we have seen above, was relatively low because of its appalling reputation and the extent of popular fears of it.

Utilitarianism: the underpinning philosophy of social policy

The utilitarian principles underpinning the New Poor Law imply something very different from the folk memory and historical records we have of it. The Benthamite maxim was that the 'greatest happiness of the greatest number ... is the measure of right and wrong'. This was seen as the crucial test for government intervention and policy. This author, however, finds it difficult to see how this was true of the New Poor Law, which imposed a harsh and cruel regime on any who came within its orbit. Utilitarianism is a philosophy that actually seems much more to have served the interests and be concerned with the 'greatest happiness' of the small minority who governed and influenced the state, had the vote and ran the Poor Law – even though everyone's happiness was meant to count equally.

It is difficult to be sure exactly how far the New Poor Law was implemented as intended. Workhouses were built in most areas and most were reorganised into Poor Law unions. However, it was not implemented as uniformly as intended, for example, the reforms were not as far-reaching in the north as in the south. Some out-relief also continued to be paid. The extreme conditions of poverty that existed at the time often made it difficult for the New Poor Law to be operated as inflexibly as was intended. At the same time the *threat* of the Poor Law hung heavily over the population. In addition what still distinguished the New Poor Law was its theoretical and ideological commitment to standardisation, uniformity and conformity. This was key to the philosophy of utilitarianism underpinning it. The aim was to ensure a *consistency* of approach which would mean that if debarred from support from one quarter, those judged capable of supporting themselves, would not be able to get it from another. This raised issues that extended beyond the Poor Law itself.

The state is not and has never been a monopoly provider of support for 'the poor' in the UK. In the nineteenth century, churches and charity still played a significant role. Strong pressures, however, developed for all help for poor people to conform with the utilitarian thinking underpinning the New Poor Law. After its establishment, there were growing concerns that the New Poor Law principles were being undermined by charitable alms giving. Charities were expected to operate along the same utilitarian lines as the Poor Law in order not to weaken its effectiveness. 'Indiscriminate' charity was seen as the enemy of 'providence', encouraging dependence.

The Charity Organisation Society (COS) was key to this and epitomised a much broader movement. Key figures in the COS, such as Canon Barnett and Octavia Hill, were also key figures in Victorian social policy, philanthropy and social reform. Founded in 1869, as its name makes clear, the COS was based on the same utilitarian principles as the New Poor Law. It was established at a time when efforts were being made to tighten up the Poor Law through major reform (Harris, 2012). It grew out of concern that some poor people were escaping the workhouse test, so its aim was to restrict the distribution of 'outdoor relief' so that paupers had to accept the test (Stedman Jones, 1984, 254–8). The Society believed that giving out charity without investigating people's circumstances would encourage indolence and dependency. It supported 'self-help' and limited government intervention (Rees, 2001). By organising local charitable giving in a systematic way, it would ensure that the overall poor relief system was coordinated and seamless and not vulnerable to the perceived depredations of the 'undeserving poor'. The COS repeatedly stressed that its function was to organise charitable activity rather than to give relief. It subjected each applicant to a rigorous and systematic investigation, to ensure that charity fulfilled its role as an individualised 'personal relationship dependent upon acceptable behaviour', while the Poor Law retained its punitive and deterrent function (Stedman Jones, 1984, 255–6). We can get some taste of the harsh and intrusive cross-questioning that made up the COS's process of investigation from contemporary case notes that still exist. It is a measure of how difficult people's circumstances might be that some had to go through such a process.

The importance of fear

Stedman Jones's London study is a key source for making sense of problems of poverty and the social and political response to them. His focus was the second half of the nineteenth century – the period we generally associate with the Victorian age – and the population with the least economic security. He subtitled his book, 'a study in the relationship between classes' and the classes he was crucially concerned with were the middle classes and those *they* saw as the 'undeserving poor'. The section of the middle class he was particularly interested in 'was the educated professional sector, those responsible for the dominant discourse on charity and social policy in the period' (Stedman Jones, 1984, xv).

What emerges powerfully from the wide range of evidence which he musters, is that the primary relationship between the classes was based on the *fear* – of the ruling class generally and the middle class specifically – of the poor. This fear seemed to be pervasive. It could not be said to be confined to those who were rich or powerful who sought to keep down poor and disadvantaged people, or those who saw the poor as their class enemy. It extended even to those who appeared to be concerned about the condition of the poor and seemed to want to improve their lot. Stedman Jones stressed that this fear was 'an underlying tone of the discussion of the casual poor in the 1880s (Stedman Jones, 1984, xvii). This enduring fear gave rise to middle-class mythologies and moral panics about 'the poor' (xxiv). They were seen as threatening and in need of change – both for their own moral sakes and for the sake of society more generally. A growing number of terms were coined to describe this feared constituency, including, the 'submerged tenth', the 'casual poor', the 'dangerous class' and the 'residuum' (Stedman Jones, 1984, 11).

How things were

It's always interesting to watch the steerage people who, no matter what the weather might be, always seem to be getting up amusements of one sort or another and to enjoy dancing round and round on a few square yards of deck until one would have thought they must have been giddy. I went several times into the second class and talked to the women and children, many of the former going out with their husbands to try their luck in the new country... Some of the men were very intelligent artisans who would be sure to succeed, and all seemed superior working men ...

The train follows White River... We frequently saw Indians and their small camps in these parts ... They are most unattractive specimens of humanity and have none of the bright grin of the negro or kaffir ...

The station at [Winnipeg] was crowded with a rougher and much lower class than I had seen anywhere further west. In Calgary it was quite different and everybody seemed so respectable.

[In New York] we lunched at the Waldorf and at Sherrys, and amused ourselves studying the beau monde of those places, and also spent some time at the Horse show. The driving teams, of four in hand, were good, and an interesting sight, also the trotting competition ... In the evening we were fortunate enough to get places for the first night of the Play of 'Lady Rose's Daughter' from Mrs. Oliphant's work, Fay Davis acting the part well, and the Play was well staged.

Lady Catherine Decies*
Paternal grandmother

* Extracts from: Typewritten copy of journal *Through Canada Stopping Calgary and Vancouver, 1902* (Decies, 1902).

The Victorian social reformers we now associate with improving the wellbeing of poor people frequently felt disgusted by them, as well as fearful of them. Thus, pioneer of the settlement movement Edward Denison observed of Petticoat Lane: 'Humanity swarms there in such quantity, of such quality, and in such streets, that I can only liken it to the trembling mass of maggots in a lump of carrion.' He said that what was worst about London's East End was the 'habitual condition of this mass of humanity – its uniform mean level, the absence of anything more civilizing than a grinding organ to raise the ideas beyond the daily bread and beer' (Stedman Jones, 1984, 258).

Beatrice Webb, founding Fabian, wrote pejoratively of 'the aborigines of the East End' (see also Chapter Eight) and General Booth, co-founder of the Salvation Army, equated East Enders (his statue still stands among them) with the 'pygmies' encountered by the explorer, Henry Stanley (Wise, 2009, 217). The housing reformer, Octavia Hill, who has become the twenty-first century poster girl of the National Trust and social housing, said: 'You will have, before you can raise these very poorest, to help them to become better in themselves. Neither despair, nor hurry, but set to work with the steady purpose of one who knows that God is on his side' (quoted in, Stedman Jones, 1984, 196).

Fear of contamination

Given such widespread negative attitudes, it is not surprising that the poor were also seen as a *contaminating* influence by the ruling and middle classes. This corresponded with their scientific understanding as well as their moral view of the poor. The problem for the Victorians was that the poor did not represent a threat only to themselves, but to others. They created wider risks and problems in society which spread beyond them and their neighbourhoods. This contamination was seen to take several different overlapping forms. These included:

- health contamination,
- moral contamination, and
- political contamination.

Health contamination

There were major outbreaks of contagious diseases including influenza, typhus, cholera and typhoid in the 1830s, 1840s and 1860s. These claimed large numbers of lives and while poorer people were less resistant and more exposed, such diseases were no respecters of class or status. They threatened the highest as well as the lowest and Victorian graveyards still bear witness to this. This led to legislation and measures to destroy insanitary dwellings, improve the quality of the water supply, impose controls on housing, particularly the housing of 'the poor' and introduce clearances to remove what were seen as the breeding grounds of 'fever' and 'miasma', the noxious gas thought to generate and spread disease. Key to these public health developments was the utilitarian, Edwin Chadwick (Wohl, 1984). Much less attention was paid to providing replacement or decent housing for poor people themselves.

When local authorities did build new housing to replace poor stock, they could also expect to come in for criticism. With the arrival of Jewish refugees in London's East End from the 1880s a new target became available. The anti-immigration campaigner and Conservative and Unionist MP, Samuel Forde Ridley, said in Parliament that it was 'grotesque' that British workmen had been cast out as a result of house building by the London County Council (LCC), so that 'alien families', code for Jewish families, could be 'comfortably ensconced in these dwellings'. His campaign was ultimately successful and resulted in the passing of the first explicit immigration legislation, the 1905 Aliens Act (Wise, 2009, 269).

At school in the 1920s

If someone had head lice, everyone knew because they shaved your head. It was shaming. But that's what they did then. If you had school dinners – and those that could went home or brought something – it was made by the older children. It was terrible.

Ida Kaufman
My mother (using her maiden name)

Moral contamination

The Victorians were no less concerned with the *moral* contagion that they attributed to the poor. This connects with the writings of the influential economist Thomas Malthus who, as we have seen, argued that population would outstrip resources and that *moral restraint* was ultimately the best means of easing the poverty of the lower classes and reducing the problem posed for society (Petersen, 1999). Prominent among Victorian concerns were the high levels of 'illegitimacy', sexual diseases, incest and reliance on drink and drugs which they associated with the poor. This is not to understate the significance of such issues. But we have little accurate idea of their scale among the better-off, or the scale of the latter's sexual exploitation of the poor, because the same scrutiny was not applied to them. This was in times when under-age prostitution was widely reported and syphilis was a major health problem across classes. There was a simplistic and condescending assumption that families forced to live in appalling circumstances would automatically be morally degraded by them. This was a short step to seeing the neighbourhoods they lived in as a moral threat to wider society which needed to be expunged. In 1926 the social reformer and Fabian, Beatrice Webb, thus wrote in her memoirs: 'To put it bluntly, sexual promiscuity, and even sexual perversion, are almost unavoidable among men and women of average character and intelligence crowded into the one-roomed tenements of slum areas' (quoted in Wise, 2009, 121).

She omitted to tell us what she thought of the sexual mores of more advantaged groups, like the Bloomsbury Set, wealthy enough to live in large town houses or arts and crafts manors. Fears of incest among families forced to live in single rooms, rather than a concern with their housing problems, was a major impetus for housing reform and indeed for the establishment of child protection charities like the NSPCC (the National Society for the Prevention of Cruelty to Children), established in 1884. While child sexual abuse appeared to be 'rediscovered' in the late twentieth century, it was a key issue in the organisation's reporting and publicity in the late nineteenth century: 'In cases of crime of an unnatural and immoral kind against girl children, the record is a black one … with, in many instances, the offenders being the fathers or near male relatives of the injured ones' (East End London NSPCC booklet, 1890–91, cited in Wise, 2009, 122).

As the century progressed, fear and distrust of this perceived rump or 'residuum' of poor people continued and even increased as there was sustained economic growth and the standards of working-class living seemed to rise. As Stedman Jones put it, the prevailing view was that: 'the problem was not structural but moral. The evil to be combated was not poverty, but pauperism: pauperism with its attendant vices, drunkenness, improvidence, mendicancy, bad language, filthy habits, gambling, low amusements and ignorance' (Stedman Jones, 1984, 11).

Medicalised concepts were extended into the moral domain. Thus, the concepts of 'moral insanity', 'moral idiocy', and 'moral imbecility', led to the emerging field of eugenic criminology, which held that crime could be reduced by preventing 'feeble-minded' people from reproducing.

The 'settlement' movement that developed from the 1880s has often been contrasted with the earlier 'case-based' social reformers. It aimed to get rich and poor people to live more closely together in society by encouraging middle-class volunteers to move into 'settlements' in poor areas. But like the Poor Law reform, the COS and Octavia Hill's housing schemes, it grew out of the social and economic crisis of the 1860s and its aims and analysis were also little different to theirs. It sought to offer a moral example and to re-educate the poor. As Stedman Jones put it: 'The traditional distinction between deserving and undeserving poor remained a central tenet of middle-class social philosophy both in its individualistic and in its collectivist forms' (Stedman Jones, 1984, 285).

Political contamination

Less often discussed has been the Victorians' fear of political contamination. Mid-century fears of political unrest, the 1848 European revolutions and the Chartists, have all been well documented. According to Stedman Jones, while the second half of the nineteenth century had seemed a time of improvement and progress, the economic crisis of the 1880s reawakened fears first raised by the economic difficulties of the 1860s that 'the residuum' was 'large enough to engulf London' (Stedman Jones, 1984, 283) There were also fears that this crisis might lead to it allying with and corrupting the broader 'respectable' working class (Whiteside, 2012). 'Separation of the respectable working class from the residuum had been a preoccupation of liberal theorists ever since the 1860s' (Stedman Jones, 1984, xx). The great worry was that if the latter's social and economic situation worsened, with increasing housing and employment problems, this would push them closer physically and temperamentally to the residuum. The result could be their becoming radicalised and disaffiliated, throwing in their 'lot with the casual poor' (Stedman Jones, 1984, 284) and creating a revolutionary threat to social order.

Social relations of Victorian poverty

From more modern perspectives, these threats, fears and moral questions seem rather more clearly rooted in economic, housing and health problems and inequalities. A major concern of the New Poor Law, like the old Poor Law before it, was that those who could work were made to work. In other words, the able-bodied poor had no escape from earning their own living. But neither Poor Law system could solve the problem of unemployed rural workers moving to towns to find work or the insecurity of casual workers' employment. If the Victorians interpreted the poverty of casual workers in terms of their laziness and immorality, modern commentators have evidenced that it was the result of economic insecurity and the routine exploitation of the workforce (Stedman Jones, 1971; Harris, 2004; Whiteside, 2012).

Insecure and under-employment

One effect of the New Poor Law was to keep wages down as people saw any job, whatever the wages or conditions, as preferable to the workhouse and Poor Law test (Wise, 2009, 75).

As Wise wrote: '"Overpopulation", not under-employment was understood by New Poor Law advocates to be the problem. (In *Oliver Twist*, Charles Dickens acidly named those with such beliefs "Experimental philosophers ... whose blood is ice, whose heart is iron")' (Wise, 2009, 76).

> **Baroness Decies**
>
> When Lady Decies (1844–1941) came back from a ball or a dinner, whatever the time – in the early hours of the morning – her personal maid would have to brush out her hair. That was her responsibility. She would have to wait up for her. And then she'd have to be up at six in the morning for her! When she was 90, the dowager still had all her teeth!
>
> *Stories my mother told us as children about my paternal grandmother.*

In this *Through the Looking-Glass* world, the dominant view was that it was the 'indiscriminate' availability of outdoor poor relief that led to the creation of a large 'residuum' of idle and thriftless able-bodied men, who were thus able to avoid working. The casualisation of employment and the inconsistency of the labour market were either ignored or downplayed (Wise, 2009, 84; Thane, 1996).

Housing conditions

Sarah Wise's study of one slum in Bethnal Green, London, the 'Old Nichol', highlighted that some of the most appalling dwellings with disproportionately high mortality rates even for the local area were also 'some of the most lucrative properties in the capital for their absent slum landlords, who included peers of the realm, local politicians and churchmen' (Wise, 2009, back cover). As late as 1887, Queen Victoria's Golden Jubilee, when there were many foreign visitors in London, levels of homelessness 'had become embarrassingly acute' (Wise, 2009, 78).

Health problems

Crammed into such slum neighbourhoods, with high morbidity and mortality rates, most poor people had to turn to the workhouse infirmary for medical help. The voluntary, charitable hospitals 'required a personal recommendation from a 'respectable' member of society and admission days were often restricted' (Wise, 2009, 83).

In her analysis of the notorious 'Old Nichol', Sarah Wise concluded that the 'quiet poor' formed the majority of local residents. As one interviewee had said: 'The predominant idea was paying the rent. That was the first and last duty of everybody, to pay the rent.' As Wise added, that was 'hardly the defining characteristic of a wild and feckless community' (Wise, 2009, 73–4). Yet this is how the Victorian social reformers seemed to see it and it is a view of disadvantaged neighbourhoods that has often been perpetuated since, with the continuing negative stereotyping of 'council estates' in the press and in television programmes.

Growing up in the East End

We lived in Parfett Street (previously called Nottingham Place*) – in three different houses in the street over the years, 14, 25 and 39. First it was in one room. I was born at number 14 where they had one room. Later we had two rooms. You've got to remember, people with eight children had two rooms. There were 40 houses in the street, on both sides, all Jews except two Christian families.

We sublet from someone who lived there. After 1937 my parents moved to Warden Street in Whitechapel, where they lived till they died. We had a kitchen and bedroom. My mother would make up the settee for me to sleep each night. They had lovely bedclothes. We had duvets and covers. People brought them over with them from Poland. No we didn't have proper curtains, we had net curtains, no carpet, we had lino and gas lamps. Nobody had carpet in those days. My mother had to get up on the chair to light the gas lamp. I thought about it afterwards, how dangerous for her. I used to play with my cousin Eve when she, her brother and her parents lived at 28 and we lived at 39. They – the Blooms – had the whole house – upstairs his workshop. He was a master tailor [married to my grandmother Dora's sister].

See also EB (1995)
Ida Kaufman
My mother (using her maiden name)

* See Charles Booth's notebooks (Booth, 2001), where he reports of the then-named Nottingham Place and surrounding streets, 'mixture of Jews, Christians and Germans' living there. In Booth's 1898–99 map Parfett Street was coloured purple, his fourth category, 'Mixed. Some comfortable, others poor'. Two streets away to the east was coloured dark blue – 'Very poor, casual. Chronic want'. Warden Street, my grandparents' last address was similarly coloured purple (http://booth.lse.ac.uk/cgi-bin/do.pl?sub=view_booth_and_barth&args=534 400,181350,1,large,0). Sarah Wise describes the colour purple as a 'catch-all' category to give Booth's maps some semblance of reflecting reality (Wise, 2009, 179). At the time of writing, estimates for house prices on Zoopla in Parfett Street are £800,000 plus.

The idea of the 'hard core pauper': a case study of the New Poor Law

As we have seen, from their earliest days poor laws and provision were motivated by the fear of a band of 'indolent' or threatening 'rogues and vagabonds' wandering about the country, avoiding or outwitting an essentially local system of relief and control and preying on villages and towns. Thus was born the idea of 'vagrants' and 'vagrancy' and the old Poor Law made increasingly punitive provision to identify, restrict the movement of and to punish and control the wide range of people it included in this category. These ranged from itinerant labourers and petty thieves, to the beggars, entertainers, actors, gypsies and fortune tellers, referred to earlier. As time passed, vagrancy legislation was modified to include whatever groups of people came to be seen as deviant, dangerous or threatening. The 1824 Vagrancy Act deemed the mere act of moving about or sheltering without a licence or means of support as a criminal offence (Ribton-Turner, 1889).

The New Poor Law, however, was a centralised system and therefore theoretically much better able than its predecessor to deal with this perceived problem. Yet it failed to do so. It made no mention of or provision for such vagrants. Initially it tried to exclude vagrants, but eventually had to compromise and admit them because of the deaths that had resulted. However, there were growing concerns that they undermined the workhouse regime and corrupted more 'deserving' inmates.

As a result, a separate system of 'casual wards' was established and their inmates known as the 'casual poor'. Inmates included men, women and children, although these were segregated. The system enforced mobility under threat of detention, requiring inmates to move on to the next casual ward after undertaking a work task. This tended to be harsh, like picking oakum (unpicking rope strands that had been coated with tar as ship's ballast or to calk their seams) with bare hands, or breaking rocks by smashing them into small pieces against an iron spike (from which came the term by which George Orwell referred to the casual wards he visited – the Spike – nearly a century later (Orwell, 1933)). Casual wards were increasingly prison-like, in some cases fitted out with cells. The numbers swelled in the 1840s and 1850s with Irish people seeking to escape the Irish Famine. They were once again the subject of increasingly repressive vagrancy legislation.

What the Victorians came to conceive of as 'hard core casuals' ended up defining the severity of the Poor Law. There was a constant official preoccupation with this group – those who were seen as not discouraged or reformed by the harshness of the regime. There was a regular concern either that conditions were not harsh enough for 'hard core casuals', or too harsh for other less undeserving paupers (Ribton-Turner, 1889; Booth, 1890).

According to Stedman Jones, by the second half of the nineteenth century:

> Vagrants were quite distinct from ordinary casual labourers, both in their habits and their economic attitudes [although] it is difficult to draw a precise line of demarcation between the two groups...Vagrancy itself was a vague term which included both the genuinely unemployed travelling in search of work, and professional tramps and beggars. (Stedman Jones, 1984, 88–9)

The casual wards established under the New Poor Law, became home both to those with no place of their own and those without regular employment, the two groups who made up 'the casual poor' so hated and feared by the Victorians. Ironically, these casual wards, symbolic of both the harshness and the failure of the New Poor Law, became one of its most visible expressions and also by far the most long lived, as we shall see later in this book.

Emerging contradictions

As the nineteenth century advanced, competing understandings, analyses and policy responses increasingly came into conflict with each other. Stedman Jones concluded that:

> The social crisis in London in the mid-1880s engendered a major reorientation of middle-class attitudes towards the casual poor. In conjunction with growing anxiety about the decline of Britain's industrial supremacy, apprehensions about the future political role of the working class, fear of the casual residuum played a significant part in provoking the intellectual assault which began to be mounted against laissez-faire both from the right and the left in the 1880s. (Stedman Jones, 1984, xxii)

Britain's position as the sole major industrial power was challenged, first by the USA and then more significantly by its imperial and economic rival, Germany. In the 1880s, Germany had introduced state-sponsored social insurance while Britain was facing an increasingly worrying 'social question'. Economic crises were raising growing middle-class fears of mass pauperism Over the period there were numerous official enquiries into social problems (Whiteside, 2012, 118–19).

Thus British policymakers were increasingly intervening to deal with the public health, housing and moral problems that they had conceived of as individual and moral problems. In so doing they were increasingly at odds with their own political, social and economic philosophies. Traditional liberal theory was not offering a solution to the problems that they faced. While issues were still often framed in individualistic, free market, laissez-faire terms, more and more policymakers were making social interventionist responses through provision for education, health and housing.

Practical policy and analysis became increasingly out of step. Thus later in the century, the Charity Organisation Society, frequently identified as a key pioneer of social administration and social work, was attacking the London School Board for providing shoes for barefoot children to attend school, on the grounds that it was encouraging parental neglect. Charitably supported free dispensaries and outpatient treatment by London hospitals were condemned for holding up the development of 'provident' habits (Stedman Jones, 1971, 270–1). Canon Barnett, social reformer and first warden of Toynbee Hall (after whom Oxford University named the site of its social work department), was still saying, 'the principle of our work is that we aim at decreasing, not suffering but sin' (Stedman Jones, 1971, 270).

Increasing consensus against the poorest

As more provision was made to deal with the worst effects of economic crisis and uncertainty, '"Able-bodied paupers", "clever beggars", and "the residuum" were still seen as a degraded force whose "demoralization" posed a threat to civilization, social order, and even the gene pool' (Stedman Jones, 1971).

The 'residuum' of the Victorians and the 'lumpen proletariat' of Marx continued to represent to middle classes, social reformers and trade unionists a reactionary and dangerous force. What is interesting, from our vantage point of the early twenty-first century, is that there could be such a negative consensus about some of the most oppressed, disadvantaged and marginalised people from these very different social and political positions. As the nineteenth century drew to its end, the political position of the working class – in both local and central government was improving and trades unions were exerting a greater influence (Stedman Jones, 1984, xvi). But this did not necessarily indicate any improvement in attitudes towards the casual poor. Thus, Ben Tillett, the dockers' leader and hero of the 1889 Great Dock Strike, said:

> Many of those who live in the black spots of misery had been so demoralized by want that they no longer had any desire for anything better … it was from these quagmires of degeneration that the hyenas of the revolution emerged. A socialist government would therefore have to think of ways and means to get rid of this scum. (Quoted in Wise, 2009, 164)

In the 1880s, there was discussion of the segregation and even preventive detention of 'loafers' and 'the unfit' (Stedman Jones, 1984, xvii, xx). Labour colonies were advocated along the lines of the colony established by the Salvation Army. Both Liberals and Fabians advocated compulsory detention and the 'elimination of the unfit'. The Fabian Canon Barnett suggested 'schools of restraint' where people could be detained for years. The liberal economist A.C. Pigou, in 1900 argued, in language that now has an even more alarming resonance than might originally have been intended: 'There is little prospect that a final solution to the problem will ever be achieved if public opinion cannot be brought to sanction, either the forcible detention of the wreckage of society, or the adoption of some other means to check them from propagating their species' (quoted in Stedman Jones, 1984, 332).

In New Poor Law Britain, the pattern of dealing with the poor who came to the authorities' attention included categorising, institutionalising and removing them. This meant their segregation in a growing range of institutions, including the workhouse, workhouse infirmary, casual ward, 'lunatic asylum', 'imbecile asylum', prison, schools for the blind, 'the deaf and dumb' and orphans. It could also mean clearances resulting from destroying their housing, communities and environments. Finally it could result in their removal to work and other colonies in the UK and the Empire. Towards the end of the century the emergence of eugenics ideas and the eugenics movement encouraged even more radical ideas of putting an end to pauperism and the poor by 'selective breeding'. Ironically for the Victorians, as Sarah Wise has highlighted, it was ultimately their commitment to laissez-faire rather than the poor themselves – as they had seen it – that seemed to put the nation at risk:

> The degeneration strand of thought would reach a peak in 1902 following the revelation of the vast numbers of working-class males deemed to be in too poor a physical condition to be accepted for [army] service ... during the second Boer War.... [This] would lead to the National Efficiency movement and a new impetus for the State to intervene to improve the British 'race', since *laissez-faire* had wreaked such damage. (Wise, 2009, 218)

Conclusion

Victorian social policy has many warnings and insights to offer that are still pertinent today. During the century we see both the creation of heavily ideologised social policy in the form of the utilitarian New Poor Law and also increasing consensus about its failure and the need to take a different turning. The story of nineteenth-century UK social policy cannot really be seen as the progressive story – as we are still sometimes encouraged to believe – of improved understanding of 'the poor' and more positive theory and policy in relation to them (for example, Alcock et al, 2012). Nor is it only a story of a monopoly Poor Law, but also of other charitable and church-led services which largely operated under a similar set of values and assumptions. What unfolds is thinking which increasingly created and isolated a group of disadvantaged and impoverished people and created a consensus around the need to control them. By the end of the century serious thought was even being given to eradicating what was seen as this troubling and damaging group of people. Yet much evidence and more and more policy pointed in a very different direction.

From such a distance of time, it is difficult to have a sense of the scale and degree of suffering, fear and misery that Victorian social policy engendered. People killed themselves and suffered desperately to keep away from it (Wise, 2009, 72). It broke up marriages, families and sometimes even communities. In the nineteenth century, if you faced difficult personal, or social and economic circumstances, this is what you could expect and may have dreaded would happen to you.

For a significant part of the nineteenth century social policy served as a stopper on the social and economic consequences of the advance of capitalism. As time went by, it also developed as a response to the needs of capitalism for a reasonably healthy, basically educated and disciplined working class, to fill both its factories and armed forces.

It is difficult to consider nineteenth-century social policy and social theory in relation to poor people and poverty without being drawn to reflect on growing parallels with our own times. There seems to be the same flight from evidence, the same scapegoating of the most powerless, the same dislocation of policymakers from most citizens, the same capacity to spread negative stereotypes of the poor widely and the same determination on the part of powerful people to understand issues in moral terms, even though they often profited from these problems and their own moral and ethical position was constantly being called into question.

In this chapter we have looked at the antecedents of the welfare state. The longstanding fear and hatred they engendered undoubtedly played a part in creating popular pressure for something different. In the next chapter, we will explore the more immediate circumstances that led to the creation of the welfare state.

THREE

The origins of the welfare state

Man becomes great exactly in the degree in which he works
for the welfare of his fellow-men.
   (Mahatma Gandhi)

The more you can increase fear of drugs and crime, welfare
mothers, immigrants and aliens, the more you control all
the people.
   (Noam Chomsky)

There is little that is not contentious about the 'welfare state'. It was a
term that Sir William Beveridge, the individual most closely associated
with it in Britain, apparently disliked – since as critics comment – he
was anxious to emphasise the limits to state responsibility (Mitton,
2012, 36; Collins, 2013, 28). While in the UK the 'welfare state' has
come to be seen as a native concept, in fact it was a term that was used
earlier in Germany in the 1920s (Gladstone, 2008, 24). Uruguay was
described as 'South America's first welfare state' as a result of reforms
made in the first third of the twentieth century (Pendle, 1952). As
time has passed, there has also been an increasing tendency to see
the origins of the British welfare state as lying further and further in
the past. In some cases this has resulted in the reframing of punitive
nineteenth-century policy in 'welfare' terms that its recipients would
doubtless find very difficult to comprehend (Gladstone, 2008, 24).

Frequently now, the Liberal government reforms of 1906–11 are
taken as a key starting point (Alcock, 2008; Baldock et al, 2012;
Whiteside, 2012, 121). Certainly these extended the role of the state
in social policy. But how helpful it is to make a linear connection with
the post-war welfare state, is open to serious question. Lavinia Mitton,
social policy academic, has argued that the welfare state was 'constrained
by being based on an existing haphazard collection of measures' and
that: 'for this reason there is ongoing debate about the extent to which
the post-Second World War structures of British welfare were laid down
in the reforms introduced prior to 1939 or whether they represented
a distinct break with the past' (Mitton, 2012, 33).

Every reform, however radical, has to build on what has gone before, however and will be more or less affected by it. This argument would equally underplay the radicalism and innovation of the utilitarian New Poor Law. What distinguishes the post-war welfare state were its *principles*. As Mitton herself acknowledges, few if any of these key principles, underpinned those earlier reforms (Mitton, 2012, 32–3). We will be looking in depth at them in Chapter Five.

Here we are concerned with what led to the creation of the welfare state. In a current social policy student textbook, social policy academic John Baldock explains that there have been two major competing explanatory accounts of the development of welfare states in the literature. He typifies these as:

- industrialisation and the social needs it generates, 'particularly unemployment and poverty' making the provision of state welfare 'more or less inevitable';
- political competition resulting in the coming to political power of the interests of industrial workers and later other social groups and movements (Baldock, 2012, 23).

Neither of these over-simplistic models on its own offers a sufficient or convincing explanation even of the nineteenth-century developments we have so far considered, although from a broad brush perspective, elements of both can be discerned. To get a clearer idea here of why the welfare state came into being when and how it did, we will be looking less at social policy and legislative developments in the preceding years, or such grand theory, and more at socio-economic and political developments and the responses that they engendered. We need to find an explanation for a shift from a Britain committed to laissez-faire, accepting state intervention only when it felt obliged to, to one where central control and state intervention could almost be said to have become the norm. What caused such a profound change?

The first half of the twentieth century was a tumultuous period for Britain, Europe and world-wide. It was marked by three interlinked and cataclysmic events, all of which affected the creation and form of the UK welfare state. These were the Great (or First World) War of 1914–18, the great inter-war depression and the Second World War of 1939–45. Two ideologies also emerged, fascism and communism, which had a global impact, continue to influence culture and thinking and which ultimately came into collision, both with each other and with western social democracies.

If we were looking for any monolithic cause for the creation of the welfare state, then we would probably turn to the Second World War. If we want to try and make more realistic sense of its origins, then we will be drawn to look at the complex, cumulative and interweaving roles played by all three of these events.

The Great War

As we look today at the village memorials with long lists of names of those killed in the Great War, it is difficult to comprehend how shatteringly different in ordinary experience this war was to anything that had gone before. Whatever suffering the Crimea, Boer and a host of colonial wars had involved, they had been distant conflicts waged by professionals. This was a different kind of war, the first European war waged on an industrial scale with all the paraphernalia of modern industry and science. We can get a taste of it from the American Civil War of 1861–65, with its mass casualties – but this was foreign territory to most Britons. While there was still romantic talk of personal death 'on a foreign field', the reality was of people routinely killed and maimed on the same scale and in the same mechanical ways as operated in Victorian factory mass production.

The war may not, as the contemporary rhetoric suggested, have 'destroyed a generation' or wiped out 'the flower of British youth', but it certainly transformed it and the nation. Britain's peacetime army had been less than a quarter of a million. Wars that once involved tens of thousands now involved millions. Now the only constraints on the size of armies and, correspondingly of casualties, were organisational and these were swiftly overcome. 'Daily wastage', that is casualties when there weren't major battles, ran into thousands. During the war, nearly nine million men and women are estimated to have served in the UK armed forces. Nearly three quarters of a million British service men were killed and 1.65 million wounded, of a UK population of 46 million (Army Council, 1921). Of these, around 240,000 British soldiers suffered total or partial leg or arm amputations (www.spartacus-educational.com/FWWamputations.htm). Following the war, there was a massive increase in death, disability and 'invalid' pensions to officers and men, widows and dependants. Nearly two and a half million men were to be entitled to a war pension – although these were far from generous (Doyle, 2012, 15). This compares with the average 3 per cent of the 28 million population of England and Wales (840,000) who were reliant on poor relief in the 1880s (Wise, 2009, 82).

If, before the war, the state had only been a distant idea for most people other than paupers, with, for example, conscription and massively increased reliance on war pensions, it became a direct reality for many millions more. The extraordinarily increased power of the state over the citizen was a defining characteristic of the war and one which took many expressions. It directly brought about a wide and profound range of changes. This included major changes in relationships, including relationships:

- *between classes.* The numbers needed for a conscript army created a new social mobility between classes, with 'temporary gentlemen' recruited as officers to make up for public school casualties and officers promoted from the ranks. The middle and upper classes came into closer and more direct contact with working-class people, leading them in the armed forces. This encouraged the 'one nation' Conservativism of later leaders and former soldiers, such as future prime ministers, Harold Macmillan and Anthony Eden.
- *between men and women.* Women were recruited into industry in large numbers during the war, gaining new economic and social independence and earning unprecedented wages (in munitions, more than £2 a week – half the wages paid to men, but far in excess of the shilling a day (five pence) received by frontline soldiers (Doyle, 2012, 37). With men in the forces, women took on more responsibilities and more young women left the family home to live independently in hostels and lodgings. There was a new flexibility and freedom between the sexes. There were also massively increased divorce rates post war (Adie, 2013).
- *between workers and employers.* Industrial relations worsened with inflation, shortages, massive rent rises and 'manpower' shortages, which were associated with increased industrial unrest, disputes and strikes.
- *between the state and its citizens.* State intervention increased on an unprecedented scale, with food control, rationing and price fixing. The 'Defence of the Realm Act' (DORA) gave government enormous powers to requisition land and factories and shape people's lives, with new licensing laws, the introduction and extension of 'British Summer Time' and even the imposition of curfews on shops and places of public entertainment.
- *between Britain, Ireland and its empire.* Because of the key military, political and economic roles they played in supporting Britain in wartime, empire nations increasingly challenged its traditional

dominance and sought a new equality and independence, both diplomatically and through revolt and resistance.

- *between government, economy and industry*. The economy was put on a war footing and centrally directed by government, with all munitions manufacturers brought under the control of a new Ministry of Munitions and required to replace men with women to free them for the forces. (Doyle, 2012)

If the Edwardian era that preceded the Great War has been presented as an age of imperial confidence, then the war itself called into question many widely accepted certainties and assumptions. It encouraged a loss of confidence and trust in their elders from young people and led to a glut of post-war books that emphasised their sense of betrayal and lost innocence (Remarque, 1929; Graves, 1960; Herbert, 1919). It was followed by an influenza epidemic which killed as many people as had the war itself. Now there were many new issues, personal and social problems to deal with, with many more widowed families, young disabled and psychologically damaged people, major increases in marriage breakdown and children born outside marriage. As well as inspiring solidarity, the Great War encouraged new divisions and antagonisms; for example, between those who fought and 'conscientious objectors'; between 'profiteers' and those who suffered from the war, between service men who could be shot for desertion and trade unions which had supported strikes and industrial action. The sense of betrayal engendered by the war, also generated other divisions; between those who felt betrayed by the establishment and ruling classes (the communists) and those who felt betrayed by Jews, other minorities and more progressive politics (the fascists). But the war also transformed understandings and experiences and offered people new opportunities and expectations.

The Great War represented a cataclysmic change for Britain which had stood outside major European Wars for nearly a century. Not surprisingly as well as the immediate changes it brought, it also had major longer-term consequences. In 1914, just over one and a half million people earned enough to qualify to pay income tax, a tiny proportion of the population. At the same time, many more, 16 per cent of the population were estimated to be living in poverty (Doyle, 2012, 21). Having been expected to 'make the supreme sacrifice', millions of returning soldiers did not even have the vote. The electorate was tripled between 1912 and the end of 1918. But it was not until 1928 that all men had the vote and there was electoral equality for women, a belated response to their wartime contribution.

Inter-war depression

The war had a severe economic cost for Britain, creating enormous debts and greatly reducing the value of sterling. However, the right of centre historian Correlli Barnett has argued that 'in objective truth the Great War in no way inflicted crippling economic damage on Britain', but it 'crippled the British *psychologically*' (Barnett, 2002, 424, 426). Lloyd George's rhetoric had been of 'homes fit for heroes'. The reality was dole queues, begging, hunger marches, homelessness and poverty on an unprecedented scale. The Victorian fear of a working class reduced to and contaminated by pauperism actually came closest to realisation in the 1930s, rather than the nineteenth century (Overy, 2009).

Before the welfare state

Life was very hard in the East End, however neighbourly it still was. You'd see the prostitutes going to the clinic at the London Hospital before the war, with deteriorated syphilis. Their faces were eaten away. I felt sorry for them. God knows what had led them to where they were.

Ida Kaufman
My mother (using her maiden name)

Unemployment was the dominant issue in British society during the interwar years. Unemployment levels rarely dipped below one million and reached a peak of three million in 1933, a figure which represented 20 per cent of the working population (not including many more who had only part-time jobs, those not registered or who could not claim employment benefit) (Laybourne, 1999, 105). This was the time of unemployment marches like the Jarrow Crusade, when people were effectively reduced to petitioning government (invariably unsuccessfully) for the dirty, dangerous and poorly paid jobs they were now denied. The reasons for the long period of economic hardship in the UK in the inter-war years were complex and varied. They had political, ideological, industrial and social origins. Initial economic problems were closely linked with the war. Reduced demand with war ending and an increased supply of labour from returning soldiers, increasing international competition, shipping losses, loss of markets, industries in need of modernisation, the effects of German coal reparations, an initial commitment to free trade, political instability, realignments and incompetence, all contributed to a damaging decade.

This was epitomised by the General Strike of 1926 and the divisions and hatreds still associated with it. The Conservative government's misguided attempt to return sterling to the gold standard in 1925, which lasted until 1931, slowed economic recovery and led to reductions in workers' wages.

William Beresford

If people think the miners shouldn't go on strike, why don't they try working in the mines?

(My mother, Ida Beresford, often quoted this to us as children, of our father in the 1930s)

Depression loomed even larger in the 1930s, the deepest economic depression the UK experienced in the twentieth century. The 1929 Wall Street Crash triggered a world-wide depression as the United States called in its debts. The UK still hadn't recovered from the effects of the Great War. Victorian staple industries which were associated with the North, South Wales and Central Scotland – coal, ship-building, steel, cotton and wool, which were in decline – were hardest hit. Jobs were cut and governments reduced expenditure in the development and investment of their home industries. Unemployment reached 70 per cent in some areas at the start of the 1930s and many families depended entirely on 'dole' payments from local government. Thus the images that have come down to us and are associated with the age, are of hunger marches, dole queues, soup kitchens, begging and homeless people.

Inter-war social policy reflected prevailing economic thinking. There were cuts in public spending, wages and in the dole. In the 1930s people who were long-term unemployed still had to rely on Poor Law relief. This unemployment benefit was subject to a strict means test, to see whether benefit could be reduced and anyone applying for unemployment pay had to have an inspection by an official to make sure that they had no hidden earnings or savings, undisclosed sources of income or other means of support. The process took into account the income and goods of the *whole* household. For many poor people this was a demeaning and degrading experience that summed up the age in which they lived. Means-testing became dirty words for millions, like the Poor Law before them. As Pearce has noted: 'Many benefits were technically on offer in the 1930s, but there seemed to be an array of means tests to stop people receiving them. By 1939 there were no fewer than eighteen different means tests in operation for benefits administered by seven different ministries' (Pearce, 2012, 71).

Living with the Poor Law in the 1930s

How did we manage? We didn't, we just had to do the best we could. Half the women in our street had husbands out of work. We never claimed relief even when I was without work...The women had to work. They took in washing if they had a mangle or went out scrubbing floors. You had to pawn to buy food, and pawn to pay the rent. You only saw Sunday best for the one day. It was washed and dry by Monday to go back in hock. The women wore heavy black shawls instead of overcoats, and the kids only had the clothes on their back. On Sunday they stayed in bed while mum washed them ready for school on Monday. We lived on leftovers; stale bread and pot herbs. We were brought up on bread and marge and bread and drip. But families stuck together and helped each other, and the neighbours were wonderful. Still they were terrible times.

Poor Law relieving officer looking back to the 1920s and 1930s

It was a miserable existence for those who were on relief. It was the minimum you could manage on. I can honestly say that I've had wives crawling across the floor to my desk on their knees weeping and begging for food. You tried to do the best you could, but you didn't have that much leeway. If the guardians or the public assistance committee made out I was giving out too much under my emergency powers, I used to quote the general consolidated order at them, that I found the need and relieved it in accordance with my statutory duty. My chief once said to me, 'It's easier to tell the auditor why you gave relief than the coroner why you didn't'.

The author
(Beresford, 1969, 723)

The Conservative Party dominated the era politically; the Labour and Liberal parties were split. Deflationary economic policies, committed to reducing the public deficit, ruled. These exacerbated social and economic problems and divisions. This was a time of massive economic change and political realignments. The 'National' governments in power from 1931 to 1940 were increasingly Conservative-led, drawing Labour leaders associated with them, into supporting traditional economics. Some Liberal and Labour leaders explored Keynesian economics. John Maynard Keynes' theory challenged assumptions of neo-classical economics that free markets provided full employment. He argued instead that state intervention was necessary to moderate 'boom and bust' cycles of economic activity (Skidelsky, 2010). However, there was no large-scale state intervention in Britain along the lines associated with the United States under President Roosevelt's 'New Deal'.

The Great Depression was never only an economic problem. Its global nature meant that it was also associated with international and ideological conflict. It encouraged the rise of fascism, including the development of the British Union of Fascists led by Oswald Mosley, formerly a Labour Party leader. Ironically the UK depression only began to come to an end with the massive programme of rearmament embarked upon by the National Government in 1936. As late as 1940, there were still a million unemployed (Overy, 2010).

The 1930s, London's East End, Mosley and the police

Policemen came round to the market stall holders for bribes every week not to move them on. They were on the side of the Mosleyites during the fascist troubles in the thirties. I saw one old Jewish man being grabbed by the beard and carted off to police cells. He had done nothing. They'd pick on the young boys. It wasn't Dixon of Dock Green.

Ida Kaufman
My mother (using her maiden name)

Compare this with another account by Victor Gregg, looking back to himself as a young man of 18 who left family poverty in Bloomsbury to sign up as an army regular before the war and served throughout the Second World War.

These were the days when opinions were formed by reading newspapers, listening to the wireless and taking part in discussions. The different papers all had their own specific points of view. The worst was the *Daily Mail*, with its rabid support of the Hitler regime in Germany and its backing of the British Union of Fascists led by Oswald Mosley and his Blackshirts.

Blackshirt gangs used to go round the streets causing mayhem, breaking the windows of Jewish shopkeepers and doing their best to put the fear of God into anyone who opposed them. The worst thing about all of this was the protection they had from the police. If the Blackshirts were involved in violence it wasn't them who ended up in court the next morning. (Gregg, 2011, 22)

The dole and hunger marches were, however, far from the whole story of inter-war Britain (Gardiner, 2004). The reality was very far from this uniform image. Britain was much more about division than homogeneity. Left of centre writer and broadcaster J.B. Priestley travelled the length of England in 1933 and concluded that there were at least three Englands: the 'old England' of cathedrals, manor houses and inns, the nineteenth century England of heavy industry and back-to-backs and the 'new England' of the Midlands and south east associated with new light industries. There were also the Englands of the 'very rich and of the poverty-stricken' (Pearce, 2012, 11). North and south painted very different pictures. While the new generation of 'social explorers' headed north to report decay, squalor and death from TB, the Midlands and south epitomised a new emerging age of production and consumption. As some people were dying through health problems brought about by lack of food, decent housing and access to medical care, others were gaining from the benefits of a new age of transport, technology and mass media.

This is the other world we read about of weekly trips to the cinema, Hollywood and 'the talkies', of mass produced fashion and domestic gadgets, of paid holidays and holiday camps, young people mobile on motorbikes and mock Tudor semi-detached houses. This was the world portrayed in films like David Lean's *This Happy Breed* (1944) and the heyday of the *Daily Mail* Ideal Home exhibition. Throughout the 1930s building was Britain's chief industry, and the suburbs began to spread (Delderfield, 1958a). Mortgages were becoming more accessible and more people from the middle and skilled working classes than ever before bought their first home, even if for most people private rented accommodation was still the norm. From 1926 to 1939, over 200,000 new houses were built every year, with the peak reaching 365,000 in 1936. Over this period we can see the flowering of modernism in art, design, architecture, literature and intellectual life, all exerting their influence on popular culture and everyday lives (Hughes, 1991).

This is not to say that the poverty and the Poor Law didn't still loom large in popular understanding and the cultural representations of the period. George Orwell summed up all the different Englands in his novels and social commentaries, as well as in his foray into fighting fascism in Spain, but he is best remembered for his inroads into poverty and the Poor Law (Orwell, 1933, 1937). He was, however, only one of many social explorers doing the rounds of slums, casual wards and street sleeping in the 1930s. Homelessness resurfaced as a symbol of poverty and exclusion in the interwar period as it had done in Victorian England. This new generation of social commentators highlighted again the failings of the Poor Law and suggested that efforts to ameliorate both its problems and harshness were inadequate and unacceptable (see, for example, Gray, 1931; Bentley, 1933; Keating, 1976). Interestingly the solutions to problems of homelessness of progressives like Orwell tended to be no more radical than those of the Poor Law itself (Beresford, 1979, 145–6).

The Second World War

The 1930s were truly a paradoxical decade. And just as life seemed to be getting better for many people, war loomed. The Second World War was the third of the interconnected elements that were to dominate and shape individual and social consciousness in Britain in the first half of the twentieth century and to influence the complex and subtle national psyche that was to follow. The Second World War could also be described as the second major consequence of the Great War, with the great depression its first. Individuals and families in their millions, had had to live with an unremitting sense of fear and anxiety since 1914, first through losses from the Great War, then of poverty and unemployment through the depression and most recently, with the rise to power of Hitler, of another European war. The declaration of war in 1939 meant that for most, there was now no doubt about more suffering and hardship to come.

This second war was also clearly the event that had the most immediate impact on people, politics and government in the following period. If we want to understand the UK welfare state and, perhaps also its subsequent development, it is this war that we perhaps must try most carefully to make sense of – even if we must also always connect its impact with the earlier war and depression that preceded it. All were key in shaping contemporary attitudes, memory and understanding. All three shared common themes, which included:

- increased uncertainty and risk
- traumatic change
- increased consciousness of individual vulnerability
- new opportunities, roles and experiences
- changes in relationships and expectations
- new lines of division, conflict and collaboration
- increased awareness of the force and limits of state intervention.
  (Marwick, 1976; Purvis, 1995; Rowbotham, 1997)

The Second World War was more disruptive than any war before it. It was fought as much by civilians as armed forces – for the first time civilian casualties internationally outnumbered military ones. Families were separated, sometimes never to be reunited; neighbourhoods destroyed and sometimes never re-established. 'As an indication of the uprooting and restless, harried movement of the population, there would be 34,750,000 changes of address among civilians alone in the course of the war' (Titmuss, cited in Waller, 2012, 27).

The creation of the welfare state is inextricably associated with the Second World War and it is questionable if it would ever have come about without it. But simplistic ideas about that war have helped to perpetuate subsequent misunderstandings about the welfare state itself. For this reason, an initial warning here may be helpful. We need to be clear what the Second World War was not. It wasn't the simple age of the Dunkirk and Blitz spirit, when cockney sparrows kept up morale and 'we all pulled together', as handed down to us by innumerable films, books and commemorative newspaper stories and TV documentaries. As Stuart Hylton's book on the home front reminds us, 'Britain won the war despite the best efforts of the bureaucrats, defeatists, profiteers and bigots' (Hylton, 2010, vii–viii). By all accounts, the prevailing feeling for most people between 1939 and 1945 was tiredness, from working long hard shifts; the dominant colour was grey and most things were on their last legs.

The war brought about massive changes, however, which offered insights, experience and examples of how things could be different. While we have some information, we can only imagine what this all meant for people. We can expect that for both ordinary people and policymakers, citizens and politicians, personally and collectively, it pointed to and opened up different possibilities, different ways of coming at issues and different solutions. And of course, the biggest issue that faced Britain was how things should be after the war.

The war brought people and groups together who ordinarily would have little or no contact, in ways that the nineteenth-century settlement movement sought to, but never achieved. Crucially this happened on the basis of class and gender, but also along lines of ethnicity, sexuality, age and disability. It resulted from the mass evacuation of children, recruitment of women to the forces, industry and voluntary work, forces billeting, the coming of American forces, government requisitioning of housing and so on. It all happened on an unprecedented scale. Thus the majority of women under 40 were working during the war, with women up to 50 added from 1943 (De La Bedoyere, 2011, 27–9). The Women's Land Army finally numbered 80,000; 100,000 women were working on the railways; nearly half a million in the armed forces (Hylton, 2010, 203–10). For many this meant an alternative to low paid shop work or domestic service. In 1939 4,837,800 women were employed. At the peak in 1943 it was 6,759,000 (Eden Camp, 2013). By 1943 a million women were volunteers with the Women's Voluntary Service set up to 'serve and protect' local communities in wartime (Malcolmson and Malcolmson, 2013).

The scheme for evacuation highlighted the level of ignorance about the lives of working-class families and children, both among the better off and policymakers. While three million schoolchildren and others were meant to leave centres of population, many didn't go or rapidly returned. As one contemporary study observed: 'only middle-class parents, accustomed to shooing their children out of sight and reach at the earliest possible age, could have been so astonished to find that working-class parents were violently unwilling to part with theirs' (cited in Hylton, 2010, 41).

Different groups had new kinds of contact with each other and began to learn new things about each other. However, this didn't always result in greater understanding. There was talk of evacuees as 'low slum types...dirty and idle' and of children 'bound to grow up into just such sub-human savages, unless we seize this opportunity of saving them' (cited in Hylton, 2010, 36–62). Some Victorian attitudes hardly seemed to have changed. Britain's class divisions seemed remarkably resistant to change. Animosity was increased by the overseas evacuation of wealthy people. 'Class resentment' was also identified against better-off women who could escape being directed into factory and similar employment by doing 'voluntary work' (Hylton, 2010, 61, 69).

The state was now intervening on a scale that was unprecedented even by the standards of the 1914–1918 war. The 1940 Emergency Powers Act meant that government could exercise complete control of UK manpower and war production. The man with this massive authority, ironically, was Ernest Bevin, general secretary of Britain's largest trade union, the TGWU (Transport and General Workers' Union) invited by Winston Churchill to be a member of the War Cabinet, 'who could now decide the job of every person between the age of 14 and 65', including those fit and unfit for military service (Eden Camp, 2013). The mining industry had still not recovered from pre-war industrial conflict and decline but was now desperately needed, so one in ten conscripts were diverted to it, despite much resistance and hostility from trade unions, miners and the 'Bevin Boys', as they were known, themselves. Bevin commanded support and respect from the trade unions, gave them a new importance in public policy and maintained collective bargaining and industrial health and safety standards (Bullock, 2002; Hylton, 2010, 69). By 1943, 400,000 people had been directed to war work, but Bevin 'never became a dictator', saying, 'I have stuck to leadership as long as I can rather than resort to drastic compulsion.' The government also demonstrated that the Keynesian goal of full employment could be achieved, with 22 million in employment in 1943 (Eden Camp, 2013).

Between 1939 and 1945, people were organised as never before. An alphabet of acronyms developed to signify the many organisations they were encouraged to join: the AFS (Auxiliary Fire Service), ARP (Air Raid Precautions), ATS (Auxiliary Territorial Service), CD (Civil Defence), the NAAFI (Navy, Army and Air Force Institutes), the WRAC (Women's Royal Army Corps), the WRENS (Women's Royal Naval Service), the LDV (Local Defence Volunteers), VADs (Voluntary Aid Detachments) and so on. Some roles were taken on as volunteers, but by no means all. For example, there were paid air raid wardens, rescue men, firemen and some women ambulance drivers. In terrible times of bombing, loss, homelessness, poverty, death and injury, people helped each other as rescue crews, auxiliary firemen, air raid wardens, messengers (including children), motorcycle despatch riders (including women) and fire watchers. The state may have organised them, but at ground level and first hand this could be and was understood in another way. People's experience was also of organising to look after *each other* and of being helped by strangers. While of course some measure of 'little Hitler' officiousness went with this, like, for example, the 'Put that light out' mentality of the air raid warden in TV's *Dad's Army*, we also know that much good was also widely associated with it. The help and support people received and gave each other, was an important experience and perhaps what gives the most truth to folk recollections of 'all being in it together', of pulling together and a sense of common purpose associated with the war (Delderfield, 1958b).

There were undoubted negatives as well, but significantly these mostly seemed to be associated with the old system, old attitudes and class assumptions. Thus the Poor Law, already widely feared and hated, came to have an even broader and more doleful impact as a result of wartime conditions. In 1939 there were still 100,000 people in workhouses. Arrangements made by local authorities to receive evacuees were rooted in the Poor Law and Poor Law attitudes. Thousands made homeless by bombing who would never have expected to have come the way of the Poor Law, suddenly found themselves at the mercy of its worst excesses and incompetence. More eyes were opened to its failings.

In late September 1940, some 25,000 people were living in London's rest centres, which were run under the Victorian Poor Law system for the destitute and were avoided by all who could possibly do so.

> One rural rest centre greeted its bombed-out guests with a
> large sign containing the following uplifting information:
> 'Behind every social problem is revealed the hidden hand
> of alcohol'. (Hylton, 2010, 136–7)

This wasn't learning about other worlds and other lives through the
mediation of social explorers, but people finding out for *themselves*
and telling each other. Meanwhile letters to the right-wing *Spectator*
magazine complained about the authorities 'thrusting filthy women
and children [evacuees] into the homes of decent ... people'. Fears
of the 'fifth column' and 'enemy aliens' provided an opportunity to
promote racist hatred and divisions, with Jews and Italians particular
targets (Hylton, 2010, 9, 14).

If traditional condescending and cost-cutting attitudes of local and
central state were increasingly shown to be wanting during the war,
there were also new wartime developments which pointed in a different
direction. This included the expansion of services to support people in
difficult times, from state and municipal restaurants where people could
get a decent meal at a reasonable cost and nursery day care provision
for the many mothers now in employment, to the building of durable
good quality prefabricated housing – 'prefabs' – to replace damaged
and destroyed stock and the equalising effects of rationing and price
regulation. Hostels were opened, maternity and convalescent homes
and play centres established. Of course, how people saw interventions
like the requisitioning of accommodation and billeting of families
made homeless by bombing, depended on their vantage point. But
increasingly the state was occupying the moral high ground, intervening
to offer help to those facing difficulties, rather than supporting its own
or other powerful interests. It also attacked the 'two sacred Victorian
cows that were on no account to be slaughtered', the sanctity of private
property and the self-reliance of the poor (Wise, 2009, 18).

While it was still a world of officers and other ranks; of factory 'girls'
and ladies 'doing their bit', major changes were taking place. From 1942
officers were selected in a different way through 'War Office Selection
Boards' (WOSBys) which placed more emphasis on competence than
class. While class distinctions were still strong – officers and 'men' lived
in different quarters, ate in different 'messes' and were awarded different
medals – even if they did the same job or showed the same courage,
the forces encouraged a new kind of social mobility. People rubbed
shoulders who wouldn't have done so previously. The services, 'going
overseas', war work, leaving home, hitchhiking and the arrival of the
Americans and other nationals, all broke down longstanding barriers

and opened people's eyes to different lives and different possibilities for their own.

Even where class barriers remained, people could more clearly see the inequalities that operated. While maximum weekly rations during the war were, for example, four ounces [113 grams] of tea a week, half a pound [1/4 kilo] of cheese and one egg or a packet of 'egg powder', luxury food was still available for those with enough money; eating out didn't require ration coupons and the high life continued at London's grand hotels for the rich, titled and con artists (Zweiniger-Bargielowska, 2002; Hylton, 2010, 77; Sweet, 2011). Class divisions still determined many things: from what people could eat, to what kind of work they were directed and even where they sheltered in a raid – a damp Morrison shelter or the converted basements of luxury hotels. In 1940 East End residents and a local councillor marched on the Savoy, demanding shelter and better air raid shelters for the East End, in 'the most serious political demonstration of the war' (Sweet, 2011, 50). Significantly, by 1942, 'Home Intelligence was reporting public outrage' at apparent inequalities: 'There is growing evidence of a feeling among certain sections of the public that "everything is not fair and equal and that therefore our sacrifices are not worthwhile"' (Hylton, 2010, 80).

Conclusion

As we have seen, the Second World War had complex, transformative and often tragic effects upon people's lives. Both the war and policy responses to it had an enormous impact on almost everybody's experience and ideas. But it wasn't just this which influenced what was to follow, including the creation of the welfare state. The war was also a time of active planning for the future. Thus, to make sense of the welfare state, as well as putting it in a long-term social policy context, we need to consider it in relation to two key interactions. These were between:

1. people's lives and their experiences of the first half of the century, culminating in the Second World War itself;
2. this war and its immediate effects on politics, policy, policymakers and opinion formers.

We will return to these in the next chapter.

FOUR

The welfare state and pressures from the war

It will be the same old story, those who can pull the strings will be all right, the other poor buggers can look after themselves.

(Army tradesman interviewed by Mass Observation, 1943, quoted in Kynaston, 2008, 45)

Keeping going fighting in the war…We had a feeling deep down inside us that we were fighting for you – and all the other babies…all these people were fighting for you, Tim.

(*A Diary for Timothy*, documentary film (Jennings, 1945))

The problems of victory are more agreeable than those of defeat. But they are no less difficult.

(Winston Churchill, 1942, in Churchill, 2011)

It's difficult in retrospect to have any idea of how catastrophic and chaotic life in Europe was by the end of the war, not least because so few signs of this remain. While the UK had not suffered the material and psychological effects of invasion and occupation, its post-war commitment to radical domestic reform, social change and equality are nonetheless amazing, particularly by today's standards of political short termism. While Britain set to work to create the welfare state, Europe was the site of an explosion of violence and brutality. This included civil war, 'ethnic cleansing' rape and murder, which were rife for years. The breakdown of law and order extended from Poland to Italy and France and Yugoslavia, to Germany and Greece (Lowe, 2013; Buruma, 2013).

With the certainty that comes from hindsight, some modern analysts have argued that: 'It is unlikely that something along the lines of the Welfare State would have been long delayed had the war not intervened' (Hylton, 2010, 214).

As Bentley Gilbert wrote in his history of social policy between 1914 and 1939:

> The Beveridge Report and the White Papers on National Insurance and the National Health Service, children's allowances and the announcement of a policy for full employment were all products of wartime experience... More important, they represented attempts to find solutions to problems of peace...The destruction of wealth between 1939 and 1945 made action more immediately necessary, but the war itself did not bring the welfare state. (Gilbert, 1970, vii)

Truth to tell though, while some commentators, as we have seen, have also made a linear connection between the 1906–11 Liberal social reforms and the creation of the welfare state, there can be no evidence for such assertions and there were no certainties at the end of the war. Instead as we shall see, it is unlikely that many members of the population would have banked on change. It was not even expected that Labour would win the post-war election and if women alone had voted, then they may not have done. As the historian Peter Hennessy has said while 'much of the thinking had been done by the late 1930s ... it took the impact of an all-in, total war, in which the entire British people were in the front line, to make [the welfare state] happen so swiftly and comprehensively' (British Academy, 2008).

What can be said, as the previous chapter highlighted, is that there were massive forces at work pointing in the direction of radical change. These forces also had a bearing on the nature and form such change might take. There were strong pressures on the population supporting such change. Public consciousness and experience were altered on a mass scale. Furthermore, for many, if not most people, 1939–45 was just the last in a sequence of appalling events over 30 years, with conflicts and economic collapse creating cumulative hardship and loss. In addition, the Second World War itself:

- brought home to a growing number of people, who now came into contact with them, the reality, unpleasantness and unhelpfulness of many old attitudes and arrangements. Now, often for the first time, many people saw 'how the other half lived'. This was particularly true of the Poor Law, the means-tested mentality of social services and the selfishness of some better-off people;
- gave many people, women and men, new opportunities and confidence, which highlighted for them what they were capable of, given different circumstances to those of their parents;

- brought into being 'for the duration' new kinds of services, accustoming people to different ways of doing things and new ways of life, that planted seeds in people's minds of the possibility of a different kind of future;
- offered millions both in the forces and on the home front, experiences of doing things together and making new kinds of relationships that they could never have previously imagined;
- socialised people of all ages into having different expectations and aspirations, from children being involved at school in discussions about the future (www.youtube.com/watch?v=vG9wCSrTbXs), and women given the chance of economic independence through the provision of collective childcare, to soldiers receiving political education from the influential left-leaning Army Bureau of Current Affairs and Education Corps (Kynaston, 2008, 39; Allatt, 2014).

A world of change

At the beginning of World War II hundreds of Jewish people had fled the bombing and landed bag and baggage in the Royal Borough of Windsor…The east end of London was catching most of the blitz and as this was largely a Jewish area they evacuated themselves to areas less targeted by the Luftwaffe. It was rumoured at the time that Hitler wanted to eat his Christmas dinner in Windsor Castle so it would not be bombed. It never was bombed so maybe the rumour was correct… The Jewish influx must have been quite a shock to the indigenous residents… Synagogues are organised by a committee … the chairman during most part of the war was Mr Lewis Gould. Mr and Mrs Gould had two daughters, Isabel and Rosita, the latter being my first head girl at Windsor Grammar School [see Rosita Rosenberg, Family section (the author's second cousin)].

(Newton, 2002, 9 and 25).

What people wanted

At a time like the present, when the dominant welfare discourse seems to be concerned with undermining the welfare state and questioning public support for it, it is invaluable to get some idea of what people actually thought and wanted at the time of its creation. It's difficult at the best of times trying to establish public views and attitudes, especially so in retrospect. In reality such views are complex, subtle and fugitive. Getting broad-based and honest opinions, rather than superficial ones, is much more difficult than tends to be allowed. However in addition to secondary sources and subsequent interviews and individual accounts, we have two valuable contemporary sources to draw upon, to make sense of what people were thinking. First was 'Home Intelligence', a far-reaching, indeed somewhat intrusive monitoring system which kept the government informed about public attitudes from 1940 to 1945. Second was Mass Observation, set up in 1936, itself an expression of new social thinking, with its aim of observing and recording the views and behaviour of the public. While often accused of having a (middle) class bias, it offers an invaluable and in-depth source of public opinion at the time (Hylton, 2010, viii).

By common consent, what the evidence does suggest is that people wanted something *different*. This was certainly the view of Richard Titmuss, the social policy academic, who wrote the history of wartime social policy. He concluded from the mass evacuation of children and withdrawal from Dunkirk that there was 'a widespread desire for major social and other reforms of a universalist, egalitarian nature' (Titmuss, 1950; Kynaston, 2008, 40). Wartime surveys also suggested that a majority of all sectors of the population favoured a National Health Service (Hylton, 2010, 216). Clement Attlee, Churchill's wartime deputy, and the economist John Maynard Keynes were agreed that 'the post-war period would produce a craving for social and personal security' (Sebestyen, 2014, 79). But the evidence seems to be clearer on what people *didn't* want, rather than what they wanted. This is perhaps not surprising since most people would have had little familiarity or involvement with the political or policy process and while they might know what they wanted and hoped for in their lives and those of their children, most were hardly equipped to think in theoretical or practical policy terms. As David Kynaston put it, of the progressive policy proposals that had been developed by Britain's progressive elite: 'How in fact *did* all these noble aspirations for a better post-war world strike the much invoked, less often consulted and still heavily (about 75 per cent) working-class people?' (Kynaston 2008, 39).

Les Norris's letter to his step-father, New Year's Day 1944

Dear Bill

So you have started doing a little farming on your own, hope it turns out to be a bumper crop and I hope I'm there to see it before harvest arrives – (I wonder)... I guess things will be very different and quite changed when at last I arrive home and I think I have changed a good deal myself... You may well imagine that we are always longing for the day of returning, also hoping that this will be the last complete year of all wars... Hope the new year brings peace, happiness and a great reunion for us all. That's all for now, Take Care, all Love, Les

Les Norris's letter to his mother, 28 June 1944

My dear Mum

... I'm pleased that Bill's corn is doing well and I wish I could see it before it turns yellow, but of course that is out of the question and I would be more than content if I can be there before the ground that it's stood in is ploughed up again... I've got to be content and even thankful just to say 'all is well'.

Well dear, that's all for now and as I say my Goodnight I'm also thinking of you and all the other dears there back home and longing as much as ever to be there with you and loving you with all my dearest and best Love

XXXXX Cheerio Darling All My Love Les X

Able Seaman Les Norris, HMS Liddlesdale
My mother-in-law Joan Croft's brother

Kynaston concludes from the contemporary evidence that there was no strong focused support for the welfare state and radical reform, but it is unlikely that most people would be equipped to think in such terms. The one thing it seems we can say with certainty is that what many people expected and many feared, was that there would be a rerun of the situation after the First World War, with economic depression and mass unemployment. They did not want a return to the poverty and insecurity of the past. They feared the 'old gang' returning, with the old market-driven cycle of boom and bust and lurking means test. 'Never again' was the phrase that resonated for millions (Calder, 1971; Hennessy, 1992). People might not be clear or able to articulate what they did want, but most could articulate what they feared. In 1943 a Mass Observation survey found that 43 per cent of people expected heavy post-war unemployment (Kynaston, 2008, 45). In 1942, Tom Harrison, co-founder of Mass Observation, speaking from their findings, said that people wanted 'equality of opportunity, better housing and education, socialism, abolition of unemployment' and much more. But there were strong feelings that these hopes would not materialise. Pessimists outnumbered optimists five to one about post-war reconstruction and writing in 2008 with additional evidence, Kynaston concluded that he was 'broadly right' (Kynaston, 2008, 42–3).

What politicians and policymakers wanted

Kynaston drew a distinction between the mass of British people and what he called the 'activators' – politicians, planners, public intellectuals and opinion formers (Kynaston, 2008, 22). But there is a third grouping to consider too, those individuals and institutions which seemed committed to the status quo. This included the Conservative Party, established church and media. Their influence was important at the time as well as since. The Archbishop of Canterbury in July 1945, for example, seemed to be thinking less of reconstruction than of a return to what he saw as pre-war Christian values:

> the increase in divorce, the declining birth rate, the spread of venereal disease, and the number of young couples who as always in wartime, wed in haste without any intention of fulfilling the primary purposes of marriage. This is partly due to the influence of war time conditions, and partly to the flaunting sale of contraceptives. (Hylton, 2010, 217)

Just as, however, many ordinary people had aspirations for change, so too had many politicians and policymakers. Post-war reconstruction was a war aim from early on in the war. There was much talk during the war of the better world that Britons were fighting for, although this was discouraged by the Conservative Party in the wartime coalition government. Prime Minister Churchill's interest in radical reconstruction was tepid, his tactics diversionary and social policy reforms that were introduced during the war under his leadership like the 1944 Education Act were very limited in their aims (Hylton, 2010, 213–14). The 1944 White Paper on employment, for example, was condemned by both Labour and Conservative leaders as a 'sham' (Hylton, 2010, 215).

This reflected a broader radical intellectual atmosphere and impulse that had gained strength during the interwar years. It was reflected in a growing interest in new ideas about housing, health and town planning. It saw the launch in 1937 of 'Penguin Specials', paperbacks dealing with social issues, the founding of the Left Book Club around the same time and its associated discussion groups, as well as the publication of the influential books by George Orwell, offering new insights on England, Englishness, social conditions and social justice, popular culture, Soviet and Fascist ideologies.

Social issues were also the stock in trade of the popular and pioneering left-of-centre photo-journalism magazine *Picture Post* which was established in 1938. It highlighted the need for a new post-war Britain throughout the war, with articles about the Beveridge Report, state healthcare and post-war Labour plans. In 1941 it ran a special edition under the title, 'A Plan For Britain' (Hopkinson, 1970). The Plan addressed the agenda embodied in the post-war welfare state: social security, full employment, education, health reforms and the need for land-use planning (Hylton, 2010, 213).

The Beveridge Report

It was, however, the Beveridge Report which was the summation of wartime hopes and plans for a better post-war Britain (Beveridge, 1942). As William Beveridge himself said, 'the purpose of victory is to live in a better world than the old world...if these plans are to be ready in time, they must be made now' (quoted in Hylton, 2010, 213).

Looking back, what Beveridge proposed can be seen as relatively modest and 'conservative: it required contributions from workers, employers and the state, had flat rates of benefit and did not even produce a bare subsistence income' (Hylton, 2010, 214). However, its symbolic significance is difficult to over-estimate. Published in December 1942 Beveridge's report was always much more than the crudely produced official document that we can now look at in archives (Beveridge, 1942). The inquiry from which it followed was brought into being by Arthur Greenwood, the Labour MP (Addison, 1975, 169) who had helped secure Winston Churchill his slim war cabinet majority vote to keep fighting the war in 1940 (Marr, 2009, xvii). Churchill gave this 'failing Labour politician with a drink problem' responsibility for questions of post-war reconstruction (Hylton, 2010, 214). This was at the time when Britain was at its lowest war-time ebb: isolated, suffering defeats everywhere and with no clear hope for any future victory. With hindsight, it seems amazing that such visionary activity was embarked upon during such dark days.

No wonder Beveridge's plans for social renewal captured people's imagination. It can be difficult now to appreciate the resonance his 300-page report had. The report gave people purpose, something to fight for, instead of solely a cruel enemy to resist. Its wartime context has to be appreciated if we are to grasp Beveridge's enormous meaning and its immense popularity. The Beveridge Report was published just after the first great military victory of the allies, El Alamein. It was a talking point in the trenches, on the airfields, at sea and in service education classes. It sold 100,000 copies in the first month (Page, 2012, 125). It was a best seller with well over 600,000 copies (mainly the abridged version) sold in a pre-blockbuster age. It even featured in the famous *ITMA* (*It's That Man Again*) radio comedy programme, with the comic Tommy Handley, saying: 'I've been up...reading the first chapter of a book called "Gone With The Want" by that stout fellow Beveridge.' It is difficult to believe that any high rated TV comedy or comedian today would celebrate an equivalent modern welfare report.

Beveridge sought to protect people from the financial insecurity associated with 'predictable risks such as unemployment, ill-health, and old age through a comprehensive system of social insurance' (Page, 2012, 125). His report proposed that all people of working age should pay a weekly national insurance contribution, in return for which, benefits would be paid to people who were sick, unemployed, retired or widowed. Beveridge argued that this system would provide a minimum standard of living 'below which no one should be allowed to fall'. Crucially it was a plan based on insurance which provided benefits without the dreaded means test (Kynaston, 2008, 25). He also based his report on a belief that there should be some kind of National Health Service. This was a policy already being worked on in the Ministry of Health (Addison, 1975, 169–70).

The Beveridge Report is often treated as synonymous with the welfare state. Certainly it was important in its development, but it is important to draw a distinction between Beveridge and the reforms introduced by the post-war Labour government. While there were overlaps, they were not the same.

The distance between the liberalism of Beveridge and the socialism of the Labour Party is highlighted by their political fates in 1945. Beveridge lost his seat as the Liberal vote collapsed and Labour were elected by a landslide. Thus we should treat with caution current comments that Beveridge himself would not have recognised or wanted the modern welfare state, since it was never simply his liberal proposals that were implemented by the post-war Labour government (Collins, 2013, 28; *The Times*, 2014). If Beveridge's proposals have been seen by some as relatively modest, the rhetoric in which they were clothed was certainly radical. He identified three guiding principles for his recommendations. These were that:

- Proposals should not be constrained by consideration of sectional interests. 'A revolutionary moment in the world's history is a time for revolutions, not patching.'
- The organisation of social insurance should be treated as one part only 'of a comprehensive policy of social progress'.

- Social security must be achieved by co-operation between the state and the individual. 'The State in organizing security should not stifle incentive, opportunity, responsibility' (Beveridge, 1942, paras 6–10).

Beveridge is best remembered for his 'five giant evils'. Significantly he framed these in personal and individual terms as: squalor, ignorance, want, idleness and disease. These have tended to be linked with specific policies and objectives by analysts over the years. Thus:

- Squalor – housing
- Ignorance – education
- Want – national insurance and assistance
- Idleness – full employment
- Disease – a national health service. (Alcock, 2008, 5)

This kind of categorisation oversimplifies and rests on important unstated assumptions about what works to deal with the difficulties people face in their lives. At the same time it reflects the kind of narrow social administrative approach to social issues which dominated professional discussion until the 1970s when it began to come under challenge from the political New Right.

This is perhaps a good time to consider three other major issues which were key inheritances from the Second World War and which all have significance for the post-war welfare state, before going on to look at the latter and its principles in more detail. The three issues are:

- the position of women
- the persistence of division
- social and psychological disruption.

The position of women

The 1939–1945 war offered many women liberatory opportunities, through employment, skill development, collective childcare and psychological, personal and economic independence from men – more so even than the Great War before it (Adie, 2013). As Raynes Minns wrote in her history of the women's front: 'Greater acceptance by the general public of women working was one of the greatest changes brought about by the war' (Minns, 1999,10). However, all this tended to be a double-edged sword. Women's new confidence and assertiveness, their increased self-determination in relation to their behaviour generally and their sexuality specifically, were constantly questioned and condemned. Issues identified as worsening social problems, like prostitution, 'venereal' or sexually transmitted diseases, population decline, children born out of wedlock ('illegitimate' children), marriage breakdown, 'infidelity' and divorce, tended to be laid at women's door. It was they who were criticised and condemned as 'permissive', 'immoral' and 'fast' (Hylton, 2010, 140–62).

Writing in 1980, Raynes Minns noted:

> In the government literature of the period we see what Britain expected of her women: from the women themselves we learn how they actually experienced the war...What seems clear is that women learnt...to handle and sometimes repair the almost total breakdown of normal life. And they did it with extraordinary spirit...Some may recall those days as the best of their lives...but for many women the breaking point was never far away. (Minns, 1999, 1).

Regardless of women's contribution and their radically changed roles, however, sexist attitudes continued to dominate in the factory, media and policy process, with, for example, the theme of 'beauty is duty'. Meanwhile, efforts to achieve equal pay for women during the war were sabotaged and gained little political support. During the war, the government made it clear that it would not 'run ahead of outside practice, and of course, sexual differentiation (sic) is deeply embedded in industrial...[and] commercial practice'. In 1944, Churchill denounced equal pay for women as 'impertinence' (Minns, 1999, 41). Family allowance, introduced during the war, only went to the mother after a coalition-breaking amendment was threatened and it was put to a free vote (Hylton, 2010, 205–10).

While the unions had supported equal pay for women during the war, their efforts afterwards seem to have been in the opposite direction as far as women were concerned. As Hylton concluded:

> Trade union pressure ensured that most of the advances women made into new areas of employment were reversed, once peace was restored. Most of the workplace nursery provision disappeared, some employers reintroduced their bans on married women employees and many more applied a very restrictive policy on working practices that made their position more difficult...by 1951 the proportion of women in the workforce had fallen back to its pre-war level (Hylton, 2010, 208, 216).

Yet by 1942 well over one and a half million women were members of the Trades Union Council (TUC). Thus while the war meant massive change for most women, raised women's issues and many women's consciousness, at the end of it all, their position neither seemed to be significantly different nor understanding or achievement of their equality, significantly advanced. Yet there were women's organisations both before and during the war, like the Women's Freedom League and Women's Group on Public Welfare which continued to raise issues around women's rights, interests and equality. The London Women's Parliament brought women together to highlight and 'discuss their many problems' (Minns, 1999, 3,11, 29, 37).

The persistence of division

We have been taught to think of the war as a time when we were 'all in it together'. While this may carry rather more conviction than Prime Minister Cameron's more recent claims in relation to government austerity policy and ideas like the 'Big Society', the war years also seem to have been characterised at least as much by division as solidarity. We can see such faultlines operating on the basis of class, interest and identity. As we have seen, there were divisions between town and country, employers and employees (with the number of strikes rising through the war years), Labour and Conservative, petty officials and the public, rich and poor and of course between the ascendant left of centre intelligentsia and prevailing reactionary thinking, so well summed up by the Colonel Blimp cartoons in the *Evening Standard*. For example,

> Colonel Blimp explains: 'Gad sir, Lord Nuts is right! The working class should be ashamed to ask for shorter hours, when the upper class is slaving themselves to the bone at dinners and balls.'

> Colonel Blimp explains: 'Gad sir, Lord Punk is right! We can't have the British Empire saved from defeat by Soviet Russia. Dash it, it would lower our prestige with the enemy.' (Quote in Hylton, 2010, 72, 101)

One official government poster that became a focus for much public anger unintentionally highlighted divisions that were widely felt.

Your courage
Your cheerfulness
Your resolution
Will bring us Victory (Minns, 1999, 11)

'The town that didn't stare'

The Second World War is where we were all definitely meant to be 'in it together'. For a short time in the war my mother lived in East Grinstead, where Archibald McIndoe's famous pioneering burns unit was established. East Grinstead formed close links with the airmen who made up the unit's 'Guinea Pig Club'. It was called 'The town that didn't stare'* at airmen with badly burned faces, hands and bodies. My mother said to me, that one day she told off other passengers on a bus, who, when some airmen got on, said, 'They shouldn't allow them out.' So much for all in it together! We have to treat received wisdom with care.

The author

* Presentation at National Portrait Gallery, 11 January 2014, Portrait of the Day, Sir Archibald McIndoe, by Anna Katrina Zinceison, NPG 5927, 1944.

We can expect that what kept people going together were not the endless imprecations from above, the wartime emergency powers, stirring posters, government slogans or even sophisticated propaganda films such as 'Millions Like Us', 'Colonel Blimp' and 'Target For Tonight'. Instead, as members of the forces reported repeatedly, what kept them from running away and deserting their positions, was 'not letting down their mates'. To this we could add women and men's primary and abiding wartime commitment to their families, friends, neighbours, workmates and children.

It is important to be aware that most, if not all, the conflicting positions on the welfare state that have become significant over the last 30 and more years can be seen as already in place, even before the Labour government that created the welfare state came to power. F.A. Hayek, at the London School of Economics, was writing *The Road to Serfdom*, his defence of classic liberalism and attack on socialism in 1944, just months before Michael Young was penning the Labour Party's 1945 manifesto: *Let Us Face the Future* (www.labour-party. org.uk/manifestos/1945/1945-labour-manifesto.shtml). Churchill also enlisted Hayek's book as part of his disastrous 1945 election campaign (James Meadway, in Loach, 2013). Hayek was a key influence on Mrs Thatcher, who later wrote of repeatedly reading this book from the late 1940s onwards (www.pieria.co.uk/articles/lady_thatchers_relationship_with_friedrich_hayek_and_milton_friedman). We should remind ourselves, that if she had been able to, Mrs Thatcher would have imposed Thatcherism *after* the war, rather than using the supposed failure of the welfare state as her argument for introducing neoliberalism 30 years later. It was Young's somewhat slimmer volume, rather than Beveridge's report that was the true blueprint of the welfare state – the antithesis of all that Mrs Thatcher held dear. This suggests that the issue was not about a growing disillusionment with the form the welfare state ultimately took, as we are often told, but an inherent opposition to its aims and philosophy, even before it came into existence. Left to those who have subsequently opposed it, there would never have been a welfare state!

Social and psychological disruption

Died of wounds 29 September 1944

Handwritten letter from Assistant Matron
  Queen Alexandra's Royal Naval Nursing Service (QARNNS)
  Royal Naval Hospital, Alexandria 4 October 1944

  My Dear Mrs Norris

  ... Your dear boy did not complain of any pain & he had a most peaceful death & did not know he was dying – once again be assured of our <u>very deep</u> sympathy.

  Yours sincerely

  MGE Maher-Loughnan

Letter from Les's shipmate Roy Otter AB (347568) to his own mother
  1 October 1944

  Dear Mother and all

  I suppose that you will know by now that Les has died of his wounds received in an action with the enemy. Yesterday the funeral took place here and we did everything we could to make it as lovely as possible. Our Gunner's Mate drilled his men to his best, and a bugler sounded the 'Last Post'. I cried then. I had to.

> *You see Les has been my best friend for nearly three years now...*
>
> *All my love Roy xxxxxxxx*
>
> *Able Seaman Les Norris*
> *My mother-in-law's brother*

The war was a time of incalculable suffering, deprivation and loss, and for many its ending on 2 September 1945 was an anti-climax, truly leaving them to face a different and uncertain future. It had been a time of mass separations: of children from parents, husbands from wives, lovers from each other, old from young. Many relationships were damaged or broken for ever, or had undergone profound change. Many had lost their homes, their families and their jobs. Juvenile delinquency had risen, schooling had often been irregular, psychological disturbance among young people had increased. When the war ended, as Minns observed, 'there was the business of living together again....[and] living together again was by no means always simple (Minns, 1999, 1). People were now returning, from combat, from prisoner of war (POW) camps, from terrible treatment as Far East POWs. Children were encountering strangers as fathers and, women, husbands who expected to be in charge – after years during which they had achieved independence. People's past lives had not just been constrained by lack of money, but also by endless rules and regulations, a narrow moral code, snobbery and secretiveness. The war had thrown all these into the air. 'Community' was still more about exclusion than inclusion. This extended to the stigmatising and exclusion of black people and minority ethnic groups, gay men, lesbians and bi-sexuals, single parents ('unmarried mothers') and disabled people. All these boundaries were also challenged and blurred by the war (Minns, 1999).

This, of course, was not a time of counselling, talking or working through people's problems. Instead many were reluctant to talk about their difficulties and were haunted for years by nightmares. These were traumatising times, storing up issues for the future in a way that was not generally well-recognised or understood at the time. One exception to this was a book published in 1946 *Living Together Again*, which tried to prepare people for the problems they might have to face after the end of the war: psychologically damaged or disfigured husbands, disrupted children, exhausted wives, 'strange behaviour', living with disability (from blitz or fighting), marital infidelity, housing shortage and rising prices. People who had been stretched during the war were now having to return to mundane jobs and lives, or even worry about finding a job at all (Bendit and Bendit, 1946). It was women, predictably, who were expected to deal with all these difficulties, women who, willingly or unwillingly, were now being forced back into the home.

Conclusion

As we have seen, it took the suffering of two world wars and inter-war depression to create the impetus for the Beveridge Report and the establishment of Britain's welfare state. The two have to be understood as the product of war, want and the most extreme suffering.

As Labour policymakers made their plans for the welfare state, there was clearly no shortage of problems for the post-war government to deal with. There were major international, political, economic, social and psychological problems to be addressed. But this was also a government committed to offering a new and better future to Britain and its people. In Chapter Five we will look at the principles that underpinned their efforts to do this, as well as address the problems they faced.

FIVE

The principles of the welfare state

We need the spirit of Dunkirk and of the Blitz sustained over a period of years.
(Labour Party Manifesto, 1945)

Here then is our new scheme of social security for all. I believe that it will increase the health and happiness of our peoples and I ask you all to join in working wholeheartedly for it so that it may bring new strengthen and well-being to our country.
(Clement Attlee, Prime Minister, 4 July 1948, quoted in Kynaston, 2008, 284)

This chapter focuses on the principles underpinning the post-war welfare state. Clearly it is important to explore both the practicalities and the principles of any policy or reform. Often success or failure can be judged in terms of the distance between the two. The ambitious nature of the post-war Labour government's reforms always made it likely that their reach would outstrip their grasp. However, in the case of the welfare state, it is likely to be especially helpful to start with its principles, because the many criticisms that have since been made about the welfare state, have tended to focus on these. Clearly there are interconnections and overlaps between principles and practice, but it is also necessary to differentiate between the two. Two key questions are raised here. First, what were the principles underpinning the welfare state? Second, where, crucially, do problems lie – with those principles themselves – as we have frequently been told by critics of the welfare state – or with their interpretation and practical implementation?

According to the social policy academic, John Baldock, 'societies in which a substantial part of the production of welfare is paid for and provided by the government have been called 'welfare states'. While the term's definition is contested: 'It remains important because of the frequency with which it is used, by politicians, in the media, and by ordinary people, and because, historically, the welfare state was at one time understood as the twentieth century's most complete answer to social need' (Baldock, 2012, 22).

As Kynaston has noted, most European countries established some kind of state welfare system after the war: 'As state-provided welfare spread across a reconstructed Western Europe during the 1950s, it was soon clear that this was far from being a uniquely British [development]' (Kynaston, 2008, 435).

While the 10 per cent of British gross domestic product (GDP) that made up public spending on social welfare was higher than that for Scandinavia, Italy and the Netherlands, it was less than that for Belgium, Austria and West Germany (Tomlinson, cited in Kynaston, 2008, 144). Furthermore, the UK welfare state was never the tail that wagged the dog: 'The welfare state was created, but in a context where it consumed a quite limited level of resources, and where it was continuously vulnerable to a resource allocation system which gave priority to exports and industry, and restrained both private and collective consumption' (Kynaston, 2008, 144).

The welfare state is also probably most misremembered and misinterpreted by its critics as an isolated welfare policy. Instead it needs to be understood as a much broader programme. This involved the nationalisation of key industries, state regulation of the economy, progressive taxation – *and* the introduction of an egalitarian welfare system (Page, 2012, 125). The Labour government never saw the solution to inequality and the achievement of 'fair shares for all' narrowly in terms of welfare policy. Its 1945 manifesto highlights the scale of its ambitions: '[The Labour Party's] ultimate purpose at home is the establishment of the Socialist Commonwealth of Great Britain – free, democratic, efficient, progressive, public-spirited, its material resources organised in the service of the British people.'

The coming of the welfare state

We thought it was a good thing – we really did – because of all the change. I remember the workhouse for one thing and all that changed. Free dental – free hospital treatment – which we never had before. You didn't have to pay a penny when the doctor came out. It was just such a change. During the war, when he was about 16 and working at Barclays Bank, John [Croft, whom she married after the war] had a grumbling appendix. He biked to the next village, to the doctor's surgery. Then about a week later, the doctor came to John's village in his car and popped his head round the door and asked John if he was alright. Then he sent a bill for five shillings! That was a lot of money then.

Joan Croft
My mother-in-law

The 'welfare state' was thus the sum of many parts. It needs to be understood as a number of interlocking value-based policies committed to the Labour party's socialist goals. We have only seen such radical proposals and policies since from right-wing governments. Negative modern readings of 'the welfare state' have effectively reordered the words to emphasis '*state* welfare'. We will return shortly to the question of why welfare was provided as it was. But the term 'welfare state' followed much more the commitment to an holistic approach to improving people's lives, which was concerned with directing *all* state policies to this end. Thus key to the thinking underpinning the welfare state was the principle that all policy truly had to be 'joined up' in pursuit of public well-being and social security for all.

The specific welfare policies that were introduced included:

- free education up to age 15 (later 16);
- the national health service (NHS) free at the point of use;
- public housing for all citizens to rent;
- a national system of social insurance benefits for all in need, to combat want. This was backed up by a scheme of non-contributory benefits for those with insufficient contributions, or whose incomes fell below an agreed level. (Alcock, 2012a, 8)

Primary school food

They clearly wanted us to grow healthy and strong at primary school in the 1950s, in line with the founding values of the welfare state. So the teacher handed out cod liver oil capsules and we each collected a little third of a pint bottle of milk from crates to drink at break times. This seemed to follow on from the bottles of concentrated orange juice dispensed at the 'baby clinics'. I loved the cold milk. Some boys would get through several bottles, from mates who didn't want theirs. But what still haunts me are school dinners. I've never ever eaten food like it since. I don't doubt that there are some people, somewhere, in some impoverished situation, who would be grateful for what we got. But for us as small children it was terrible. What I remember most was the meat that was full of fat and gristle. And then there was the swede, a soggy orange sweet mess that has meant I have never been able to eat swede since. Not all the food was so bad. Unlike some, I acquired a taste for the marmalade pudding and custard.

But what was worst was that some of the dinner ladies forced us to eat anything we tried to leave. They'd check our plates and send us back to the table. However small I'd try and make the left-overs at the side of the plate, it might not be good enough. I still remember one dinner lady standing over me, to make sure I ate every last bit. That only happened once as I remember. After that I put whatever was left over in my handkerchief to throw away when I got home. My mother told me about a girl's mother telling her that she'd wondered what the terrible mess in her pocket was and it was the lumpy custard that she had spooned in, in similar desperation. I've wondered since, why was the food so bad? Did it have to be? Clearly not. It felt like a punishment at the time. Was someone ripping off the money and buying cheap? How was this in keeping with the idealised war-time posters that so often showed the nation's children as the hope for the future? And why did some dinner ladies behave so oppressively to us as small children? Was this what state education meant to them – acting like the little Hitlers of the welfare state's critics?

The author

Some key principles

The Labour Party in 1945 made a manifesto commitment to 'introduce state provision to meet major welfare needs' and to do this on a comprehensive basis. In so doing it endorsed the Beveridgean principle of seeing it as the state's duty to remove the evils facing people, 'as the representative body of all citizens' (Alcock, 2012a, 8). Thus intervention was not so much seen as a right, as a responsibility of the state. At the heart of the reforms, explicit in the term 'welfare state', was the belief that the state had this responsibility for its citizens. It is this sense of responsibility that is central to the reforms. It is a key principle upon which the welfare state was based. Not only was the ending of Beveridge's 'giant evils' seen as a collective responsibility in society, but they also were understood in social rather than individualised terms. Thus although terms like 'ignorance', 'idleness' and 'squalor' are often individualised and attached to people as personal characteristics or failings, both the Beveridge Report and the founders of the welfare state identified them as social problems with social origins.

It's often difficult to separate policies from principles and many of the principles underpinning the welfare state ran across policies rather than being associated with any one. These principles were also closely inter-connected because they followed from the same government commitment to and understanding of what it saw as its socialist mission. Some of these principles were self-declared, others implicit in the post-war government's reforms. Some of them almost go without saying: the commitment to equality, to equality of opportunity and to social justice, and don't really need to be detailed here. Different analysts might also frame these principles in different ways. Here the aim is to explore them, consider some of the problems that beset them at the time, as well as others identified since.

The ambulance men

We'd gone to my granny and granddad's. I must have been about five or six. Children tend to remember things as big. I remember things there as small. Granny was lying on the bed. The ambulance men had come into the room – I don't know why I was in it. When they started to lift her from the bed, the sheets fell back. I saw her ulcerated leg. It looked as though there was a large black hole in it. I must have cried out in fear and surprise. She spoke in Yiddish. She had never learned to speak, read or write English. My mother told me much later she said, 'Why does the little one cry?' (As my mother used to say, 'always she was thinking of other people'.) And I remember the ambulance men putting her nightdress back in place very carefully, covering her again. I remember how respectful and solicitous they were to her. And then they carried her down to the ambulance. I will always remember the kindness and respect with which they treated her – and my mother feeling the same.

The author

Public ownership

At the heart of the proposed welfare state was the policy of bringing industries and services into public ownership, and the method adopted to do this was nationalisation. Nationalisation effectively meant that services and industries were taken out of private ownership into the control of the government. The objective was to avoid the short-termism, cycle of boom and bust and inequality that had characterised the market-led inter-war economy. In more recent times, the state has tended to take over the market's loss-making failures (memorably, British Leyland, Network Rail and the banks) and the private sector has taken over the state's profitable and valued successes (of many examples, air–sea rescue, the utilities and telecommunications). Between 1945 and 1951, nationalisation included transport – from airlines to canals, road transport to railways – coal mines, iron and steel industries, power/ utilities – water, gas and electricity, communications, and the Bank of England. The aims were to improve conditions and safety for workers, to make industries politically accountable, invest them with social goals and divert surpluses from private profit to the public purse. The task facing nationalised industries was a huge and perhaps impossible one. They were meant to combine a commitment to public service with ensuring commercial efficiency, when the prospects for adequate investment were poor and services like the railways and mines had been under-resourced, run-down and often conflict-ridden during the war.

Full employment

The principle and objective of full employment was framed by the Labour Party in its 1945 manifesto in terms of 'jobs for all'. Through government intervention, the aim was to put an end to the 'slumps' and high levels of unemployment after the Great War and during the inter-war years. The government saw the maintenance of a high and stable level of employment as a primary aim and responsibility. This was this implicitly taken to mean a formal level of unemployment of no more than 3 per cent. It only rose above that in the 1970s and averaged half in the years before. The classic Keynesian approach adopted to achieve this was: 'To invest in public works and publicly funded projects while attempting to influence private capital investment and expenditure by raising and lowering interest rates' (Timmins, 2001, 133).

To ensure that production could be maintained, workers were to be ensured 'good wages' and raised standards of living. However, as has frequently been highlighted since, full employment was generally interpreted narrowly in terms of the full employment of 'able bodied' *men*. The creators of the welfare state did not break from the tradition of seeing women's primary place as in the home as wives, mothers and carers. Women were largely restricted to unskilled work and work designated for women and any attempt to secure equal pay and conditions was ignored or over-ruled (Kynaston, 2008, 415–21; Nicholson, 2012, 336). Three hundred thousand ex-servicemen and women and civilians had been disabled by the war. The 1944 Disability Employment Act offered sheltered employment, reserved occupations and employment quotas for disabled people, rather than their equal inclusion in the labour market. The employment quotas were never achieved, even by public employers and those disabled people who were employed tended to be restricted to marginal jobs like lift attendants, piano tuners and in sheltered workshops (Barnes, 1991a; Historic England, 2015).

Social citizenship

The welfare state's proponents saw it as having a key role to play in the protection and promotion of the economic and social well-being of its citizens. This was articulated by the sociologist T.H. Marshall, who introduced the concept of social rights, which he understood as being people's welfare rights. He believed in an evolution of rights in England acquired through citizenship, beginning with civil rights in the eighteenth century, political rights in the nineteenth, and social rights in the twentieth. He identified the welfare state as a distinctive combination of democracy, welfare, and capitalism, which he saw as protecting people from the instability, harshness and arbitrariness of the market. The welfare state's policy provisions and legislation was seen as compensating for inequalities arising from the market, in contrast to the Poor Law which sought to police and regulate people disadvantaged in society and through the market (Marshall, 1950).

What such thinking did not take account of, as subsequent critiques from feminist, black and disability rights perspectives have highlighted, were the inherent biases of such concepts of citizenship which were very much tied to the thinking of their time. From a feminist perspective, Marshall's work is of limited value because of its narrow focus on able-bodied men and failure to take account of the social rights of women and barriers to their achievement (Rummery, 2002; Lister, 2003; Borsay, 2005). The efficacy of Marshall's principle has also been more generally called into question since. In his 1982 analysis, Julian Le Grand concluded that 'the strategy of equality through public provision' had failed. Looking at healthcare, social services, education and transport, he said that the better-off benefited more from it than the poor, as they were able to make better use of welfare state provisions (Le Grand, 1982, 151–3), a finding that has since been modified, but not rejected (Timmins, 2001, 485). Having said this, anyone with experience from the days of the Poor Law would have been unlikely to want to exchange the new arrangements for the old, whatever such limitations they might have had.

Progressive redistribution

The Labour government saw the state's role as to reduce inequality – both material and in terms of life chances and well-being. This was done both through fiscal policy and the provision of public services. Surtax and death duties were increased sharply. During the late 1940s, the middle class lost financially as the working class gained. The salaries after tax of the former fell as the wages of the latter rose. At the same time, as we have seen, the middle class benefited from the health service and free secondary education and many of the social reforms were financed by transfer of income within lower income groups themselves (Kynaston, 2008, 173).

Breaking the Poor Law link

What particularly distinguished the new welfare state from what had gone before, was that it sought to break the key Poor Law link between needs and income. Historically, through both the old and new Poor Laws, getting help was conditional on how much money people (or even their families) had. People would not receive support unless they could demonstrate that they were either poor, impoverished or destitute. Thus all services, from maternity-, child- and healthcare to support for older people and people with learning difficulties, were accessed on the basis of income rather than need. Now with the universalist National Health Service, state housing and secondary education, for example, eligibility was according to need rather than resources. You did not have to be poor to qualify for free healthcare under the new NHS. The new welfare state drew a distinction between income maintenance and the meeting of other needs, with separate state policies and services established for each. While as we will see later, this link was never absolutely broken (see Chapter Six), it was a fundamental founding welfare state principle and signalled political revulsion from the longstanding tradition of Poor Law means-testing. At the same time, it raised a key issue, which has remained unresolved ever since, of who defines the need to be met. This is an issue we shall return to later in this book.

Universalism

One of the principles that the post-war welfare state is mostly closely associated with is *universalism*. Universalism is itself a system of redistribution, aiming to ensure entitlement to goods or services to all, regardless of their status, income or circumstances. It is contrasted with selectivism, where those seen as most in need are targeted for help, or particularism, which aims to respond to the particular needs of particular groups. Universalism has become most closely associated with benefits and social security policy. The post-war Labour government sought to offer protection against loss of earnings due to sickness, old age or unemployment in line with the principles of Beveridge. They were opposed to means-testing because of its associations with the Poor lLaw and the widespread fear and hatred of this. Yet the post-war Labour government's income maintenance policies were generally not based on universalism, except insofar as it was hoped to be achieved through compulsory contributions from all who were employed. Instead Labour's social security reforms were underpinned by a system of social insurance, with non-contributory and top-up payments from the means-tested 'national assistance' system.

The positives associated with a universalist approach are that no stigma is attached to receiving help, all can access it and its administration costs are relatively low. The negatives are that better-off people who may be seen as not needing help receive it as well, suggesting wastefulness, and that historically universalist approaches have underplayed and failed adequately to acknowledge and recognise difference and diversity. These are issues to return to when we explore alternatives to traditional social policy approaches. Child benefit (originally Family Allowance) was the main example of universalism in post-war social security policy, paid to all out of general taxation. However, the service that has most strongly been associated with universalism and continues to do so, even if it is no longer fully a service 'free at the point of delivery' is the National Health Service, again, paid for out of general taxation and available to all.

A new nurse in a new NHS

On 27 February 1947 I went to Sunderland to commence a four year State Registered Nurse training course. Everyone had to live in the nurses' home and we were allowed one late night out a month – until 11 pm. The working week was 48 hours with one day off...

At first before the advent of the NHS, we had no penicillin or sulphonamides. Infectious patients were treated with good nursing care – tepid sponging for high temperatures and frequent applications of kaolin poultices for chest cases ... All bedbound patients were turned frequently, had at least four-hourly pressure care, received daily bed baths and attention paid to their nutrition and fluid balance. With the advent of the NHS in July 1948 things got gradually better, for example penicillin and other drugs became available.

(Originally published in *The Messenger*, the Magazine of the Parish Church of St Nicholas, Lincoln, Summer 2013, Issue 7)

Doreen Croft
My partner Suzy Croft's aunt

Also associated with this idea of universalism are notions of solidarity rather than division; of 'togetherness' rather than separation. It has become a cliché of the Second World War that it encouraged and foregrounded such a spirit of togetherness. Not only did the war extend people's experience of such togetherness and collectivity, but this also seemed to chime with a longer-standing mood. The holiday camps that had mushroomed before the war were based on similar commitments to communality and collective organising. Interestingly they seemed to thrive over the same period as the kind of thinking that underpinned the welfare state – from the 1930s to the 1960s. They also often acknowledged the position of women, taking conventional domestic tasks from their shoulders and in Billy Butlin's words, providing the 'perfect holiday for mother' by providing free childcare (Ferry, 2010, 26–7).

Decommodification

Closely associated with universalism is the principle of decommodification. Decommodification was a theme running through post-war reforms and an underpinning principle. What it means is people being able to have their needs met, not on the basis of payment or an 'exchange' or commercial relationship, but through the intervention of the state and the provision of public services. Thus the meeting of social need was separated from profit-making. It was based on a *social* relationship; based on the state accepting a social responsibility. Instead of having to purchase goods and services, or receiving them out of 'kindness' or the inequality of traditional charity, people could receive them out of entitlement and as of right. Linked with this was the development of another idea: the 'public service' ethos or ethic – signifying a different value basis for behaviour in state provision. We can see the decommodification of healthcare, housing and education through the development of the NHS, council housing and state education. This can be seen as a revolutionary development, even in a welfare state which had strong Fabian and Liberal roots. Here was a vision of an entirely different and new social relationship, highlighting service and equality.

Why the centrality of the state?

In early twenty-first century Britain, with neoliberal ideology dominant, the idea of turning to state control and provision to achieve major political and social change, as the founders of the welfare state did, would probably find few takers. We have now had a generation of governments inclined to the right, which have energetically sold consumerist choice and distrust of state intervention. But it was not like this in 1945. Private enterprise and the market were fundamentally tarnished by the memories of profiteering in the Great War and associated with the disastrous inter-war economic crises. The state was an obvious choice for the post-war government. Even from this distance, it is easy to believe that much of the analysis of the Labour Manifesto would have resonated with millions. Thus the Manifesto said: 'Great economic blizzards swept the world in those years. The great inter-war slumps were not acts of God or of blind forces. They were the sure and certain result of the concentration of too much economic power in the hands of too few men.'

More to the point, the state had a track record of achievement. At the outset of the Second World War, much of British industry was subjected to state regulation or control, even if not nationalised as such. This had worked during the war and was associated with victory. Clement Attlee, the Prime Minister, understood this and in a general election political statement included as part of a Pathé newsreel said: 'We have shown that we can organise the resources of the country to win the war. We can do the same in peace.'

It is perhaps not surprising that coming out of a world at war where the UK had ultimately survived by extending the role, power and control of the state, the welfare state was also an approach based on belief in the essentially virtuous and corrective role of the state and state intervention.

Tony Benn remembered as a young Labour MP thinking: 'We presented (the policies) in terms of the kind of list of objectives you might have in wartime. This is what you've got to do. We'll do it. And it was credible for that reason' (Loach, 2013).

It is also difficult to believe that returning service men and women – who were particularly likely to vote Labour – would have had many misapprehensions about the state, having been under its firm control and discipline. Their allegiance was perhaps more a measure of what they thought of the free market.

Charity, the third sector providing health and welfare services, also had limited appeal as an agent of change. The war had demonstrated to many more in the population that old Victorian charitable attitudes died hard. Much charity continued to be characterised by paternalism, condescension and control. Thus, for example, the report of a county organiser for the Women's Voluntary Service (WVS, now Royal Voluntary Service) in 1939, regarding the planned evacuation of families: 'I think this scheme is impracticable and unworkable, and it can never be successful. The low, slum type form the majority of the mothers, some of them out for what they can get, most of them dirty, many of them idle and unwilling to work or pull their weight' (quoted in Hylton, 2010, 46).

The local representative for the National Society for the Prevention of Cruelty to Children in Chester 'tried to have an 8pm curfew imposed on evacuee families' (Hylton, 2010, 47). At the same time, whatever the hopes of some leftist radicals, the welfare state was never a monopolistic state system. There was always still private education, health and housing. BUPA health insurance for instance, was founded in 1947! Being on the receiving end of charity was nobody's ideal, except perhaps for the philanthropists for whom it brought status, a sense of self-importance and the warm feelings associated with 'do-gooding'. The term 'welfare state' also highlighted the essentially benign nature of the state as the reformers seemed to understand it.

There can be no question that with nationalisation, conditions and safety for workers improved in industries like coal mining. However, the rhetoric that went with nationalisation spoke of much more and was often of a shift not just from private to state, but from 'the bosses' to the people. After the appointed day, 1 January 1947, signs outside the pits said: 'This colliery is now managed by the National Coal Board on behalf of the people' (Loach, 2013). However, it didn't necessarily feel that there had been any transfer of power. Despite the Attlee government's pronouncement that 'Today the mines belong to the people', in reality the same people held influence over the operation of the mines at national and local levels and many of the same attitudes remained. The first chair of the National Coal Board appointed by the Labour government was Lord Hyndley, previously managing director of a private colliery and a director of the Bank of England, with no past commitment to nationalisation (Loach, 2013). A contemporary researcher found that members of the Colliery Consultative Committees that had been set up felt disenchanted and powerless: 'our suggestions are completely disregarded and little encouraged …We have as little say about the colliery as before' (Kynaston, 2008, 203). Nationalisation was not routinely associated with democratisation. This did not vary with leaders to the left or right of the Labour Party. Nationalisation as understood by leading Labour politicians like Herbert Morrison did not include democratic control, either from the public or the shop floor. 'The assumption was that the managers of these public corporations would be exemplars of scrupulous, objective professionalism – and that the workers in them should know their place' (Kynaston, 2008, 24).

As Kynaston concluded, a similar faith in the beneficent, public-minded expert underlay the creation of the modern welfare state (Kynaston, 2008, 24). The primary goal of policymakers seems to have been to establish benevolent good quality state services, rather than democratic ones. This was strongly reflected, for example, in Aneurin Bevan's commitment to building high quality public housing, with high minimum standards, with gardens and bathrooms, rather than just more public housing. Coming out of an age where most people had to be content with grossly inferior healthcare, schooling and housing, this may have seemed an ambitious enough goal. Although, it seems to have been overlooked subsequently, Bevan's achievement in producing so much decent housing seems to have been as much valued by its recipients and as great an achievement, as his creation of the NHS. Having a decent home at last, which his reforms made possible for many hundreds of thousands of people, was for them, like a dream come true (Loach, 2013). Kynaston has also called into question from the evidence, how much either workers or public *wanted* or expected to be involved in or have control of the new nationalised industries and services (Kynaston, 2008, 141). 'Few miners seemed to equate nationalisation with workers' control, whatever that might mean' (Kynaston, 2008, 188). Furthermore, the charitable and private sector equally could not be said to offer democratic control – except that the latter could to some degree promise consumerist choice for the narrow and privileged part of the population who could afford to go 'private'.

While the idea of nationalisation itself seems a radical and innovative one, the way it was implemented often appears to have been much more cautious and pedestrian. Thus:

> Too many 'non-believers' were appointed to the nationalised boards, including not just businessmen but a motley crew of peers and retired generals...The criticism, though, that would resonate most through the years, at least from the left, was that a golden opportunity had been missed to institute a meaningful form of workers' control. (Kynaston, 2008, 140)

So while, for example, the National Dock Labour Scheme that was introduced guaranteed registered dockers a minimum amount of work, they remained casual workers hired by the day until 1967. As Sir Harry Keen, who qualified as a doctor just before the inception of the NHS and was a great defender of it, suggested, what sense of control there was under nationalisation, took a different form. 'There was a real feeling of ownership about the NHS when it started. People felt that they were doing it themselves, that it was their possession and they've lost that' (Loach, 2013).

Visiting Granny in hospital

We went to visit Granny in hospital. I think it must have been after she had had a stroke. I must have been about six. My abiding memory is of a large waiting room that was dark and cavernous, with long dark wooden benches to sit on. I needed to have a pee. My mother took me to find a lavatory. We couldn't find one. It was so dark, she told me to have a pee in a corner. I almost can't believe it happened now, but it did. There was nowhere else to go and everything was dark, oppressive and in shadows. According to my mother, this was the old workhouse infirmary, she called it 'Bancroft Road'.*

Then my granny had another stroke. She was readmitted to the same old hospital. My mother went to see her in the ward. She came back crying and told me and my sister, 'She was just lying there. It was boiling hot. The flies were buzzing around her. There was no one around to help her. God forgive me I wished to God at that moment that she would die. It was pitiful to see. No help. She couldn't do anything for herself.' My granny died soon after this. For my mother, whatever the intentions of the NHS, what she was seeing was indistinguishable from the past.

The author

* There was a workhouse here between 1858 and 1881. It was demolished and a new infirmary opened, Mile End Infirmary in 1883. It became a London County Council (LCC) hospital in 1930 and then part of the NHS in 1948. In 2013 after numerous reorganisations and transfers it came under the management of the Barts Health NHS Trust (see Barts Health NHS Trust, 2015).

The gap between principles and practice

Tony Benn spelled out the limitations of nationalisation as it was implemented.

> The way nationalisation was done was under a centralised system, top-down. The Chairman of the National Coal Board ran all the pits in the same way the private owners used to and I am not saying it wasn't a better system than the old system, because it was. But at the same time, the

idea that the people who worked in an industry had any say in how the industry was run was a completely foreign idea (Loach, 2013).

Perhaps not surprisingly the post-war welfare state fell short of the principles and ideals with which it was associated. In some cases, policies failed to match up to such aspirations. Thus, for example, the 1944 Education Act, the product of the war-time National rather than post-war Labour government, retained a tripartite system of schooling based on selection for '11-plus', which greatly restricted the educational experience and opportunities available to most working-class children, who were largely consigned to 'secondary moderns' with inferior resources and a limited curriculum (Kynaston, 2008, 150–3).

Maureen and the 11-plus

My mother told us that one of the teachers said that my sister only got through the 11-plus exam 'by the skin of her teeth'. That remark stuck with me. It seemed such a cruel and damning one and it tells you a lot about the 'sheep and goats' attitudes that it encouraged at the time. I felt it got through to my sister. She never did well academically at secondary school, more I think to do with lack of confidence than anything else. She made a life for herself instead in New York. Sadly much of the culture of grammar schools seemed to be about focusing on those who were seen to be the brightest.

The author

Perhaps more significantly, the welfare state was both ahead of its time and *of* its time. It was built on brave new ideas, but tied to the mindsets, hierarchies and realities of its age. As we have seen, this conditioned and restricted how its pioneering principles were interpreted and implemented in at least three ways. Thus these principles were:

1. shaped by the art of the possible, at a time of inadequate and diminishing resources, when it was what was feasible rather than what was ideal that often had to be adopted;
2. implemented by a narrow white male political and policy elite which was tied to its time, class and identity. This narrow group, with a correspondingly restricted understanding, perpetuated the exclusion from and marginalisation in both policy process and delivery, of women, lesbian, gay, bisexual and transgendered people, black and minority ethnic groups and disabled people. As

Virginia Nicholson has observed, in 1945, as before, 'the deeply embedded consensus that women's proper destiny was wifehood and motherhood continued to block the way ahead...the political patriarchy was in no mood to embrace sex equality in the workplace or anywhere else' (Nicholson, 2012, 336). We need to remember that this was an age when suicide was illegal and homosexuality was still strongly criminalised to the extent that many gay men were imprisoned and permanently stigmatised. In 1948, even as the Empire Windrush was bringing nearly 500 Jamaicans to England in search of work, a group of Labour MPs was suggesting that the government should 'by legislation if necessary, control [black] immigration in the political, social, economic and fiscal interests of our people' (Kynaston, 2008, 275).

3. largely dependent for their realisation on the old guard; traditional groups, structures and cultures to introduce, undertake and manage the changes which were intended. This was an old guard familiar with very different, traditional ways of doing things.

To sum up, the welfare state sought to challenge traditional ruling values, but was largely located within them. It sought to replace old approaches with ideas of public service, equality and shared ownership, but was still informed by prevailing assumptions and prejudices of its age. The process of change was led by and drew on people and structures mainly drawn from the old, who exemplified and perpetuated such biases and exclusions. While its initiators recognised the weaknesses and limitations of the market, they did not adequately recognise or address the weaknesses of the top-down state.

> **One size doesn't fit all**
>
> The school that I go to [a local mixed secondary school], it deals very well with bullying, but how do I put it – the thing about attendance. There's a rewards trip at the end of the year, mainly to Alton Towers – and if your attendance is below 95 per cent you can't go – and mine was, because I was ill with asthma attacks.
>
> *Charlie Hatton*
> *Grandson, aged 11*

There were some bright new exceptions like the 1951 Festival of Britain. This was bold, innovative and immensely popular, with its face turned firmly to a brave new future (Banham and Hillier, 1976). But generally, the post-war welfare state's failure adequately to address diversity, its general lack of citizen, patient and service user involvement and its reliance on a narrow corps of experts, seem more a reflection of the period in and from which it emerged, rather than applying narrowly or in isolation to the welfare state itself. Sansom suggests that Kynaston's insight is that: 'culturally Britain in the decade following the Second World War retreated into a 1930s view on many social issues ... there were highly censorious attitudes to subjects like illegitimacy, homosexuality and divorce, and the belief that women belonged in the home resumed' (Sansom, 2013).

This can help us to understand the appallingly cruel treatment in the early 1950s by the police of Alan Turing, the inventor of the computer and hero of wartime codebreaking, leading to his suicide (Leavitt, 2007), as well as the harsh treatment of single mothers well into the 1960s (Robinson, 2015).

In his autobiography, the broadcaster John Humphrys gave a feel of the times when he said of the BBC: 'It reflected life in Britain accurately enough: well mannered, class-ridden, deferential and exceedingly dull' (quoted in Moran, 2013, 94).

These limitations of the welfare state may also have more to tell us about social policy in general, rather than just about this particular innovation. This is an issue which we will consider further in Chapter Eight where the focus is on social policy more generally. Sufficient to say perhaps that social policy as a discipline did not really begin to address issues of diversity until Fiona Williams' textbook of 1989, *Social policy: A critical introduction, issues of race, gender and class*, more than 40 years after the publication of the Beveridge report (Williams, 1989). Right-wing critics of the welfare state have been ready to criticise its failure to address diversity, but years later, they themselves have frequently failed to respond to it, generally with even less justification. Moreover, their criticisms of the welfare state have tended to be rooted in the nature and limitations of the 1940s welfare state, as though it did not undergo significant reform and development in ensuing years, including under Conservative and neoliberal governments.

Conclusion

By the early 1950s, the NHS was in operation. It was making a real difference. People could see a doctor for free and get their medicine paid for, instead of having to buy it at the chemist. But as I was already seeing as a small child, old institutions, old cultures, attitudes and approaches still existed. You couldn't knock down the Poor Law at a stroke even if you could legislate it out of existence. The hospital in which my grandmother Dora died, may have been part of the new NHS, but it still felt like the Poor Law. However, if its legacy meant that the buildings and structures were often still the same, for me the new spirit of the post war welfare state has always been epitomised by the behaviour of those two ambulance men to my granny, their kindness, competence and most of all respect to this Jewish immigrant family. It was the people working in the welfare state that made possible its transformative potential.

Meanwhile the founding principles of the welfare state, principles, as we have seen, such as, universalism rather than residualism, public versus private ownership, social citizenship as opposed to consumerism, continue to be the subject of front page discussion and controversy. While these principles have undergone significant reinterpretation, reconsideration and redefinition since the 1940s, they are still often subject to criticism as if they have not moved on from the way in which they were originally interpreted and implemented. For its right-wing critics, the post-war welfare state has become a kind of straw man fixed in their minds as if it were stuck in its original 1945 incarnation, incapable of taking account of the massive cultural, demographic and social changes that have since taken place. Yet despite their suggestions that the welfare state is an anachronism, irrelevant and outmoded, it is still very much a live issue, especially whenever the NHS comes to be mentioned. Furthermore, while the contemporary interpretation of welfare state principles can be seen as tied to their time, many of its principles can be seen as much more enduring. In the next chapter we will look more closely at what the welfare state has meant to people, particularly on the receiving end, over the years since its inception.

SIX

The welfare state: whose consensus?

No-one can seriously deny that, whatever else Thatcherism represents, it embodies a genuine ideological break with the social democratic post-war consensus
  (Phil Lee, *Marxism Today*, May 1983)

The Conservative Policy is simply more (or rather less) of the same.
  (Ian Gough, *Marxism Today*, July 1980)

(The above two quotes originally juxtaposed by Taylor-Gooby, 1985, 71)

How can wealth persuade poverty to use its political freedom to keep wealth in power? Here lies the whole art of Conservative politics in the twentieth century.
  (Aneurin Bevan)

Political consensus?

The period between the 1940s and late 1970s has frequently been described as one of political consensus or 'settlement' over the welfare state. Conservative governments of the 1950s supported 'the spirit of the reforms and maintained their basic structure'. As Alcock observes: 'The cross-party consensus on state welfare was so strong that it even acquired an acronym – Butskellism – comprised of the names of the Labour Chancellor (Gaitskell) and his Conservative successor (Butler)' (Alcock, 2012a, 8).

Between 1945 and the election of Mrs Thatcher in 1979, there was cross-party political and policy support for the welfare state including collectivism, a mixed economy and state health and welfare services. This embraced Keynesian economics and nationalised industries. Kynaston has noted:

There was no meaningful attempt to reform, let alone dismantle the NHS or the welfare state more generally;

the only industries to be denationalised were steel and road haulage; the goal of full employment remained sacrosanct; rent controls stayed in place, at least for the time being; and the position and privileges of the trade unions were positively enhanced. (Kynaston, 2010, 72)

While this consensus is contested by some social policy commentators, a strong case can be made for some such ideological convergence between Labour and Conservative parties. As Robert Page has written: 'The possibility of an emerging post-war economic and social consensus based on support for the mixed economy (private and public enterprise), 'Keynesian' interventionism, and the welfare state was given added weight by the growing influence of revisionist thinking within Labour circles' (Page, 2012, 128).

The social policy academic Hugh Bochel concludes that as with the Liberal reforms of the early twentieth century: 'The Conservatives, particularly under Macmillan's premiership, maintained a commitment to full employment, an incomes policy, and social welfare, including developing further some parts of the welfare state' (Bochel, 2012, 66).

While the welfare state was essentially implemented by the post-war Labour government, the reforms they advanced had wider support. Lord Beveridge was, of course, himself a Liberal and the state education plans were introduced in 1944 by RA Butler, Conservative member of the wartime coalition government. So right from the start, although of course there were tensions (Page, 2012, 125), the welfare state reforms were rooted in a broader political alliance and consensus and could show some consistency with earlier Liberal reforms. Page, however, is also cautious about the existence of such a consensus. Perhaps it is better seen as a cessation of hostilities between major political parties because of other more pressing issues and problems, not least economic difficulties, as well as a lack of strong drivers or widely accepted prescriptions for something different. Of course over this period, there were undercurrents of criticism and rejection of the welfare state from the political right and free market ideologues, which had their flowering in the 1970s. But what we can say is that in principle, welfare state policies remained very much the same over this long period. During it, funding for welfare benefits and services in Britain (and indeed other European countries) grew year by year as a proportion of national income, and the major political parties shared a consensus that the core institutions of the welfare state were a good thing (Baldock, 2012, 24; Lowe, 1993; see also British Academy, 2008).

Public consensus?

While it has long been accepted that there was significant political consensus about the welfare state during the course of its first 30 or so years, what can be said about *public* attitudes to the welfare state over the same period? Was there a consensus in support of the welfare state there too? As we saw in Chapter Four, there was no unanimity about the setting up of the welfare state. Divisions seemed particularly to relate to people's class, status and politics. What did the welfare state feel like to 'ordinary' people; the mass of people who made up the electorate? What did they feel about it and what was their experience of it? Was there the same underpinning support for it among those who were intended to be the benefactors of the welfare state as among the major political parties?

Primary school

I started Wix's Lane primary school aged four. In those days there was no nursery or nursery class. It was straight into school, first infants, then 'big boys'; with both teaching and break times to survive. If the classroom was the place where you learned to conform with teachers and the education system, then the playground was where you had to deal with your peers' prevailing values. I can't imagine what complex model of masculinity ruled at the time or what its relationship was with broader assumptions about patriarchy and competition in education. Boys had quickly been separated from girls, but the model seemed to be one closely linked with physical strength and prowess, skill at games and not being different. When this unpleasant mixture ignited it was shouts of 'fight', 'fight' and a circle would form. What I enjoyed were the 'tag' and 'cowboys and Indians' games where you'd have the solidarity of a team and the help I got early on to join in from one kind and gentle boy, Max, with glasses, who wore what were then known as 'brothel creeper' shoes.

What I still remember was the sense of threat at any time, if you did the wrong thing – whether with teachers or other pupils. Both school and pupils were concerned with hierarchy and control. Without being able to articulate it, I quickly realised that this was not a place for difference. This is where I learned to dread 'school'. This encouraged me to develop a false sense of security about home. How all this connected with the lofty ideals associated with the welfare state, I have no idea. Maybe I was experiencing the time of transition. Looking back in general (despite the inroads that some teachers' and children's humanity could make) this seemed to accord more with models of state education being about beginning the process of creating a conformist, disciplined and subordinated workforce than much else. Perhaps that is where I began to formulate one of my key conclusions about social policy – which seems to be shared with many other service users. Whatever the philosophy or rationale attached to it, the reality in human hands has the potential to be nasty and brutish.

The author

These were times of increasingly evident conflict on grounds of race, gender, citizenship status and sexuality. The 1950s witnessed the beginning of a major cycle of black commonwealth immigration to Britain and also the re-emergence of fascist and extreme right political parties and violence. This was the time of both the Notting Hill riots and Rachmanism (Lowe, 2005, 268). But the most important conflict politically in relation to the welfare state was along lines of class. The Conservative Party returned to power in 1951, even though it actually gained fewer votes than Labour. Its victory was seen as a victory for the middle classes, who repeatedly expressed their irritation with what they saw as the constraints and regulation of the previous government. This despite a point repeatedly made that they particularly benefited from the National Health Service and from Labour's later ending of the 11-plus education selection system (Le Grand, 1982). What evidence is available also suggests a broader discontent and weariness with what was seen as pettifogging bureaucrats, officiousness and controls (Kynaston, 2010). However, how much these problems followed from the policymaking approach of the Labour administration and how much from the difficult economic times they were working in, following a war that virtually bankrupted Britain, continues to be unclear.

Craig and Bentley

Childhood memories aren't restricted to what happened to us; they also include things that happened in the world that impinged on our consciousness – even at an early age. So for me there was the Queen's coronation, the 'conquest of Everest', the sinking of the Andrea Doria, the shadow of the Korean War and the Bentley and Craig case. Derek Bentley was hanged for the murder of a policeman, PC Miles, Craig was too young to be executed although he fired the fatal shot. It is difficult to separate what you come to know afterwards from what you knew at the time as a small child. All I know is that I was conscious of the headlines – about the notice of 'execution', Mr Sydney Silverman campaigning against 'capital punishment' and a sense of something awful happening.

My dominant memories of the 1950s are less of rock and roll and more of dark and dreary streets and the injustice of 'executing' a boy we came to realise had learning difficulties, who was under arrest when the fatal shot was fired, which was itself a ricochet and words 'Let him have it, Chris' that almost certainly were never said. This wasn't the only high profile public injustice of the time. There were also the Ellis and Evans and Christie cases. Ruth Ellis had been abused by the partner she shot and Timothy Evans was undoubtedly executed for a murder committed by the mass murderer Christie. It is important to remember that the post-war Labour government had managed to create the welfare state in an age that was still so harsh and dominated by massively powerful traditional institutions and elites.

The author

There are other developments between the 1950s and 1970s that we need to take account of in exploring public attitudes to the welfare state. The context for such attitudes, at personal and political levels, was changing. First it was a time of increasing individual material improvement (if national economic decline), summed up in the famous 1957 comment attributed to Prime Minister Harold Macmillan: 'you've never had it so good' (Lowe, 2004). But if as David Kynaston has said, by the early 1960s, consumerism was inexorably taking hold, under cost-cutting Conservative administrations, transformatory urban redevelopment embodied a shift away from Bevan's high housing standards, to alienating high-rise. If some had 'never had it so good', perhaps some had forgotten, or had never known what it was to have it so bad as in pre-war market-driven days (Kynaston, 2014). Some contemporary sociologists were concluding that workers were now more interested in 'greater individualisation' and a bigger pay packet than collective struggles and achievements (Goldthorpe et al, 1969; Kynaston, 2014, 157–8). However, subsequent secondary analysis of their data, suggests considerable continuities in working-class attitudes and identities (Savage, 2005).

Second, it was also a period of liberalisation. The period became strongly identified with the beginning of challenges to continuing discrimination on grounds of gender, ethnicity and sexual orientation. Following the recommendation of the Wolfenden Report, Britain decriminalised prostitution but banned solicitation and other related activities with the Street Offences Act of 1959. Other legislation passed included the Abortion Act, 1967, the Equal Pay Act, 1970, the Sex Discrimination Act, 1975, the Race Relations Act, 1976, and the Sexual Offences Act, 1967, decriminalising consensual homosexual acts between men aged 21 and over in private. These were radically changing times, with music that reflected this, from Johnnie Ray and Elvis Presley in the 1950s, through the Beatles and Rolling Stones in the 1960s to the Sex Pistols, Clash and Queen in the 1970s. There was also the emergence of Rhythm and Blues, Northern Soul, Hip Hop and Rap. There were also chart toppers over the period from Petula Clark, Winifred Atwell, Max Bygraves, Frank Ifield and Clive Dunn, reminding us that how diverse and multicultural, taste, personal preferences and interests had become in the UK.

Trying to make sense of popular attitudes to the welfare state raises the whole complex issue of how 'public opinion' is identified, formed, interpreted and measured. From the late 1930s, the creation of organisations like Mass Observation and Gallup Poll had highlighted a new interest in 'public opinion'. However, they equally made clear how problematic it is to explore and understand it. The more subtle qualitative techniques used by Mass Observation raised questions about how representative what they tell us is. On the other hand, public opinion polls and surveys are very blunt instruments to try to elicit and capture that most complex, hidden and elusive of things – what people really think (Taylor-Gooby, 1985, 22). In their 1980s' study of press and public attitudes to welfare, academics Peter Golding and Sue Middleton observed that the validity of such surveys: 'is frequently the object of considerable criticism within social science and, though often confused and naïve, this criticism has bequeathed a healthy scepticism about some of the more pretentious claims of some survey researchers' (Golding and Middleton, 1982, 159).

We know that how people respond to questioning depends on how they are asked, why and who by; whether it is an individual or collective experience.

During the war through documentary and feature film, posters and other propaganda, the government had tried to inform and influence public opinion, for people to feel positive about what they were fighting for, to keep going and to have a better peacetime life to look forward to. According to Lowe, by the mid-1950s, government had limited its ambition to 'the superficial manipulation of public opinion rather than an active attempt to win people's minds' (Lowe, 2005, 109). The German social theorist Jürgen Habermas concluded that public opinion is highly susceptible to elite manipulation (Habermas, 1991). In Chapter Seven we will consider that issue in more detail when we look at modern welfare reform and the way that the 'public' appears to have been enlisted to support such reform through a complex and symbiotic relationship between mass media and government.

Meanwhile we need to be careful regarding the quantity, quality and interpretation of the data available about contemporary public opinion on the welfare state during its so-called 'golden age' between the 1940s and 1970s. The social policy academic, Peter Taylor-Gooby, has suggested that 'survey data on public attitudes was thin on the ground for this period … it cost a lot more to do surveys then and they didn't have the computers etc we have now to analyse them' (personal communication, 18 September 2013). Rodney Lowe, historian of the welfare state has some interesting observations to make about public opinion in relation to the welfare state over this period:

- He noted that even in the late 1940s, it was recognised that 'one-third of the population was either "chronically ignorant or apathetic"' about the welfare state. This view:

    would seem to be confirmed by later polls. In 1956, for instance, 49 percent of mothers polled neither recognized nor could define the term 'welfare state' and in 1964 there was discovered a 'widespread civic illiteracy over the cost of the social services' (Lowe, 2005, 107).

- He was persuaded by arguments that people's support for the welfare state tended to be selective and selfish. They would pay higher taxation for services they saw as benefiting themselves, like the NHS or pensions. They were less enthusiastic about expenditure they felt helped minorities, like lone parents or unemployed people (Lowe, 2005, 107).
- He offered the example of workers' resistance to technological change and wage restraint, as evidence of a lack of support for the principles of the welfare state, citing the classic study of the affluent car workers who were motivated by individual material, rather than collective social improvement (Lowe, 2005, 108).

These findings, however, could additionally be read as highlighting a lack of public education and understanding about the welfare state. The views above which Lowe and others related to selfishness, can also be understood as the kind of inconsistency that might result from people's ignorance and naivety about policy. We must remember that the welfare state created post-war, was very much a top-down rather than a participatory affair. As we have seen, it was not based on people's involvement and therefore did not seek their understanding and ownership. Its strength was seen to lie in the improvements it was intended to bring to people's lives, not in a changed relationship between them and government. Lowe concluded that there was public support for the welfare state: 'Public opinion, both expressed and perceived, strongly supported welfare policy between 1945 and 1975 and, as the most authoritative study of electoral behaviour in the 1960s has concluded, "the rise and endurance of the welfare state was directly related to this fact"' (Lowe, 2005, 107).

He also, however, offered a warning about how substantial and reliable this support was: 'Public opinion was also contradictory and restrictive, and this severely constrained the positive role that the welfare state could play in the resolution of Britain's underlying structural economic and social problems' (Lowe, 2005, 197).

Certainly it seems unlikely that public opinion was simply subject to a crude reversal from the late 1970s. It is difficult to believe that popular support for Thatcherism grew from a zero base. Instead we can expect that public opinion over welfare state issues in its first decades was complex, fragmented, and perhaps most important, inadequately addressed, prioritised or understood. According to Taylor-Gooby's evidence, there was no strong shift in public attitudes to public welfare, privatisation or welfare for women coinciding with the arrival of Mrs Thatcher as prime minister: 'To the contrary, the main services [were] as strongly supported as they have been at any time since the war' (Taylor-Gooby, 1985, 51).

Golding and Middleton, however, highlight an international shift to more hostile media attitudes to poverty and welfare from the mid-1970s as the economic situation worsened (Golding and Middleton, 1982, 4–5).

Efforts made before this to educate, inform or even manipulate public opinion in support of the welfare state appear to have been very limited. But that would be consistent with the lack of interest then shown more generally in engaging the public in the welfare state. After all, why would government and policymakers need to know people's views if they weren't seen as having a role to play? Also why would people formulate and offer their views if they weren't welcomed or wanted? Of course the uncomfortable answer that was subsequently to emerge, is that if people don't have a particular sense of involvement and ownership in something like the welfare state, then whether it is in their interests or not, they can be expected to be much less likely to support, defend or identify with it, or indeed the political party that was most closely associated with it.

Thus, while there may have been popular support for the welfare state from the 1940s through to the 1970s, it seems very unlikely that there was any public consensus about this. It is also not clear what it would have been based on. As we have seen, there also appears to have been little attempt made to build such a consensus and the views of ordinary people do not seem to have been seen as of central importance by contemporary policymakers.

Another part of the problem is that we probably don't know as much as we should about what people's experience of the welfare state actually was like. This is because historically there seems to have been limited interest in finding out from people on the receiving end what they thought about its services and support. We have little material that provides a flesh and blood picture of the day-to-day reality of the welfare state and its services. Social policy analysts seemed at least as concerned with offering their views about people as enabling us to hear theirs about their worlds. For example, this was how Rowntree and Lavers presented one of their 'case studies' in a 1951 survey of 'life and leisure':

> Miss R is a copy-typist in a large office. She is 21 or so, and lives in a bed-sitting room. She finds it difficult to make both ends meet but is happy because she is free, because she has plenty of boyfriends and plenty of entertainment. She is quite promiscuous and sees no harm in it. Indeed, she doesn't see why people make so much fuss about it; it just seems natural. (Rowntree and Lavers, 1951, 92)

We don't have nuanced accounts of what the welfare state seemed like to people on a personal level; how it was experienced. People themselves, on the other hand, often lacked the power, resources, status and access to get their views represented. We do know that the new mainstream services (and we will consider those for particular groups later) were not universally popular. For example, according to the evidence offered by Lowe:

Social security

Within ten years the social security system was no longer popular. 'Most services, concluded one poll of public attitudes towards the welfare state in 1956, are felt to be helpful by those who use them. This is least likely to be the case where national insurance and national assistance are concerned' (Lowe, 2005, 170, drawing on Political and Economic Planning (PEP), 1961, 192).

Health

The popularity of the service as a political ideal contrasts with its increasingly criticised record as a practical deliverer of healthcare (Lowe, 2005, 176).

Housing

A survey of public attitudes towards the welfare state in 1956 revealed that housing was 'the only service about which there were widespread complaints' (Lowe, 2005, 247). Council housing was also associated by many of its tenants with paternalistic control, which in some cases extended to internal and external inspections to check that gardens were maintained and homes kept clean and tidy. However, contemporary tenants of charitable and private rented housing could expect the same intrusion (Burnett, 1986).

Education

The tripartite school system improved educational standards and increased educational opportunity, but commanded little public support. Together with the unpopular and discredited 11-plus exam, it perpetuated social divisions according to class, gender and disability (Kynaston, 2010, 410). The 'secondary moderns' quickly came to be seen as rebadged state provision for low achievers, receiving relatively fewer resources than grammar schools. The introduction of 'comprehensive' schools to overcome these problems was undermined by a populist middle-class movement to retain grammar schools (Lowe, 2005, 204–45).

We must also remember that there was no one welfare state over the period from the 1940s to the mid- and late 1970s. There were changes in emphasis, political commitment and indeed principles. Some principles were enlarged, for example, those relating to poverty and equality, while others diminished, for instance the commitment to local autonomy and independence. The welfare state was constantly underfunded. While there may have been some general political consensus over this period, it cannot be said that Conservative administrations gave the same priority or commitment to the welfare state's founding principles as its post-war founders had. Similarly, Fabian commentators in the 1960s and 1970s felt that Labour governments of the period had slackened in their enthusiasm for reform and needed to be firmly reminded of their responsibilities (Alcock, 1997, 197–201).

Also when we think of public attitudes towards the welfare state, much depends on what comparisons were or are being made. Were people making them with their previous life, with the opportunities they did or did not have on the private market, or with an ideal, or what was felt to have been promised? How did the welfare state compare with before or alternatives? It is probably impossible now to establish a reliable or detailed picture. Certainly we can expect that the welfare state always generated controversy, as well as deep affection from some, frustration from others, particularly with its close-up detail and dislike from others who felt that their own earlier freedoms were inhibited by the greater equality and choices it brought for more.

The welfare state and marginalised groups

The normality of abuse

When I worked in a pre-Seebohm welfare department in the late 1960s, we sometimes went to a local old people's home for meetings and in-service training, Nye Bevan Lodge, named after the founder of the NHS. It was a lovely light 1960s building. Such outside use of residential services has often since been encouraged – bringing in 'the community' and highlighting that residential services actually are part of it. It wasn't until later that I found out that Nye Bevan Lodge was the site of appalling abuse of residents by staff which had continued without intervention for a long time. This included staff charging residents for bathing, punishing those who complained, leaving one resident's feet for a long time in extremely hot water, opening windows and removing blankets at night so that some people got pneumonia and died. There were falls caused by 'altercations' with staff, residents being made to eat their faeces, physically man-handled and 'helped to die'. One man who had seen a Nazi concentration camp as a soldier in the second world war, compared Nye Bevan Lodge to it (Glendenning, 1999, 181).

The author

So far we have considered the post-war welfare state in relation to its mainstream services. What about its specialist services and services for particular groups? It is here that problems become even more apparent and the gulf between founding welfare state principles and practice become particularly evident. A number of groups which had historically been marginalised did not seem to fare much better under the new welfare state arrangements. Indeed they don't seem to have been recognised as part of the mainstream population. Among these were homeless and disabled people, people with learning difficulties and mental health service users. The experience of each of these groups during the welfare state's 'golden age' highlights some of its broader limitations. They also relate to problems of abuse, neglect, institutionalisation, poverty and poor housing design all of which gained high visibility over this period of so-called political consensus, although it should be said that problems of abuse seem to be a constant and ongoing feature of social policy for marginalised groups. In this next section we look in more detail at these as case studies with much wider ramifications for the welfare state and social policy generally and their futures.

Single homelessness

In the 1960s, homelessness, like poverty, seems to have been 'rediscovered' as a social problem. It was mainly conceived of in terms of family homelessness; that is to say homelessness involving children. This led to the setting up of the housing charity, Shelter, and the famous high profile BBC TV Play for Today, *Cathy Come Home* (Sandford, 1976a). But there was also a parallel problem and parallel play which highlighted how differently different forms of homelessness were conceptualised and treated at the time. This was the problem of 'single homelessness' or 'single homeless people'. Here the play, *Edna, The Inebriate Woman*, by the same playwright, Jeremy Sandford, had as its central character a woman tramp or vagrant who was presented as having mental health problems, while Cathy was personified in terms of a photogenic young couple who'd lost their home (Sandford, 1976b). This reflected the prevailing approach at the time (which still survives to some extent). This framed single homelessness as an individualised problem of personal pathology, taking little account of housing and broader structural issues in people's homelessness. Discourse about family homelessness, in contrast, highlighted problems of housing supply and access. While family homelessness was generally defined in terms of a lack of permanent housing, single homelessness was defined much more narrowly in terms of people associated with rough sleeping, use of common lodging houses and hostels and government reception or resettlement units for people adjudged 'without a settled way of life'. There was long and strong resistance to recognising the problems of homelessness including among young single people and members of black and minority ethnic communities, relating to lack of access to housing and entitlement to rehousing (Beresford, 1975a, 1979). While little was done to address problems of single homelessness in the 1960s and early 1970s, there was an upsurge of interest in first-hand and journalistic accounts that echoed the experience of the 1930s (for example, Walton-Lewsey, 1963; Fletcher, 1966; Sandford, 1971; Marshall, 1971; Wallich-Clifford, 1974 and 1976; Wilcox, 1977).

The reception/resettlement centres, which were the government provision made to meet such needs, some of which continued in existence until the late 1980s and 1990s, were the direct descendants of Poor Law casual wards for vagrants. Some were even located in the same Victorian buildings. Their definition of single homelessness was essentially a perpetuation of nineteenth-century Poor Law definitions of vagrancy. While the aim of the welfare state had been to separate services from benefits, these resettlement units provided under the 1948 National Assistance Act were the continuing embodiment of the Poor Law and its principles. They retained the direct Poor Law link between money and meeting need. They offered short-term stay and overnight accommodation to people judged to be destitute. Homeless single people (mostly men) who turned to this service were asked to prove that they were destitute (had less than ten shillings or 50 pence) and were required to do a task of work during the day, exactly as had been required by the old nineteenth-century 'spikes'. This was the only service other than benefits provided under the National Assistance Act, which had been intended to break that link between poverty and need. We should remember that this anachronistic left-over of the New Poor Law was still in operation well into the 1980s when the likes of Madonna, Boy George and the Pet Shop Boys were topping the music charts (Foord et al, 1998).

Institutions, neglect and abuse

Another way in which the legacy of the poor law seemed to live on was in the continued existence of many large institutions established during the nineteenth century. Such 'subnormality' or 'mental handicap hospitals', 'lunatic asylums'/psychiatric hospitals certainly did not disappear with the creation of the welfare state. Despite the then Minister of Health, Enoch Powell's famous 'water towers' speech in the 1960s, intended to signify their end, many of these continued to operate until the community care reforms of the early 1990s and some rebadged have lingered much longer, particularly in Scotland. Thus if the welfare state put an end to the workhouse for people who were primarily poor (except in the case of single homelessness and reception/resettlement centres), this was not the case for a number of other groups (who were still also likely to be impoverished). Provision for all these groups was strongly based on a medical model. This took the source of the problem as being within the individual, caused by some personal inadequacy, deficiency, abnormality or pathology.

The problems of institutionalisation associated with these groups began to be highlighted in the 1960s (notably by Goffman, 1961). There was a series of high profile scandals in the UK in the 1960s (Stanley et al, 1999). The groundbreaking work of Barbara Robb, published in *Sans Everything*, helped to bring to lasting public attention the scale of neglect and abuse in such services for mental health service users, older people and people with learning difficulties (Robb, 1967).

In *The Last Refuge*, the sociologist Peter Townsend, evidenced the restricted lives lived by older people in these large long-stay institutions (Townsend, 1962). Significantly, he sought and included the views of older people themselves in this study. (A follow-up study found that 25 of the 173 institutions originally surveyed still existed as registered care homes in 2005 (Johnson et al, 2010; Weicht, 2011)!) The poor law mentality of segregating and congregating particular devalued groups in institutions was perpetuated in other ways after the establishment of the welfare state. Charities such as Leonard Cheshire were set up providing services in smaller but nonetheless institutional residential settings for disabled people.

All of these were strongly based on a medical model, which saw the source of the problem as within the individual, caused by some personal inadequacy, deficiency, abnormality or pathology.

Psychiatric services

The Victorian coupling for people experiencing mental health problems, of special hospitals, long-stay, compulsory 'treatment', custodial regimes, mainly based in large institutions, continued apparently unaffected by the coming of the welfare state. The historical thriller *Dominion*, by CJ Sansom, set in an alternative past where the Nazis controlled the UK, paints a well-researched, atmospheric and chilling picture of the psychiatric system in the early 1950s. It is a world of big shabby buildings, appalling food, batch living without privacy, padded cells, straitjackets, routine ECT (electro-convulsive therapy) and psychosurgery, with new drugs like Largactil starting to be used (Sansom, 2013). Almost half of NHS hospital beds in the 1950s were for people with mental health problems, but the system was still locked in the past (Kynaston, 2010, 628).

What led to change was not so much new progressive thinking as a number of other developments. These included the high cost of maintaining the old dilapidated and deteriorating institutions; high profile human rights abuses associated with them (Gostin, 2010) and the advent of new 'antipsychotic' drugs like Largactil (chlorpromazine hydrochloride, marketed in the US as Thorazine) which provided new chemical rather than physical way of controlling patients. Despite its serious and damaging (side) effects, Largactil was to be a standard drug for responding to 'schizophrenia' for half a century.

Becoming a mental health service user

I remember one afternoon, after collapsing in the street with a panic attack, huddled against a shop window, frightened to move, and then with help, managing to make my way to the health centre to get an emergency appointment with the GP. I didn't know what was happening to me. I was terrified. When I got there, the bureaucracy swung into action. I was told to take a seat. I sat worried and fearful. The doctor walked through the surgery, empty apart from me. He had been my doctor for some time. He walked past me without even looking look in my direction. Some time passed before he called me in and I remember no helpful guidance from that consultation. That memory typified for me how the system seemed to see people with mental health problems. It also highlighted for me the difference between bringing a physical and a mental problem to the doctors.

The author
(Beresford, 2010c, 8)

The psychiatric system seemed to stand well to one side of the social justice rhetoric of the welfare state (Lowe, 2005, 201). Larry Gostin was legal officer at Mind in the 1970s and his strategy was to take cases before the European Court of Human Rights, 'where we won landmark rulings on the rights of the mentally ill'. He has written:

> I read daily dozens of letters sent by persons with mental illness in prisons, hospitals, nursing homes, and the community. One case stands out among the many that shocked the conscience, Adrian Clarke...When I arrived at Broadmoor [special hospital], his psychiatrist refused permission to see him, saying that he was too dangerous. After threatening litigation against the hospital, I was permitted to enter his isolation room. The stench was so overpowering that I could hardly breathe. The room was filled with pots of urine, and faeces were caked on the walls. Clarke was crouching in a corner, naked and cowering. The

room had only a tiny translucent window with bars, with little light, and no ventilation. He had been confined there for 5 weeks and allowed out 20 minutes in every 24-hour period. (Gostin, 2010, 5–6; see also http://studymore.org. uk/mpu.htm#PeterWhitehead)

We should remember that this was the same Broadmoor to which the mass sex attacker Jimmy Savile was given free rein around the same period, appointed by the health minister to a key role in its management (*Guardian*, 2012).

Housing and high-rise

Finding somewhere to live

When I came back to London in the early 1970s, I tried to find somewhere to live in North Battersea, where I grew up. With massive redevelopment under a strongly entrenched Labour council, great swathes of the area I had known since childhood were bulldozed and replaced with high-rise estates. At this time the area to be demolished was what was known as Prince's Head after the local Edwardian pub on the corner (halfway between Battersea Park and Clapham Junction). A long row of shops along Falcon Road were to go, including our local Sainsbury's, together with row after row of terraced houses. I was told that they were due for demolition but in the meantime were being let to people in housing need as temporary lets. So I went along to the office – a room in one of the houses. There I met a man who was lounging on an armchair. He was the right person to ask he told me. He'd been given responsibility for this large area of housing by the council. I was homeless. I told him about my situation. He said he'd get back to me. I never heard from him. I went a couple of more times and it was clear that this was a personal fiefdom and I wasn't going to get any joy here. He told me he was Johnny Savile, Jimmy Savile's brother.

There was no good reason for this large-scale demolition. It helped destroy our locality. Happily a decent low-rise housing estate, the Kambala was built here, unlike the many high-rise blocks that had gone up elsewhere and some local people were rehoused there. But this could have been achieved by improvement, not so-called 'slum clearance'. In 2012, following the outing of Jimmy Savile, I read more about his brother, who had died in 1998. He had been accused of raping a patient in a local psychiatric hospital in the 1970s (Springfield, where I was to be a patient in the 1990s). He was sacked from the hospital where he ran the radio station in the 1980s 'for gross misconduct'. I shudder to think what happened to young people in vulnerable times who came the way of Johnny Savile and his cronies when he was in the powerful position that I encountered him.

The author
(MailOnline, 2012; Daily Star, 2012)

Perhaps the most frequently cited example of the distance between welfare state policy and the people for whom it was intended, was the issue of 'tower blocks' or high-rise council housing. It became a cliché for the failure of welfare state policymakers to listen to what people on the receiving end wanted or had to say. This issue takes us back to much earlier debates before and during the war when progressive architects and town planners saw town planning as the solution to housing and social problems. Their idea of town planning was also very much a top-down one, without 'people's actual participation in the act of planning' (Kynaston, 2008, 48). The need for policy was accentuated by the massive amount of housing destroyed or seriously damaged by wartime bombing.

However, there were *two* conflicting camps of experts. One set of architects and town planners wanted people to live in modernist high-rise blocks of flats in the inner city. The other favoured rebuild in spacious, airy new towns in mixed communities (Kynaston, 2008, 30–9). While the proponents of city flats largely won the day, what people themselves seemed to want (although if they were ever asked, they generally weren't listened to), was to live in small suburban houses (some critics, including George Orwell, sneered about public preferences for these to be in mock Tudor style), which would offer them better amenities and more privacy (Kynaston, 2008, 50–5 and 154–68). This issue perhaps also highlights more deep-seated problems with architecture, which still seem to have problems recognising that buildings are meant to be for the people who use them and that form should follow function, rather than vice versa.

By the 1960s, the policy talk was of 'streets in the sky' (Kynaston, 2010, 421), with architects' models that featured all the necessary community services and amenities. In the event, inadequate funding meant that much of this was lost in the realisation and tower block estates came to be associated first with corrupt councillors, officials and architects, cost saving and broken lifts and then with 'problem estates' and 'problem people' (see www.independent.co.uk/news/people/obituary-t-dan-smith-1487528.html).

Welfare state housing policy had travelled a long way from the 1949 Housing Act enacted by Aneurin Bevan as Housing Minister, which sought to open up state housing to be a universal service for all classes and to support local social mix as well as reinforcing his commitment to high quality housing. Ironically it was not socialist preoccupations with centralised planning that led to the shift to the tower block estates of the 1960s, but rather Tory Prime Minister Macmillan's policies which resulted in the building of cheap, mass-produced high-rise tower blocks. Many subsequently degenerated into what came to be seen as 'new slums' (Glendinning and Muthesius, 1994). Kynaston has described this development as 'the beginning of the long, painful process of "residualisation", by which those living in local-authority housing would sink ever further below the average income and status of the population as a whole' (Kynaston, 2010, 416).

Conclusion

The conventional view has been that there was public support for the welfare state post-war, but this was lost over the years as its inadequacies became apparent to people. People were also put off because they saw the welfare state as unduly advantaging those who were idle and deviant.

The old East End

When we stayed at my grandparents' house in the East End in the early 1950s, I remember the sounds of the rag and bone men early in the morning, the clip-clopping of their horse and cart and the rich smell of the food my grandmother cooked. I remember going to the market; it smelled different, it was noisy, exciting, with signs in Hebrew script and lots of Jewish traders, who were friendly to me as a little boy. If I close my eyes now, I can feel and see it. I remember going to one stall where there were stringy looking chickens for sale. They came with the giblets – the 'kishkas' – in one I could see small half formed eggs and the men chopping and laughing. It seemed a strange world, but I knew it was my world as a little Jewish boy, although my mother didn't want us to see it like that. There was strong shame in her about having been Jewish and poor. Much later when I went back with her to these places and saw the new generations of immigrants, this time from the Indian sub-continent, the inheritors of my grandparents' home and neighbourhood, it gave me a strong sense of fellow-feeling for them and brought my mother's world closer. This was a world that was part of the greater Jewish world destroyed in Europe by the Holocaust. And this London East End Jewish world itself – the world that Webb and Booth also knew in their own ways – had little time left to run when I saw it and was already beginning to disappear.

The author

We do know that the welfare state failed adequately to address diversity in relation to age, gender, sexuality, ethnicity and disability. What the reading here also suggests is that there was never such a strong consensus of public support for the welfare state, before, during or after its creation, as has often been implied. There was division on class lines and the welfare state certainly fell short of meeting the rights and needs of particular groups. These groups had bad experiences, where the welfare state, instead of supporting their social citizenship, could be seen further to be denying and undermining it. Significantly many of these groups, poor and disabled people, mental health service users and people with learning difficulties, were either politically weak or actually disenfranchised.

What in retrospect seems especially important is that internal economic difficulties, the failure of economic and industrial leaders to address these effectively and of trade unions successfully to work for effective alternatives, combined with growing international economic problems, became the opportunity for the political right, rebadged as the political New Right, to come to prominence. But it did this with the same old views with which it had opposed the Labour Party and Labour government and their welfare state proposals in 1945. However, these can also be seen as having revolutionary implications for the welfare state of the late twentieth century.

Change happened when any attempt at political consensus ended. The Conservatives were able to gain power in 1979 in alliance with a predominantly right-wing press and drag public opinion behind them. Critically, the founders of the welfare state didn't engage or involve the population in their reforms as workers, citizens or service users. In no way could the latter be said to set the agenda. Instead they were there as a stage army. The founders of the welfare state did not adequately educate them about the welfare state or give them a sense of ownership that would either lead them to identify with it, or encourage them to defend it. The public/electorate were instead lay figures in the process, to be pulled this way and that by politicians and other opinion formers. Their own opinions were not central, powerful or even particularly sought. Labour failed to enlist ordinary people's support for its post-war project. Mrs Thatcher's Conservative Party merely co-opted them. In the next chapter, we will look at the dramatically different future that lay in wait for the welfare state from Mrs Thatcher onwards and how much this future has actually been a matter of going back to the past.

SEVEN

Back to the past

And, you know, there is no such thing as society. There are individual men and women, and there are families.
(Margaret Thatcher)

We must absorb your curious customs. Drive on the left, politics on the right. Animals in the home, children safely in boarding school. Hate privilege, suck up to the privileged. Love money, despise the rich.
(Russian spy school leader referring to British culture and tradition, in *Danger Man: Colony Three*, 1964, directed by Don Chaffee)

Blair once said that if he did not leave behind a fairer Britain, he had failed. He failed.
(Toynbee and Walker, 2010, 96)

It is worth noting that UK national politics since 1979 have been strongly signalled in terms of their departure from the past. Thus Mrs Thatcher was associated with a grouping which was defined as new, the political *new* Right. The Labour government that followed the years of Thatcherism first under Mrs Thatcher and then Mr Major determinedly rebadged itself as *New* Labour, pursuing a new *third* way ('not state, not market'), committed to '*modernisation*' (strange perhaps in a self-consciously *post*-modern age). The Conservative/ LibDem coalition in power between 2010 and 2015 presented its policies as an innovative meld of those of its two constituent parties. Interestingly in his acceptance speech as Prime Minister of a majority Conservative government in 2015, David Cameron broke with this tradition, stressing his commitment to old style 'one nation' Toryism. Yet he promised in his manifesto what the Institute for Fiscal Studies described as the deepest cuts in welfare and the state for 80 years (Emmerson, 2015). Writing in 1985, Peter Taylor-Gooby explored two competing analyses of the Thatcher welfare reforms (Taylor-Gooby, 1985). One understood them as revolutionary, the other as an incremental extension of previous Conservative thinking. Whichever

119

we accept, both acknowledge the ground-breaking nature of Thatcher's policies and plans for welfare, either pushing further than before, or in a different direction.

There is no question that for those, like me, who grew up under the welfare state, Mrs Thatcher's policies and those of her successors, have felt like a break with the past. The talk has constantly been of ending old shibboleths, 'breaking out of the box', challenging 'sacred cows' and questioning old assumptions. There has truly been radical change in the UK. Specifically there has been a constant questioning of the 'welfare state'. Our economic base has fundamentally altered. Although there is no longer any claim to overseas empire, the UK has been involved in overseas military conflict for much if not all of the time. People's expectations of government and the state and their role in relation to their own lives have undoubtedly changed. There is even a pervasive idea and sense that Mrs Thatcher radically changed our personal behaviour, making us more selfish, competitive and individualistic (www.historyandpolicy.org/opinion/opinion_111.html).

Certainly there seems to be agreement that Mrs Thatcher and her successors were bent on taking us somewhere different from where we had been before, even if there are disagreements about their motivation, intended destinations and how similar or different they are to each other. There are, for example, different views about whether Mrs Thatcher's crusade was ideological, economic or moral (Sutcliffe-Braithwaite, 2012). While UK governments since 1979 have had differences from each other, they have had one thing in common. This has been their primary commitment to the market, rather than the state, as a vehicle of policy, including social policy.

Mrs Thatcher and her governments' preoccupations in relation to social policy have been well rehearsed and don't need restating at length. They included seeking to:

- reduce state intervention – they disliked the state and saw it as inefficient and intrusive;
- reduce welfare spending – which was seen as a drain on wealth creators, damaging the economy and encouraging dependence among its recipients
- re-emphasise and increase the role of the market in society and reduce the role of the state;
- encourage people to make their own provision to meet their needs in the market place. (Alcock, 2008, 8–9; Glennerster, 2012)

The historian Correlli Barnett gave crude expression to what seem to have been the underpinning fears and assumptions of anti-welfare statists when he wrote of the New Jerusalem 'dreams [of the welfare state, turned into]…a dank reality of a segregated, subliterate, unskilled, unhealthy and institutionalised proletariat hanging on the nipple of state maternalism' (Barnett, 1996, 304; see also Kynaston, 2008, 145). Thatcher's Conservative Party abandoned attempts to develop comprehensive, state-led, paternalistic schemes to tackle poverty. It attempted to marginalise the importance of state welfare for the middle classes. It wanted to residualise welfare, so that it was only a safety net for the poorest. Its approach to social policy also sought to uphold the traditional nuclear family. It rejected the idea of the state supporting employment, industries or regions, or bridging bad time, seeing this as encouraging inefficiency and dependence, instead leaving these to market forces.

Mrs Thatcher's plans did not, however, work out as intended. There are uncomfortable statistics which her advocates have been reluctant to be reminded of. First there was no real reduction in the proportion of the gross domestic product (GDP) devoted to welfare spending during the period of her leadership because of the huge increases in unemployment (www.historyandpolicy.org/opinion/opinion_111.html). Total public spending increased by an average of 1.1 per cent a year in real terms over her era. Thus if the aim was to cut the size of the state, Thatcher's welfare policy failed (Eaton, 2013). Second, we are also now learning that Mrs Thatcher was prevented by her own government from carrying out as radical reform of the welfare state as she intended. The original plan extended to compulsory charges for schooling alongside a drastic reduction in resources going to the public sector, the break-up of the NHS, full-cost university tuition fees and ending the link that then existed between welfare benefits and prices (Travis, 2012). However there was no consistency in Mrs Thatcher's policymaking. While traditional industries like steel, ship building, coal mining and British car production were allowed to wither, every personal and political support and encouragement was, for example, given to the arms industry. Ironically this led to it becoming one of the largest industrial sectors in the UK, and the UK becoming one of the world's biggest and most 'successful' arms producers, in complete contradiction to Mrs Thatcher's ideological assumptions and predictions (Johnson, 1991). The path set by Mrs Thatcher has continued under successive governments since. There has been:

- an emphasis on moving away from state services and provision to privatisation and outsourcing
- a continuing rhetoric emphasising the strengths of the market
- an increasing trend towards and pressure on people to make their own provision to meet their needs, rather than relying on state support.

Their approaches have embodied some new elements, crucially:

1. monetarism
2. new public management ideas
3. financial and other redistribution through privatisation and outsourcing/contracting-out
4. a rhetoric of choice and consumerism
5. globalisation
6. trade union reform.

Monetarism

Thatcherism is associated with the economic theory of *monetarism*. This places a priority on controlling inflation over controlling unemployment. It regards inflation as the result of there being too much money in the economy and the theory is to control the money supply in order to control inflation, rather than trying directly to limit price and wage increases (Bochel, 2012, 67). Not only has the underpinning argument for monetarism been called into question (for example, Fischer, 1996), but while consistently argued for by Mrs Thatcher and supporters of monetarism succeeding her, it has not been consistently carried out (Alcock, 2008, 210). To fudge, this, the calculation of the 'public sector borrowing requirement' (PSBR) is held down by the ruse of subtracting the proceeds of privatisation as well as taxes from government expenditure and by not counting the massive costs incurred by public–private partnership schemes like the private finance initiative (PFI) (Pratten, 1987).

New public management ideas

Post-1979 enthusiasm for the market meant that its business methods were seen as the solution for the perceived problems of the state and imported or adapted wholesale. They reinforced trends to bigger organisations and more bureaucracy in public services that were already emerging in the 1970s.

Working in a welfare department

For a short time I worked in a pre-Seebohm welfare department. Our office was in the same building as a local day centre, making for ready contact with service users. In those days social services were divided into children's and welfare departments. Welfare departments worked with older and disabled people and were seen as very much the poor relation, with far fewer qualified or graduate staff. When departments were combined into social services departments (SSDs) in 1971, this was mainly under the leadership of managers, frequently male managers, from children's departments. The only graduates in my team were the team manager and me. But it was a team with much local knowledge, skill and experience, empathy and understanding. These were people to whom local service users could readily relate. Team members were much closer in class and culture to the people with whom they worked than in many subsequent SSDs. I found out later, that few of the staff lasted long after reorganisation. SSDs established a pattern of hierarchical management and bureaucratisation that continues to overshadow social work and which initiatives like patch and community social work – where the aim was to decentralise services and bring them closer to local people – sought unsuccessfully to challenge. Current pressure for more 'elite' recruits to social work parallels this development. It also shows similarly little understanding of the loss of experiential knowledge and other skills valued by service users that this can be expected to result in (SWAN, 2014).

The author

The assumption underpinning this 'new public management' (NPM) was that by importing ideas from the private sector, the public sector would be made more efficient and cost-effective (Hood, 1991). NPM has been associated with the introduction of markets, managers and measurement into public services (Ferlie et al, 1996). If public services were previously meant to be shaped by ideas of public service, now this was to be achieved by market methods and philosophy. 'This often involved introducing markets or market-like mechanisms into services, putting services out to competitive tendering or separating purchasers and providers, or commissioners and contractors' (Clarke, 2012, 266).

The new systems placed a heavy reliance on new information technology systems to provide better data faster and strengthen managerial oversight and control; the separation of 'strategy' and 'delivery' with improved delivery to be achieved through a system of 'target' setting and to monitor this, the massive expansion of processes of audit, inspection and scrutiny. All this was to be brought about by expanding and improving management, drawing on private sector models, experience and personnel.

Given the poor state of the UK's private sector in the 1970s, which could hardly be blamed solely on state intervention, its appalling labour relations, inefficiency, lack of strategy, reliance on industries that were increasingly seen as obsolescent (a view that extended to the New Right), this could at best be seen as a naive gamble, at worst, as unjustified and unrealistic. Certainly the adoption of NPM in public services and social policy has been consistently called into question. Running a more complex system has meant that costs were increased. Reliance on unproven IT systems has repeatedly resulted in costly problems as well as diverting workers from their primary tasks and responsibilities. Preoccupation with bureaucratic targets to 'manage performance' has resulted in a 'target culture' which has frequently undermined and corrupted the essential goals and purpose of services. Increasing management has extended rather than reduced bureaucracy, stifled initiative and undermined workers' motivation, creating a cult of 'managerialism' and 'micro-management' (Alcock, 2008, 59, 293–4; Clarke, 2012, 266–7).

An insight into this was offered by the American academic George Ritzer, who first coined the phrase *The McDonaldization of Society* in 1993, to highlight the destructive way in which public services were being reshaped in the image of fast food production (Ritzer, 2008). The social work educator, Donna Dustin, has offered an in-depth case study of how this has had an impact on social work and social care, exploring in depth in care management the four key principles associated with McDonaldisation. These are *efficiency*, based on narrow economic and bureaucratic judgements; *predictability*, through reliance on standardisation and a procedural approach; *calculability*, reducing everything to numbers and finally, *surveillance*, closely controlling and monitoring workers (Dustin, 2007). The Munro Inquiry into child protection subsequently highlighted the consequences that this has had; reducing the amount of time social workers can spend in direct contact with clients, increasing bureaucracy, creating a tyranny of inadequate IT and increasing the risks and costs associated with provision (Munro, 2011). In 2004, the childcare expert Nigel Parton highlighted what he saw as the damaging effects of such managerialism over a generation of high profile child abuse tragedies, from Maria Colwell to Victoria Climbié (Parton, 2004). The culmination of such systemic problems of management and leadership ignoring appalling problems of child abuse across police, social services and the council, can be seen in the case of the Rotherham scandal. Here despite whistleblowing efforts by youth and social workers, the sexual abuse of a conservatively estimated 1,400 children over a long period continued and was ignored by senior managers and leaders (Jay, 2014).

The Mid-Staffordshire Hospital scandal is another high profile example of the potentially damaging effects of market driven target-based approaches to performance and efficiency. Senior management determined to gain independent 'foundation hospital' status for the service, determinedly pursued targets to achieve this which had a grossly perverse effect on the actual performance, efficiency and humanity of the hospital and its staff. As a result large numbers of vulnerable patients are believed to have died, many others and their families to have suffered. Significantly some of the senior staff involved went on to achieve major promotions and success within and beyond the NHS, none have been sanctioned, only more junior staff disciplined (Francis, 2013; Beresford, 2013a).

'Regulation' was meant to be the way in which service quality and 'outcomes' were maintained, but there was an inherent tension between the role of the state as restrictive regulator and of the market presented as creative innovator, experimenter and entrepreneur. The result has been a history of inadequate regulation and regulators often culturally closer to the market than to its consumers. Regulation has also been an essentially bureaucratic process framed in terms of maintaining paper 'standards', reinforcing the association of state intervention with bureaucratisation, as well as proving a blunt and sometimes ineffective instrument for safeguarding people's rights and interests, particularly those of powerless people at vulnerable times (Francis, 2013).

Financial and other redistribution through privatisation and outsourcing/contracting-out

The process of creating large-scale public services and the organisations to run them which began in the nineteenth century, the development of utilities by local authorities and then the post-war policies of nationalisation, all incurred major costs. They also represented major resources in public ownership. This extended from the massive stock of council housing, through to the real estate and capital tied up in the nationalised industries and their infrastructure of support. The policies of privatisation pursued by governments since 1979 not only shifted responsibility for policy and services from the state, but also represented a major redistribution of money and resources. If the aim of the post-war Labour government had been to pursue progressive policies of redistribution in relation to taxation and services, in order to equalise the 'social citizenship' of the people, then such privatisation policies can be seen as travelling in the opposite direction, representing a regressive form of redistribution. This came to be described by the former Prime Minister Harold Macmillan, a 'one nation' Conservative, associated with the Butskellism of the 1950s, as 'selling off the national silver' (Warner, 1998). This process did not stop with the financial redistribution, it was accompanied by a loss of parks, amenities, school playing fields and public buildings as these increasingly went into private hands. Even swathes of city centres have become private space lost to the public with the expansion of commercial shopping malls.

What this meant was that what had been in the public purse was now transferred to private and corporate hands, frequently, critics argued (and continue to argue), at 'knock-down' prices. By offering such new, often under-costed markets to the private sector, it could be argued that it was featherbedded and its innovative edge undermined, rather than encouraged and strengthened. Furthermore while one of the arguments underpinning privatisation was that it would open up the market to competition and a wider range of suppliers, the general trend has been to a very small number of large multinational, sometimes overseas owners. This has been the pattern for the railways, public utilities, bus and coach travel. Kevin Farnsworth has also highlighted the as yet under-explored issue of the degree to which such welfare corporatism has led to for-profit organisations being subsidised by the state (Farnsworth, 2013).

Mrs Thatcher's 'right to buy' policy enabled council tenants to buy their homes at a discount. Since then two million council homes are estimated to have been sold. Michael Heseltine as the Minister first responsible, said, 'no single piece of legislation has enabled the transfer of so much capital wealth from the state to the people'. Critics said 'Why pay for your home twice?' Significantly, many council tenants no more felt that they owned their homes because they were in public ownership, than miners before them had felt that they owned their pits following the nationalisation of the coal industry.

This was undoubtedly one of Mrs Thatcher's most popular and effective policies and has been maintained in some form or other ever since. However, council house sales policy helped increase the cost of housing, excluding an increasing number of people from having their own home, increased problems of homelessness and insecurity and encouraging council housing to become a commodity for speculative investment. The remaining stock of council housing has increasingly been concentrated in disadvantaged areas and estates, further isolating and stigmatising tenants (Murie, 1989; Grant, 1992; Jones and Murie, 2006; Sommerlad, 2013).

A rhetoric of choice and consumerism

Advocates of the New Right argued that state welfare reduced the choices open to people to meet their needs and maximise their opportunities, instead strengthening bureaucracy and the power of professionals (Alcock, 2008, 9). Historically, the market was advanced as offering efficiency and freedom. From the 1970s, the neoliberals also emphasised the gains it could bring in extending the choice and control that they assert the market offers people in their private lives, to their dealings with public policy and services (Pascall, 2012, 271). This was to be achieved by replacing a relationship based on the public service ethic, with an exchange relationship resting on marketisation and purchase of service. Redefined as 'welfare consumers' and public service 'customers', people would be able to regain control of provision by owning or having a stake in it and through enhanced opportunities to choose what services they wanted. From being passive clients and claimants, people would become active consumers.

Having a baby – then and now

When I had my first baby, Catherine, in 1976, the GP did all the ante-natal care. If there was any problem, they had a relation with the local hospital. The whole thing was based on a relationship with your GP – who was excellent – Mr Smith (real name!). If there were any problems, they would deliver the baby in the local hospital – the GP would come over to the hospital. I went to ante-natal classes at the local clinic run either by a midwife or health visitor, it was just down the road. They gave us loads of information about the labour, birth, what to do after the baby was born, all word of mouth, from women who knew what they were talking about. When I had Catherine in the hospital, she was a forceps delivery, so the GP came. You stayed in for seven days and, in that time, they showed you how to bath the baby, how to do its nappy (not disposables then), breast and bottle feed and so on. After you went home, you saw the midwife and health visitor for what seemed like months. Sadly by the time I had our last daughter, Ruth, in hospital in 1992, the system was collapsing. I had to make my own way to the lavatory after the birth although I had been badly torn, I had nothing to eat all day.

Now it seems you have to sort out your own ante-natal classes yourself. You have to pay for them. Not on the NHS. The health visitor comes just once after you

127

have the baby unless they identify a problem. She has a checklist and then you are given lots of written information, which of course starts to be prescriptive and dictatorial – what's recommended. In other words, you should do this, you should do that. All written. So before it was women's advice. Now it's written instructions! Our daughter Rebecca, you can see her (in 2014), trying with her first daughter, to keep to what they say. A kind of tyranny of how things are meant to be, so that if you are a tired, depressed new mother, you are vulnerable. How do you keep it in perspective? You haven't got the experience to know that all babies aren't the same.

Suzy Croft
My partner

Important early expressions of such consumerism were the rights to comment and complaint included in the 1989 Children Act and the 1990 NHS and Community Care Act (Means et al, 2008). Under Mrs Thatcher, this new relationship was symbolised, as we have seen, by the right to buy your own council house and to purchase shares in the newly privatised utilities. By the time of Mr Major such consumerist policy had descended to farce with the introduction of 'cone hotlines' (originally 0345 504030, later 08457 504030) where people could check on progress in completing road repairs (http://en.wikipedia. org/wiki/Cones_Hotline). Under New Labour, it was typified by a preoccupation with consultative exercises and seeking public views through 'focus groups', which has come to be known as 'focus group politics' (Peck and Phillips, 2008). Under the Coalition government, it was most strongly expressed in their slogan for the National Health Service, 'Nothing about me without me' – an individualised version of the rallying cry stolen from the disabled people's movement – 'Nothing about us, without us'!

While the rhetoric of consumerism has loomed large in the marketisation of welfare, it doesn't necessarily sit comfortably with the realities of public policy, however (Barnes, 2012). This may apply, for example:

- because some recipients of welfare/social policy are involuntary (for example, mental health service users, offenders, parents and other family members associated with the neglect or abuse of children);
- where services are needs or means-testing, and people are adjudged ineligible for support, yet cannot afford to purchase it independently;
- where the market has not been sufficiently developed to offer choices;

- where it is not judged economic to respond to complex or unusual needs.

> ## Care work today
>
> I feel proud to live in a country with an established welfare state. It's wonderful, and how it should be. I refuse to accept that it is necessary to inflict spending cuts on this treasured possession in the name of austerity. For example, we continue to spend billions on nuclear weapons, further armament and questionable wars; expenditures which in no way reflect our progression into the twenty-first century as an advanced, intelligent and enlightened race. And yet through manipulation of the media, scapegoating and fear-mongering, the government is able to lie and manipulate, fooling us to believe that they are acting with integrity and goodwill.
>
> The welfare state is great. I am indebted to the NHS for the countless times they have aided me in times of agony. Skateboarding would never have reached its dizzying heights if it weren't for the NHS!
>
> Currently, I am working part-time as a care worker. I visit an elderly, 101-year-old gentleman, who lives with his son who has learning difficulties. This man is a war veteran, who served in the Second World War, surviving a parachute drop and two years in a POW camp. His son has severe mental health problems, and is unable to care for himself. I visit their house in the morning, to help with daily tasks. They live in squalid, nasty conditions. I have very little nutritious, acceptable food on offer to cook for them – microwave and tinned meals. I myself am not specialised or trained in caring, and am paid £7 an hour for the work I do. This is the best on offer for this veteran and his son.
>
> *Harry Hutchins*
> *Nephew*

The shift to market models also certainly does not seem to have put an end to problems of abuse, neglect and poor treatment in services like health and social care, as we have already seen. Indeed some critics would suggest that the primary focus on making a profit and the lack of transparency that comes from a preoccupation with competition and commercial 'confidentiality' and 'sensitivity' may actually increase the risks. The move has been to fewer, bigger, multinational companies and finance houses, less and less transparent, as they adopt increasingly deregulated market forms, like that of being a private equity or 'zombie' company. Private equity firms now account for 11 per cent of the market in social care and supported living, supply 8 per cent of care homes and 10 per cent of services for people with learning difficulties – and their market share is growing (Boffey, 2014). William Laing, of consultancy, Laing & Buisson, who reported in 2012 on private equity has said, 'It makes pots of money' (quoted in Boffey, 2014). 'Those profits – which are made before debt payments and overheads – don't appear on the bottom line of the health firms' company accounts, and because of that corporation tax isn't paid on them' (Boffey, 2014).

It really is difficult to see how the individualised customer is king or queen in a world of distant and powerful corporations which are not directly politically accountable. For all the consumerist rhetoric, we may wonder how much closer to being participatory marketised welfare is than the original welfare state. There seems to be little evidence of it.

Globalisation

The term globalisation has been increasingly used since the mid-1980s. The sociologist Anthony Giddens defined it as: 'the intensification of worldwide social relations which link distant localities in such a way that local happenings are shaped by events occurring many miles away and vice versa' (Giddens, 1991, 64).

In neoliberal discussions, economic globalisation has come to be understood in terms of the opening up and deregulation of commodity, capital and labour markets (Fotopoulos, 2001). Dominant discussions about globalisation highlight the limited power of nation states in relation to international corporations. However, critics suggest that this can equally be understood in terms of the ideological reluctance of such states to restrict large corporations, in the context of powerful international 'free market' organisations like the International Monetary Fund (IMF) and World Bank. This then becomes a self-fulfilling prophecy (Yeates and Holden, 2009; Holden, 2008). The actual effects of such globalisation have been to perpetuate low wages and poor working conditions in the developing world and encourage the export of money and other wealth from there to the west, while restricting the mobility of people whose poverty is thus increased and perpetuated, in the opposite direction. This has, for example, been reflected in the increasing internationalisation of services like health and social care in the UK, with large multinational corporations playing an increasingly significant role and increasing reliance placed on low paid migrants (and in some cases people without citizenship status) to make up the labour force in low paid areas of public service employment, like social care.

Trade union reform

The trade unions occupied a powerful place in British policy and politics entering the last quarter of the twentieth century. This was in strong contrast to their position during much of the nineteenth century, when free market economics did not face the same constraints that they could later impose. As a result, through a series of seven Acts between 1979 and 1990, Mrs Thatcher gradually restricted the rights of trade unions, making it more difficult for them to take effective collective action (Bochel, 2012, 67).

Back to the future?

The political shift from state to market from the late 1970s onwards in the UK, and indeed in many other countries, did not mean that longstanding problems associated with the market had been resolved. Also, as we have seen above, new developments like monetarism, NPM thinking, regressive redistribution through privatisation, consumerism and globalisation, all brought their own new problems and challenges. None of them could truly be said to resolve earlier problems associated with the market, although they have all generated new discussions and raised new issues for understanding it and the way it is interpreted and taken forward (Bourdieu, 1999; Finn, 2008; Aspers, 2011).

In its obituary editorial on the death of Mrs Thatcher, the left of centre *Guardian* newspaper reinforced what seems to be a broader conventional wisdom, that regardless of all the problems and divisions she initiated, there can be 'no going back to the failed post-war past' (www.guardian.co.uk/commentisfree/2013/apr/08/margaret-thatcher-editorial). The ideological shift in UK politics which began with Mrs Thatcher's governments and which has ever since been strongly associated with questioning of the post-war welfare state and its principles, has been presented as a break from this past. It is offered as a move to a new approach. It emphasises that the welfare state has become an increasing anachronism over the years as social, economic, demographic, cultural and political conditions have changed.

Little or no evidence is, however, offered for such increasingly common casual assertions about 'not going back' to what is presented as an outmoded welfare state. However, there does seem to be at least one element of truth in them. For what Mrs Thatcher and her political successors actually seem to have done *is* gone back to the past – but it is to an even earlier past – to a pre-post-war welfare state past – the failed past of the market. It was this to which they have sought to return us, the past of market failure.

> ## Hoping not to use it
>
> The welfare state is something that I know is there, but I hope never to use. It is a security blanket, a back-up, a last resort. If it is to be used, it's not to be relied upon. If you are using the welfare state, you are disadvantaged. You are ill, unemployed, or in some way deprived to the normal. That is unless you are over 65, when everybody regardless of wealth should be entitled to a state pension. It is an important principle of living in the UK that there is a provision for those 'in need', and I hope that austerity measures do not squeeze the life from this important provision. As a UK taxpayer, I hope to be contributing to the welfare state for my whole working life. As a 29 year old, I hope never to have to benefit from this contribution; until, that is, my retirement.
>
> *Toby Hutchins*
> *Nephew*

Truth seems to have been an early casualty in the heavily ideological discussions and assumptions that have dominated modern analysis of the welfare state. For example, the post-war welfare state is presented as a failed *monolithic* creation. Yet as Alcock has noted, there was never a state monopoly of welfare. There were, for example, always 'pay beds' in the NHS and public schools continued to flourish. Charitable and private sector provision kept going strong over the whole of the period and by the 1950s was even expanding, notably in the housing sector (Alcock, 2008, 144). Commentators like Hadley and Hatch in the late 1970s and early 1980s criticised the over-bureaucratisation of state provision and called for a welfare pluralist approach to provision, placing a particular emphasis on the need for an expanded role for the voluntary sector (Hadley and Hatch, 1981). But they only served to destabilise existing state services and act as a stalking horse for the dominance of the private sector in social care and social services, which ultimately has shown itself to be even more bureaucratic (Beresford and Croft, 1984; Alcock, 2008, 59, 293–4; Clarke, 2012, 266–7). Meanwhile the failings of the voluntary sector, even though long evident and again highlighted at this time, were largely left unaddressed (Kramer, 1981). Nor was the economy from the 1980s significantly improved by political moves to the right, but, increasingly unregulated, rather went through major depressions and crises from 1987 and 2007 (Alcock, 2008, 210).

Discussion about the welfare state and the need for change continues to make constant media headlines. But the dominant right of centre discourse has restructured the focus and form of discussion about social policy by adopting a deliberately, perhaps mischievously, narrow understanding of 'welfare'. While the words welfare and welfare state are used interchangeably (Collins, 2013), discussion tends to be limited to welfare benefits and the people receiving them. From the founding of the welfare state, this was always one of its most contentious areas, where consensus was most questionable. But of course the 'welfare state' included – and still includes – very much more. This extends to the national health service, education, transport, planning and other policies. While these may also come in for right-wing political attack, there is, of course, also recognition that services like the NHS command enormous support and affection from the population. So they are decoupled from attacks on benefits and claimants to reinforce the effectiveness of these attack and in order to secure populist support.

Milton Friedman, the American free market economist, claimed that 'the thing that people do not recognise is that Margaret Thatcher is not in terms of belief a Tory. She is a nineteenth-century Liberal' (cited in Cowdrill, 2009, 5). While there is some disagreement about this, it seems to hold for her beliefs in the role of the state and the nature of the economy. The former left-wing Conservative cabinet minister Ian Gilmour described such neoliberalism as old style nineteenth-century liberalism dressed up in twentieth-century clothes (Gilmour, 1992, 9). It is important to remember that neoliberal ideas were not a creation of the 1970s and 1980s. As we saw in Chapter Four, advocates like Hayek and Friedman had their right-wing supporters even in advance of the establishment of the welfare state. Mrs Thatcher was one of them and referred to reading Hayek's writing as early as the late 1940s. At that time, however, because of strong public and political memories of the social and economic hardships of the inter-war years, they had little political resonance and found little popular favour. Neoliberalism, however, has played an increasingly influential role in global politics and economics since the late 1970s and has certainly dominated the UK scene in its various governmental iterations to the present. It has come to be associated with a radical and laissez-faire capitalist set of ideas, that have strong echoes of Victorian politics and ideology (Harvey, 2005). The neoliberal policy agenda is committed to limiting the role of the state and emphasising individual rights and individual freedom. And so, neoliberalism is committed to the transfer of public services and functions, like health, education and social care, to the private sector, seeing the supportive role of government as limited to encouraging citizens to look after themselves.

Thus it becomes increasingly difficult to see the shifts in politics and policy from the late 1970s, while cast in terms of the 'new', as anything other than a determined return to the past. As Alcock has written about neoliberal critiques, there is little new about them: 'they drew on classical liberal thinking from the nineteenth century and before' (Alcock, 2008, 9). There is an enormous irony here. While the welfare state had been developed in order to address the problems originating in the inefficiencies, inconsistency and inequalities of the market, now the market is presented as an alternative to the deficiencies of the welfare state! In one fell swoop through an alliance in the UK of right-wing press, dominant political interests, powerful market organisations and institutions, what was the problem is now recast as the solution. This is a disturbing sleight of hand and the limited critical discussion of it (highlighted by comments like those expressed in the left of centre *Guardian* above) is both disturbing and a sign of the narrowness of debate about welfare and the welfare state.

If any evidence were needed of the problematic nature of the market in relation to providing services and meeting need, then it is to be found in the series of very high profile scandals associated with it and UK neoliberal policy over the last 30 years. These include:

- the pension 'mis-selling' and other financial services scandals – from salesmen persuading people to ditch valuable final-salary occupational schemes for riskier personal pension schemes based on the stock market, through endowment mis-selling to unhelpful and unnecessary 'payment protection insurance' (Dunn, 2009);
- problems of abuse and neglect in private provision for older and disabled people, and children continuing unabated, with high profile cases like Winterbourne View (described by the Minister as a 'national scandal' (www.bbc.co.uk/news/uk-england-bristol-20078999)), and Orchid Grove in 2011, where five older people died, the tip of an iceberg of restrictions on 'soft rights' through inadequate and poor quality residential and domiciliary care as well as serious criminal cases;
- the failure of the global company G4S to provide security at the 2012 Olympics resulting in the army having to be drafted in (www.telegraph.co.uk/finance/newsbysector/supportservices/10070425/Timeline-how-G4Ss-bungled-Olympics-security-contract-unfolded.html);

- ATOS apologising for wrongly assessing people with long-term sickness in nearly 40 per cent of cases appealed, as fit for work in 'work capability assessments' (WCAs) undertaken for the Department for Work and Pensions (Ramesh, 2013);
- the 'horsemeat scandal' with high proportions of horsemeat found in 2013 in supermarket burgers and other processed meat sales (Lawrence, 2013);
- the widespread and routine use of phone hacking by the media empire of Rupert Murdoch, who was closely associated with Prime Ministers Thatcher, Blair, and Cameron (www.thedailybeast.com/articles/2013/10/30/murdoch-s-news-of-the-world-editors-admit-to-phone-hacking.html);
- the collapse of UK banks resulting in a state rescue package 2008–09 (http://www.bbc.co.uk/news/business-11462440).

Most if not all of the much vaunted promises of Thatcherism have failed to materialise. We have not become a nation of small shareholders. Privatisation of public provision has hardly resulted in meaningful consumer choice in relation to transport or utilities, now significantly owned by monolithic, often overseas corporations or even state organisations. Instead of becoming a 'home-owning' democracy, more and more people are having to turn to a poorly regulated private rented sector (Meek, 2014a; 2014b; Chakrabortty, 2014). What is interesting, in the light of this catalogue of disaster and broken promises, is that political fascination with the market continues. Despite its evident failures and problems, it still seems to command widespread political support. Thus in 2014, we still had former Prime Minister Tony Blair warning his party 'not to demonise business arguing that the financial crash did not mean that people had "fallen back in love with the state"' (Wintour, 2014). Perhaps this is less difficult to understand in the UK, once we take account of the strong links that have developed between politicians, government, private sector, market organisations and dominant right-wing media. Neoliberal politics have also exhibited the same preoccupations as their nineteenth-century predecessors – whose power-base similarly rested on powerful alliances between media proprietors, property owners, politicians and ideologues. Neoliberal discussions of the early twenty-first century are remarkably similar to their nineteenth-century antecedents. This is again manifest, for example, in frequent attacks on and the scapegoating of:

- immigrants – previously framed as 'aliens' and interlopers (then Jews and Irish people), now as 'asylum seekers' and 'benefit tourists' (Wise, 2009);
- people reliant on benefits – formerly framed as 'the undeserving poor', now repathologised as 'skivers rather than strivers';
- lone parents – cast by the Poor Law as 'moral imbeciles' and now pressed back into employment, regardless of their responsibilities as parents;
- disabled people, people with learning difficulties and mental health service users – previously conceived of as 'defective', now stigmatised as 'dependent';
- young unemployed people – in the past presented as potentially criminal, disruptive and a threat, now defined as 'NEETS – not in employment, education or training' and similarly highlighted as potentially criminal, disruptive and a threat.

There is also the same determination to keep public spending down (ironically, often undermined by the inefficiency and damaging effects of laissez-faire economics. There are also similar moral undertones to policy and practice. If the founders of the welfare state assumed that human nature was essentially altruistic and benign – with people wanting to do things for each other, then the model underpinning the New Political Right onwards has been one that assumes the inherent selfishness of people, who would be prepared to lie and do each other down. Given the commitment of neoliberal politics to individualism, 'self-help', and competition, this could be seen as another of its self-fulfilling prophesies, imputing to others a mindset which has characterised its advocates.

While as we have seen, twenty-first century neoliberalism displays some differences to its nineteenth-century predecessor, many of the same social problems of the past have resurfaced (Harvey, 2005). Crucially these are problems of inequality and poverty.

Inequality

As the social policy academic Peter Taylor-Gooby has argued, 'egalitarianism had no place' in Conservativism from the mid-1970s. Labour party reappraisals after four success electoral defeats also led to vaguer commitments to spreading 'opportunities and life chances as widely as possible' and equality of opportunity, combined with a new emphasis on 'individual responsibility' (Taylor-Gooby, 2012, 30). While the Blair and Brown governments introduced targets for reducing child poverty, and levels of income inequality dropped slightly in the early twenty-first century, the general trend has been to the widening of the gap between rich and poor in the UK. This is a trend that has been increasing and accelerating over the years. It has been reflected in widening inequality in relation to class, income, wealth and health. We have also even seen the re-emergence of the same inequalities and divisions between the north and south in the UK. These were the inequalities which the post-war welfare state had sought to reduce and succeeded in reducing significantly.

The Black report on inequalities on health highlighted increasing inequalities during the Thatcher years, with social class differences in mortality and morbidity widening (Townsend and Davidson, 1982; Smith et al, 1990).

> The Report concluded that these inequalities were not mainly attributable to failings in the NHS, but rather to many other social inequalities influencing health: income, education, housing, diet, employment, and conditions of work. In consequence, the Report recommended a wide strategy of social policy measures to combat inequalities in health. These findings and recommendations were virtually disowned by the then Secretary of State for Social Services (Gray, 1982; see also Wilkinson, 1986).

In 2010, the Marmot review of health inequalities reported a worsening situation, evidencing 'huge differences in people's life expectancy and [impairment]-free life expectancy between people in different social positions' (Pascall, 2012, 263; see also Pickett and Wilkinson, 2009). 'Social inequalities in health arise because of inequalities in the conditions of daily life – the conditions in which people are born, grow up, live, work and age – and the fundamental drivers that give rise to them: inequities in power, money and resources' (Marmot et al, 2010, 37; see also Pickett and Wilkinson, 2009; Marmot and Wilkinson, 2006).

Marmot concluded that much of the rest of Europe takes better care of its families than the UK. Life expectancy for women and death rates among the under-fives are worse in the UK, where there is also more child poverty (Boseley, 2013). Marmot also highlighted that while governments had been planning to raise the pension age, 'more than three quarters of the population do not have [an impairment]-free life expectancy of as long as sixty-eight' (Marmot et al, 2010, 38). Health inequalities are also identified in relation to gender and ethnicity (Pascall, 2012, 264). More attention is also being paid to the geography of inequality and the increasing problems and extremes this is highlighting. Social geographer Danny Dorling makes the case that in the UK, the gaps in life expectancy between regions, between cities, and between neighbourhoods within cities now surpass the worst measures over the last hundred years. In almost all other affluent countries, inequalities in health are lower and people live longer (Dorling, 2013; see also Wheeler et al, 2005; Dorling and Thomas, 2011).

Poverty

The advent of new right/neoliberal governments also heralded the return of large-scale poverty. Increasingly this has become poverty among employed rather than unemployed people, following the US model. New Labour's 'third way' introduced targets to reduce child poverty and went some way to achieving them. It did this while emphasising people's individual responsibility for their circumstances, equating social inclusion with having paid work and topping up low wages with tax credits and benefits. These marked a return to the old Poor Law 'Speenhamland system' of topping up wages with 'out relief'. This was rejected by the 1834 New Poor Law which saw it as increasing inefficiency and encouraging dependence. Certainly in the twenty-first century, it has enabled employers to perpetuate low pay, subsidised by the state, and then for right-wing critics to attack such public subsidies, further reducing incomes.

Using the commonly accepted measure of the proportion of households below 60 per cent of the adjusted median average income, according to Pete Alcock: 'The figures reveal that the proportions or people in poverty ... have remained high since the 1980s, with only some improvement in the early years of the new century under Labour' (Alcock, 2012b, 183).

By this measure, 22 per cent, more than a fifth of the population, were living in poverty in the UK in 2008/09 – an increase of 'over one and a half million over four years' (Alcock, 2012b, 183). Differing risks of poverty for different social groups, like disabled people and members of minority ethnic groups, can also be identified. The situation worsened following the coming to power of the Coalition government in 2010. According to official figures, 'an additional 900,000 people were plunged into poverty during the first year of the coalition government, including 300,000 more children'. The entire increase of children in poverty in 2011/12 came from *working* families

(Butler, 2013). In 2015, at the time of writing, the visible signs of the return to the nineteenth-century past are the expansion of 'food banks', the mushrooming of pawnbrokers and 'payday lenders' and people on low income being faced with the brutal choice between 'heat' or 'eat' for themselves and their children.

This period of neoliberal politics and policy has also seen the re-emergence of equivalent notions to the Victorian 'residuum'. This first took the form of a disaffiliated and dangerous 'underclass' highlighted by Charles Murray (Murray, 1996) and has more recently been presented in terms of 120,000 'troubled families', regarded as disproportionately damaging, disruptive and costly to the public purse (Casey, 2012; Welshman, 2012; 2013). Not only have neoliberal policies created more social problems, but by reducing resources to deal with them through prioritising residualising approaches to social policies, these have been exacerbated. Furthermore while supporters of the market have criticised the post-war welfare state for its failure to address gender and other difference, their policies have similarly maintained traditional inequalities, as well as in some cases reinforcing them.

Conclusion

We have seen how many citizens and service users were not necessarily convinced of the welfare state's actual achievement through their own experience of it. Its reach often seemed to exceed its grasp and in many ways initially, it was the prisoner of its own time. Mrs Thatcher and her neoliberal successors were able to build on this, with a rhetoric that carried wide resonance. Thus, it may not have taken Mrs Thatcher, her politics, followers and fellow travellers to make many people aware of the shortcomings of the welfare state. But they were able to use people's own doubts and questioning of the welfare state, to offer a convincing critique of its shortcomings. Crucially, however, this has not necessarily meant that they have been able to offer something new or capable of overcoming such limitations in its place. Instead neoliberal ideology has overlaid longstanding problems of free market social policy with additional ones of over-bureaucratisation, inefficiency and managerialism. The state has tended to be replaced by large corporations, often multinational corporations, with minimal processes for democratic accountability.

There is also an irony, that in a climate of thought where state has been presented as 'bad' and market 'good', the National Health Service, despite initial opposition, the qualified ways in which it was implemented and current efforts to privatise it by stealth, continues to be enormously popular with people and remains a key political issue. Ever since Mrs Thatcher's attacks on the NHS, all major political parties seek to convince the electorate that the NHS is safe in their hands. Yet the NHS still most closely reflects the founding principles of the post-war welfare state – of a service run from the centre, free at the point of delivery and largely paid for out of general taxation. Equally the policy which by common consent is least popular, efficient, understood and fit for purpose, is social care; the policy least altered by the welfare state reforms and which has been at the vanguard of Mrs Thatcher's and her successors' market-based reforms.

Meanwhile we are witnessing, under neoliberal politics and social policy, growing inequality, poverty, division, want and social problems – the conditions which ironically provided the impetus for the creation of and popular support for the welfare state. More recently identified problems of inequality around identity remain unresolved, while old material problems which the welfare state set out to eradicate, have resurfaced with force and intensity. The same wastefulness, inefficiency and human suffering that were associated with neoliberalism's nineteenth-century laissez-faire predecessors have regained ground (Wilkinson and Pickett, 2009). But while this unproductive search for solutions in old inegalitarian approaches to social policy still dominates, less visibly other new roads have also been identified and taken and we will shortly be examining those. First though, if we are to make better sense of why we have got to where we are, it is perhaps time to look more carefully at social policy as a *discipline*.

EIGHT

What's wrong with social policy?

As the UK's leading experts on social policy and the welfare state, we urge the government to reconsider the benefit cuts scheduled for 1 April and to ensure that no further public spending cuts are targeted on the poorest in our society.

(Letter to the *Guardian* newspaper from Professors of Social Policy, 27 March 2013)

Many of us wrote to the prime minister previously urging him to reconsider the social security benefit cuts scheduled for 1 April 2013 and to ensure that no further public spending cuts were targeted on the poorest in our society. Unfortunately our pleas went unheard.

(Letter to the *Guardian* newspaper from Professors of Social Policy, 6 May 2015)

If there was a flaw at the heart of the classic social-democratic welfare state, it was the assumption that those operating it were by definition altruistic and trustworthy, together with the accompanying assumption that those receiving its benefits should be passive, patient and grateful.

(Kynaston, 2008, 145)

Many of us were brought up to think of nineteenth-century social reformers like Dr Barnardo, Elizabeth Fry, Octavia Hill, Lord Shaftesbury and Robert Owen as heroes of a progressive age, motivated by increasing humanitarian concern. In fact, as we might expect, both their motives and the times were much more complex and ambiguous. For example:

- Shocked by the appalling conditions of women and children in Newgate Prison, Elizabeth Fry (1780–1845) introduced a strict system for supervising the women and imposed compulsory sewing duties and bible reading.

- Octavia Hill (1838–1912), the housing pioneer, regarded poor relief outside the workhouse as 'a profligate use of public funds' (Wyatt, 2000, 2). She 'argued that although workers' houses were often badly built ... they were tenfold worst because of the tenants' habits' (Cunningham and Cunningham, 2012, 27). Despite the seasonal nature of employment in London, she insisted on rents being paid regularly as evidence of 'habits of energy and punctuality' (Stedman Jones, 1984, 265). She was described by an admirer, as 'ruling over a little kingdom of three thousand loving subjects with an iron sceptre twined with roses' (Bremner et al, 1965).
- Dr Barnardo (1845–1905) is still remembered as a major pioneer in child protection and Barnardo's continues to be a high profile children's charity. Yet in his own lifetime he was condemned for his vanity and overbearing ambition. He faced public scandal accused by his numerous enemies of financial dishonesty, cruelty to children, immorality and deception and for not being entitled to call himself Doctor as he did (Pettit et al, 2013).
- Robert Owen (1771–1858), the factory reformer began as a follower of the utilitarian Jeremy Bentham, but increasingly became a socialist. He created his own paternalistic utopian regime at New Lanark for his workers, but distrusted the 'industrialised poor' and thought that their independent action would lead to chaos (Miliband, 1954).

This is a helpful reminder to avoid simplistic and superficial understandings of the nature and purpose of social policy. Many of the social reforms and reformers we first learned about at school, are better understood as committed to moral and utilitarian rather than humanistic concerns. Their interest was often less to do with the personal welfare of the people and groups involved and more with what they saw as the ugliness, inefficiency, immorality, evil and wider damage that they associated with them. Thus housing reformers were motivated by concerns about immorality and incest; penal reformers with the degradation and moral reform of criminals, public health reformers with the contaminating effects of impoverished areas on the wider community, education reformers to ensure that there was a sufficiently skilled and disciplined workforce and the poverty reformers because they saw the existing system as encouraging indolence, increasing the numbers of 'the poor', extending their immorality and putting the fabric of society at risk (Stedman Jones, 1971).

The new science of social policy

The history of social policy, from its nineteenth-century origins onwards, has constantly been bound up with ideas of 'science' and being 'scientific'. This can be traced to the emergence of such ideas in the eighteenth century, with the advent of the 'enlightenment' and 'age of reason'. Philosophy, policy and politics were no longer to be rooted in religion, as they formerly had been, but instead on intellectual and deductive truths and centred on rational choice, utilitarianism and secularism (Oakeshott, 1962). Starting with the natural sciences and then extended to the 'social' and 'human' sciences, they were based on systematic and rigorous methods of establishing knowledge through testing, practical experiment and measurement. Thus the nineteenth century became both the age of scientific discovery and also the time of 'social reform' and innovation.

The aim was to reform society on the basis of reason, rejecting faith and old beliefs and advancing human knowledge and understanding through 'scientific methods'. This meant measuring, testing, experiment, investigation and enquiry. The 'scientific revolution' of the eighteenth and nineteenth centuries followed from this new age and social theoreticians and reformers borrowed from the increasing interest in empiricism, scientific rigour and increased questioning of religious orthodoxy that was first expressed in the natural sciences. In England, such ideas were particularly associated with the emergence of the Whig party and the development of liberal political thinking and political philosophers such as John Locke (Porter, 2001). Underpinning these ideas was the belief that human beings could create a more democratic, free and equal society through their own reason rather than relying on god, faith or any other outside agency.

In social policy in the nineteenth century, these ideas found expression in the utilitarianism that underpinned the New Poor Law, as well as in other social reforms like those relating to public health. Utilitarianism was also seen as an ethical theory compatible with science. While there may be question marks over whose interests utilitarianism actually served, what is indisputable and of critical importance to understanding it, is its preoccupation with an almost mechanistic ordering of society and its population through social reform. The utilitarians were essentially social reformers. They believed that criminals should be reformed, not simply punished. They supported suffrage for women and those without property and were opposed to slavery.

Jeremy Bentham, the philosopher most closely associated with utilitarianism, was also strongly influenced by science, particularly the systems of classification developed by the Swedish botanist Carl Linnaeus, known as the father of modern taxonomy. For example, Bentham developed the idea of the 'panopticon' or scientific prison where all inmates could be seen and therefore controlled by a supervisor at any time. He was preoccupied with 'rationalising' human activity whether the law, economics, sex or social policy. Bentham was opposed to cruelty to animals and supported a meritocracy (Richards, 2005).

These same preoccupations with a systematised, centrally controlled regime underpinned the New Poor Law. In this way it was felt that resources would be properly and most cost-effectively used, consistency would be ensured and there was least likelihood of the system being open to abuse. The New Poor Law can be seen as the starting point of a new interest in and understanding of social policy based on 'expert' conceptualisation, theory, categorisation and measurement, resting on what were seen as 'scientific' principles. The legacy of such so-called scientific approaches on social policy is no less important than that of the Poor Law itself, although in its case, there was no similar date of cut-off or abolition.

It wasn't only state services that were based on these principles. The Charity Organisation Society (COS) founded in England in 1869 claimed to use 'scientific principles to root out scroungers and target relief where it was most needed' (Rees, 2001). Charity organisation societies were an international movement and saw themselves as using 'scientific' philanthropy to organise charities to avoid the damaging effects they associated with what they called, 'indiscriminate giving' (Mowat, 1961).

The social policy trinity

From its nineteenth-century beginnings, social policy has been as complex and ambiguous as its pioneers. A number of important strands can be traced in its development, all of which seem to be as important today as they were in the past. They can both help us to understand the shortcomings of present policy, as well as the reasons for their continued existence. Three key characteristics have been associated with social policy: first in this trinity is that it is scientific, second that it has its own corps of experts and third, that they provide the evidence base to justify it.

A distinction that is often drawn and which has already emerged in Chapter One, is between social policy (or public policy as it tends to be called in the US) as an activity of policy-making, and as an *academic* discipline. So, as Alcock says, 'social policy refers both to the activity of policy-making … and to the academic study of such actions' (Alcock, 2012a, 5). However, there is a further distinction that needs to be drawn. This is between social policy as an academic discipline and as an *analytical* approach. Clearly the two are related, but social policy as an analytical approach has a longer history and is perhaps of more central importance here, both in trying to make sense of existing practical social policy and improving it for the future.

As we saw earlier in Chapter Two, the development of social policy, as such a distinct area of policy analysis and planning, can be traced back to the nineteenth century. Often the criticism made of researchers and theorists is that they are too distant from the real world – abstracted inhabitants of ivory towers. In a powerful sense, the opposite has been true historically of social policy. So while distinctions can be drawn between social policy as theoretical analysis and political activity, in fact the two have long been closely intertwined. The people who have played a key role in theorising and writing about social policy have also often been closely involved in the shaping of policy itself. They have had an important hands-on, or influencing role in policy formation and development. Thus there have been no barriers between the two – analysis and policy – no great distance separating them, with little likelihood of a challenge to any bias, or of independent critical examination. This is except where the prevailing ideology of one is opposed to that of the other, and then there tends to be another set of problems.

This has been true from the earliest times, from utilitarian thinkers such as Edwin Chadwick, through social reformers such as Beatrice and Sidney Webb and the Fabian movement they helped found, to founders of the welfare state, notably, William Beveridge, Clement Attlee and also Richard Titmuss. Prime Minister Attlee whose government established the welfare state, was, as a young man, secretary of Toynbee Hall, the East End settlement, and also a lecturer at the London School of Economics (LSE). Beveridge was director of the LSE between the wars and the Webbs were co-founders of the LSE and Titmuss its first Professor of Social Policy. Now we can also learn about the hierarchies and sexual politics of Titmuss's time, with the 'difficult women' pioneers who were marginalised and the devotees fostered as 'Titmice' (Benn, 2014; Oakley, 2014). The same links between practice and analysis are to be found in later generations too, with the distinguished social policy academic, David Donnison, Chair of the government's Supplementary Benefits Tribunal and the present Richard Titmuss Professor of Social Policy at the LSE, Julian Le Grand, a senior policy adviser to former Prime Minister Tony Blair and one of the principal architects of the government's 'quasi-market' reforms in healthcare and education. Such links have also extended to right-wing thinkers. Thus, Friedrich August Hayek, the free market economist, was an academic at the LSE before exerting a key influence on Margaret Thatcher's social and economic policy. Such connections have loomed large in UK social policy and have had a significant bearing on its nature and formation.

Key social policy case studies

This can be seen as particularly significant given some key shortcomings of social policy analysis from its nineteenth-century beginnings. Three key early social policy researchers and commentators, Henry Mayhew, Charles Booth and Seebohm Rowntree provide case studies of the issues raised. With a background as a writer, Mayhew's work, most closely associated with his massive study, *London labour and the London poor* (first published in 1851), has been distinguished from that of other social researchers as more journalistic and superficial, with detailed accounts of people's lives and characteristics, offered as in their own words (Mayhew, 1950 and 2009). However, he also offered his own interpretation of the causes and structure of poverty and he was as critical of 'indiscriminate charity' as the Charity Organisation Society. Indeed his reporting of vagrants' and beggars' 'frauds and deceits' were included in the COS's recommended reading lists in the 1870s (Stedman Jones, 1984, 267 and 10). However, it would be a mistake to dismiss Mayhew as just another impressionistic social explorer. As Stedman Jones has noted, his plan was to undertake a comprehensive social survey of London and he offered an embryonic theory to help explain the economic behaviour of London's poor, although he himself still seemed to accept implicitly the idea of a destructive 'residuum' (Stedman Jones, 1984, 14, 263).

Indeed Mayhew can be seen to exhibit the key characteristics of early social policy analysts and commentators; their ideological commitment, moral underpinnings and tendency to moralise, their curiosity and emphasis on 'science' and being 'scientific'. We can also see this in the work of the two other leading social researchers and reformers of the time, already mentioned, Charles Booth and Seebohm Rowntree.

Charles Booth, a rich businessman and amateur statistician, published his massive 17-volume survey of *Life and Labour in London* between 1889 and 1903 (Fried and Ellman, 1969), Booth saw himself 'as a disinterested investigator, using scientific methods of inquiry to state more clearly the nature and extent of the actual problem [of poverty]' (Wise, 2009, 170). According to Wise, his 'sensual enjoyment of poor London' was associated with a determination to establish its causes and extent. But as she has highlighted, in Booth's work there was a constant tension between moral judgement and his search for scientific, 'pure' and objective data (Wise, 2009, 169). He wanted to move beyond what he saw as anecdotal and impressionistic accounts of poverty, like Andrew Mearns' *The bitter cry of outcast London* (Mearns, 1883), but he was also constrained by his own moral and ideological agenda. Eventually he proposed regulated 'labour colonies' to which those he regarded as 'Class B' should be sent. These were people he included as mostly 'shiftless, helpless, idle or drunkards' (Wise, 2009, 176). He thought the problem of poverty was overestimated, wanted to establish its true proportions (as also did Seebohm Rowntree) and saw the 'moral deficiencies' of the poor as one of the three major causes of the problem (Wise, 2009, 171–8). He divided London's East Enders into eight categories and created a 'poverty map' coloured according to these different designations. As Wise has commented: 'It looked like empiricism, but wasn't. Who in all seriousness could look at the map and believe that it tells us anything about actual, lived human experience? ... The map is an elaborate concocted fantasy of a city that never existed' (Wise, 2009, 178–9).

A similar pattern emerges with Seebohm Rowntree, the last in this trio of major pioneering social policy researchers and reformers. Another successful business man and also a committed Quaker, in his work, there is the same complex mixture of values, moralising and claims to being 'scientific'. He undertook a series of large-scale poverty surveys in York over more than half a century, from 1899 until 1951. As Alcock has observed, 'Rowntree paid much attention to arriving at a precise definition of poverty in order to demonstrate that those who were poor ... needed support or improvement' (Alcock, 1997, 7). However, this search for scientific authority was always undermined by moral and value judgements. Thus he identified two groups of people as being in poverty. These were those seen as in 'primary' poverty because they 'lacked the wherewithal' to purchase what Rowntree decided were the 'necessities of healthy life', and those in 'secondary' poverty, who had enough money, but didn't spend it as he judged fit (Alcock, 1997, 71).

Traditional tensions in social policy

There were numerous other ways in which Rowntree's poverty standard was neither 'objective' nor 'scientific'. He based nutritional standards on experiments with prisoners, takes no account of the realities and subjectivity of people's lives, cultures, expectations and experience. In 1922 the trade union leader, Ernest Bevin, highlighted some of the problems when he bought the then recommended diet of scraps of bacon, fish and bread and asked a researcher if this was appropriate for a labourer doing a day's heavy work (Atkinson, 1989, 27). Rowntree framed poverty narrowly in terms of 'nuclear' family households, with a male breadwinner, ignored differences between men and women and modified his definition of poverty in his three major surveys as times, conditions and what might be seen as 'necessities' changed (Alcock, 1997, 15).

Mayhew and Rowntree highlight differences in traditions of social policy analysis and reforms, but also their overlaps and similarities. Tensions between 'scientific' and 'subjective' approaches to social policy seem to have existed as long as there has been formal analysis of social policy. Mayhew sought to collect first-hand accounts and provide descriptive accounts. He described his book, *London labour and the London poor*:

> as being the first attempt to publish the history of a people *from the lips of the people themselves* (emphasis added) – giving a literal description of their labour, their earnings, their trials, and their sufferings in their own 'unvarnished' language; and to portray the condition of their homes and their families by personal observation of the places, and direct communion with the individuals. (Mayhew, 2009, Preface)

Rowntree was committed to what he saw as a scientific approach to social policy. In contrast, there was talk of the 'vivid picture' that Mayhew painted and 'the artist's fascinated interest in violence and horror...providing a mine of odd and intriguing information' (Mayhew, 1950, jacket cover). Ultimately if the artificially 'cold science' of Rowntree is both disconcerting and disconnects the reader from the poor people he investigates, in the enduring sociological tradition of social tourism, where the researcher investigates society's 'denizens' – its poor, criminal and deviant, Mayhew also reinforced the gulf between the observer and the observed. This is admittedly in a different way to Rowntree, but the two have the same effect. What we see in both cases are the interpretations and viewpoints of the researcher rather than the researched. In their different ways, both the pseudo-scientific approach of a Rowntree and the more journalistic forays of a Mayhew emphasise 'otherness' and separation, rather than being part of a process of enabling and advancing understanding, inclusion and a shared humanity.

Moralising masquerading as science, opinions as objectivity, outside interpretations as first-hand accounts and precise measurement as accuracy, typified the approaches of these founding fathers of social policy. It also characterised the origins of social policy more widely. This was also true of the analysis, implementation and teaching of social policy.

Such social policy, based on pseudo-science, was shaped by a coterie of upper-class pioneers. This was a time where 'we' were a narrow, privileged class-based elite who could look on others almost as specimens in a world of their making. This applied widely, not just in academic pursuits. The researcher Beatrice Webb, whom we encountered earlier, in Chapter Two, served as a female rent collector for Octavia Hill in Aldgate, worked for her cousin Charles Booth on his London survey and then married Sidney Webb. The Webbs played leading roles in the formation and development of the Fabian Society and Fabianism, with their commitment to non-revolutionary, evolutionary socialism. Fabianism placed an emphasis on empiricism and drew heavily on the research of Booth and Rowntree. The Webbs were signatories to and largely wrote the Minority Report of the Royal Commission on the Poor Laws of 1909, which called for state welfare and an end to the Poor Law (Booth signed the Majority Report supported by key figures in the Charity Organisation Society) (Alcock, 2012a, 6–7). They were also influential in the Labour Party, which they saw as the vehicle for advancing their programme of social reform. Fabian politics were closely linked to the establishment and development of the Labour Party. Together and with others, the Webbs founded the London School of Economics, a focus for research, education and for training the social workers and others to populate their proposed welfare system. The LSE Department of Social Science and Administration was informed and guided, in Alcock's words: 'by a strong ideological commitment to Fabianism, in particular the use of academic knowledge and research on social problems to create pressure on the state to introduce welfare reforms' (Alcock, 2012a, 4).

Theirs seems to have been a very small world. Given the nature of early nineteenth-century British society, this is perhaps not surprising, but its influence has clearly lingered much longer. William Beveridge was a researcher for the Webbs on the Minority Report and Sir Stafford Cripps, Chancellor of the Exchequer in the post-war Labour government, was Beatrice Webb's nephew.

Beatrice Webb can be seen as the mother of British social policy and the same tensions identified among its other founders can also be seen in her and her work. The struggle between 'objective investigator' and observer, moralising outsider and human participant, also looms large in her account of her early undercover activities as a female investigator in the East End, disguised as an unemployed 'trouser-hand'. In her detailed analysis of the social explorations of privileged women in the nineteenth-century East End, Gabriel Mearns highlights emerging contradictions and inconsistencies. As Mearns says, Webb analyses local women anthropologically 'as almost a species apart', committed to 'scientific research', offering a 'Darwinian reading of the [East End] setting' (Mearns, 2011).

Despite her concern not to impinge on the behaviour of the people she was investigating, it is difficult to imagine that the women she encountered would have taken her at face value. At the same time, it is apparent from her own notes, that for all her emphasis on scientific research that avoided engagement with its 'subjects', there is such engagement, as Webb experiences her own human subjectivity and vulnerability and the women she works with in turn are kind and supportive. This does not, however, enable her to stand outside her own narrow 'scientism' reflected in her racist talk of: 'Jewish girls with flashy hats, full figures, and large bustles; furtive-eyed Polish immigrants with their pallid faces and crouching forms; and here and there poverty-stricken Christian women' (Webb, 1888, 301, cited in Mearns, 2011).

It may be suggested that views like this were common in her day and need to be understood in the context of their time. The Jewish girls she worked with may have had a different view of such commonplace discrimination, which was also reflected in routinely disablist and classist views expressed by such social reformers.

Worked as a milliner* in East End sweatshops in the late 1920s and 1930s

If things were quiet – and there were some terrible times – then they didn't want you. There was no work. Other times, if there was a rush, you could be working till midnight. They locked you in. They locked you in. God knows what would have happened if there had been a fire. We worked with felt. It was all steam and damp. No wonder I got arthritis later with the damp.

Ida Kaufman
My mother (using her maiden name)

> * Prostitution was historically notorious among dressmakers and milliners because of the seasonal nature of the work (see Perkin, 2002).

What in retrospect can appear most alarming is the enduring nature of the judgementalism and snobbishness of mainstream social research. Thus, the high profile Nuffield television enquiry which explored the effects of television on children in the 1950s, concluded about one programme series that was especially popular with children, *Ask Pickles*, that they: 'comprised mainly duller children from secondary modern schools [and] being duller they were also the most gullible and most cliché-ridden' (cited in Moran, 2013, 96).

The Fabian legacy

Fabianism was the dominant strand in British social policy analysis and practice until Mrs Thatcher came to power. It was also influential and exported internationally. It has rested on three key commitments. These have been to:

- 'scientific' analysis
- the production of evidence to inform and influence public policy
- the key role of the 'expert' in this social policy process.

As we have seen, a consistent preoccupation in early social policy analysis was with defining and measuring social issues and conditions. This commitment to 'scientific evidence' rested on its proponents' belief in the importance of such evidence in informing and influencing public policy. Central to this was the role they gave themselves in this process as professional 'experts'. The issue on which they particularly focused their 'scientific examination' was poverty. In the words of the historian Bernard Harris, for the Webbs,

> solutions to the problems of poverty lay in the correct application of professional knowledge appropriate to the cause of destitution...Professional analysis should inform the provision of state services appropriate to cure poverty: medical care for the sick, residential care for the old, work for the unemployed, disciplinary camps for the 'workshy', and so on. (Cited in Whiteside, 2012, 119)

Becoming a social policy academic

I had got my first 'real' job. It was in 1975, to be a 'lecturer in social administration' at the new department formed at Lancaster University. I was travelling up on the train to start work. It took three and a half hours in those days. The journey really emphasised the big step I was taking, going to live further away from home than I had ever done. I got talking to an older woman on the train who was heading home to Scotland. I told her what I was doing. What was interesting was that she immediately assumed that I must have experience in social policy or social services; that I had a background in working in or running them. I remember thinking and saying to her that she had a good point and feeling that I certainly didn't have such a body of knowledge or experience. After all how would you teach about something you didn't really know about first hand? My six months working as a 'welfare officer' hardly qualified. She planted a seed which grew and grew. What were we doing talking about things that we really only had second hand knowledge about?

The author

Two key and widely held assumptions can be seen to underpin this approach. First, essentially that in social policy, 'knowledge is power' and if the right data is properly collected, it makes possible progressive change and, second, that the people to gather that knowledge and to make such change are people like the Webbs. It's perhaps no wonder that Max Beerbohm caricatured Sidney Webb as manipulating figures of people, like a child playing with toy soldiers (Beerbohm, 1914). As Kynaston has commented, 'A similar faith in the beneficent, public-minded expert underlay the creation of the modern welfare state.' Beveridge himself was the epitome of such an expert and he was also committed to such experts, taking the view that 'we shall need to have planning on a national scale' to win the war on squalor (Kynaston, 2008, 24, 31).

This top-down elitist approach to social policy, with its cult of the expert, dominated UK social policy thinking and practice for many years (Kynaston, 2008, 35–6). However, both of its two core assumptions are value rather than evidence based. It mistakes the political process of social policy development for an administrative one – which it is not. Poverty is ultimately a political and contested concept, not an objective scientific one. This means that what critics call Fabianism's 'arithmetical tradition', of using empirical evidence to influence political opinion, does not necessarily work (Alcock, 1996, Ch 1).

This quickly became apparent with the rise of the political New Right in the late 1970s. Mrs Thatcher was not interested in the Fabian evidence and her governments certainly felt under no obligation to respond to the limited political pressure it could actually bring to bear. The Fabian approach had always been a narrowly based one, emphasising its own expertise, discouraging wider involvement and lacking popular support. Right-wing academics, think tanks, pressure groups and organisations emerged under Thatcherism, like the Institute for Economic Affairs, the Centre for Policy Studies and the Adam Smith Institute. They offered a counter to Fabian thinking and findings. The political New Right, and subsequently the neoliberals, have been able to dismiss the traditional Fabian social policy approach as controlling, excluding, elitist and protecting its own professional interests.

They have presented themselves as the supporters of ordinary people's aspirations; defenders of the 'plebeians' against the 'patricians'. They have highlighted the paternalism of Fabianism and its failure to listen to the public. They have presented themselves instead as offering the promise of choice and control through being customers and consumers in a welfare market. Fabian social policy has never seemed able to offer a counter story that carried comparable conviction with the public. Whatever the reality of such right-wing claims, they certainly seem to have had some popular resonance. The post-war welfare state, based on a Fabian approach, had failed to involve citizens, patients and service users. It created a coupling in people's minds between state provision and top-down paternalism. The political New Right determinedly reinforced this stereotype. However, we should remember that such lack of involvement has been characteristic of Fabianism, but is not necessarily inherent in state provision, or a necessary characteristic of it. This is an issue we will revisit later when exploring future approaches to social policy.

Meanwhile, it is important to recognise the enduring legacy of Fabianism in British social policy. A new generation of Fabian academics and reformers emerged in the 1960s and this time their target was Labour governments that they felt had failed on social policy reform (Townsend and Bosanquet, 1972; Bosanquet and Townsend, 1980). As Pete Alcock, a current social policy academic in the same tradition, wrote: 'The assumption underlying the whole arithmetic tradition of Fabian political influence was a belief that governments of welfare states should ... resolve, or at least relieve, social problems such as poverty' (Alcock, 1997, 200).

The importance of Peter Townsend

Most visible and perhaps most important of these commentators was Peter Townsend who became the personification of Fabian and mainstream analytical social policy critiques of poverty. He was a key modern Fabian thinker and activist. Townsend and his colleagues rejected the 'absolute' or 'subsistence' model of poverty (having enough to sustain life) pioneered by Seebohm Rowntree. They argued instead for a 'relative' model of poverty by which: 'Individuals, families and groups in the population can be said to be in poverty when they lack the resources to obtain the types of diets, participate in the activities and have the living conditions and amenities which are customary... in the societies to which they belong' (Townsend, 1979, 31).

This was a definition which included many more people in poverty than its predecessor and therefore highlighted perceived failures of the welfare state and Labour governments. At the time it was presented as the 'rediscovery of poverty', as though those who were directly experiencing poverty, didn't count as being aware of this for themselves (in the same way that the 'discovery' of America ignored the experience and knowledge of native Americans!). Again it was offered as a 'scientific' definition of poverty. Again, it was underpinned by the same ideological, moral, cultural and value judgements as previous attempts at objective definition. It also came in for criticism from other progressive poverty analysts for oversimplifying complex definitional problems (Veit-Wilson, 1986; Sen, 1983).

Townsend drew a sharp line between the relative approach to poverty he spearheaded and traditional absolute and subsistence models. This distinction dominated discussions and developments about poverty from the 1970s. However, since then, poverty academics have highlighted that the two definitions are not so different from each other, with Rowntree's approach having relative elements and Townsend's absolute ones (Alcock, 1997, 70–2). While the relative definition purports to be 'scientific', as David Piachaud suggested, any cut-off line to demarcate poverty is arbitrary and based on a subjective judgement of an acceptable minimum standard for a given time (Piachaud, 1981).

Much more important was the response from the political New Right. Mrs Thatcher rejected relative poverty as rooted in ideas of material equality, for which she said, with some accuracy, that there was little public or political support and was thus able to isolate and stifle opposition to her anti-state welfare, pro-market social policies. Furthermore when people with experience of poverty began to be involved in discussions about the concept of poverty, few of them seemed to support the relative model, emphasising that it offered a poor basis for broad-based campaigns in which they would be likely have any sense of ownership (Beresford et al, 1999).

Fabian social policy did not recover from Mrs Thatcher's attacks, instead it largely shifted to the right, first as 'welfare pluralism' and then as part of the 'third way' (Beresford and Croft, 1984; Giddens, 1998). Since then New Labour governments have been associated with increasing extremes of material inequality. People on benefits have continued to be stigmatised, with an increasing proportion of people on low incomes now in employment, although still dependent on state support (MacInnes et al, 2013).

Bumping into Peter Townsend

In the late 1980s, when I, my partner Suzy and our children were still living on poverty-level unemployment benefits, we bumped into the social policy academic Peter Townsend, with whom I had had some correspondence before, at a *Community Care* magazine annual lecture we had both gone to hear. He was friendly and asked how things were with us, and I briefly told him that we were having a struggle. He replied, with no apparent sense of incongruity, that he understood, as his last two or three research grant applications had been unsuccessful!

The author

Fabian social policy not only came under attack from the political right in the late 1970s and 1980s, but also from the Marxist new left. The latter's proponents rejected the Fabian consensus and empirical approach and argued that the post-war welfare state had failed to solve social problems as envisaged and that instead it had worked to support capitalism rather than to challenge it (Ginsburg, 1979; Alcock, 2008, 8). Now after 30 plus years of neoliberalism this critique itself looks simplistic. The state is certainly not neutral and its benevolence cannot be assumed, but can be more and less supportive of the rights and needs of citizens. Very real differences can be seen between the Labour state of the late 1940s and the coalition from 2010. Equally very real differences emerge in relation to redistribution and the degree to which the state seems preoccupied with the social control of its citizens. Ironically, academics such as Taylor-Gooby, who challenged old Labour state welfare, went on to be part of the social science establishment under later neoliberal ideology (Taylor-Gooby, 1985).

As Alcock has stated, the traditional Fabian social policy approach, with its claims to objectivity and science, 'experienced a significant setback in the 1980s' (Alcock, 1997, 201). Ironically, Townsend published his magnum opus on poverty in the same year as Mrs Thatcher became prime minister (Townsend, 1979). Right-wing governments were not impressed by isolated experts such as Townsend and could shrug off their criticisms. Lacking popular support the latter could exert little political pressure on governments which rejected their values, assumptions and sense of self-importance. Yet this did not put an end to the traditional social policy approach of producing evidence for experts to advance. This can be seen to be alive and well, for example, in the work of the Joseph Rowntree Foundation on poverty through the 1990s and into the present (MacInnes et al, 2013; Hills, 2014). However, over this period its effectiveness seems to have been limited, with ever diminishing returns. Looking back to the 1980s and the radical regressive redistribution that took place under the Thatcher governments, it is difficult in retrospect not to question the wisdom of strategies like Townsend's. Problems of poverty through the loss of traditional industries, large-scale unemployment, regional decline and cuts in welfare services increased greatly during the 1980s.

There seems little sense in maintaining an approach to anti-poverty campaigning which rested on a notion of equality that then carried little political force and was advanced by campaigners negatively associated with the Fabian left. Did it really serve the interests of the growing number of people in poverty to base campaigning on such an approach, which was closely associated with political opponents of the government? It seems likely that it would have been wiser instead to have been working to build a much more broadbased, popular and strategic campaigning approach. We will return to this issue in the next chapter in relation to disability where some of the answers to these questions may begin to emerge.

Eugenics and the reliance on 'science'

There can be little doubt that the influence of Fabianism on the welfare state and state welfare, with its preoccupation with being 'scientific' and the elite 'expert', has done damage to both. A high point of this problem was its long-term espousal of 'eugenics'; the idea of selective breeding, sterilisation and reducing the number of perceived 'unfit' people. This was long a group closely associated with people who were poor. Looking back with our knowledge of the Nazi holocaust and Aktion T4 killing many thousands of disabled adults and children, as well as German authorities forcibly sterilising many more, it is difficult to understand the ready support that eugenics commanded internationally, from the US, the UK, Sweden and beyond (Gallagher, 1990; Close, 2011, 7). However, the list of its supporters in Britain reads now like a Who's Who of the left, the Fabian left and social policy reformers. This includes the Webbs, Beveridge, Marie Stopes, Harold Laski and John Maynard Keynes. Perhaps as Jonathan Freedland has suggested their naïve belief in 'science' encouraged them to think that 'nothing was more cutting edge and modern than social Darwinism' (Freedland, 2012).

Such eugenic thinking underpinned the 1913 Mental Deficiency Act which sought to identify 'feeble-minded' children through IQ tests, who were then sent to segregated schools (Kerr and Shakespeare, 2002). In the early 1900s members of the Eugenics Society advocated the ideal of a scientifically planned society and supported eugenics by way of sterilisation. This is said to have influenced the passage of the 'Half-Caste Act', and its subsequent implementation in Australia, where children were systematically and forcibly removed from their parents, so that the British colonial regime could 'protect' the Aborigine children from their parents. The human rights lawyer, Geoffrey Robertson, criticised Fabian socialists for providing the intellectual justification for the eugenics policy that led to the stolen generations scandal (Robertson, 2008). Such views on socialism, inequality and eugenics were widely shared in the Fabian Society and among Fabian analysts and reformers in the early twentieth century (Badcock, 2008). Such interest has also resurfaced in the twenty-first century with the development of bioethics and genetics and their application to issues of disability, mental health and parenting (Beresford and Wilson, 2002; Burdett, 2014; Kerr and Shakespeare, 2002).

The scientism of the right

Ironically 'sociobiology' is now being used as a rationale for the political right to attack welfare. The social policy academic Hilary Land has noted the same contemporary search for 'scientific' justification from the political right, as in the past there was from the political left. 'Eugenics ... underpinned the belief in the naturalness of inequalities and hierarchies in the first half of the twentieth century ... Sociobiology is now providing a similar ideological basis for undermining the arguments for a universalistic welfare state' (Land, 2012, 52).

Now the emphasis is on what is offered as the essential *selfishness* of human nature. Such genetic determinism, epitomised by the work of

Richard Dawkins sits comfortably with the current neoliberal emphasis on individualisation and competitiveness (Dawkins, 1976, 38). This is truly a philosophy of 'every man (and woman) for him/herself'. Again, ironically while the argument is presented as scientific and seeks the respectability that this is seen to afford, it is actually metaphysical and can neither be proved nor disproved, resting as it does on subjective ideas like altruism and selfishness. However, it provides a conceptual framework which has been widely and effectively used to encourage us to see ourselves as different to and as having the right to question the honesty and motives of people seeking support or relying on welfare benefits. It has not only been the political New Right and neoliberal governments of Mrs Thatcher and the coalition which have signed up to such a selfish model of human nature. This was true too of New Labour and seemed to underpin its espousal of the unevidenced idea of 'the underclass', as well as its rhetoric that 'more than a million people' needed to be taken off disability and sickness benefits, which they were inappropriately (and often dishonestly) claiming, rather than honouring their obligations to be in paid employment. The assumption was that people would only do the right thing through a system of 'sticks and carrots' (Prideaux, 2006).

Such a view of human nature as essentially selfish stands in strong opposition to the thinking underpinning the creation of the welfare state. Politicians who had experienced the camaraderie, shared experiences and responsibility that went with serving in the Great War and who had seen people pulling together both in the Blitz and the forces in the Second World War, readily put their trust in a notion of most people's inherent altruism. For theoreticians like Titmuss and Marshall, 'welfare policies were mechanisms for extending altruism beyond the family'. Societies could foster or discourage people's inherent altruism (cited in Land, 2012, 51). His groundbreaking study of voluntary blood donation was an exposition of his (and the welfare state's) belief in and commitment to, ideas of a shared sense of citizen social responsibility and obligation in society (Titmuss, 1970).

The real meaning of choice

Right-wing and neoliberal approaches tend to be based on a view 'that only the poor need state welfare provision – the middle classes and the wealthy can [or should] look after themselves' (Land, 2012, 52). Thus they have long been associated with residual or 'safety net' approaches to collective welfare intervention and support. This makes a mockery of their consumerist rhetoric of choice and control. For neoliberals the search is always for reductions in collective services and support, with a longstanding commitment to cutting back public welfare systems (Ellison, 2012). This leaves more and more people out in the cold, ineligible for their support, but also unable to pay for it themselves. This is the current situation we are seeing with English needs and means-tested social care. It also means that those who need or seek such welfare support are increasingly likely to be isolated and scapegoated as a result.

The rationale of such a residual model of welfare is that it targets resources more effectively and prevents people inappropriately benefiting from the system and becoming unnecessarily dependent on it. However, the evidence has long been that means-testing actually deters people *entitled* to such support – such under-claiming has long been strongly associated with older people. It also *encourages* uptake from people with less claim who are not discouraged by negative stereotyping, stigma and threats – a lesson that had already been learned by the Poor Law in the nineteenth century. Or put another way, the only people ready to seek such conditional support would be those too desperate not to and those who were unaffected by being 'badmouthed'. Welfare service users talk about 'those who shout the loudest' benefiting from such arrangements.

Ironically, in reality, by isolating and stigmatising a group, residual welfare is more likely to perpetuate the kind of notional 'welfare class' that its proponents associate with universalist services. The former approaches are also often associated with social control, because there is a greater enthusiasm with regulating perceived deviance than with providing support. Thus, instead of addressing structural problems and barriers that people may face, or reforming inadequate mainstream services such as, for example, schools or mental health provision, separate special provision is made. People may only get appropriate support through the attachment of a negative label or status. 'Intermediate treatment' for 'young people in trouble', developed in the 1970s, offers just such an example. It was intended to provide positive opportunities and experiences for 'such' young people. Meanwhile other young people, who were not seen as a problem, tended not to get those opportunities or experiences. Thus paradoxically, a residual system, frequently framed in moralistic terms of 'deserving' and 'undeserving', may actually work to reward those it identifies negatively, while ignoring the needs of the rest (Beresford and Croft, 1981a). Of course, as with the workhouse before it, while unit costs may be high, by limiting access overall, this can offer the promise of savings, in a narrow financial sense, by leaving most people without help.

Julian Le Grand, one of the main architects of the current 'choice' agenda used the metaphor of knights and pawns, knaves and queens to highlight changing approaches to and understandings of welfare policy. He saw the post-war welfare state as framed in terms of altruistic and knightly public servants, with service users as passive pawns. In the mid-1980s by contrast, public servants were seen as self-interested knaves and service users as consumers and queens (Le Grand, 1997; Kynaston, 2008, 145). Certainly there was little provision for participation in the post-war welfare state. But as John Welshman has argued in his critique of Le Grand's conceptualisation, under neoliberal policy and provision, service users and claimants are more likely to be criticised as dependent and dishonest than treated like royalty (Welshman, 2007). In its practice and process, neoliberal social policy has shown itself little different from its earlier Fabian counterpart. Beyond the consumerist rhetoric, neoliberal social policy has demonstrated no greater capacity for being participatory than its post-war predecessor. It also reflects the same commitment to self-defined experts, with its own large corps of management and other consultants, advisers and theoreticians.

Reinforcing division

Social policy has long been used to maintain and reinforce social divisions, notably, in relation to gender, sexuality, age, ethnicity and disability, through prescribing narrow discriminatory roles. Additionally, by basing itself on the belief that state support is only needed by a marginal part of the population, neoliberal social policy, like all 'safety net' approaches to social policy, is both almost inherently divisive and encourages division. First, it requires that you have to prove that you are one of the eligible group (one with which most are reluctant to identify) and second, it highlights the distance between you and other people. Encouraging division becomes both means and end for such policy. While such social policy was first conspicuously apparent with Mrs Thatcher's governments, it continued under New Labour (with the negative stereotyping of 'irresponsible' teenage lone parents, 'dangerous' mental health service users, 'anti-social' young people and the 'underclass'). It reached new heights under the coalition government with attacks on asylum seekers, Eastern European immigrants, 'benefit tourists', disabled people, 'baby boomers', travellers, people with public sector pensions and others on welfare benefits. There is every sign this direction of travel will continue in the wake of the 2015 general election. Such negative criticism has mostly been directed at groups on the basis of their relation with the health and welfare system. At a time when nationally standards of living, average wages and levels of child poverty, inequality and social mobility have all worsened, repeatedly immigration and benefit claimants are highlighted by the media as major public concerns. Significantly anti-immigration and welfare benefits rhetoric figured centrally in Conservative election campaigning in 2015 and was followed by the election of a majority Conservative government, contrary to the expectations of pollsters and politicians.

The whole point of the post-war welfare state was to make possible progressive redistribution to compensate for the arbitrariness and inequalities of the market. Thus people who couldn't manage on their own, people facing particularly difficult times in their life course and families that needed outside help, could all get support. Titmuss summed this up clearly and simply: 'As adults, people are constantly moving in and out of the territory of socially provided or subsidised services according to varying need and circumstances. In old age, as in childhood, most people take out more than they put in' (cited in Kynaston, 2010, 76–7, speaking on BBC radio Third Programme, February 1952).

Understanding this, of course, depends on people being able to recognise this reality and to identify with such situations, with people experiencing them and able to associate themselves with them. We know that public opinion has always been complex in relation to these issues, especially when sought in conventional ways through relatively blunt instruments such as questionnaire surveys. In essence, post-war, the broader public seemed to support welfare state services from which they could readily see themselves as benefiting, and were more suspicious of those they saw as for other groups. As Taylor-Gooby stated in 1985, drawing on what he suggested was the most definitive study yet made:

> Support for the mass welfare state services of pensions, the NHS and education is tempered by concern at unemployment and low-pay benefits, council housing and lone person's benefits. Perceptions of redistribution and of the welfare state as a whole show strong support for the principle of state welfare with some concern at the cost and the extent of transfer to other groups. This is the only justification for the 'welfare burden' model in public opinion. (Taylor-Gooby, 1985, 52)

More recently, under New Labour and coalition governments and then with Conservative political campaigning, we have seen policymakers, in collusion with right-wing and tabloid media, make determined efforts to alienate such public opinion from marginalised groups and negative experiences with which people do not want to identify. It is important to remember the point that even when the welfare state in its early days had cross-party support and significant public support, large sections of the media were opposed to it, sending strong negative messages (Kynaston, 2008, 280–1; Golding and Middleton, 1982, 228).

The presentation of welfare reform policy and its media coverage under the Coalition government were eerily similar to the picture that emerged 30 years earlier from Peter Golding and Sue Middleton's study of press and public attitudes to poverty in the late 1970s. Perhaps one difference, second time round, was that disabled people have been a particular focus of both political and media hostility (Briant et al, 2012). Golding and Middleton reported the same vitriolic press attitudes and found that people had a very limited knowledge and understanding of the welfare system, over-estimating levels of and ease of access to benefits. Attitudes to claimants (which also embodied broader prejudices) were especially hostile among the low paid and unskilled and even among claimants themselves. One *Daily Mail* journalist told the researchers, 'We don't cover tax evasion much because if you asked people 95 per cent would say social security fraud is more important.' This pattern has persisted, even though the cost to the public exchequer of tax evasion tends to be far higher (Golding and Middleton, 1982, 106–7, 148, 159–85). This seems to say at least as much about the agenda of the media, as about the actual priorities of the public.

As Golding and Middleton wrote in 1982: 'Two carriers that might have kept aloft a banner for the poor and welfare [were] the Labour Party and the left press' (Golding and Middleton, 1982, 213).

However, both were already compromised and by the second decade of the twenty-first century, the Labour Party's position on welfare reform was barely distinguishable from the Conservative Party's in principle and UK mass media's centre of gravity had shifted far to the right. It is often suggested that with regard to poverty and welfare, the media and policymakers follow public opinion. This carries little conviction. They set the agenda; they play a crucial role in shaping public opinion. The argument that policymakers have no choice but to appeal to public opinion rests on several unevidenced assumptions, notably, that:

1. 'public opinion' can be separated from their influence;
2. public opinion is necessarily reactionary;

3. crude opinion surveys that focus on policymakers' preoccupations offer accurate or helpful indicators of public opinion.

In recent years, we have hardly seen policymakers follow public opinion in response to key issues like MPs' abuse of expenses; bankers' bonuses and the costly state bailout of the banks. The example of capital punishment is helpful here. Repeated public opinion surveys, particularly after high profile murders, have shown popular support for a return to capital punishment. As yet no major party as a result has committed itself to it (and now polls show public support for the death sentence falling) (C Davies, 2014).

Social policy and direct voices

At the beginning of this chapter, I made the point that three facets of social policy were closely, often unhelpfully inter-related: social policy analysis, the discipline and the practice of social policy. Admittedly, in another equally important sense, this has not been the case. This relationship is where there has tended to be a big gap – between social policy theoreticians, academics and policymakers and the people that social policy most closely affects, particularly at its heavier end. Thus there is also a fourth dimension of social policy that demands to be considered – its relation with people on the receiving end – service users. So far what we have seen is how qualified, under-developed and unequal that relationship has tended to be. Given the key role that social policy has always played in providing responses to those most facing disadvantage in society, who have fewest resources to provide for themselves, this is especially important. It has meant that social policy has a history as both analytical approach and policy, of providing *its* solutions to people's problems and imposing them on them, rather than being centrally informed by their views of themselves and the world, their experience or understandings.

Not all those who have been concerned with social issues, social problems and social policy have, however, adopted the top-down route of either Fabian left or residualising right. There have been some key commentators who have sought to give priority to the voice and experience of people on the receiving end of policy, through interviewing and speaking with them, rather than merely enlisting their interpretations of their views as a data source – the traditional approach of social policy investigators from Mayhew onwards. Over the period both of the heyday and fall from grace of the UK welfare state, there have been writers and others who have been committed to accessing the direct voices and views of citizens and service users in relation to welfare and social policy. Two key examples from the UK have been Tony Parker and Colin Ward; one from the United States was Studs Terkel. They provide a link with the second part of this book and it is worth exploring their contributions in more detail, both because this highlights their particular value, as well as the fact that there could have been and have been alternative approaches. Significantly they all came from backgrounds and traditions outside social policy, including publishing, political action, journalism and broadcasting. This extends a pattern and reinforces an issue that has emerged for me in writing this book. I have found some of the most illuminating writings and discussions about social policy to have come from historians, geographers and sociologists, rather than from social policy academics themselves.

Tony Parker

The first of this trio is Tony Parker (1923–96) who is remembered as an oral historian and popular author. Following his own experience as a wartime conscientious objector and miner, his interest began with prisons and the experience of prisoners on release. The focus of his first three high profile books were two recidivist criminals and the commonplace murder of a young man (Parker, 1962, 1963 and 1965). In these and other books, through focusing on people's own accounts of their lives and experience, he made possible fresh understandings that transcended the conventional wisdoms and negative value judgements of their time. He carried out lengthy interviews with participants and tried to write up what they said 'without comment or judgement'. The criminologist Keith Soothill described him as 'the best interviewer of criminals and other marginal people since the Second World War' (Soothill, 2001). The psychiatrist Anthony Storr called him 'Britain's most expert interviewer, mouthpiece of the inarticulate and counsel for the defence of those whom society has shunned and abandoned' (*Sunday Times*, 15 February 1970, cited in https://en.wikipedia.org/wiki/Tony_Parker_(author)).

Parker wrote about women prisoners, council estate tenants, homeless people, lone parents, sex offenders, inmates of a psychiatric prison and many more (Soothill, 1999). He focused on people, but highlighted much broader social and policy issues. Keith Soothill, who has perhaps written most about him, concluded that his motivation was 'a passionate resentment of the inequality and unfairness of modern Society ... His interests and sympathies lay chiefly with the underdog or the outsider (Soothill, 2001). If Fabian social policy analysts and commentators and their Victorian predecessors seem to serve more as mediators of the accounts and experience of their subjects of study, then Parker seems to have been committed to a very different approach. He prized advice he received from a friend who told him: 'Shut up and listen to what prisoners say: when it comes to trying to understand, you won't – but do the best you can' (cited in Soothill, 2001).

Colin Ward

Colin Ward (1924–2010) was a major British anarchist thinker, writer and activist. His wartime experience in the army led to him becoming an anarchist. He subsequently worked as an architect and paradoxically also as education officer for the Town and Country Planning Association, which had long been associated with centralised planning and the garden city movement (Hardy, 1999; Kynaston, 2008, 159–63). However, key ideas for Ward were self-organisation, self-management, mutualism, self-help, local democracy, self-build and 'bottom-up' planning. He coined the term 'self-help socialism', in contrast to free market self-help. Instead of bureaucratic and large organisations, he was interested in how small groups of people could organise things together in non-hierarchical ways. Thus early on he was committed to participatory ways of working and a very different approach to the state-led post-war welfare state (Tonkin, 2010).

A Fabian Society blog, *Next Left*, highlighted Ward's opposition to the 'Fabian tradition':

> This comes across very clearly in his work on housing where he was always highly critical of state-heavy efforts, led by middle-class housing professionals, to provide housing *for* the working classes. In this context, he argued for the alternative left tradition of cooperative self-help in the form of tenant cooperatives, self-build projects and squatting. (White, 2010)

The writer and social commentator Ken Worpole said that Ward: 'was fond of contrasting the vocabulary of self-organisation, with its friendly societies, mutuals, co-operatives and voluntary associations, with the nomenclature of the state and private sectors with their directorates, corporations, boards and executives' (Worpole, 2010).

Ward creatively brought together two traditions, the theoretical tradition of anarchism and the practical traditions of working-class and popular self-help, which aimed to make the world a better place for ordinary people (Worpole, 2010). Particular focuses for his work were housing and education. He became involved with, 'championed the worlds' of and helped give voice to allotment-diggers, unofficial smallholders, prefab dwellers, caravan habitués, rural squatters, estate children, multi-tasking traders, do-it-yourself artisans and house-builders (Tonkin, 2010). He was also interested in children and young people and how they could be more engaged in their environment, both urban and rural and how it could be more responsive to them (Ward, 1978; 1988). Through Ward, the subjects of distant and top-down social policy were brought centre stage and their issues highlighted on *their* terms.

Studs Terkel

Studs Terkel (1912–2008), a political liberal, blacklisted from television during the McCarthy era, was born in New York to Russian Jewish immigrants. He was a broadcaster and historian. He wrote oral histories of the Second World War, the Great Depression, people's working lives, race, aging and much more, interviewing ordinary people, 'through prison inmates to the wealthy' (Terkel, 1970; 1974; 1984; 1992; 1995). His first book of oral history interviews, *Division Street*, about twentieth-century urban America, came out in 1966. His last, *Will the circle be unbroken?*, about death and dying, was published in 2001, nearly half a century later. His long-running radio programme, *The Studs Terkel Program*, was on air each week day between 1952 and 1997; 7,000 tape recordings of Terkel's interviews and broadcasts were donated to the Chicago History Museum. In 2010, the Museum and the Library of Congress announced a collaboration to preserve digitally these recordings. The Library of Congress described them as: 'a remarkably rich history of the ideas and perspectives of both common and influential people living in the second half of the twentieth century. The Museum President said that, "for Studs, there was not a voice that should not be heard, a story that could not be told"' (Library of Congress, 2010). 'He believed that everyone had the right to be heard and had something important to say. He was there to listen, to chronicle, and to make sure their stories are remembered' (Library of Congress, 2010).

Terkel, like Parker and Ward, foregrounds people's own voices. He offers rich, flesh and blood accounts of public policy, social issues, America and the twentieth century.

There were also direct links between the three of them. Colin Ward wrote an obituary of Tony Parker (Ward, 1996) and Tony Parker wrote a book (published posthumously) about Studs Terkel (Parker, 1997). These were not the only such writers and commentators of the time who particularly valued people's first-hand accounts, instead of merely using them to flesh out their own views and ideas. Over this period there have certainly been others who have been committed to accessing the direct voices and views of people on the received end of policy. They include, for example, Raphael Samuel, founder of the History Workshop movement (Wise, 2009, 292), Ray Gosling, broadcaster and gay rights activist (Mayes, 2013) and Ann Oakley, novelist and sociologist whose books include ones focusing on women's experience of childbirth and housework (for example, Oakley, 1979). They came from many different backgrounds, experiences and disciplines. Theirs is a genre and tradition that demands closer examination, which so far the academic discipline of social policy has barely given it. Crucially, here, they provide a link between the first part of this book, which is concerned with past and present welfare and social policy and the second part, which explores possible futures. The link is the voice of the subjects of social policy. These social commentators sought to give expression to it.

Some bridges are also to be found between traditional social policy and such efforts to foreground the voices and viewpoints of people with direct experience. A key example of this is the work on poverty of Ken Coates and Richard Silburn in Nottingham from the 1960s. They carried out a community study under the auspices of the Adult Education Department of the University of Nottingham with a group of students, which subsequently gave rise to a film directed by Stephen Frears (Coates and Silburn, 1967). They built on the work of Peter Townsend and Brian Abel-Smith, but they drew definitions and understandings of poverty from what poor people themselves had to say. As they wrote, poor people, 'must be seen not simply as isolated individuals, abstracted from society, but as human beings formed in the very society from which they are to a greater or lesser extent excluded' (Coates and Silburn, 1970).

Conclusion

We have seen how historically the analysis, discipline and implementation of social policy have all been closely inter-related, but have generally remained at some distance from their subjects and their subjectivity. Instead the pioneers and key figures of social policy have emphasised its 'scientific' nature and their central role as experts both to interpret and to shape it. This has been true from the Fabian left to the neoliberal right. The post-war welfare state was based on such a model and its key limitations, its lack of participation and its paternalism, can be traced to this. The UK, US and Scandinavian welfare systems all had their origins in this approach. Such a pseudo-scientific/expert-based approach has brought major problems, like the mainstream espousal of eugenics and the failure to maintain popular support.

While mainstream social policy has continued largely to be imposed top-down, some significant differences have emerged. While groups long seen as the particular subjects of social policy, such as disabled, older and poor people, have continued to be treated as different and often also as defective or deviant, the response to them has significantly changed. Where traditionally there was a sense of some responsibility to support them, with the advent of globalisation and neoliberalism, there has been a new stress on them looking after themselves, however difficult this might be. For disabled commentators such as Mike Oliver, both of these represent disabling social policies, the former imposing dependence, the latter a false notion of 'independence' – being left to manage on your own (Oliver, 2009, 77–8). However, over this same period, as we have seen, there have been others coming at social policy issues in much more personal ways, respecting and highlighting people's own viewpoints, voices and experience. In the next chapter we will begin to look at how people themselves have sought to give voice to their own experience, knowledges and ideas.

The unacknowledged demand for involvement

In 1977 we carried out our first research on people's participation. The study was prompted by the public participation exercise mounted in North Battersea by Wandsworth Council in preparation of its statutory 'borough plan'. At this time Wandsworth was controlled by a Labour council which regarded itself as radical and progressive. We surveyed 580 households in the area and found that less than a third of people even knew about the exercise and only about 1 per cent – about 450 of the local population of 35,000 – took part in it in any way – and they were grossly unrepresentative with a preponderance of middle-class participants. At the time, more than two-thirds of the local population were council tenants. Of the people we interviewed (n 637):

• 57 per cent thought that the council planning department knew little or nothing of what they wanted. Only 2 per cent [thought] that it was well informed;
• 94 per cent thought that the council didn't ask them what they wanted;

- 62 per cent thought that the council took little or no notice of their needs and wishes.

These views extended to all social groups. People's responses revealed an overwhelming sense of powerlessness. Their lack of participation seemed to have much more to do with their lack of trust in the local authority than any imputed 'apathy'. The prevailing emotion we encountered was anger against the council, turning into resignation and sometimes despair among older people. Two-thirds of the representative sample we interviewed said that they wanted more say, offering proposals for how this could be achieved. Participants identified what they saw as key issues for local people, with four major areas of need emerging, first the inadequacy of local services and amenities, second, the need for more and better council housing, housing repairs and maintenance, third an improved environment, with better cleaning, traffic, noise and pollution control and coming a poor fourth, improved law and order. People wanted a different more participatory approach to meeting local needs, offering them more say in decision-making. Young people felt particularly excluded.

This study gained a high profile locally and nationally and led to no noticeable change from the Labour council. In 1978 it lost control to a Thatcherite Conservative Party and there has never been a Labour council in Wandsworth since.

(Beresford and Croft, 1978; 1982)

PART TWO

The way to the future

> We are tired of being statistics, cases, wonderfully courageous
> examples to the world, pitiable objects to stimulate funding.
>   (Paul Hunt, 1966a)

In the first part of the book we saw the very limited role that people
on the receiving end of social policy have tended to play in its
conceptualisation, formulation and delivery. In this second part we
are concerned with a very different approach to social policy, where
they are at its centre. At the heart of this can be found people's desire
to speak and act for and organise themselves. If the social policy that
we have had has mainly been the result of what some people have laid
down for others, then what is offered here is the promise of future
social policy that is shaped and owned by the people for whom it is
intended. These ideas and proposals do not start from a blank sheet.
There are many precedents and early examples. Together they offer
a blueprint for changed participatory social policy as well as insights
for how to achieve it.

NINE

The beginnings of something different

I am proposing the formation of a consumer group to put forward nationally the views of actual and potential residents of these successors to the workhouse. We hope in particular to formulate and publicise plans for alternative kinds of care. I should be glad to hear from anyone who is interested to join or support this project. – Yours faithfully,
(Paul Hunt, letter to the *Guardian*, 20 September 1972, that led to the establishment of the British Disabled People's movement)

In the last chapter, we saw how mainstream social policy has historically largely ignored the first-hand accounts and experience of those on the receiving end of social policy or reinterpreted them as it has seen fit. We have learned about the enduring tradition of analysts and social explorers offering their own interpretations of the views and lives of poor and dispossessed people. Finally, we encountered new generations of social commentators in the second half of the twentieth century who sought to privilege people's own accounts. This can also be seen as part of a much broader development of seeking to access the first-hand voices of marginalised groups and people, as well as them seeking to develop and offer their own accounts themselves. It represents a major attempt to enable people to speak for themselves, instead of being spoken for – the beginning of a fundamental change for social policy.

Accessing people's views, people's histories

This commitment to foreground the lives and activities of 'ordinary' and marginalised people came to prominence from the late 1960s to the 1980s. It can be seen as linked to two developments. First, these were times of fundamental political and economic change that particularly threatened disadvantaged individuals, communities and regions. Second, they were also associated with the emergence of the new social movements: the women's, black civil rights and LGBT (lesbian, gay, bisexual and transgendering) movements. These all challenged oppressive dominant white heterosexist conceptualisations of themselves and developing their own critiques and analyses of their lives and their positions in society.

There were earlier precedents for such grassroots accounts and histories, in the nineteenth and early twentieth centuries, with such writers emerging through adult education classes, political clubs, trade unions, local libraries and other initiatives (Pollard and Smart, 2012, 22), but they flowered in the latter part of the twentieth century. If the impetus came from the major social changes then taking place, such developments were also made possible by new technologies. Thus in the 1960s and early 1970s, cheap tape recorders became available to document rising social movements like the civil rights, feminist and anti-Vietnam War protests. Offset litho, Letraset, duplicators, Tipp-ex, screen printing, photocopiers, Super 8 cine cameras and early word processors, made it possible to reach large and new audiences effectively and economically.

Two inter-related movements emerged, both committed to accessing first-hand voices and previously hidden histories, both of which continue in existence. Here the focus is particularly on the UK, but they had their international equivalents. These movements were the oral history and community publishing movements. They shared the same commitment to access and preserve the experience, views and ideas of 'ordinary' people, particularly groups facing exclusion, oppression and disadvantage. The British Oral History Society was established in 1973, reflecting a desire to move from the history of kings and queens and privileged interpreters, to the lives and history of individuals and groups who had been under-represented and ignored in historical accounts, including homeless and young people, minority ethnic communities, trade unionists and local tenants. By the second half of the 1970s the Society also included feminist historians and others interested in women's history. The related History Workshop movement's main aim was to promote the tradition of 'history from below' and 'people's history', 'setting up an alternative means for producing historical knowledge which had roots deep in the subordinate groups of British society' (Schwarz, 1993, 23). It built on plays and performance as well as interviews, testimonies and discussions.

The community and alternative publishing movement that developed focused around community needs and local issues such as housing, redevelopment and council services. It was international, as well as national and local in scope, producing reporting, poetry, stories and fiction, first-hand and community accounts. It involved writers' workshops, alternative and radical newspapers, print shops and bookshops, distribution companies and was often organised cooperatively and collaboratively. It was emphatically bottom-up and participatory in nature (Mathieu et al, 2012; Pollard and Smart, 2012). As David Morley and Ken Worpole have written, 'a defining feature of this movement is representing the richness of [people's] experiences in ways that they had chosen and determined' (Morley and Worpole, 2009, 28). This was a struggle that was rooted much more broadly than in conventional politics and economics, trade unions and employers. Originating in community activism, it went on to form women's, LGBT and BME groups and address their issues. It has involved a wide range of groups, including immigrant communities, rural and 'queer' communities, homeless people, older people, people with learning difficulties and people in custody (Pollard and Smart, 2012, 23 and, for example, Nelson, 1978; Hemmings, 1982; Cardus, 1989; McClenaghan, 2009). Well-known examples of such publishers include QueenSpark Books in Brighton, Guildhall Press in Derry and Sheba Feminist Press.

The Federation of Worker Writers and Community Publishers was formed in the UK in 1976 to develop skills in participatory writing and publishing activities, to encourage people to be heard and read – and write and read creatively – especially those who were socially excluded. Federation members have been self-running organisations, a mixture of writers' workshops, community publishers, community-based writers' groups, adult literacy organisations, and literature development organisations, both in Britain and overseas. The Federation's aims were to publish work by and for particular communities and to enable marginalised groups to express themselves through writing, performing and publishing (Pollard and Smart, 201). Sheba, established in 1980, summed up the broader approach of such publishing, aiming to publish:

> women who wrote about what it was like to live as an ordinary, non-privileged woman in post-imperial Britain in the second half of the twentieth century... being ready to publish writing by women of colour, or lesbians, or working-class women; it means recognising the multiplicity of voices within these communities – a multiplicity which is frequently overlooked by a world quick to categorise and dismiss. Sheba has built its reputation around its commitment to diversity, to difference, and to open and critical debate. (http://mith.umd.edu/WomensStudies/ReferenceRoom/Publications/about-sheba-press.html)

This was a development that clearly connected with social policy and its subjects, sometimes explicitly and specifically and sometimes more generally. Yet it is largely a tradition that has not been explored in social policy texts and discussions, despite its implications and significance for them. The development of first-hand accounts through oral history and community publishing represents an important challenge to traditional social policy, with its devaluing of subjective experience and its emphasis on 'science' and 'expert' analysis.

The key way, however, in which the subjects of social policy have been able to engage with it and speak for themselves, has been through the emergence of their own welfare movements and organisations. This has been the starting point for both a new understanding of and approach to social policy and it is to this which we now turn.

The emergence of service user movements

Between the late 1960s and 1980s a range of organisations and movements of welfare state service users also emerged. A number of reasons for this development can be identified. These include dissatisfaction with the services and support they were receiving, a sense of injustice, a new assertiveness linked with more liberatory political times and the emergence of broader movements, as well as new political challenges to the welfare state coming from both the political New Right and the radical left (Campbell and Oliver, 1996). These movements included movements of disabled people, mental health service users, people with learning difficulties, looked after young people, older people and people living with HIV/AIDS. Such service users were associated with health, welfare and social care services. This was an international development. It took place both in advanced western industrialised societies and also developing countries. Local, regional, national, European and international organisations were established.

The earliest established and best known of these movements is the disabled people's movement, which began to establish itself in the UK and internationally in the late 1960s and 1970s. The early prominence of the disabled people's movement has meant that some of the other 'user movements' have been overlooked or unhelpfully incorporated into it. It is also unlikely to be helpful to see all welfare users through the prism of disability. However, while there are differences in the history, nature, culture and objectives of each of these movements, they have some important concerns in common. All attach central importance to:

- their right to speak for themselves
- their equal worth as human beings with other people
- their right to participate and be involved in society
- their human and civil rights and needs being met. (Oliver, 1996; Beresford and Campbell, 2004; Campbell, 2009)

These service user movements also saw links between themselves and the 'new social movements' that emerged internationally particularly from the 1960s and 1970s, including the environmental, anti-nuclear and anti-war movements, the black civil rights, women's and the gay men, lesbians, bisexuals and transgender movements. What distinguishes these latter movements is that they grew out of the sense of oppression and discrimination felt by the groups who established them. The welfare service user movements also connect with broader discussions about 'movements'. A number of social theorists identified the emergence in the late twentieth century of a wide range of groups, which they conceived of as 'new social movements' (Touraine, 1981; Oliver, 1996). Characteristics associated by theorists with new social movements include that:

- they remain on the margin of the political system
- they offer a critical evaluation of society
- they imply a society with different forms of valuation and distribution
- the issues which they raise transcend national boundaries and they adopt an international perspective. (Oliver, 1996, 157; Oliver and Barnes, 2012, 173)

Some disabled commentators have described the disabled people's movement as such a new social movement (Oliver and Zarb, 1989; Davies, 1993). Others have seen it as a liberatory movement. Tom Shakespeare, for example, has distinguished between post-materialist and liberation movements and argued that the disabled people's movement belongs to the latter category (Oliver, 1996, 158). He has said that: 'Most of the struggles mentioned ... are about resource allocation; women, black people and disabled people are crucially concerned with their economic exploitation and poverty' (Shakespeare, 1993, 258).

These movements represent people's determined efforts to speak and act on their own behalf – to 'self-organise' – and develop aims, ideas, ways of working and cultures of their own to achieve their own self-defined goals (Jordan and Lent, 1999; Lent, 2002). What unites welfare service user movements and many of the new social movements is that they are both based on identity and people's efforts to define their own identity. They have all sought a revaluation of their social roles and worked to develop more positive identities.

Being involved in service user led organisations

How many times have I heard disabled people and other service users talk about 'light bulb' moments in their life! For me it was going to the first meeting with other mental health service users. *I could be myself*, it was a wonderful feeling. I didn't have to pretend or deny my difficulties. There was understanding and familiarity. We didn't have to be careful, apologetic or be other than who we were. It was a liberating feeling. And then I began to learn there were different ways to make sense of what had happened to me and that 'it wasn't just me'. I got more involved and people were sensitive to different things that were difficult for different people. It wasn't just about a sense of acceptance, but also a chance to do something. This isn't like 'charity work' or 'rehabilitation'. It is a sense of being part of something much bigger, that is desperately important in our world, but largely ignored as such. And it is about coming at it *together* in a different way. Of course it is not a fantasy of consensus and everyone getting on with everyone else. But I have truly seen and experienced on a routine basis, shared understanding and supportiveness that it is not common elsewhere. And I have seen the emergence of new wonderful ideas that give me hope for all our futures.

The author

The service user organisations and movements that emerged in the latter part of the twentieth century may have been the fullest flowering so far of such collective action, but they were certainly not the first (Barnes, 1997; Campbell and Oliver, 1996). In the 1890s, the British Deaf Association and the National League of the Blind were formed. These are identified by the disabled people's movement as the very first organisations run *by disabled people* for themselves (BCODP, 1997, 9). In the 1920s, unions of disabled war veterans were formed and in 1920, members of the National League of the Blind, a union of blind workers, marched to a rally in London to demand better pay and working conditions, anticipating the famous Jarrow March (GMCDP, 2010, 6). In the 1920s the Blind Persons Act was passed, introduced and supported by disabled people (Close, 2011, 7). Past centuries are studded with accounts of people whom society saw as mad protesting that they were misunderstood (Porter, 1987). Peter Campbell, the survivor activist identifies much earlier examples of activism and protests by 'mad persons' from the seventeenth century onwards (Campbell,1999; 2005; 2009). It is interesting to ponder how modern social policy might have developed if instead of the major figures of the nineteenth and early twentieth century advancing their own ideas and prescriptions, they had supported, encouraged and accessed those of people with direct experience of poverty and other social problems. Campbell dated the modern UK survivor movement to the mid-1980s and traced its origins to earlier mental patient groups from the beginning of the 1970s and acknowledges the support it gained from radical mental health professionals (Campbell, 2009). Already by 1982, the socialist activist, Peter Sedgwick, was writing of survivor movements in Belgium, France, Germany, Holland, Scotland and the United States, as well as England (Sedgwick, 1982).

The social policy community response

Thus we can trace elements of a different history, from the nineteenth century, and even before, of people's own thoughts, feelings and ideas, even though this is generally sketchy and much was unrecorded. While such hidden history and collective action from people on the receiving end of policy from the time of the Poor Law – and even before the emergence of modern social policy in the nineteenth century, can be identified – contemporary social policy appears to have paid little if any attention to it as either a subject of analysis or of study. The same lack of interest and attention also seems to have persisted into the twenty-first century.

In 2010, I wrote a chapter for the UK Social Policy Association's annual review, exploring the relationship between current academic social policy and service users (Beresford, 2010a). The points I made then still seem to hold true. Typically recent and current social policy textbooks to be found on library and bookshop shelves, even those offered as standard texts or key introductions, tend to have little or nothing to say about, or to report, from people as welfare state service users (for example, Pierson and Castles, 2006, Pierson, 2006; Alford, 2009; Fitzpatrick, 2011a; Alcock, 2012a; Baldock et al, 2012). They seem to have particularly little to say about the organisations and movements developed by such service users. Thus, for instance, a social policy text whose focus was specifically 'social welfare movements' acknowledged in its introduction that it 'barely discusses' the modern service user movements, like the disabled people's and psychiatric system survivor movements (Annetts et al, 2009, 12). Yet these can be seen as the movements most closely associated with social policy, indeed in some cases, being traceable to and generated by it and in the case of the disabled people's movement, as we have seen, with a modern history stretching back more than a generation to the early 1970s (Campbell and Oliver, 1996).

When in 2009, for the first time, the Association organised a plenary session at its annual conference on 'user involvement' in social policy, the session was presented by an academic, Marian Barnes, who did not come from a service user perspective or movement and the Chair of a carers' organisation, Pat Thomas. It is difficult to imagine a session relating to any other issue of diversity or social movement: the women's, black civil rights, or LGBTQ movement, where the same approach would have been adopted and such a session led by someone not sharing the identity under discussion. In 2012, the Social Policy Association published the fourth edition of its *Student's companion to social policy*, which is intended as the definitive introductory text for social policy students. This included chapters on disability and welfare users, neither of which was written from a disabled person's or service user's perspective (Priestley, 2012; Barnes, 2012). The Research Excellence Framework is the official process established for grading academic research and allocating research funding. In 2014, this highlighted the importance of 'impact'. The sub-panel for social work and social policy did not include any representative, either as a panel member or assessor, from a service user or user movement perspective, relating to disability studies or on the basis of experiential knowledge, despite efforts being made for such a perspective to be considered.

Such discussion continues to be under-developed. Academics like Marian Barnes, who have focused on such issues, particularly in the context of health and social care, are unusual (M. Barnes et al, 1999). There has been at least some rhetorical sign-up to the virtues and value of public involvement and the engagement of service users in political social policy, if only because of the shift to market-based consumerism. However, academic social policy discourse has had only a very limited engagement with welfare service users and their movements and has not developed a significant cannon of work addressing or critiquing them. Much more attention has been paid in academic social policy to the supply-side of social policy than the role of its recipients or 'consumers'; to what might be called the viewpoints of 'the demand-side'. We can only guess why this is. It seems likely that the inherent paternalism of traditional Fabianism, which has been the dominant strand in UK academic social policy discourse, with its presumption of the 'expert' construction of social policy, has a bearing on this. We will return to this later when we return to the knowledge base of social policy. What this suggests is a continuity in social policy attitudes towards service users' voices, views and collective action from the nineteenth-century origins of social policy analysis to its present day equivalent. This is summed up by the comments from social policy professors offered at the beginning of the previous chapter.

One last comment should perhaps be made about the failure of the academic discipline of social policy to pay serious attention to the direct voices of welfare service users and to consider the roles they do or might play in social policy. This is in some contrast to the attention that the emerging discipline of 'disability studies' – whose origins lie in the disabled people's movement – has paid to social policy (see, for example, Oliver and Barnes, 1998). This offers additional and significant insights into social policy, which we will be looking at in due course.

If the response of the social policy community and discipline to the emergence of welfare service user movements seems at best muted, their development nonetheless seems far-reaching in its implications and transfigurative in its consequences, both for social policy and far beyond. Not only is it difficult to see how their development can be ignored, but it also offers fundamental insights for social policy. This becomes increasingly apparent when we look more closely at the founding of such movements.

The UK disabled people's movement

The modern welfare service user movements are not all the same, as has already been indicated and as we will see further in the next chapter when we explore their principles in more detail. However, it is worth focusing to begin with particularly on the disabled people's movement, as it was both the first to form in the UK and has also probably been the most influential of these movements.

When documenting any 'history', it is important to remember that there can be many starting points, many different branches to be followed and many, sometimes competing, connections that can be made. This is a point that Jane Campbell and Mike Oliver, disability activists, made in their history of the UK disabled people's movement (Campbell and Oliver, 1996). It was in Le Court Leonard Cheshire residential home that Paul Hunt, 'whom many of us regard as the founder of the modern movement' (Campbell and Oliver, 1996, 53), first developed the ideas and philosophy which were to inform the Union of Physically Impaired Against Segregation (UPIAS). Thus a strong argument can be made that the founding of the British disabled people's movement was inextricably linked to the Leonard Cheshire organisation. Paul Hunt's edited collection of disabled people's accounts is now identified as one of the key texts in the development of the disabled people's movement and disabled people's thinking (Hunt, 1966a; Barnes et al, 2002, 5). As Mike Oliver has written:

> Paul Hunt was influential not only through his writings. He also became a key participant in the Union of the Physically Impaired Against Segregation (UPIAS). This was a newly formed collective of disabled people who, after meeting regularly to share their experiences and further their personal struggles collectively, came to the conclusion that disability was a form of social oppression. (Oliver, 1996, 25)

The Union of Physically Impaired Against Segregation was established in 1972. It can be seen as a key starting point for the development of the British disabled people's movement. Paul Hunt and other disabled people believed that by being 'shut away' and 'incarcerated' in residential homes, they were being denied choice and freedom over their own lives, that other people in this country were taking for granted (Hunt, 1966b). They did not believe that the institutional discrimination that they faced on a daily basis could be challenged or contested from within and thus in 1977, they formed Project 81. Their aim was to leave residential care and live as equal members of society in the community. They planned to organise their support needs, their funding and to find accessible housing within the following five years. Some of them succeeded in doing this. In January 2014, a celebration was held to mark what was seen as the thirtieth anniversary of the independent living movement, when the first of these disabled people, John Evans, left Le Court to live an independent life.

A fellow resident of Paul Hunt at Le Court Leonard Cheshire residential home, Peter Wade, believed that it was possible to make change and improve disabled people's lives working with existing powerholders. He was equally committed to equality and freedom from social oppression, but he believed that the best way for people to achieve this was by working within the established system. To this end, he and others joined RADAR (the Royal Association for Disability and Rehabilitation) and the Leonard Cheshire Foundation. However before he died, he changed his view completely and did not believe that it was possible to work with large organisations for disabled people, with a real hope of changing them. As the historians of the disabled people's movement Campbell and Oliver wrote: 'Peter Wade's experience was, and still is, a very common one for those who strive to change traditional "caring" organisations from within, and is a major reason why the BCODP (British Council of Disabled People) adopted a policy of organising quite separately from such bodies' (Campbell and Oliver, 1996, 57).

What is helpful to remember here, is that it was two former residents of a Leonard Cheshire home, Paul Hunt and Peter Wade, who had an enormous influence on the development of the British disabled people's movement. Each embodied, at an early stage, different, often competing approaches to making change and seeking to transform the lives of disabled people. This is a reminder of the central role the Leonard Cheshire organisation (now Leonard Cheshire Disability) played in the development of the UK disabled people's movement. For this reason it is worth looking more closely at Leonard Cheshire – the organisation and the man.

Leonard Cheshire

The Leonard Cheshire organisation has played an important part in disability policy since the creation of the welfare state. It was founded in 1948, when it established its first 'home' for disabled people. Leonard Cheshire Disability is now a large international organisation. It describes itself as offering over 150 services in the UK, include care at home, residential services, respite care, day services, resource centres, independent living units and services for people with an acquired brain injury. It also works internationally with over 250 services in more than 50 countries (http://www.lcdisability.org/?lid=19). Historically, however, the Leonard Cheshire organisation can be seen to be more than just a major service provider. It has also had a profound influence on thinking, policy and provision for disability more generally. This can be traced, at least in part, to the powerful and enduring influence of its founder, Group Captain Leonard Cheshire, VC, OM, war hero and visionary.

As well as his own writings (Cheshire, 1943, 1961, 1981, 1985), many books have been written about Cheshire (Boyle, 1955; Braddon, 1956; Morris, 2000). This last biography reminds us that Nehru, the first Prime Minister of India, compared him to Mahatma Gandhi and that he was commended for canonisation by the actor Sir Alec Guinness (Morris, 2000; Beresford, 2001). In 2002 in a BBC public poll, he was identified as one of the 100 'greatest Britons' (Wells, 2002).

Leonard Cheshire had at least three significant roles in public life; as bomber commander, witness to and supporter of the wartime use of nuclear weapons, and founder of the foundation named after him.

He became an important internationally known public figure. His first big project after the war was to set up 'classless colonies' based on 'united effort and mutual support' in England and 'the dominions'. Organised on the basis of a hierarchical democracy 'with a military tinge', these sought to blend community, cooperation and private enterprise. Like many earlier utopias, they quickly collapsed. They are strongly reminiscent of kind of colonies and utopias established in the nineteenth century and like many of them, rapidly failed. However, they can be seen as the foundations on which he then established Le Court as the first Cheshire home, to be filled with 'the disabled, the unwanted, the helpless, TB patients and the dying' and then set up the Foundation which was named after him.

Leonard Cheshire can also be seen as a kind of early Mother Teresa. He too was interested in taking 'unwanted invalids' off the street and offering a place to people who were dying. He was dismissive of the British post-war welfare state, as paternalistic and materialistic. He took St Teresa of Lisieux who died of TB in her 20s as his 'pattern' or prototype. Faith became his guiding star. The unity of Christendom and the restoration of England as a Catholic nation was his 'supreme desire' and work with sick and disabled people followed from this. 'Family' and 'community' were key concepts for him and from the start his idea was that homes like Le Court should be both. The Foundation grew out of his personal philosophy based on ideals of the family, community, mutuality and self-help (Morris, 2000). These ideals were inculcated into both the organisation and service users. Although he died in 1990, in some ways Leonard Cheshire's presence is still powerful and important. His picture, quotations and books, as well as his papers, are still important in the mythology of the organisation.

The historic relationship between the Leonard Cheshire organisation and the disabled people's movement has been one characterised by conflict and mutual dislike. It is highlighted in the comments of key figures included by Jane Campbell and Mike Oliver in their history of the disabled people's movement. For example:

> I was a resident at Le Court ... There was no flicker of recognition of what we were saying. One felt that there was no contact at all, no understanding. At one stage he (Leonard Cheshire) came and suggested that we all gave up our Christmas dinner and sent the money to a Cheshire home in India and he was astonished that we didn't even discuss it. He just thought that it was absolutely appalling ... It was virtually a diktat which the residents just wouldn't

have contemplated. It was just a totally false proposal and it was based on some really very, very grossly misguided assumptions about disabled people. He assumed that we were just being selfish and ungrateful and exceedingly uncaring in refusing to discuss it. But in fact it was to do with lots of other issues as well. It wasn't to do with the state of people in India at all. It was all to do with the fact that he should come along and make that suggestion. (Phillip Mason, quoted in Campbell and Oliver, 1996, 42–3)

I knew about the Cheshire homes but Paul (Hunt) introduced me to the real criticisms about them, about the institution approach. It seemed to me that the clearest perception of what was wrong with disability was in relation to these homes. It was around the issue of controlling your life and the ability to get out of the homes and to get into the community, which then raised the income issue. (Vic Finkelstein, quoted in Campbell and Oliver, 1996, 54).

Charity and the disabled people's movement

Dominant attacks on the UK welfare state from the last quarter of the twentieth century onwards were primarily framed in terms of the deficiencies of *state* welfare. What is interesting about the critiques that emerged from the disabled people's movement was that it represented a revulsion more from *charitable* than state welfare. Yet such charitable provision has repeatedly been offered by both welfare pluralist and neoliberal analysts and commentators as part of the solution that they see to the shortcomings of state welfare. Commentators from the emerging UK disabled people's movement identified a number of characteristics of such charities which they saw as problematic, if not oppressive. First, as Vic Finkelstein (1980) argued, the segregation of disabled people, whether in separate schools, hospitals, homes or colonies, encouraged the growth of a wide array of non-disabled disability 'experts' and professionals, who were themselves effectively dependent upon the continued dependence of disabled people. Second, these charities, which were frequently impairment specific, like Guide Dogs for the Blind, the British Epilepsy Association and the Muscular Dystrophy Association, stressed the seemingly inevitably dependent nature of disability and disabled people. This could, of course, be seen as the reason for their existence. Third, such charities have traditionally been, and in many cases continue to be, run and organised by non-disabled people. Thus disability charities have traditionally been based on an individualised model of disability and consolidated the idea that disabled people are dependent. They implicitly suggest, as Mike Oliver, the disabled academic and activist has written, that disabled people 'require the "charitable" assistance of well-meaning professionals, voluntary workers or politicians' (Oliver, 1990, 115). Thus the disabled people's movement has long associated disability charities with segregation, institutionalisation and the perpetuation of dependency. Such charities have also been consistent with the top-down model of policy and provision which has characterised modern social policy, with a key role reserved for 'experts' as analysts and mediators, perpetuating the exclusion and dependence of service users.

The UK disabled people's movement developed its own critique of the origins and historical role of disability charities. It was a very different analysis to that either of Victorian, Fabian or neoliberal social policy. It was based on the centrality of two developments. First, was the economic change resulting from the industrial revolution and the rise of a capitalist or free market economy in the nineteenth century. Second, was the subsequent and related shift in social policy signalled by the establishment of the utilitarian New Poor Law in 1834 and the introduction of segregation as a way of dealing with difference, including difference based on disability. The change in social and economic conditions had enormous ramifications for people with impairments. As Colin Barnes has commented:

> First, a family dependent upon wage labour alone could not provide for its members during economic depression, so that large groups of dependents were created by industrialisation. Secondly, the system of Poor Law relief which had survived since Elizabethan times was directly at odds with the ascending free market economy. Waged labour made the distinction between able-bodied and the non-able-bodied poor crucially important, since parochial relief to the able-bodied poor interfered with labour mobility. (Barnes, 1991a, 15)

The Victorian Poor Law reinforced a distinction between the 'deserving' and the 'undeserving' poor. While groups like unemployed paupers and unmarried mothers were included in the latter category, disabled people were more likely to be associated with the former. There were, however, rising concerns about the damaging and contaminating effects which perceived 'defectives' and 'defective stock' could have on the

British nation and empire. This was intensified from the late nineteenth century, as we have seen, by the rise of the eugenics movement. The solution adopted was the segregation and congregation of people and groups seen as morally, mentally and physically deficient in asylums, workhouses and hospitals (Foucault, 2001). This served as both an efficient means of containment and as a warning to others. The massive expansion of institutions can thus be seen as a direct result of the rise of capitalist economy.

The desire to make provision that was less rigorous than the Poor Law for groups seen as more deserving resulted in a general expansion of charities in the nineteenth century and the specific development of disability charities. Many of the large modern disability charities, including, for example, the Royal National Institutes for the Blind (RNIB) and the Deaf (RNID) were established at this time. Such charities not only served to distinguish between the 'deserving' and 'non-deserving' poor, they also separated disabled people into their specific impairment groups. Even after the ending of the Poor Law they continued to segregate disabled people in institutions, although these became smaller. Disability charities operated as part of broader structures of moral and medical surveillance focused on disabled people (Borsay, 2002).

Disability charity advertising: a case study

Charitable advertising provides a helpful case study for understanding both the traditional ideology of disability (and other) charities and the objections of the disabled people's movement to them. David Hevey, the disability filmmaker and writer, has identified a three-stage process for such charitable advertising based on: branding, attitude change and functional status (Hevey, 1992). The first stage highlights the negativity of impairment, but the possibility of help from charity. This phase is particularly associated with imagery which disability activists see as oppressive and negative, highlighting 'the tragedy' of disability. In the second stage the role of charity in offering care or cure is emphasised. Finally we see that disabled people can overcome their difficulties – with the help of charity. Hevey stresses:

> the point I am making by outlining these three stages is to show the process that is common to many charities who wish to position themselves through advertising. It is likely that this trend will continue to grow. The notion of a process of charity image making is also important to

grasp…because some people are being seduced into seeing the different stages as a 'positive' move on from the previous one. All charity advertising, must somewhere in its poster posit the notion of its particular brand of impairment being dependent on charity. (Hevey, 1992, 41–2)

Colin Barnes, the academic associated with the disabled people's movement, made similar points around the same time and 20 years later they still sum up the pattern of much disability charity advertising (as indeed they do for advertising in relation to third world disasters and development).

Images of the disabled person as pitiable and pathetic are still the most common in charity advertising… Others focus on the 'courage and bravery' of individual 'super cripples'. Besides emphasising the abnormality of the individuals concerned, this approach reinforces the perceived inadequacy of the rest of the disabled population. A more recent development…is the stress on the 'abilities' rather that the 'disabilities', of disabled individuals – normal able-bodied attributes are emphasised while impairments are conveniently overlooked. (Barnes, 1991b, 4; see also Barnett and Hammond, 1999)

The apparent purpose of charity advertising is to raise funds. But the relationship between charity advertising and fundraising is more complex. A Charities Aid Foundation report identified door-to-door collections as the most effective means of raising money, while advertising campaigns were much less successful. 'One of the least-used methods of prompted giving was responding to advertising appeals. Indeed, only 1 per cent were found to respond to this method' (quoted in Hevey, 1992, 44.

Such advertising is often not primarily aimed at fundraising. Instead, it mainly serves to reinforce the link between disability, or a particular impairment and the charity concerned; to raise the public profile or 'brand' of the charity, and to support and reward local volunteers and fundraisers for their efforts. It does this, as we have seen, by linking disability or a specific impairment in people's minds with a particular charity; by exploiting fear of disability and demonstrating the dependency of disabled people upon the charity.

Disabled people tend to be presented as the beneficiaries of charitable fundraising. However, often the association of the charity with disability and impairment is so effective, that its disabled service users become key fundraisers themselves as a way of 'doing their bit'. The 'branding' – or linking between the charity and disability – is so strong that many service users may see the charity as working for them, rather than colluding in their oppression, as the disabled people's movement has generally conceived of it.

Breaking the social policy tradition

If there is one abiding theme which emerges from the history of social policy and the counter histories of service users, it is the central role of self-appointed professional 'experts'. These have almost invariably been experts without direct experience of the issues they discuss, who have played a key role as analysts, mediators and shapers of policy and practice. They offer their policy prescriptions, justified by the rationale that these are in 'people's best interests'. If social policy were a religion, then they would have been its high priests. Just how big a departure and how much of a challenge the emergence of welfare user movements and organisations could be to traditional social policy approaches and understandings, can be seen from discussions held early in the history of the disabled people's movement between a traditional organisation *for* disabled people and a founding organisation *of* disabled people, where control lay formally and explicitly with disabled people. What perhaps makes this especially significant is that the traditional approach was mainly represented by Peter Townsend, who as we have seen was a key figure in modern academic social policy and social policy reform, and the new approach which included as spokespersons two key founding members of the emerging disabled people's movement, Vic Finkelstein and Paul Hunt.

One document brings together the very different traditions of these two ideological and campaigning positions. This is the *Fundamental principles of disability* published in 1976 (UPIAS/Disability Alliance 1976). It has come to be understood in the disabled people's movement as one of, if not the most important statements in its development. While rarely mentioned in social policy discourse, in the field of disability studies it is seen as a defining document in the development of disabled people's collective action and an articulation of the key ideas that they were developing. It is because of this that it is discussed in some detail here. If there is one primary source that readers of this book should check out directly for themselves, because of its transformative implications and effects, it is this one. The *Fundamental principles* is not, as might first be expected, simply a straightforward statement of the values and beliefs of members or representatives of the developing disabled people's movement. It is actually a dialogue or debate between members of a disabled people's organisation, UPIAS, and of the Disability Alliance, an organisation which included both disabled and non-disabled people. The aims of Disability Alliance were to relieve the poverty of disabled people and improve the living standards of disabled people. It was founded by Peter Townsend as a non-disabled person in 1974 and he played a key role in it, as he did in the discussion with UPIAS. UPIAS has been described as 'the first disability liberation group in the UK, and one of the first in the world' (http://www.labournet.net/other/0107/upias1.html). The establishment of both organisations can be linked to the collapse of the Disablement Income Group (DIG) in 1972. As Adam Lent stated in his discussion of British social movements: 'the Disability Alliance – a new body under the leadership of Peter Townsend aimed to make up for DIG's failings' (Lent, 2002, 107).

Thus in essence, this was an exchange between one of the new organisations of disabled people and one that reflected the traditional model of being an organisation for disabled people – including some of them – but not controlled by them. Perhaps even more important, not only does the document record a formal discussion between the two organisations, but each had the opportunity to read, finalise and agree this and then to offer additional commentaries of their own. So here we have that rarity in history, a record that has been agreed and authenticated by the parties involved, where we know that how their arguments are presented, where there are differences and conflicts, can be taken to be accurately represented. This offers a unique insight into contemporary thinking about disability, particularly disability in relation to poverty, from the different vantage points of these two organisations. What makes it even more significant and relevant here, is that these different vantage points reflect much broader competing perspectives. These are crucially that which is lodged in traditional Fabian (and indeed other top-down) approaches to social policy and campaigning and that which emerges from the new self-organisation and collectivity of disabled people within their own organisations.

The agreed aim of the meeting between the two organisations, subject to their 'prior agreement' to a set of 'fundamental principles of disability' identified by UPIAS, was to explore how disabled people 'could become more active in the disability field' and consider a 'long-term programme of action' to make that possible (UPIAS/Disability Alliance, 1976, 3). These 'fundamental principles' were that:

disability is a situation, caused by social conditions, which requires for its elimination:

a. that no one aspect such as incomes, mobility or institutions is treated in isolation;

b. that disabled people should, with the advice and help of others, assume control over their own lives;

c. that professionals, experts and others who seek to help must be committed to promoting such control by disabled people. (UPIAS/Disability Alliance, 1976, 3)

Although both organisations said that they had signed up to these principles, UPIAS was not convinced that the Disability Alliance and Peter Townsend actually had, instead seeing them as:

- pursuing the income issue in isolation – 'it is only one aspect of [disabled people's] oppression';
- maintaining an approach with 'a small number of [non-disabled] experts' having the central role and most disabled people left 'largely passive';
- seeking to educate the public through 'expert' information, with a 'narrow concentration on parliamentary pressure' (UPIAS/Disability Alliance, 1976, 4) rather than working for the 'mass participation of disabled people' which UPIAS saw as crucial;
- not making serious efforts to involve disabled people (UPIAS/ Disability Alliance, 1976, 4).

UPIAS interpreted Peter Townsend's and the Disability Alliance's focus on a comprehensive state income for disabled people as perpetuating their social and economic dependence. It regarded the Alliance's reliance on a medically based model of assessing disability – what people 'couldn't do', rather than a social model – providing the support they needed to live independently – as keeping control with social administrators and taking it from disabled people. UPIAS were critical of what they saw as 'the willingness of the incomes "experts" to use disabled people to give authority to their own social interests' (UPIAS/Disability Alliance, 1976, 16). Peter Townsend, on the other hand, genuinely seemed unable to understand, wondering why they were 'making such heavy weather of them' (UPIAS/Disability Alliance, 1976, 8) and saying that the failure to ensure large-scale involvement of disabled people in the Disability Alliance was no more than 'a problem of time and organisation' (UPIAS/Disability Alliance, 1976, 6).

Townsend described the setting up of the Disability Alliance as 'very much a spontaneous development' (UPIAS/Disability Alliance, 1976, 4). The response of UPIAS was: 'you set up a spontaneous ad hoc organisation, putting forward policies to the government in the name of disabled people without involving them' (UPIAS/Disability Alliance, 1976, 14). On the issue of disabled people's involvement, Townsend said that 'one might wish that there may be a much heavier representation of organisations of the disabled within the Disability Alliance in the future' (UPIAS/Disability Alliance, 1976, 6). The UPIAS view was that the Alliance relied on 'organised groups of experts to speak for disabled people', which increased their disempowerment (UPIAS/Disability Alliance, 1976, 6).

UPIAS was strongly critical of Townsend's approach to the meeting, which had been agreed long in advance and was formal, when he spoke of giving an 'off-the-cuff reaction' to their fundamental principles (UPIAS/Disability Alliance, 1976, 4). The gulf between him and UPIAS seemed to stretch even further when, for example, he said 'I think I am speaking here for a very large number of disabled people' (UPIAS/Disability Alliance, 1976, 4) or he justified the involvement of non-disabled 'experts' rather than disabled people as 'just to give dignity to an exchange of correspondence with the Prime Minister' (UPIAS/Disability Alliance, 1976, 16).

In their commentary UPIAS made it clear that they saw Townsend as patronising and excluding, unable to understand or attach value to their ideas or principles. One point which UPIAS found particularly difficult to accept was Townsend's assertion that it was not possible for him to say which was cause or effect – poverty or disability. He said:

> You must understand, a social scientist who is asked to make a declaration about cause and effect takes up a very complicated position about factors which are so associated as to make it difficult, in lay terms, to distinguish cause from effect. I have to make that point. (UPIAS/Disability Alliance, 1976, 8)

The UPIAS response was to say:

> Imagine a lecturer going into a class to talk about sociology, starting by saying that he had not thought very much about the fundamental principles of sociology. (UPIAS/Disability Alliance, 1976, 12)

Vic Finkelstein for UPIAS:

> pointed to the dramatic difference in approach between the
> Alliance and the Union evident at the meeting. "Putting out
> more pamphlets to the public", he said, "is only different to
> what has gone before in terms of degree. If it did not work
> before, why is it going to work in the future?" Forming
> an umbrella organisation has not touched the fundamental
> issues, and unless you raise and investigate these questions
> "what is disability, and how come we are impoverished in
> the first place you are not going to deal with the causes of
> disability, and it may well be that your approach will help
> to perpetuate them".
>
> Peter Townsend then asked, "Who do you have to
> persuade about what are the causes of disability? We are
> trying to educate the public about disability … I mean, what
> is the alternative?" (UPIAS/Disability Alliance, 1976, 7)

The Disability Alliance described itself as: essentially an educational
forum in which disabled and non-disabled people alike are coming
together to press for fundamental changes in attitude and policy
(UPIAS/Disability Alliance, 1976, 23). UPIAS not only rejected the
approach to disability adopted by Townsend and the Disability Alliance
– their narrow focus on poverty. They also rejected their model for
making change. They saw this as based on:

> A relatively tiny group of individuals/small group of
> non-disabled "experts" write, discuss and print pamphlets
> advocating State Charity. These are then circulated to the
> public in the name of disabled people before we have had
> a chance to evaluate their contents critically. (UPIAS/
> Disability Alliance, 1976, 17)

This approach rested on a process of self-defined 'experts' 'educating the
public', where there was no clearly worked out process or explanation
of how this would or could work. Meanwhile Townsend and other such
experts would mediate and negotiate with government. UPIAS were
critical of the 'amateurism' of such 'experts'. Reading the transcript
of the discussion nearly 40 years on, what comes across strongly is
Townsend's apparent inability to understand the concerns of UPIAS
and their resulting frustration. It is a conversation that in some senses
seems to have no meeting points, where the discussants often seem to

be talking at cross purposes. While UPIAS was very serious about its principles, Townsend seemed to see these as merely political points to acknowledge, then continuing with his original agenda and process. He mistakes principles for rhetoric and appears neither participatory nor committed to self-organisation in his proposals. It is perhaps not surprising that UPIAS concluded that the Disability Alliance had 'accepted our fundamental principles without even understanding what they had accepted' (UPIAS/Disability Alliance, 1976, 15).

Adam Lent, in his examination of British social movements, concluded: 'The meeting was supposedly designed to see whether UPIAS could join the Alliance and whether Alliance members would be allowed to affiliate to UPIAS. In effect, however, it simply emphasised the irreconcilability of the old moderate approach and the new, self-organised radicalism' (Lent, 2002, 107–8).

Not only were the process, aims, and the understandings of the two organisations far apart from each other, but this distance was exacerbated by the apparent inability of either party to understand the other. The dialogue between the two organisations highlighted the enormous distance between traditional Fabian approaches to social policy and new participatory ones, where groups on the receiving end of social policy challenged the right of others to speak for them, developed their own collectivities, ideas and theories, rejecting traditional 'expertise' and emphasising the expertise that came from direct or lived experience. We encounter two different cultures and ways of thinking: one, UPIAS, committed to formal democratic process, the other Disability Alliance, rooted in the exigencies of conventional political and policy process. Anyone familiar with conventional political process would recognise Townsend's pressure politics methodology, while UPIAS explicitly criticised it for its lack of both principle and effectiveness.

It is also perhaps important to consider the personal politics embodied in this meeting. I personally find it hard not to admire the courage and determination of the UPIAS contingent. It is easy to overlook this, but here was a small group of disabled people, who had experience of all the usual barriers and exclusions faced by disabled people, without external credibility or authority beyond their movement. Despite the power and authority invested in figures like Townsend (subsequently described in one obituary as 'one of the global giants of social science and a leading campaigner for social justice' (Walker, 2009)), they stuck to their principles and articulated them carefully and clearly and engaged in equal debate with much more powerful forces.

Conclusion

In this chapter we have seen the growing interest from the 1960s in developing and hearing first-hand accounts, particularly those of disadvantaged and marginalised groups. We have also seen how social policy failed to respond to this development. It culminated in the emergence of movements of welfare service users. These began to articulate determinedly and powerfully their own experience and demands. This was not just a challenge to disability policy, but also to social policy generally. Mainstream social policy, especially academic and analytic social policy, has continued to be slow to address these, still often paying them and the movements that generated them little, if any, attention. Yet these movements have both offered new critiques of conventional social policy and have also fundamentally challenged its assumptions, process and direction of travel. In the next chapter we will look more closely at some of the principles that have informed and been strongly articulated by these movements.

TEN

A new set of principles for social policy

Nothing About Us Without Us
(Campaigning slogan of the international disabled people's movement)

Disability ... the social oppression of people with impairments ... like racism, sexism, heterosexism and all other forms of social oppression ... is a human creation. It is impossible, therefore, to confront one type of oppression without confronting them all and, of course, the cultural values that created and sustain them.
(Barnes, 1996, xii)

It is perhaps not surprising that a state welfare system based on self-appointed experts imposing their analyses and ideas on others has often failed to command popular support. The market alternative has been given a much homelier and more familiar feel by its advocates, as if buying and selling public services is the equivalent of the weekly shop or buying a new sofa. However, as we have seen, this model is no less mediated by experts and ideologues and the individualised consumer is hardly king or queen of the system. We have now also seen how many disabled people have experienced charities as similarly excluding and patronising. This raises fundamental questions about how social policy might be developed, organised and undertaken in radically different ways, which address and overcome such failings and limitations.

Why poor treatment?

Here we may turn to the new welfare service user movements for insights and guidance. First though, before moving on, we should perhaps take a more careful look at longstanding problems associated with welfare services. These have tended to be framed in terms of the poor quality of some services, sometimes linked with abuse and neglect, as well as the denial of more general human and civil rights. Sadly, these problems can be traced back almost to the inception of the welfare state and have been identified under governments of all political colours. Thus the succession of high profile childcare tragedies and scandals from Dennis O'Neill in 1944, through Maria Colwell in 1973 and Jasmine Beckford in 1984, to Victoria Climbié in 2000, Baby Peter in 2007 and Daniel Pelka in 2012 (Hopkins, 2007). In Chapter Six, we heard about the widespread and appalling abuse of older people, people with learning difficulties and mental health service users exposed in the 1960s. This century there have been repeated scandals of older people in residential services beaten by 'care' staff, disproportionately high death rates at Stafford and other hospitals and the torture and brutalising of people with learning difficulties in Winterbourne View and beyond. Welfare service users, especially disabled people and mental health service users/survivors, have long complained about the quality and suitability of the support services they receive.

As we have seen in this book, the political right has regarded the welfare state itself as at the heart of whatever is wrong with its services. It has argued that state intervention tends to patronise, create and perpetuate dependency and provide 'one size fits all' solutions. However, the evidence accumulated here does not confirm that there is anything inherently problematic with state welfare services. We have also encountered problems in charitable provision and explored the many weaknesses of market-driven models for providing services and support. But even the pressure to neoliberalism does not explain all the longstanding problems associated with welfare state services particularly for marginalised and vulnerable groups.

My father's suicide

My father committed suicide in 1985. He was 59. He took an overdose of aspirins. He had had another bad period of depression. He dreaded going back into psychiatric hospital, as he had done some years before. What can we say about mental health services when people would rather be dead, than seek help from them?

Suzy Croft
My partner

The longstanding prescriptive nature of social policy offers a more convincing explanation for this. It has applied to both left and right of centre social policy, although it is particularly associated with Fabianism. Both have minimised the overlaps between service users and providers. Neither, as we have seen, seems to have valued the contribution or involvement of service users; their ideas or experience. Fresh insights have been emerging recently about this devaluing of service users. These relate to several major abuse cases, which have come to be known as the Rochdale, Rotherham, Cyril Smith and Jimmy Savile scandals. There are some significant overlaps between them. All have involved the large-scale sexual abuse of children and young people, including both boys and girls. They can't be dismissed as historical, associated only with a particular class or culture or any particular sector of services. This was particularly evident in the case of Savile.

All have involved children and young people who are particularly vulnerable and at risk, frequently children in state care. Yet instead of such care ensuring their safety, it seems to have meant that they have been left particularly unprotected. The identity of service user seems especially to have exposed them to abuse. Often they have neither been valued nor listened to. Instead of supporting their empowerment, services have contributed to their disempowerment, reinforcing inequalities of power. They and their views have been considered suspect and they have been discredited by police, social and health services. While they are often regarded as 'damaged goods', unreliable and problematic, those who actually damaged them, have frequently escaped exposure or punishment during their lifetime. (Girl A, 2013; Wanless, 2013; *Guardian*, 2014; Chesworth, 2014).

A different set of principles

Over recent years, service users and their organisations have, however, developed a series of their own principles for advancing policy and practice. One of their abiding concerns has been to develop policy and practice that are supportive and empowering rather than restrictive, isolating, oppressive and patronising. There has been a remarkable consistency in these principles across movements and internationally. First though, it may be helpful to turn again to the movements themselves, to look at them more closely. While it would be a mistake to overstate their impact, it has already been significant. It has led to major changes in ideas, culture, practice, policy, processes and legislation on a global scale. Groups that had previously often been hidden, have gained a greater individual, as well as political and cultural presence in societies. In countries like the UK, their viewpoints have begun to permeate the mainstream, just as they have made major steps along the long road to inclusion and equal rights (ODI, 2008). This, as we have said, is also an international development, finding various expressions in North America, Europe and the majority world (Aspis, 1997; Campbell and

Oliver, 1996; Morris, 1996; Oliver, 1996; Priestley, 1999; Coleridge, 1993; Charlton, 1998; Oliver and Barnes, 1998; Barnes et al, 1999).

These movements, however, are far from homogeneous. Different pressures can be discerned in their development and they are not necessarily monolithic in nature. In the UK, for example, the older people's movement has strong links with former trade unionists and workplace activity and has had a particular focus on pensions policy (Carter and Beresford, 2000). In the US, on the other hand, a 'grey power' movement had early origins. In Australia, Grey Power is a political party, first registered in 1983, which has run candidates in political elections. In the US, the Gray Panthers were founded in 1970, and from 2005 supported a progressive platform including increases in welfare payments, lifelong public education, the abolition of the death penalty, legalisation of same sex marriage, reproductive rights and the legalisation of medical marijuana (Sanjek, 2009). While the UK disabled people's movement has tended to be seen as separatist, the mental health service user movement has been identified as more consumerist and tied to the service system. Academics Marian Barnes and Polly Shardlow, for example, comparing mental health service users' and disabled people's organisations and groups, distinguished between the strategies of the former, which they saw as based on a consumerist approach and of the latter based on 'citizenship' (Barnes and Shardlow, 1996; Barnes et al, 1999).

Some user movements, notably the UK survivor movement, have gained support and linked up with radical and critical professionals (Campbell, 1999; Survivors History Group, 2012). Others like the UK disabled people's movement have tended to keep away from them. There are now strong traditions of people with learning difficulties speaking up for themselves collectively in many countries, with common issues identified relating to securing funding and effective supporters (Tilley, 2004).

Movements have also developed at a different pace in different countries. In the US, disabled people's activism was encouraged by the large numbers of newly disabled veterans created by the Vietnam war. The Independent Living Movement (ILM) that developed in America also grew out of disabled students' determination to secure access and support to complete their studies, giving rise to the development of centres for independent living (CILs) internationally (De Jong, 1983; Hahn, 1986). The UN's International Year of Disabled Persons in 1981, the Decade of Disabled Persons that followed from 1983 to 1992, the first and second Asian and Pacific Decade of Disabled Persons (1993–2002 and 2003–12), the African and Arab Decades of Disabled Persons

(2000–09 and 2003–12) all encouraged the expansion of activism and self-organisation (Oliver and Barnes, 2012, 149).

There has been some suggestion that 'people with impairments' might be seen as one diverse group of disabled people (for example, Oliver and Barnes, 2012, 171). Certainly there are overlaps and some of the self-organisations that have developed have operated across different 'user groups'. On the other hand, many mental health service users/survivors and many older people do not identify as disabled people and they, like some of the other groups associated with impairments, also see themselves as having their own distinct movements (Beresford et al, 2009; Wallcraft et al, 2003; Hoban et al, 2013). They are therefore often reluctant to be conflated with 'disabled' people, when they see themselves as having a different and unique identity and collective history of their own. Disabled identities are sometimes contested also, for example, with respect to deaf people, some of whom prefer to identify as a linguistic minority, rather than a group or movement of disabled people (Oliver and Barnes, 2012, 171; Corker, 1998).

As has been said here, these different movements have had varied histories, characters, culture and traditions. They often see themselves as different and there are competing interpretations of their nature and indeed, in some cases whether a movement actually exists at all. However, they have also had much in common. A common set of principles can be seen as having been developed by them. Not only are these inter-linking principles of central importance for understanding these movements, but they also offer an alternative framework for considering and advancing public policy, including social policy, more generally. Even though different ideologies have informed these movements – feminist, Marxist and social democratic – and they have included both conservatives and radicals, such conventional values and politics have been transcended by an underpinning commitment to these over-arching principles. These principles include: speaking for ourselves; self-organisation and collective action; social approaches; being rights-based; independent living; and living in the mainstream.

Speaking for ourselves

Going into hospital after being diagnosed with diabetes

I thought it was good because you had something to do while in bed: reading or watching a film. When I was allowed to get out there was a play area at the end of the corridor. I thought the staff were very jolly. I think it's good that I get all my things [for diabetes] free. It's good that we get money sent to us each month because of the diabetes. If we didn't have the welfare state it would be frustrating that you might not have enough money. I hope it carries on being like this.

Hannah Croft
My niece by marriage, aged eight

People wanting to speak for themselves instead of having others speaking on their behalf has been both the central reason for the development of welfare service user movements and also a key principle underpinning them. It has been both means and ends of service user organisations and movements; both at the heart of their process and their goal. Although such an aspiration and goal might seem unremarkable, as has been shown, the history of modern social policy has been one of largely excluding its subjects' first-hand voices. This cannot be seen as merely accidental or unintentional. As we have seen, the essential model on which social policy has been based, has been one of having experts *without* direct experience acting as interlocutors and mediators.

It has, however, not only been policymakers and analysts who have mediated the views and accounts of people as service users. Frequently health and social care professionals have done the same, perpetuating their own understandings of people's issues, rather than service users'. As they gained a public voice, service users also began to highlight the way in which their families were encouraged to speak on their behalf, rather than their being encouraged or supported to speak for themselves. Services frequently attached more legitimacy to the views of 'carers' than service users, creating and exacerbating conflicts and divisions between the two. For a long time, this has been an obstacle between the two groups, which overlap in practice, as has been highlighted by disabled people's and service users' organisations (Oliver, 1983; Campbell and Oliver, 1996; Oliver and Barnes, 1998).

All the service user movements have given priority to developing their own accounts and their own viewpoints (Campbell and Oliver, 1996; Campbell, 1999). People with learning difficulties, with their supporters, developed the idea and practice of '*self-advocacy*', to highlight the centrality of them being able to speak for themselves (Barron, 1996; Aspis, 1997; Bersani, 1998; Goodley, 2000). This was an early development in their collective action and made explicit their determination to have a voice of their own rather than to be spoken for. Thus they added to traditional ideas of 'advocacy' and 'advocates' – which all rested on an assumption that to make their voices heard people had to be spoken for (Williams and Shoultz, 1982). Significantly the civil rights movement of people with learning difficulties/disabilities has often been called the 'self-advocacy' movement and this term has also entered the vocabulary of other movements like the mental health service user/psychiatric system survivor movement. But particular issues had been raised in relation to people with learning difficulties because of traditional assumptions that people written off as 'idiots', 'imbeciles' and 'subnormals', in policy, practice and legislation, were incapable of 'speaking for themselves'. With the advent of self-advocacy, it became clear that while the category of 'learning difficulties' was used to include a very wide range of experience, abilities and impairments, with support and imagination, a way could be found for everyone to express their preferences, whether they used verbal language or not, regardless of the level of 'intelligence' that was attributed to them (Atkinson and Williams, 1990; Goodley and Ramcharan, 2010; Docherty et al, 2010). Low levels of literacy and other communication barriers have also restricted the extent to which people with learning difficulties have been able to speak on their own behalf. Additional barriers particularly faced them because they were frequently segregated in institutions throughout the twentieth century. People included in the category of having 'autistic spectrum disorders' (ASD), which has tended to be associated with communication problems, have also demonstrated their own capacity to speak for themselves, both collectively and individually, identifying instead as part of the neurodiverse movement (Milton, 2014; Milton and Moon, 2012).

Self-advocacy also always meant more than only *speaking* for yourself. It also means *acting* for yourself and being able to take greater control of your life. It has also been seen as a collective as well as an individual activity, developing a shared voice as service users.

Jan Wallcraft, the survivor activist and researcher, has highlighted the importance of self-advocacy for the survivor movement.

> [T]here is an emerging 'psychiatric survivor' or 'self-advocacy' discourse...which is distinct from professional and academic discourses. The key to this discourse is the power of the individual client, service-user or patient to self-define and to make choices, which is a fundamental contradiction to the discourse of psychopathology, which... has allocated this power to psychiatrists...Self-advocacy is based on personal, not professional experience, and it therefore proposes a radically different power dynamic to that of any other discourse. (Wallcraft, 2001, 83, 62)

Wallcraft contrasts self-advocacy developed by service users/survivors and their allies, with biomedical and psychosocial models. She says that it: 'challenges the power of professionals and their right to define and treat so-called mental illness. It emphasises the value of personal experience in knowledge creation and the importance of regaining power and control'.

A health emergency

Last year, feeling 'not right', I walked along a London street and rested on a wall. I couldn't go down the hill in front of me. Asking the way, I went slowly to a nearby surgery. People everywhere, they could not help: "You'll have to call 999."

I rang. I handed myself over to the empathic men in green. "Heart not happy", they said. Straight into the operating theatre at the wonderful local hospital staffed from every nation. Impossible to imagine there is better in the world. Perhaps it was heaven, for it could have been.

My heart has recovered, nourished by the sheer humanity of every person I have encountered in rehabilitation and beyond. The welfare state? Yes, the raw reality of human goodness. It has no price, for mercy and love cost not less than everything. It is our agreement that we will remember and take care of each other.

Robert Croft
My wife's cousin

Self-organisation and collective action

An early and defining activity undertaken by most if not all the service user movements was to set up their own groups and organisations. This was not because there were no organisations representing their identities or issues. Internationally there have long been organisations for different groups of disabled people, mental health service users, older people, people with long-term conditions, looked after children and so on. In many countries like the UK, by the time service users began to organise, these often included large, well-resourced and influential organisations, as emerged in Chapter Nine. But almost invariably such charities were led by non-disabled people and non-service users. As a result, service users increasingly raised concerns that often these charities did not reflect their priorities, or advance their agendas, as well as not involving them fully and on equal terms.

The disabled people's movement first drew a distinction between:

- organisations *for* disabled people – traditional voluntary or charitable organisations that were not controlled by disabled people; and
- organisations *of* disabled people – the new self-organisations which disabled people themselves controlled (where at least a majority of the board were themselves disabled people).

As we saw in the previous chapter, the discussion between the Disability Alliance and the Union of the Physically Impaired Against Segregation (UPIAS) highlighted the difference between these two kinds of organisations. The Leonard Cheshire Foundation which was the catalyst for the creation of the UK disabled people's movement (see next chapter) also was and continues to be one of the major such traditional disability charities. Service users, their organisations and movements have been critical of them for a number of reasons. These include that many of them:

- as service providers perpetuated the segregation, inferior status and stigmatisation of service users through offering separate, institutionalising, often inferior services;
- are narrowly 'impairment-based', for example, catering for people on the basis of diagnostic categories such as 'schizophrenia', cerebral palsy and visual impairment, rather than highlighting the common barriers and exclusions that they face, thus also disadvantaging people with less common or high profile conditions;
- as charities, reinforce the marginal status of service users through their use of negative stereotypes and images and preoccupation with their own organisational interests. (Drake, 1996, 150–8)

An organisation of disabled people was seen as one which they *controlled*. While the definition of such control is complex and we will return to it later, as a baseline, this has been taken to mean that the governing body of the organisation is made up of at least a majority of disabled people. More recently some commentators have suggested that this distinction between organisations *of* and *for* is no longer helpful as traditional charities have changed and greater complexities have been recognised (Shakespeare, 2006). Others have argued that many traditional charities have increasingly blurred the distinction, but have not fundamentally changed in nature or aims (Branfield et al, 2006). Making this point, Mike Oliver has written: 'we believe that the term "disability movement" has been usurped by the big charities and a variety of government quangos. Not only do they steal our ideas but our name as well' (Oliver, 2009, 134).

Service users have seen organisations which they control both as key to achieving social and political change through collective action and also as a route to their own personal empowerment. As Oliver and Barnes have observed: 'For many people with impairments, engaging in collective action was liberating and empowering psychologically and a source of positive identity' (Oliver and Barnes, 2012, 171).

Service users repeatedly refer to getting involved in their own groups and organisations as the most effective way of increasing their confidence, self-esteem and skills. Getting together in collective action is not only the best route to making positive change in themselves, but such personal development is key for effective and inclusive collective action to bring about broader social and political change. Their own 'user-led' and 'disabled people's' organisations provide the basis for both. The concept of 'empowerment', which was developed by the black civil rights movement in the United States has also featured centrally in their discussions and development (Shera and Wells, 1999). It has also become closely associated with self-organisation. While it is an idea which has often been weakened and diluted by being used carelessly and vaguely and it has also been appropriated by the market, it continues to be valued by many service users. This is because it acknowledges and encourages the importance of both personal and political change and their inter-relation. Thus service users have drawn a distinction between:

- personal empowerment – highlighting the need for change within us, and
- political empowerment – the need for wider change,

while emphasising the need to address both if people are to be truly rather than tokenistically involved in making change (Beresford and Croft, 1995).

Self-organisation has also taken different forms. Some disabled people's and service users' groups and organisations have placed a particular emphasis on offering mutual support, some on social action and some have highlighted a combination of both (Sutherland, 1981; Campbell, 1999; Wallcraft et al, 2003). There has been a different emphasis in different movements. The mental health service user/ survivor movement, for example, has understandably tended to stress people's need for emotional and crisis support, while people with learning difficulties have tended to have a particular, sometimes complex reliance on non-disabled supporters (Dowson, 1990).

Democratic disabled people's organisations were established all over the world. This included Disabled Peoples' International (DPI) and in the UK, the founding of the British Council of Organisations of Disabled People (BCODP) (Oliver, 2009, 99). Vic Finkelstein, pioneer of the UK disabled people's movement, saw disabled people's own organisations as having a key role to play not only in their own liberation, but also as a route for disabled people 'to be part of a far wider struggle to create a better society for all' (Finkelstein, 2009, 148). He saw them as 'centres for *integrated* living' developing services, training, employment and opportunities for disabled and other people. We shall return to his ideas in subsequent chapters when we look more closely at a new participatory approach to social policy and support.

Social approaches

The creation of the welfare state was underpinned by socialist thinking which rejected narrowly individualistic explanations of poverty and disadvantage. Instead it highlighted the social origins of many of the contemporary social problems that people were facing, including notably Beveridge's 'five giant evils'. Yet despite this radicalism, it still largely seemed to rely on individualistic understandings in relation to many of the marginalised groups in society. This was certainly the case as far as disabled people, mental health service users, people with learning difficulties and, indeed, older people were concerned. As Mike Oliver and Colin Barnes, pioneers of the UK disabled people's movement, have written:

> The overwhelming majority of the population with and without impairments internalize the personal tragedy view of disability...social policies in respect of disability have been influenced, albeit unknowingly, by the core ideology of individualism. However, recently peripheral ideologies have shifted away from the ideologies of disability as personal tragedy and towards disability as dependency. (Oliver and Barnes, 2012, 139–40)

The welfare state's ending of the Poor Law link between income and the meeting of need, represented a major departure in policy. But this did not extend to any fundamental shift in the models underpinning policy and practice. Many people included in these groups continued to be institutionalised, in subnormality and psychiatric hospitals and old people's homes. Furthermore, the dominant model underpinning policy and practice responses to them continued to be a medicalised individual one, which primarily framed them in terms of something being wrong with them. This was not called into question by the founders of the welfare state. But this is exactly what the emerging service user movements did, beginning with the disabled people's movement. It was not until these movements began to develop that this really happened. Significantly, the policy most directly linked with such groups, social care, was also the policy that underwent least change with the advent of the welfare state. Indeed in the case of social care, it is as if the Poor Law was never abolished or superseded. A direct link can be traced to the present system in England which is still means tested (Cozens, 2013).

Key to service users' questioning of medicalised individual interpretations of their experience has been the social model of disability developed by the disabled people's movement. The first expression of this was to be found in UPIAS's *Fundamental principles of disability* (UPIAS/Disability Alliance, 1976). This stated: 'In our view, it is society which disables physically impaired people. Disability is something imposed on top of our impairments, by the way we are unnecessarily isolated and excluded from full participation in society' (p 3).

The individual model of disability saw the problem as lying in the disabled person; this social model, elaborated by Mike Oliver and others, drew a distinction between:

- impairment or perceived impairment: the absence or lack of functioning of a person's limb or sense; and
- disability: the negative societal response to people seen as having such impairments, reflected in the negative and discriminatory attitudes, barriers and exclusions that they face.

As Mike Oliver has said, this: 'thus turned the understanding of disability completely on its head by arguing that it was not impairment that was the main cause of the social exclusion of disabled people but the way society responded to people with impairments' (Oliver and Barnes, 2012, 43). 'In the broadest sense, [disability] is about nothing more complicated than a clear focus on the economic, environmental and cultural barriers encountered by people who are viewed by others as having some form of impairment – whether physical, mental or intellectual' (Oliver, 2004, 21).

The social model of disability 'breaks the causal link between impairment and disability. The reality of impairment is not denied but it is not the cause of disabled people's economic and social disadvantage' (Oliver and Barnes, 2012, 22).

There has long been interest in the social relations of issues such as disability and 'mental illness', reflected, for example, in a concern to explore social factors associated with their incidence. This has been a focus of disciplines such as social psychiatry as well as an interest of related progressive professionals. Mental health service users, particularly, have sought to challenge mainstream preoccupations with individual pathology to consider the part that material conditions and social structures may play in the development of distress and psychological trauma (Ramon and Williams, 2005; Tew, 2011).

The social model of disability, however, goes much further than this because it challenges traditional categories and conceptions of disability and sees disability as a particular form of social oppression (UPIAS/Disability Alliance, 1976). Interest in such a social model of understanding has extended to other service user groups, from mental health service users and people with learning difficulties to people with alcohol and drug problems and people living with dementia (MHF, 2015). Disabled people sometimes talk of encountering the 'social model' as a 'light bulb moment' in their lives. It enables them to think afresh about themselves and their lives. Instead of having to feel guilty or inadequate as a result of their impairment or their need for additional support, it transforms their understanding of their relationship with society, giving them new confidence and sense of equality (Campbell and Oliver, 1996). Vic Finkelstein stressed that 'disability' should be understood and addressed as a social (that is, comprehensive) and not as a personal (that is, individual) phenomenon (Finkelstein, 2009, 146). Since then debate about the social model has developed and extended, engaged with new issues and been the subject of much controversy and challenge. The relationship between impairment and disability and the disabling effects of impairment have come under scrutiny (Thomas, 2007). Its impact, however, has continued to be transformative, at both an individual and policy level, nationally and internationally.

Being rights-based

Historically, social policy has largely framed welfare service users in terms of their 'needs'. This is perhaps hardly surprising. Whatever the response envisaged, whether sympathetic or hostile, through Poor Laws and welfare states internationally, they have tended to be seen as a problem in need of solution. And the problem has essentially been framed in terms of their individual deficits, even where these might be recognised as having social origins. This has been the case whether the problem has been seen as madness, homelessness, disability, poverty, older age, parenting, childcare or disease. What has also generally been true is that these needs have been conceptualised and constructed by individuals and organisations who do not share their experience. Thus, much social policy has been based on the prescriptions of one group for another and this has frequently meant the imposition of ideas from above. For a long time this reflected the actions of more powerful over less powerful people. In the twentieth century, with modern social policy, it reflected the emergence of professional groups, charged with the role of categorising people according to *their* definitions of their 'needs'.

This has been a theme of discussions and writings from both the modern welfare service user movements and the earliest expressions of such groups first-hand accounts and collective action. They have challenged 'needs-based' discussions, even when these have sought to be or were presented as progressive, rejecting them as ineffectual and diversionary (Doyal and Gough, 1991; Oliver, 1996). What has distinguished the modern movements is a new emphasis on service users' *rights* to counter needs-based approaches to them. In countries such as the UK and the US, there developed both a rhetoric of 'fighting for our rights' and a framing of thinking and campaigning in terms of disabled people's rights and achieving them. This extended to both civil and human rights, individual and collective rights. All groups of service users began to talk of their restricted citizenship and called for change. In the UK the first major research project commissioned by the disabled people's movement and undertaken by a disabled researcher explored and evidenced the extent of discrimination that disabled people faced (Barnes, 1991a). As Oliver has written:

> Disabled people ... began to take to the streets when our concerns and wishes were either ignored or derided; notably in support of fully accessible public transport and against disabling media images ...These actions were singularly successful ... All this forced both government and disability charities to take notice ... So much so that, in 1995, after many false starts the Disability Discrimination Act became law. (Oliver, 2009, 137)

Oliver, Barnes, Finkelstein and other disabled activists, however, not only highlighted the weakness of the legislation – 'neither comprehensive nor enforceable'. They also cautioned that an isolated approach to a 'rights-based' approach to disability, particularly one which was narrowly legalistic and focused on parliamentary lobbying and the traditional political process, rather than grassroots collective action, was unlikely to be successful (Oliver, 1990; Barnes, 1991a; Finkelstein, 2009). So while the rhetoric of rights and a commitment to rights has been central among service user movements, its complexities and ambiguities have also been highlighted.

Independent living

The Poor Law, social policy and welfare, through their whole history, have been predicated on the idea that people should be able to 'stand on their own two feet' and manage on their own. If they aren't managing, then the key and recurring questions have been, is this because they can't, or they won't? Do they need or deserve help, or not? Because judgements have been based on such a distinction, where support has been seen as appropriate, it has tended to be strongly associated with dependence. The post-war welfare state recognised the role of structural factors in creating and perpetuating social evils/problems, such as unemployment and ill health. But by and large, it still conceived of disabled people and other long-term users of health and social services as dependent and defective.

This analysis has been fundamentally challenged by all service user movements. The issue was first and most clearly articulated by the disabled people's movement in their philosophy of 'independent living' which developed from the 1970s in the UK and the US. Instead of seeing service users as sick, defective or deviant, requiring professional intervention, it has highlighted their right to and need for self-respect, self-determination and equal opportunities. As the feminist disability commentator Jenny Morris has said, the philosophy of independent living rests on a number of key values or assumptions:

- All human life is of value.
- Anyone, whatever their impairment, is capable of exercising choice.
- People who are disabled by society's reaction to physical, intellectual and sensory impairment and to emotional distress have the right to assert control over their lives.
- Disabled people have the right to participate fully in society. (Morris, 1993, 21)

The philosophy of independent living in turn followed from the social model of disability. Independent living is enshrined in the UN

Convention on the Rights of Persons with Disabilities (UNCRPD). In this philosophy, disabled people internationally have turned traditional understandings of independence on their head. Instead of them taking them to mean people managing on their own, they have reinterpreted them to mean people having the support that they need to live their lives on as equal terms as possible with non-disabled people. Thus such support is not understood as being to compensate for disabled people's inability to do things for themselves, but as far as possible to *enable* them to do things for themselves, like having a job, a home of their own, be a parent, contribute to their communities and so on, like anybody else.

By framing support in these terms – to help equip people to live their lives on more equal terms with others – rather than of just 'looking after them', a very different understanding of what is needed and what this can make possible emerges. This 'shook up uncritical assumptions about independence, such as the idea that disabled people should aspire to physical independence or self-reliance'. It also challenged conventional ideas about 'caring' (Garabedian, 2014, 81). It meant that where disabled people and other service users were traditionally seen as needing to be 'cared for', institutionalised, or provided with an income, because they could not live 'independently', with the right kind of support they could live *independently*. Service users argued that with such personal and social support, they could live in their own home, gain skills, have families and relationships, be active citizens, take part in voluntary action and in many cases be in paid employment. This is seen to apply to all groups of service users, of working age and beyond.

While the philosophy of independent living has made some impact on policymakers, 'in a service-led and resources-poor system of social care' like that operating in the UK, independent living opportunities for much of the disabled population have so far been limited (Pearson, 2012, 240). As Townsley and others' research showed (2009), independent living across Europe was seen by governments as an unwelcome expense in a difficult economic climate and this was underlined by subsequent serious cuts in personal budgets in the Netherlands.

Living in the mainstream

Having suitable support, however, is only one of two key elements of the philosophy of independent living. The other is the removal of the barriers and restrictions which have prevented disabled people and other welfare service users from living in society on equal terms with other people. Historically, social policy has been more concerned with segregating and congregating such groups, reinforcing such barriers, rather than reducing and removing them. This applied to their accommodation, education, employment and sometimes even extended to separation of the sexes and restrictions on sexual relationships and reproduction. Given their experience of such separation and isolation, with the inferior life chances and opportunities that have tended to go with this, it is perhaps not surprising that disabled people have laid such an emphasis on challenging their exclusion.

Right from the beginning of the independent living movement, with the establishment of the first Centre for Independent Living in Berkeley, California, in 1972, the goals have been to facilitate the integration of disabled people into the community (Centre for Independent Living, 1982). Making it possible for disabled people to take on this role, as we have seen, was to be achieved by providing a comprehensive system of support services. But wider change was also needed in society if it was to be open to them so that they could maximise these opportunities for involvement. Thus the philosophy of independent living has always also meant transforming society, its institutions, amenities and services so that they were accessible to service users, regardless of their personal impairments or the difficulties that they faced.

Independent living stands in some contrast to two other philosophies which have developed outside of service users, which have both been presented as concerned with enabling their inclusion and integration in society. These are normalisation and recovery. Significantly both were developed by professionals rather than service users; both had their origins in the US and both have been seen by some as having progressive and liberatory potential.

Recovery

'Recovery' is an idea which has become central in UK mental health policy and practice in recent years and is influential internationally (British Psychological Society, 2015). It has been presented as a movement, as well as gaining the support of many mental health service users/survivors and their organisations. This is because of the idea's inherent ambiguity. As a concept, recovery 'is understood in myriad ways with no agreed-upon definition or framework for supporting people' (Morrow, 2013, 324). For mental health service users/survivors, the attraction of 'recovery' lies in it appearing to reject conventional ideas of writing them off as permanently damaged, pathologised or deviant. The official rhetoric associated with it is positive and appealing. Thus the Mental Health Commission of Canada (MHCC) has defined recovery as: 'a journey of healing that builds on individual, family, cultural and community strengths, and enables people living with mental health problems and illnesses to lead meaningful lives in the community, despite any limitations imposed by their condition' (MHHC, 2009, 8).

It is therefore perhaps not surprising that offered in such terms, while apparently originally a professional model imported from the United States, it has gained widespread service user interest and support. The emphasis on 'recovery' is presented as improving life chances, although service users highlight the need for better quality support from services and don't define recovery as professionals do (Gould, 2012). Service user definitions, however, do not carry the same authority and legitimacy as official ones. Ownership of the idea of recovery seems to lie with dominant policymakers, in individualised medicalised understandings and is also subject to over-arching neoliberal political ideology. As critical academics such as Marina Morrow have written, their conceptualisation of recovery:

> suffers from its individualistic framing as a personal journey, which has neglected a wider analysis of social and structural relations of power in mental health (eg, racism, sexism, homophobia and the power of psychiatry to define experience) that signal system discrimination, on people's experiences of mental distress and how these interact at an individual and social level. (Morrow, 2013, 325)

Recovery is essentially based on a medical model – 'getting better' (Harper and Speed, 2012). Thus unlike the idea of independent living, pioneered by disabled people, which takes account of disabled people's ongoing need for support, recovery suggests that it would be possible to withdraw support as people 'recover', ignoring the reality for many mental health service users/survivors that their need for help and support may be varied, continuing or recurring.

Such a model, however, is clearly likely to have an appeal as part of a neoliberal approach to policy, when spending on services is in decline and services face continuing cuts. The associated UK policy emphasis on 'reablement' has encouraged a notion of 'throughput' in services, with support withdrawn when people are regarded as sufficiently 'recovered' rather than its importance being recognised in maintaining their well-being. 'Recovery' has also been strongly linked with neoliberal policy commitments to get people into paid work. Thus seeking and securing employment has come to be seen as a key objective for and measure of 'recovery', however arbitrary the process of people having to find a job or the nature and quality of such employment.

Normalisation

'Normalisation' (which has also come to be called 'social role valorisation' (SRV)) has similarly been an influential and high profile approach to disability and support for disabled people. While it originated in Denmark in the late 1950s and spread to other Scandinavian countries, it has been particularly associated with the United States and Wolf Wolfensberger who popularised such ideas. In its first incarnation, it was concerned with offering people as 'normal' a life as possible (Emerson, 1992). At first glance it seems to have much in common with the aspirations of many disabled people and other service users to challenge their segregation and isolation. This is because of the emphasis it has placed on destigmatising people and them being able to live 'ordinary lives' and be part of the mainstream, no longer confined to segregating and professionalised services. Normalisation has been particularly focused on people with learning difficulties, although it has also been adopted in relation to other groups of disabled people and service users.

Wolfensberger's SRV emphasised the 'creation, support and defence of valued social roles for people who risk devaluation' (Wolfensberger, 1983, 234). Initially these ideas had cautioned against professional dominance in the lives of disabled people through the creation and perpetuation of 'human service industries' which fed off them. Later in its history, however, it was outside 'experts' who became central in proselytising normalisation and interpreting disabled people's socially valued roles and activities (Barnes et al, 1999, 73–4).

Critics from the disabled people's movement argue that normalisation is primarily concerned with integrating disabled people into existing society, rather than changing society so that they are no longer treated as different and defective (Oliver, 2009, 87–105). It fails to locate disabled people's experience within a political framework (Fulcher, 1996, 168). A major aim seems to be to secure higher status for them through their association with roles, people and activities that are conventionally valued. An example from the United States that I encountered, early on, which was seen as positive, was of a young man with learning difficulties who had joined a gun club. As the recovery model seems to be primarily concerned with isolated change in the individual, so has normalisation, where such change has extended from making changes in the behaviour even to the appearance of people with impairments (Oliver and Barnes, 2012, 91).

Conclusion

Historically, the dominant logic of most social policy internationally has been to prevent people in capitalist economies, who otherwise would, from becoming totally impoverished – and then either a threat or a risk. Groups such as disabled people and mental health service users/survivors have been seen to be inherently dependent and incapable. Thus the emphasis on income maintenance and maintenance services, which have frequently been inferior, stigmatising and segregating – and sometimes routinely abusive. With the international development of neoliberalism, this has been accompanied by new commitments to reduce public expenditure on social policy and a new emphasis on such groups' integration into the labour market, regardless of its effects or effectiveness. The service user movements have rejected such approaches to social policy and called for an end to such models based on individual deficit, deviance and inadequacy. They have demanded both a different process and different goals for social policy and this has been embodied in their own values and aims.

A series of values and principles underpin the welfare service user movements which emerged in the last quarter of the twentieth century. These can be seen to be the antithesis of traditional mainstream social policy of the political left, centre and right. They are embodied in neither neoliberalism nor Fabianism. Instead of the emphasis on outside 'experts', professionalisation and 'scientific objectivity' which has dominated modern mainstream social policy, these principles prioritise service users' own involvement, voices, rights and inclusion. Key to service users' shared understandings has been that they face oppression, discrimination and barriers in western and other societies and that these are generally reinforced rather than challenged by social policy. Instead they see themselves as the best *experts* in *their own* lives, identities and experience. All emphasise the importance of the 'lived experience' and 'experiential knowledge' of being a service user. All highlight that these have traditionally largely been excluded from social policy discussions and developments. In the next chapter we will examine such knowledge or knowledges more closely and their development through service user involvement in research and service user controlled research.

ELEVEN

Reconceiving research

The real challenge, therefore, for research in the twenty-first century is how to build an enterprise that exposes the real oppression and discrimination that people experience in their everyday lives without merely contributing to the classification and control of marginalized groups who seek nothing more than their full inclusion into the societies in which they live.
(Oliver, 2009, 118)

We do not see things as they are. We see things as we are.
(The Talmud)

Disability is a human rights issue requiring political action rather than a social problem requiring welfare provision.
(Oliver, 1992)

As research was key in the foundation of modern mainstream social policy, so it has been in the emergence of the welfare service user movements that have challenged traditional understandings of social policy. In the history of modern social policy, social research has been both a related and an inextricably intertwined activity. It is also closely associated with the development of the discipline of sociology. Social research, like social policy, was tied to twin commitments of being scientific and involving 'experts' as mediators of knowledge and experience. Modern social policy was developing around the same time as the new 'science' of sociology and began with many of the same preoccupations as it did. These ranged from the individualism, social Darwinism and 'survival of the fittest' thinking of theorists such as Herbert Spencer (Taylor, 2007), to the interest in eugenics and the categorisation of disabled people associated with thinkers such as Henry Goddard (Zenderland, 1998). A direct line can be traced from Spencer's laissez-faire thinking through Friedrich Hayek, Milton Friedman, Ronald Reagan and Margaret Thatcher, to current neoliberalism. We have seen how Fabians from the Webbs, Beveridge and Titmuss were also closely associated with eugenics, although this tends to be left out of or downplayed in modern discussions of them.

Social research has consistently occupied a central position in mainstream social policy, reflecting the latter's concern to be seen as scientific and based on measurement. As we have seen, there is a longstanding tradition of surveys and studies, particularly statistical studies, which have been offered as the evidence base and justification for social policy and shaped its and wider understandings of the world and the people with whom it is concerned. True to its origins, historically, social policy research was predominantly positivist in its approach, committed to a view of reporting a 'real' and objective world, rather than acknowledging its role in manufacturing the versions it offered and perpetuated.

Research is sometimes treated as a marginal activity, dismissed as an 'ivory tower' pursuit, whose products are largely left to gather dust on library shelves. This ignores and denies the significant role it plays in advancing and legitimating powerful institutions and dominant accounts. Significantly, research was one of the first major focuses of the emerging UK disabled people's movement. Again the initiative related generally to the services disabled people were receiving and, specifically, to the Leonard Cheshire Foundation.

Leonard Cheshire, disability research and the disabled people's movement

The Leonard Cheshire organisation played a special role in the development of disability research. It was in the context of their services that a major challenge to traditional approaches initially to disability research and then social research more generally, was first made. It was a challenge which came from disabled people themselves. Ironically this questioning of conventional approaches to disability research grew out of an attempt by disabled people to enlist the support of conventional research and researchers to improve the quality of their lives and the control they had over them. They turned to research in the hope that it would offer independent verification of the discrimination, exclusion and oppression that they experienced. Disabled people's questioning of disability research and their pioneering of new approaches to research can be traced to this incident. It is still identified as a watershed in the development of disability research (Mercer, 2002, 229).

In 1962, residents of Le Court, a Leonard Cheshire residential home, approached the Centre for Applied Social Research at the Tavistock Institute. As Paul Hunt, one of those involved, wrote:

> We were at the time struggling for representation on management to extend the range of control over our lives and prevent the reinstatement of infringements on our individual liberty as expressed in such freedoms as, to choose our own bedtimes, drink alcohol if we chose, freedom for the sexes to relate without interference, freedom to leave the building without having to notify the authorities, etc. (Hunt, 1981, 38)

The residents had in fact decided that if they could get academic 'experts' to conduct independent research into the institutions in which they lived, then the oppressive regimes and the institutional degradation and discrimination to which they felt they were subject, would be exposed. As Paul Hunt went on to say: 'We had thought naively that "experts" on "group dynamics" such as Miller and Gwynne [the researchers who became involved] would be likely to support (and promote elsewhere) our struggle to build a community life in which residents took a really active part and shared in decision-making' (Hunt, 1981, 38).

The research, the residents hoped, could then be used to give their voices added credibility, validity and worth, and thereby help them gain control over their lives. However, things did not go according to plan. Eric Miller and Geraldine Gwynne, the two researchers who undertook the study, wrote what has come to be regarded by the disabled people's movement as 'one of the most oppressive pieces of work ever published' – *A life apart* (Miller and Gwynne, 1972; Morris, 1993, 86). The study was supported by the then Ministry of Health and Paul Hunt emphasised that it was influential. It was included as a set book for the important Open University course, 'The handicapped person in the community' and widely used on training courses for social work and health students (Hunt, 1981, 38).

Miller and Gwynne rejected the residents' wish for more independence and autonomy as 'unrealistic' and went on to explain that the psychological problems of 'cripples' and 'incurables', far from being the result of disabling social arrangements and institutionalisation – the issues which residents wanted explored – were, rather, the inevitable result of being disabled. Furthermore: 'the problem of providing residential care for the physically handicapped and chronically sick are in many ways intractable and will remain so until and unless there is a pronounced change in the values of society, which makes the parasitism of some of its members more acceptable to all' (Miller and Gwynne, 1972, 15).

The residents of Le Court residential home and other service users who took part in the study felt betrayed. It was the conceptualisation of disabled people in this study as unproductive 'parasites' which led Hunt and subsequently other members of the disabled people's movement to conceive of researchers and social scientists as parasites themselves: 'The real parasites are those like Miller and Gwynne who grow fat by feeding on other people's miseries ... They come out with the blatant admission that they see the institutions issue as "socially important" and "technically interesting" and as promising "both a theoretical and practical pay-off"' (Hunt, 1981, 43).

Miller and Gwynne discussed at length their efforts to conduct 'balanced', 'detached' and 'scientific' research. Hunt, however, highlighted the study's bias, demonstrating that it was entrenched in an individualistic/medical perspective of disability, which understood 'the problem' to be the disabled person and their impairment. This was seen as the barrier to inclusion. More recent critics have supported this view: 'The aim of such research has been primarily to identify "the problems of the disabled" and to suggest interventions at the individual level designed to ameliorate or palliate these problems' (Drake, 1996, 161).

Hunt criticised the study's terms of reference as narrowly interpreted to mean 'to understand and try to tackle the problems of operating these [residential] institutions' for disabled people, rather than exploring them and their role more fully in their overall context, taking account of disabling barriers.

> There is no essential difference between Miller and Gwynne's behaviour in relation to segregated institutions for people with physical impairments and the behaviour of social scientists who advise, say, on concentration camps for a racial minority, and who do not see the necessity to help the inmates to struggle for their freedom, but just limit themselves to comparing one camp with another, telling the inmates it is unrealistic to think of escape, and making recommendations for training the authorities to run the camps more efficiently. (Hunt, 1981, 42)

It was, however, the allegiance of the researchers which was the most central issue of concern to Hunt and other disabled people (Hunt, 1972b). This issue is highlighted here because it has continued to be central and contentious in disability and service user research. The researchers seemed to see themselves as trapped between two irreconcilable interests (Miller and Gwynne, 1972). Paul Hunt later wrote:

> Long before publication of their research findings in *A life apart* in 1972, it was clear that we, the residents, had been conned. It was clear to us that Miller and Gwynne were definitely not on our side. They were not really on the side of the staff either. And they were not even much use to the management and administrators. They were in fact basically on their own side, that is, the side of supposedly 'detached', 'balanced', 'unbiased' social scientists, concerned above all with presenting themselves to the powers-that-be as indispensable in training 'practitioners' to manage the problem of disabled people in institutions. Thus the fundamental relationship between them and the residents was that of exploiters and exploited. (Hunt, 1981, 39)

For Hunt and fellow disabled residents there was no neutral position. Researchers had to decide on their allegiance and be clear about it.

> Faced with any socially oppressed group, social scientists have a choice of only two alternatives: either a firm commitment to serve the interests of the oppressed group and end their oppression, or a commitment to serve the interests of the oppressors to continue their oppressive practices (which last they also do by serving their own interests). There can be no middle way. (Hunt, 1981, 42)

Real world research?

Every academic in the UK quickly gets to know the rules of the game. They must publish in 'high quality' peer review journals. They must get 'grant capture'. This is academic research twenty-first century style. No matter if the number of journal readers can be counted on two hands, or there is little point to the research that gets funding. Of course this might not greatly affect the sum of human happiness if the field was early English literature or ancient archaeology, although that might be open to debate. But at least no deaths are likely to occur. But when it comes to subjects such as social policy, there are real life connections; real life and death issues may be involved – and the prevailing academic imperatives do little to help and may do much to harm. Perhaps it is understandable that many welfare service users, since the earliest days of the disabled people's movement have therefore been suspicious of research and the academics and institutions who undertake it.

The author

A new approach to research

This viewpoint effectively provided an early basis for the research manifesto of the UK disabled people's movement. It is a view which has been the subject of much heated debate and disagreement since. Whatever different opinions individuals may have about this position, it is one which continues to have importance in disability studies and research. More than 40 years after the Miller and Gwynne study, many disabled people and disabled researchers still judge disability studies in relation to it. The issue of purpose and allegiance in research cannot be ducked. While social policy research has long highlighted its rigour, reliability and impartiality, what Hunt and other disabled people were saying was that it was inherently biased by the models upon which it was based and because it reflected the prevailing interests of the service system rather than treating disabled people with equality.

As Oliver says, it is not only disabled people who have become alienated from both the process and product of research. This has also been true of other marginalised and oppressed groups, including, women, black people, poor people, LGBT people and people from the developing world (Oliver, 2009, 108). He sets out what he sees as the key limitations of conventional research:

> First, it has failed to accurately capture and reflect the experience of disability from the perspective of disabled people themselves. Second, it has failed to provide information that has been useful to the policy-making process and has contributed little to improving the material conditions under which disabled people live. Third, it has failed to acknowledge the struggles of disabled people themselves and to recognise that disability is not simply a medical or welfare issue, but a political one as well. (Oliver, 2009, 108)

The Miller and Gwynne episode prompted disabled people to develop and undertake their own research. Since then many other groups of welfare service users have also developed their own research, including mental health service users, people with learning difficulties, people with alcohol and drug problems, older people and so on (Beresford and Croft, 2012). This has come to be known as emancipatory disability research, survivor research and most commonly user-controlled research.

Crucially the new 'service users' research is concerned with changing the role and relations of research with research participants. This is reflected in a *changed role for research*:

- from extending professional knowledge, power and control to the liberation and emancipation of research participants. This is to be achieved through working for people's individual empowerment and broader social and political change;

and *changed research relations*:

- from inequality – dominant researcher and subordinate research 'subject', active researcher and passive research "subject", with minimal overlap – to the equalising of relations between the two, increased inclusion and involvement.

This means:

- professional non-user researchers researching *with* rather than *on* research participants; and
- service users as both dedicated researchers and involved in aspects of the research process which is under their control.

Disability researchers Emma Stone and Mark Priestley (1996) identified what they saw as six principles characterising the emancipatory or user-controlled research paradigm. These were:

- the adoption of a social model of disability as the ontological and epistemological basis for research production;
- the surrender of falsely-premised claims to objectivity through overt political commitment to the struggles of disabled people for self-emancipation;
- the willingness only to undertake research where it will be of some practical benefit to the self-empowerment of disabled people and/ or the removal of disabling barriers;
- the devolution of control over research production to ensure full accountability to disabled people and their organisations;

- the ability to give voice to the personal while endeavouring to collectivise the commonality of disabling experience and barriers; and
- the willingness to adopt a plurality of methods for data collection and analysis in response to the changing needs of disabled people. (See also Priestley, 1997.)

In 2005, the National Institute for Health Research's INVOLVE, a government advisory body on public patient and user involvement in health and related research, published the first detailed exploration of the definition and potential of user-controlled research (Turner and Beresford, 2005a). This study was based on both a survey of existing user-controlled research and feedback from service users with an interest in such research. INVOLVE's aim was not to impose a single definition of its own on user-controlled research, but to get a clearer idea of service users' thinking about its definition. This revealed considerable consensus among service users about how user-controlled research might be defined. The views of other stakeholders, like mainstream researchers, have not yet been sought in a coherent way. INVOLVE (2007, 23) subsequently offered its own short definition of user-controlled research, drawing on this study, which states that:

> User controlled research is research that is actively controlled, directed and managed by service users and their service user organisations. Service users decide on the issues and questions to be looked at, as well as the way the research is designed, planned and written up. The service users will run the research advisory or steering group and may also decide to carry out the research.

User controlled research is not so much associated with particular research methods as with using methods that are consistent with its overall values and principles (Barnes and Mercer, 1997). It has led to important innovations in both qualitative and quantitative research methods (Beresford and Croft, 2012, 21). This has included more participatory and user-controlled randomised controlled trials and systematic reviews (for example, Rose et al, 2003; 2005; 2008; 2009).

This closely connects with Oliver's view that 'the crucial issue in developing more useful and less alienating research is that of control' (Oliver, 2009, 114). Thus service user or user-controlled research is usually taken to mean research that is actively initiated, controlled, directed and managed by service users and their organisations, exploring subjects and questions that concern them. Such research is not characterised by or tied to qualitative or quantitative research or particular research methods. However it does have implications for research methods and employs these in ways which are consistent with its participatory, democratising, liberatory and egalitarian goals.

Now a wide range of service user groups and movements are undertaking their own user-controlled research. As well as people with physical and sensory impairments, this includes people with learning difficulties, older people, mental health service users, young people and people with drug and alcohol problems. While this development has not been equally spread among all welfare service user groups and is more developed among some than others, it is now recognised as a mainstream research approach (Beresford and Croft, 2012, 17, 22–4).

A wide range of benefits are associated with user-controlled research. These include:

- the use of service user researchers, who have credibility with and gain the trust of other service users;
- supporting service users to gain new confidence, skills and experience;
- prioritising service users' own concerns and agendas instead of just supporting those of state and service systems, because service users are more likely to ask the research questions that service users see as important;
- a social perspective-based approach to research which takes account of the wider context of service users' lives and does not just see them narrowly in terms of personal deficit and pathology; and
- a particular capacity to achieve change, both because it is a priority of this research approach and because the central involvement of service users and their organisations means that there is a constituency committed to using the research findings to bring about change (Beresford and Croft, 2012, 25–9).

Research suggests that user-controlled research can have a significant and positive impact on research, participating service users, services and national policy (Cotterell et al, 2011).

From 'experts' to experiential knowledge

It is the development of service user research that has brought the issue of user or experiential knowledge to prominence and highlighted the role and significance of experiential knowledge. But this, in turn, needs to be considered in the broader context of 'user' or 'public and patient' involvement in politics, public policy and practice. There has been increasing interest in and emphasis on such involvement internationally in policy and politics. This has been developed in many areas, including professional education and practice, policymaking, management, service planning, research and evaluation. Different competing ideologies, models and understandings of user involvement have developed within the framework of this terminology. While these have taken many forms, at least one key distinction can be drawn. This is between:

- the consumerist/market-inspired involvement that has grown in significance since the shift to the political right in countries such as the UK, that took place from the 1980s; and
- the emergence of service user movements, starting with the disabled people's movement in the 1970s, with their interest in involvement to increase their say and control and to democratise policy and services. (Beresford, 2002)

There have been different, if overlapping, strands of interest in such user involvement, with the former advanced by the state and service system and the latter by service users, their organisations and their supporters (Campbell and Oliver, 1996; Beresford and Campbell, 2004; Campbell, 2009; Beresford, 2012).

This has also been reflected in the emergence of interest in user involvement in knowledge development and exchange. This has mainly focused on user involvement in research, although knowledge development extends beyond this, of course, having both individual and collective expressions. What distinguishes discussion about user involvement in the context of research and knowledge production is that it is ultimately concerned with knowledge that draws on direct or 'lived' experience. It is, as we have seen, concerned with experiential knowledge or knowledges.

Going to the childminder

Do you like Suzie and Danny the child minders?

Yes

Do you play?

Yes, cards.

Have you got friends there?

Yes, Lewis, Rayonne, Bella, Tayum.

Elsie Beresford Coyte
Granddaughter, aged nearly two

If broader state and research interest has been in user involvement in research, among welfare service user movements, as we have seen, the concern has been with user-*controlled* research. This has provided the basis for developing and sharing welfare service users' own knowledges. The key quality that distinguishes service user knowledges from all others involved in the field of welfare and social policy is that they are *experiential*. As Borkman (1976, 446) has put it: 'Experiential knowledge is truth learned from personal experience with a phenomenon rather than truth acquired by discursive reasoning, observation or reflection on information provided by others.' Thus, service users 'know' from their direct experience. Their knowledge has been described in different ways: as experiential or direct knowledge; as lived experience; and as from 'experts by experience'. Cotterell and Morris (2012, 58) highlight two important elements of experiential knowledge: first, that 'it arises from personal participation in the phenomenon and incorporates a reflective stance on this experience'; and, second, that the individual holds belief and trust in this knowledge 'based on their experience of the phenomenon in question'. This highlights the importance of people being able to think through their direct experience outside the constraints of prevailing ideas, rather than having to fit it into them and using it to inform and formulate their own ideas, models and theories.

Service users' knowledge alone is defined by and primarily based on direct experience of disability, distress, learning difficulties and so on, and associated policy and provision from the receiving end. It grows out of their personal and collective experience of policy, practice and services. This is not to deny the existence or validity of 'practitioner' or 'carer' knowledge(s) or the fact that they are based on direct experience. However, they are based on direct experience of being a practitioner or carer, not of experiencing distress or disability, as are service user knowledges. Service user knowledges are not based solely on an intellectual, analytical, occupational or political concern.

Traditionally, however, as we have seen, social policy practice and research have been dominated by 'expert' knowledge, whether framed as scientific, professional, academic, research or disciplinary knowledge. Academics from a range of disciplines (for example, psychiatry, psychology, education, sociology, social policy, history), as well as numerous different professional groups (for example, psychiatrists, psychologists, psychiatric nurses, social workers, criminologists, lawyers), have laid claim to specialist knowledge resulting from academic research or 'practice' in the area of disability, poverty, 'mental health' and so on.

Service users have historically been excluded from the knowledge-production processes of social policy and its service system. Knowledge about them has been produced by people generally without their experiences, or at least who do not identify as having them, or of having a history of using such services. Such 'knowledge' has been underpinned by and has highlighted individual 'deficit', 'deviance' and 'pathology', and has been used for many years to justify the segregation and institutionalisation of mental health service users. The dominant epistemology has worked to prohibit service users from being producers or knowers of their own knowledges. Social policy knowledge has been based on the 'knowledge claims' of others about the experience of service users. They have played the key role in interpreting service users' experience, while the latter's own interpretations have, as has been argued, been excluded or devalued.

Barriers in the way of service user research and knowledge

Service user knowledges have become both more visible and more influential. Yet, at the same time, they remain contested and contentious and continue to be marginalised. They face practical, ideological, professional and methodological barriers. It is these barriers that we turn to next. Service user organisations and service user researchers consistently report that they have inferior access to research funding, face problems of credibility and are seen as having less legitimacy (Faulkner, 2010; Beresford and Croft, 2012). However, most of these difficulties seem to relate to the methodological challenges that face user-controlled research. Powerful hierarchies for the production of knowledge and evidence still operate in research. These continue to privilege quantitative research methods such as randomised controlled trials (RCTS) and systematic reviews as 'gold standards' for investigation, despite their demonstrated limitations, and put less weight on qualitative research approaches (Cohen et al, 2004; Glasby and Beresford, 2006). While all forms of user involvement research come in for some measure of methodological questioning, user-controlled research has been the subject of particular challenge (Rose, 2009; Sweeney et al, 2009). This is perhaps not surprising, given the challenge it has itself represented to traditional positivist research approaches and assumptions. Oliver has criticised mainstream research for being, 'based on methodological individualism underpinned by an investigatory foundationalism'. Ultimately explanation is sought in individuals rather than social forces or structural features (2009, 112–13).

As Oliver (2009) argued in his critique of Hammersley's (2000) defence of 'objective social research' or 'foundationalism': 'Almost all social research continues to proceed on the foundational assumption that there is a real world out there ... independent of our conceptions of it ... and that by using appropriate methods we can investigate it and hence produce worthwhile and workable knowledge about it' (Oliver, 2009, 113).

Thus user-controlled research can both expect and has already frequently experienced, challenges as biased and lacking in rigour. Its apparent links with a democratic approach to participation highlight its ideological relations. As we have seen, it advocates are honest that it is primarily a political activity, aiming to improve people's lives, rather than a neutral 'fact-finding mission' to produce 'data' or evidence for library shelves (Beresford, 2009). It is concerned with making positive change, rather than solely with generating knowledge. As a result, fundamental questions are raised about the relation of user-controlled research to traditional positivist research values of 'objectivity', 'neutrality' and distance, even though user-controlled research, like other new paradigm research has made its own challenge to these (Hammersley, 2000; Sweeney et al, 2009; Rose, 2009; Beresford, 2003a; 2007). Findings from such research can expect to be questioned as partial and partisan. Questions are raised about the problems which user-controlled research may pose because one sectional interest is seen to be dominant – that of service users. It is challenged in relation to criteria of 'validity' and 'reliability'. Questions are raised about who is a 'service user' and the 'representativeness' of service users involved. All these create major barriers in the way of user-controlled research securing equal recognition and resources alongside other more traditional research approaches, both quantitative and qualitative (Beresford and Croft, 2012, 30–2).

The discriminatory effects of exclusion

The emphasis on 'being scientific' and 'objective' in traditional social policy and social research – and inherent in a positivist model – highlights the need for and possibility of research which is 'neutral', 'unbiased' and 'distanced' from its subject. The unbiased value-free position of the researcher is seen as a central tenet of such research. By claiming to eliminate the subjectivity of the researcher, the credibility of the research and its findings are ostensibly maximised. Such research, the argument goes, is rigorous and reliable and can be replicated in similar situations and always offer the same results. Research which does not follow these rules and which is not based on this value set has long been seen as inferior, with less valid and reliable results. This, however, really devalues first-hand or 'experiential' knowledge, yet we know that in ordinarily life, we place a particular value on such knowledge. Thus the importance attached to 'first-hand' and 'eye witness' accounts. User involvement in research and user-controlled research, of course, place a value on such experiential knowledge and giving it value in the process and findings of such research is one of their defining features. However, service users' knowledge flies in the face of traditional positivist research values, which grant it less value, credibility and legitimacy. Often, as we have seen, in social policy, it has been ignored or marginalised. Meanwhile the knowledge claims of researchers without such direct experience are seen to be stronger (Beresford, 2003b).

What this means, however, is that if an individual has direct, lived experience of problems such as disability or poverty, or of oppression and discrimination, when such research values are accepted, what they say – their accounts and narratives – will be seen as having less legitimacy and authority. Because they will be seen as 'close to the problem', they cannot claim they are 'neutral', 'objective' or 'distant' from it. So, in addition to any discrimination and oppression they already experience, they are likely to be seen as a less reliable and a less valid source of knowledge. By this logic, if someone has experience of discrimination and oppression, they can expect routinely to face further discrimination and be further marginalised by being seen as having less credibility and being a less reliable source of knowledge. This further invalidates people who are already heavily disadvantaged. Thus such research can play a key part in the subordination and 'othering' of people. This has unfortunately been a role historically played by much social policy research, where problems only come to be seen as 'real' when they are reported by researchers and other 'experts'. Then it is their interpretations and versions of issues and phenomena which are accepted. This issue of marginalising the knowledge of different groups, has been explored by the philosopher Miranda Fricker in her discussion of 'epistemic injustice', where someone is wronged specifically in their capacity as a 'knower' (Fricker, 2007). The Canadian researcher Maria Liegghio has talked of 'epistemic violence', defining it as: 'a very denial of a person's legitimacy as a knower – their knowledge and their ways of knowing – that renders that person out of existence, unable to be heard and to have their interest count' (Liegghio, 2013, 124).

It may, therefore, perhaps be time, to rethink assumptions about credibility and legitimacy in research. One assumption, which may particularly need to be re-examined is this: 'the *greater* the distance there is between direct experience and its interpretation, the more reliable it is'.

It is perhaps time instead to explore the evidence and the theoretical framework for testing out whether: 'the *shorter* the distance there is between direct experience and its interpretation (as for example can be offered by user involvement in research and particularly user-controlled research), then the less distorted, inaccurate and damaging resulting knowledge is likely to be' (Beresford, 2003b, 22).

A new basis for social policy knowledge

While research is not the only source of knowledge, it is an important and valuable one, especially given the weight conventionally attached to it. The approach to research developed by the disabled people's and other service user movements offers the prospect of a different knowledge base for social policy, a different more inclusive policy process and transformed understanding of bringing about change and the role that research may play in that.

The traditional 'social administrative' model has been based on belief in a cycle of self-defined experts

- defining, measuring and interpreting 'the problem'
- carrying out research
- as a basis for making change.

The lesson from history is that such an approach neither reflects the reality, nor works. Its underpinning premise that 'something should be done' – and therefore will be – is misplaced. We saw this made explicit earlier in the discussion contained in the report *Fundamental principles of disability* (UPIAS/Disability Alliance, 1976). The policy process is presented as a scientific one, when it is actually a political one. Instead of the 'neutrality' that is suggested, there has actually long been a complex process susceptible to the biases and preconceptions of researchers and research funders, as well as the preoccupations of policymakers, politicians and the service system. It was this hidden train of bias that the disabled people of Le Court first highlighted and rejected.

User-controlled research, on the other hand, makes possible a collective process of developing knowledge or knowledges which centrally includes rather than excludes the perspectives of people on the receiving end of policy:

- enabling service users to reconceive themselves and their situation
- including their identification and interpretation of issues that concern them
- making possible their engagement in a process of change, providing a vehicle for achieving this.

Mike Oliver and others have called for a research which is concerned not with investigation, but with *production*. As he puts it:

> We do not investigate something out there, we do not merely deconstruct and reconstruct discourses about our world. Research as production requires us to engage with the world, not distance ourselves from it…Thus the research is not an attempt to change the world through the process of investigation but an attempt to change the world by producing ourselves and others in differing ways from those we have produced before. (Oliver, 2009, 116)

Service user research, accountable to and controlled by service users and their organisations, offers a way of achieving this. Some service users have described user-controlled research as a form of collective self-advocacy. It offers them the chance to develop their own narratives, framed in terms of their own experience, understandings, models and theories. It helps make it possible for us all to see ourselves and the world we live in differently, as a basis for making change in both. This is a process of production, not just of inquiry. The disabled people's and service user movements stress the importance of democratising the production of knowledge and challenging exclusions and 'epistemic injustice' (Barnes and Mercer, 1997; Fricker, 2007).

Such a changed and inclusive epistemology can also provide the basis for a changed approach to social policy, one which builds on the removal of barriers and inequalities between researchers and researched, 'knowers' and 'known', challenging traditional divisions between social policy, its makers and the people whose lives it affects. This epistemology is now beginning to have an impact on social policy discourse. People are not only undertaking research on worlds and circumstances of which they have direct experience, but they are articulating this and developing theory around it (McKenzie, 2015b; O'Hara, 2014b).

Conclusion

While it may not have been intended, the exclusion of welfare service users from social policy research and the marginalisation of their views from its knowledge base, have perpetuated a paternalistic and controlling approach to social policy. This has been true of both Fabian and neoliberal social policies. The development of their own research by welfare service users, beginning with the disabled people's movement, has made it possible for service users to extend and share their experiential knowledge and make it a basis for collective action. This challenges both the processes and the assumptions of traditional social policy, as well as making it possible to develop a different user-led approach to policy. The traditional 'expert' based model of social policy knowledge formation has 'othered' service users. It is only when the 'experts', as researchers, academics, researchers, social and political commentators 'authenticate' service users' experience through adding their 'authority' that it is given credence. This diminishes service users and their knowledge.

We have seen this recently with the radical and harsh welfare 'reforms' of the Coalition government that was in power between 2010 and 2015. This threat certainly did not abate with the subsequent election of a Conservative government committed to swingeing cuts in welfare. Disabled people and other service users' rapidly warned of the destructive, sometimes life-threatening consequences the Coalition's reforms were having. However, concern only mounted slowly as conventional experts eventually added their support to this view. What service users themselves said was not seen as sufficient to influence those in power. However, user-controlled research produced by user-led organisations, such as the Spartacus group, began to challenge this tradition, gaining a high profile for service users' own knowledge and findings. Underpinning the traditional inequalities and exclusions of social policy are epistemological inequalities and exclusions. Welfare service users and their organisations have increasingly highlighted and sought to challenge these with their own user-controlled research. They highlight its importance as part of the spectrum of knowledge production, as well as for the knowledge it produces in its own right. It would be a mistake though, to assume that the battle between 'expert' and experiential knowledge is over, or that the latter is now securely established. Politicians, policy institutions and the rest of us have put our trust in 'expert knowledge' too long for our deference to it to disappear quickly. However user-controlled research is likely to have a key part to play in producing a different kind of social policy. In the next chapter we go on to look at this.

1. Baby Timothy, from the 1945 documentary *A Diary For Timothy* by Humphrey Jennings, hoping for something better after the Second World War (see pp 5 and 365)

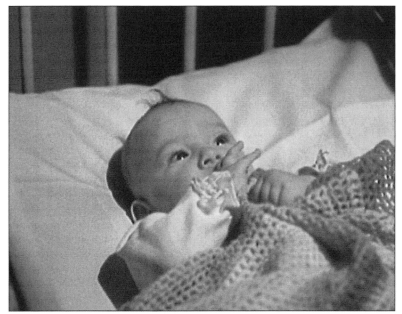

2. Goronwy, the Welsh coalminer in *A Diary For Timothy:* 'One afternoon, I was sitting thinking about the past, the last war, the unemployed, broken homes, scattered families and then, I thought, has all this really got to happen again?' (see p 9)

3. Headlining the twenty-first-century attack on the welfare state (see p 13)

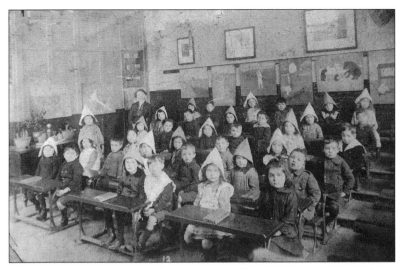

4. My mother's class at the East End Jewish School she went to (Ida, front row, second from right) (see p 38)

5. The author at Wix's Lane Primary School, Battersea, class photo mid-1950s (indicated by arrow) (see pp 101 and 362)

6. The author and partner Suzy Croft as young activists in front of the famous Southend mural by Brian Barnes in which they feature (see p vii). (See also https://www.youtube.com/watch?v=ASpA3Mb1Hrg)

7. My maternal grandparents together as a newly married couple. Check out who sits and who stands (see p 363)

8. Granddad Barnet in uniform, recruited as a conscript to the Imperial Russian Army around the end of the nineteenth century before fleeing to England as a refugee from pogroms (see p 363)

9. The real Downton Abbey: my grandmother, Baroness Decies (seated, second from right), with friends and family, at home in a world of inequality, over-privilege and entitlement (see p 363)

10. Catherine Decies, my paternal grandmother, studio portrait in her baronial robes for the state opening of Parliament in 1903 (see pp 36, 41)

11. 'Mr Sidney Webb on his Birthday', cartoon by Max Beerbohm. 'Here Webb, a kneeling adult-child, unpacks his new box of toy figurines and lines them up in parade-ground fashion...Webb is lining them up in pairs, and with outstretched arm each policeman is ordering about or arresting the citizen next in line' (Gibbons, undated, 15) (see p 152)

12. Springfield Psychiatric Hospital, Tooting, opened as the Surrey County Lunatic Asylum in 1841. At its peak in 1950 it held more than 2,150 patients. I was a patient in Willow Ward, my alma mater as a service user (see p 114)

13. My mother as a young girl (one of Beatrice Webb's 'furtive eyed, full-figured Jewish girls with their pallid faces and crouching forms') (see p 150)

14. My mother as a young woman working in the East End sweatshops, wearing the kind of hat she made as a milliner (see p 150)

15. My father (in the middle) at the same time in his life, having fun playing polo with friends (see p 55)

16. John and Joan Croft's (my parents-in-law) wedding, June 1946 (see p 82)

17. Able Seaman Leslie Norris RN, my partner's uncle, killed in action 1944. Hoping desperately to see the next harvest at home, he didn't live to see the better world he was fighting for (see p 68)

18. Leslie Norris's final resting place in Alexandria (see p 355)

19. Baby Isobel aged 11 months, 2015. 'Are you going to make the world a different place – you and the other babies?' (see p 365)

Photograph credits

1. Courtesy of BFI (British Film Institute) National Archive
2. Courtesy of BFI (British Film Institute) National Archive
3. © Peter Beresford
4. © Peter Beresford
5. © Peter Beresford
6. © Peter Beresford
7. © Peter Beresford
8. © Peter Beresford
9. © Peter Beresford
10. © Victoria and Albert Museum, London
11. © Ashmolean Museum, University of Oxford and the Estate of Max Beerbohm
12. © Peter Beresford
13. © Peter Beresford
14. © Peter Beresford
15. © Peter Beresford
16. © Peter Beresford
17. © Peter Beresford
18. © Peter Beresford
19. © Peter Beresford

TWELVE

A new approach to social policy

What can people be usefully employed upon once the current product line disappears?

(Phil Asquith, Shop Steward, Lucas Aerospace Alternative Plan, 1978)

We saw a libertarian future for social work coming from 'community control'. We argued that this needed to include the control and involvement of 'service users, workers and local people'. We thought it was important that all three overlapping constituencies should be included, rather than any one's inclusion being at the expense of the others.

(Beresford and Croft, 2004, 54)

Whether a product is regarded as profitable or not really depends on the value that a government or society puts upon it. For example it is regarded as profitable to make Harriers [military jet aircraft], but not profitable to make kidney machines. Now it's the same customer, the government, so it just depends on what price the government's put on it and does one expect a school or a hospital to be profitable.

(Mike Cooley, Trade Union Leader, Lucas Aerospace Alternative Plan, 1976)

By the mid-1970s, the UK's increasing economic difficulties and the failure of successive governments to grow and develop the welfare state meant that its principles were weakened and its practice diluted. Thus by the time Mrs Thatcher came to power, the welfare state that existed was no longer the welfare state that had been envisaged or implemented after the war. This may have made Mrs Thatcher's task easier, harnessing populist feelings of dissatisfaction with the welfare state, but her goal was undoubtedly to destroy it, whatever its specifics.

The mid-1970s, however, could equally have been a time for welfare state *renewal* – as happened in some other European countries – seeking to advance it in line with emerging political and cultural ideas, changed demographic and cultural pressures, social and other developments that had taken place since its inception. While this largely did not happen in the UK, there were strong radical forces seeking to make such progressive change. These were often forces operating internationally. This time, unlike the period post-war, there were also strong progressive interests in both diversity and participation – the key components lacking in the post-war welfare state. These times also saw, as we have noted, the emergence of new social movements, including the welfare service user movements. Other grassroots developments were also taking place. All of these offer insights into and examples of other directions that welfare state reform might have taken and how such change might have been achieved.

There were also important new, leftist developments in academic social policy in the 1970s. The proponents of the post-war welfare state left the issue of the democratisation of the state unaddressed and unresolved. This is probably because of their implicit belief in its progressive role as an agent of change. However, post-war commentators coming from socialist and Marxist perspectives were concerned with both the regressive and progressive role of the state; its capacity to control as well as liberate and support. Thus discussions from that of John Saville in 1957 (Saville, 1957) to Ian Gough in 1979 (Gough, 1979) were concerned with exploring the relationship of state and the welfare state to the achievement of socialism. They sought to critique the complexity of these relationships, not just seeing the welfare state as an agent of repression and also trying to explore progressive ways forward for the welfare state. There was a growing sense from the political left that the welfare state had lost its reforming edge and its roles and relationships were increasingly ambiguous and regressive and needed to be reconceived (Hill, 2012).

An extensive Marxist critical literature on the welfare state developed in the 1970s. This sought to challenge dominant social policy narratives. It was associated with the political new left and built on the work of figures such as Gramsci, Adorno and Althusser, the journal *New Left Review*, and groupings such as the International Socialists (subsequently Socialist Workers Party) and International Marxist Group. From the late 1970s, a burgeoning Marxist or critical social policy discourse developed. This was embodied in both activism and high profile literature.

Thus there were new academic series such as Routledge and Kegan Paul's 'Radical social policy' and Macmillan's 'Crisis points' series. There were critical texts on education and schooling, pensions policy and social security, health and housing and most of all ideology, citizens and the state (for example, George and Wilding, 1976; Willis, 1977;

Corrigan, 1979; Darke and Darke, 1979; Ginsburg, 1979; Widgery, 1979; Simpkin, 1979; Shragge, 1984; Taylor-Gooby, 1981; 1985). This development was also linked with the establishment of the discipline of 'cultural studies' and the inspiration of Stuart Hall as director of Centre for Contemporary Cultural studies at Birmingham University. A renewed interest in 'deviance' and social control and the development of the 'new criminology' was associated with both new radical critiques and methodology (for example, Cohen, 1972; Taylor et al, 1973; Rock and MacIntosh, 1974). New journals were established, such as *Critical Social Policy*, which was run as a collective, seeking to connect theory and practice, academic work and activism, traditional leftist politics and the new social movements. The late 1970s and early 1980s also saw the first flowering of a related 'radical social work' movement. As well giving rise to a new and influential social work literature (for example, Bailey and Brake, 1975; Corrigan and Leonard, 1978), it led to the establishment of *Case Con* in 1970, 'a revolutionary mag for social workers', supporting squatters and trying to prevent children being put into care (www.socialworkfuture.org).

Since the 1970s, however, the UK has experienced a range of increasingly neoliberal politics that more and more seem to be taking public policy and, indeed life, for many people, in uncharted and unsustainable directions. The period of Blair and Brown particularly emerges as a time of lost opportunity and of failure for social policy. While in 1997 the electorate showed its desire for real change, a new brand of costly market-driven policy and deregulation was introduced – the 'third way' – which reinforced Thatcherism. Not only did it prop up the inefficiencies of the market and low wage employment, through costly privatisation, tax credits and benefits policies, subsidising private employers. The latter, ironically, flew in the face of nineteenth-century liberalism, which abolished the Speenhamland system of topping up low wages with outdoor relief. It also framed welfare in mechanistic terms of sticks and carrots, casting people as inherently selfish and dishonest rather than potentially altruistic and mutually supportive.

Yet throughout this period from the 1970s onwards, there is another history. Strong counter discourses also developed and were maintained. While these have constantly been threatened by attempts to destroy, subvert and co-opt them, they have survived to encourage values and initiatives committed to equality, engagement and inclusion, at odds with the prevailing neoliberal ideology. Just as in retrospect we can see that those who later worked to derail the welfare state were already present at its inception, trying to ensure that it was still-born, so now we can also see the emergence of a range of innovations and developments opposed to modern neoliberalism which represent a serious and on-going challenge to it. They not only offer an alternative to its ideas of 'welfare reform' and the basis for a modern reinterpretation of the welfare state's founding principles. They also provide pre-figurative examples of what a new welfare society might look like and be capable of achieving. So far we have largely only looked at the role of welfare service user movements in challenging traditional approaches to social policy and beyond. In this chapter we will also be looking at a range of other developments over the period and their wider implications for change.

The initiatives detailed here are diverse and for some readers, grouping them together may seem idiosyncratic, although many inter-relations can actually be identified between them. Some of them may seem less obvious and familiar candidates for consideration than others. They are not offered as a definitive list. Each of us may have our own to offer. What is important is that through all the period which has seen the hardening of neoliberal economics, ideology and politics, such counter-developments have emerged and in some cases flowered. This is not a phenomenon restricted to the UK. It is a truly international development, taking different forms in different settings. All these developments offer insights for broader public policy and social policy specifically. As well as examining them individually, we will also explore some of the common themes that emerge from them. We begin with three developments that all relate to transport. The first is rooted in the economic decline associated with the 1970s; the second two, with changes in transport and political and ideological attitudes towards it. All relate to social, cultural, economic and ideological change and development.

Economic decline, the British motorcycle industry and revitalisation

The decline of the British motorcycle industry has come to be seen as a vanguard case study of broader UK economic decline. It was a world leader for decades, with famous names such as Norton, BSA, Vincent, Triumph, Velocette, AJS and Matchless. It was a race winning industry and highly successful in international markets particularly the USA. At the same time, it was long featherbedded by Britain's 'empire' market and the limited choice open to the domestic market, by the lack of strong overseas opposition and because many working-class people simply couldn't afford a car. This changed with the arrival of the 'Mini', innovative Japanese competition and marketing and the 'wind of change' that blew over Britain's empire. With a lack of investment, a leadership that showed less and less understanding of its product and markets, the industry turned out essentially the same machines, relying on short-term profitability. Meanwhile the Japanese, developing new standards of engineering, sophistication, reliability, innovation and economy, were producing a wide range of machines from mopeds to super bikes (Boston Consulting Group, 1975; Hopwood, 1981; Koerner, 2013).

After the initial success of the 1945 Labour government, the post-war trend was one of economic decline. 'Britain fell further and further behind … as controls were abandoned in the fifties (under Conservative governments)… But the fifties saw Britain decline faster than ever compared to Japan and Germany. Ignoring the siren call of free trade, the defeated nations achieved economic miracles' (MACE, 2012).

The advent of Thatcherism reinforced this trend. Between 1979 and 1981, 1.6 million jobs were lost in the UK. Birmingham alone (where many motorbikes had been produced) lost a third of its manufacturing jobs between 1979 and 1983. Britain's share of world trade in manufactured goods declined from 25 per cent in 1950 to around 7 per cent in 1985 (MACE, 2012). By 2020, the UK share of world trade from all sources, it is estimated, will have fallen to 2.3 per cent. (Ashcroft, 2012, 5). The shift from manufacturing to financial and other services created an over-reliance on inadequately regulated banks and financial industries culminated in the economic meltdown of 2008 and subsequent draconian cuts in public spending and welfare services.

Meriden and Triumph

The motorcycle industry, however, has more to tell us than about Britain's economic and manufacturing decline. It also offers two major insights into alternatives that might be possible. The first of these was the Meriden Co-operative. With the run-down of the British motorcycle industry, workers at Triumph's Meriden plant, which had been threatened with closure, staged a two-year work-in and then set up independently as the Meriden Motorcycle Co-operative with support from a new Labour government, particularly from the then Minister for Trade and Industry, left-winger Tony Benn (Winter, 2014). They stayed in business even after the collapse of the only remaining large manufacturer NVT (Norton Villiers Triumph) in 1977 and managed to keep going until 1983, the venture lasting overall nearly ten years, despite their insecure finance, obsolescent models and heavy Japanese competition. They were also able to design the first new Triumph engine for 20 years, link with a valued local polytechnic design department, get new overseas orders and with worker directors, work in different non-hierarchical ways which placed a value on people's expertise, experience and commitment.

As members of the Co-op said at the time:

> I believe in the Triumph, we are going to make Triumph the best bike in the world again.

> We are trying to achieve a lot, and with the attitude here, we will achieve.

> The first time we get into the black is the first time we've proved our point, not just to ourselves, but to the outside world. (BBC TV, 1983)

Over the years, the Co-op's numbers fell from 750 to 200 members. They learned the need for financial and management expertise, as well as technical skill and enthusiasm. They worked flexibly and sometimes without pay. They encountered all the difficulties of self-management and cooperative running when cash strapped in an economic and political context antagonistic to such values and ventures. The Meriden Co-op grew out of conflict and difficulty and certainly experienced both, so it is important not to sentimentalise it. But it also offered encouragement to workers much more widely that there was an alternative to traditional employment structures and contemporary anti-labour attitudes and was an exemplar of something different. The sit-in and formation of the cooperative were the subject of much media interest, including David Edgar's 1976 play, *Events following the Closure of a Motorcycle Factory*. It managed to develop its products through adversity and gave hundreds of workers experiences of worker participation that they would never otherwise have had, albeit often under dire circumstances (BBC TV, 1983; Wilson, 1991; Rosamund, 2009).

The Co-op also kept a flame alive that helped make possible the second significant development for manufacturing and the economy that has come out of the UK motorcycle industry (Beresford, 2014). This truly was a case of the phoenix emerging from the ashes, with the rebirth of Triumph motorcycles in 1991. An English property developer and builder, John Bloor, with no personal interest in motorcycling, bought the Triumph factory site and the company rights. Triumph now outsells its Japanese competitors, has a wide range of models, both modern and retro. It is now also selling more motorcycles than the old Triumph did in its heyday, with factories in England, Thailand, India and Brazil. Significantly this came from the vision and determination of one man, who was able to avoid turning to the stock market for finance. In 2013 Triumph employed 1,600 workers and sold more than 52,000 motorcycles, with a revenue of more than £1/3 billion. Eighty-five per cent of sales were overseas (Griffin, 2013). While Triumph's models have been based on a successful modular and incremental approach, one possible weakness is that they have not followed the route that was originally successful for the British industry and later the Japanese, of including in their range small and entry level bikes that widened the customer base and built customer loyalty, but even that gap now seems to be being filled by Triumph. They have demonstrated the economic viability of returning to sophisticated UK manufacture, created high quality employment, and challenged strongly entrenched conventional wisdoms.

Organising around enthusiasms

Academics Paul Hoggett and Jeff Bishop coined this term – organising around enthusiasms – in relation to freely given activity which took the form of work while remaining leisure rather than employment and where people might indulge their passions collectively by participating in groups (Hoggett and Bishop, 1986). Here we consider two such examples, heritage steam railways and the canal system.

Heritage railways

Two major changes in UK rail transport policy took place in the 1960s. These were the ending of steam on the railways and the Beeching cuts which resulted in the closure of many railway lines and major reductions in local rail services. This followed from an increasing commitment to private road transport, a desire for railways to be economically self-sufficient and a narrow search for economy, which no longer accepted the need for subsidy or for rail transport to be seen as a social service. In the event it became clear by the end of the 1960s that such a strategy would still not take the rail system out of deficit. However, it also had another unforeseen consequence. It led to the mushrooming of a heritage rail network in the UK (which has equivalents in other countries). While there had been forerunners for such recreational steam trains since the 1950s and even before, this really took off from the 1970s, resulting in the creation of a widespread network of heritage railways.

Heritage railways are now estimated to be worth £250 million to the UK economy, according to a 2013 report by the All Party Parliamentary Group on Heritage Rail. There are now over 100 heritage railways and tramways, which attract tourists and provide local employment as well as valuable skills training. In 2011 they had 10.3 million visitors and 7.1 million passengers. Forty-five years after the end of steam on British Rail, over 750 steam locomotives are operating on heritage railways. A total of 520 steam charter trains – more than one a day – ran on the national rail network in 2012 in addition to the heritage lines. As well as being an economic generator in their own right, these railways also serve as such for their local communities attracting visitors and income. It is estimated that for every £1 that is spent on the railway, a mean average figure of £2.71 is added to the local economy (APPGHR, 2013).

Thus these railways support tourism, local economies and in some cases offer day-to-day transport, providing alternatives to crowded roads in the holiday season. The Parliamentary Group concluded that apart from the economic benefits, heritage railways also provide employment for over 3,700 staff nationally and a productive outlet for 18,500 loyal volunteers. They also offer skills training for younger people and gains for the well-being of older people involved as volunteers and helpers. The heritage railways offer apprenticeships, maintaining skills in engineering to overhaul and maintain engines and rolling stock (APPGHR, 2013). Starting in 2008 with the creation of *Tornado*, an A1 Pacific like those that ran post-war on the East Coast Main Line, they have even begun to build new steam engines. Nor can heritage railways be dismissed as just a haven for men and 'nerds'. Now there are generations of children who will never have known steam in day-to-day travel, who come to wave flags for it and indeed in turn bring their children to do the same. The APPGHR report also observed that:

> A gradual change has also been noted from a male dominated activity in the 1980s to a broader base of voluntary support involving women and indeed whole families today. Not only do they allow more to be achieved, but also actively involve a younger group of volunteers which have rejuvenated and refreshed the declining number of ageing male volunteers who were the pioneers. (APPGHR, 2013, 30)

Ironically as the UK's railway system has declined in efficiency, raised fares and relied on increased state subsidies since its privatisation in the 1990s, the heritage railways have flourished (Murray, 2002; Wolmar, 2005).

The canal system

The UK canal system provides our second example. After the Second World War the British canal system, which had expanded and flourished in the eighteenth and early nineteenth century, was dying. By the 1950s the network was basically defunct with many canals silted up and effectively closed. Work traffic had almost ended. However, this was turned round by activists such as Tony Rolt, a key figure who had written an influential book about canal travel in 1944, which led to the establishment of a voluntary organisation to campaign for greater use of the canals (Rolt, 1944; 1950). This movement met with strong opposition from the authorities when it sought to reopen, restore and reuse the canals. Activists organised 'moor-ins', including a famous one at Stourbridge where direct action was taken, illicitly excavating the silted up canal, so that boats could come together and gain public support. Supporters also organised then and still do to clean up canals and make them usable again. Barbara Castle, the then Minister of Transport, passed the 1968 Transport Act, which supported canals and the canal system which the Treasury had wanted to close (although she and the Labour government went back on their commitments to halt the Beeching railway closures). Initially campaigners sought to renew both work and recreational traffic on the canals and recreational traffic has abounded. Thanks to their efforts there are now large working canals and a comprehensive and developing network of cruising canals.

There are now *more* narrow boats than there were in nineteenth century, with more than 20,000 people living on canals and 200,000 having their holidays there (Parker, 2011). There is even some renewal of working traffic. While there are tensions between the voluntarist origins of the modern canal movement and government ideological commitments to privatisation, which extend to the canal system and its management, like heritage railways, it continues to be a significant economic and cultural force in modern UK society. It has generated new industries building and maintaining boats and the canals themselves, as well as having positive environmental effects (Squires, 2008).

Diversity and involvement

Both the post-war welfare state and its successors have come in for particular criticism for their perceived failure to address two issues to which increasing importance has been attached. These issues, which appear inter-related – are diversity and participation. Thus, the welfare state has repeatedly been presented by its critics as paternalistic and monolithic, reinforcing social divisions, through treating everyone the same. The suggestion, particularly from the neoliberal right, has been that these issues demarcate the essential failings and inherent limitations of the welfare state. Here, though, we will consider the emergence and development of these two issues and the welfare state's response to them. This may draw us to a different conclusion: that the welfare state actually has a particular potential to address participation and diversity, although this has constantly been mediated by efforts to undermine or cut back the welfare state.

Diversity

The post-war welfare state, as we saw earlier, showed little recognition of the need to address diversity, in the sense of embracing difference and treating it with equality. Instead it generally reinforced existing social divisions, particularly in relation to gender and sexuality. It was only in relation to class and disability that this seemed to be different. Concern with class followed from the government's socialist commitments; with disability, in recognition of the many people war-disabled. However, government disability policy was still characterised by disabled people's segregation and marginalisation and, as we have seen, working-class people, by and large, had little involvement in the implementation of welfare state reforms, even though many benefited from them.

Meanwhile the views and experience of the many people and groups who continued to face discrimination and inferior treatment relating to their ethnicity, gender, sexuality, culture, faith, age or impairment, remained unacknowledged. They were denied full and equal citizenship, both within the UK generally and specifically within its welfare state. Ideas of equality were still far from inclusive and a vision of social justice based on inclusive equality only came with the struggles of the last quarter of the twentieth century (Witcher, 2013). It was only with the emergence of new social movements from the 1970s, that their experience and the issue of diversity began to be placed on political and policy agendas. This arose with the articulation of the collective demands of these groups – to speak for themselves, to define their own roles and identities and to challenge those imposed upon them by others, and, to secure their empowerment (Jordan and Lent, 1999; Lent, 2002; Annetts et al, 2009). While these movements began to influence social policy practice, it was not until 1989, for example, that the first major text which addressed the issue of diversity in social policy, was published, Fiona Williams' *Social policy: A critical introduction* (1989). However, it did not even consider, let alone address, the issue of disability discrimination. This reflected a broader tendency to create hierarchies of difference, placing different values on its different expressions.

This has increasingly been challenged as more complex and inclusive understandings of identity and difference have developed. This came particularly with the emergence of ideas of 'intersectionality'. Intersectionality, the study of intersections between forms or systems of oppression or discrimination, which originated in black feminist discussions, highlights that we are made up of multiple identities and can't regard or treat these in isolation (Crenshaw, 1991). Instead we need to recognise the interactions that take place between them, since these are frequently mutually reinforcing. Feminist sociologists, such as Imogen Tyler, discuss the stigmatising effect of people being classified by others and the importance of rethinking such categorisation and the importance of people being able to define themselves. She argues that class analysis should be intersectional and not narrowly based on paid work or people's economic position (Tyler, 2013).

The new social movements represented a fundamental challenge to conventional thinking, politics, policy and ideology. This included challenging the traditional positivism of (Fabian) social policy, with its emphasis on 'scientific' evidence, objectivity and analysis dominated by a narrow range of white, male, middle-class, non-disabled 'experts'. The development of the movements was reflected in the increasing visibility of other first-hand perspectives in both the analysis and formulation of social policy. This had an increasing impact on the welfare state.

This was reflected in the challenging of the Beveridgean 'male breadwinner' model of welfare and the introduction of anti-discrimination, equalities and 'family-friendly' legislation, policies and practice. Just as leftists and trade unionists offered blueprints for how a more progressive welfare state might look from the 1970s, so the new social movements began to exert an influence on welfare state policy and practice. Issues such as rape, domestic violence and child sexual abuse, began to gain public profile as social problems, with the beginnings of social policy responses. The gay liberation and emerging

LGBT (lesbian, gay, bisexual and transgender) movement developed their own support and information services, attacked the medicalisation of homosexuality and fought for equal rights in parenting, fostering and adoption. Queer studies and within them, queer theory, offer an analytic viewpoint with much wider implications for making sense of identity and sexuality in relation to social policy (Marcus, 2005). They also seem to be encouraging links with other areas of study and movements, for example, disability studies (Goodley, 2013). We have already seen that the emergence of welfare service user movements resulted in pressure for equal rights for older and disabled people.

Inequalities on the basis of ethnicity began to be highlighted as structural issues, instead of only being problematised in relation to individuals. Feminist approaches and research, as Kath Woodward observes, questioned 'the basis of universal categories such as citizenship and equality and of naturalistic concepts such as the family and in deconstructing these conceptualisations, reveal[ed] their gendered nature' (Woodward, 2006, 86). There has been increasing recognition that there are many different forms of family and family models and different models of parenting. This is the daily experience of more and more children brought up in them (Williams, 2014). With the racialisation of British post-war politics, first assimilationist/integrationist perspectives dominated, then multicultural approaches became popular and, in the 1980s, anti-racist perspectives emerged. However, as Laura Penketh has commented, 'All three perspectives continue to have varying degrees of influence in contemporary society and should not be "chronologically compartmentalized"' (Penketh, 2006, 104).

The setting up of the Commission for Racial Equality 1977 and the passing of the Race Relations Act in 1976 represented political recognition of the need to challenge discrimination on the grounds of nationality, race, colour, ethnic or national origins. We can also see the impact on social policy, for example, with Labour Minister Barbara Castle's introduction in the 1970s of the Equal Pay Act, the Invalid Care Allowance for single women and others who gave up their jobs to care for disabled relatives; of non-contributory invalidity pension for disabled people who had not qualified for invalidity pension; and reforms in child allowances.

We should, however, be careful to avoid over-estimating the improvements that have taken place. Social policy in relation to 'race' continues to be dominated by a preoccupation with control, with racism still identified as institutionalised in the police service and health and welfare systems (Fryer, 1984; Cohen et al, 2002). Mental health policy has long offered an appalling case study of such discrimination, with black and minority ethnic service users less likely to access valued support and more likely to come within psychiatry's custodial provisions (O'Hara, 2014a). In practice, the prevailing political and policy process has been remarkably resistant to the advancement of diversity and equality. This is not, however, necessarily due to any inherent incompatibility between valuing diversity and the welfare state. Efforts have been undermined by the waning influence of left-of-centre ideas and the increasing impact of neoliberal thinking. Since the late 1970s, there has been increasing pressure to reform and restructure the welfare state in line with neoliberal aims. This has discouraged the prioritising of equality and diversity issues and actually tells us more about inherent antagonisms between equality issues and the market than between them and the welfare state. The development of 'anti-discriminatory' and 'anti-oppressive' practice in social work (ADP and AOP) offers a case study. While the thinking underpinning such anti-oppressive practice has had its own limitations (sometimes being embedded in the discrimination it seeks to challenge – see, for example, Wilson and Beresford, 2000), it represented a serious attempt to address diversity in policy and practice. However, it helped result in social work coming under sustained attack from the political right for being 'politically correct' and 'over-concerned' with the structural relations of disadvantage and inequality (Butler and Drakeford, 2001; Narey, 2014).

Involvement

In the previous chapter we discussed the centrality of the concepts of involvement and participation to the emerging service user movements of the last quarter of the twentieth century, particularly in relation to user involvement in research and knowledge production. However, these concepts also went through a wider process of intellectual and practical development through this period. There was major interest in them across policy areas and across academic disciplines. If the founding 'fathers' of the welfare state and its main policy areas showed little interest in or sensitivity to people's involvement, it was not long before this came in for serious challenge. There was a new emphasis in public policy on 'public participation' and 'community involvement' – in local planning, community work, social work and social action. The 1968 Seebohm Report which laid the basis for the creation of social services department highlighted the need for local and service user involvement (Seebohm, 1968). By 1971 a new Town and Country

Planning Act introduced legal requirements for public participation in land use planning in line with the proposals of the 1969 Skeffington Report and initial provisions in a 1968 Act (Skeffington, 1969; Damer and Hague, 1971).

These were the first statutory requirements for involvement, to be followed over the years by others in other policy areas, from transport and education, to housing. New professions and activities emerged which placed a new emphasis on engagement and participation. These were mostly prefaced by the warm-sounding word 'community', such as community architecture, community social work, community newspaper, press, space, theatre, enterprise and venture. Certainly the developing welfare state did not seem be inherently opposed to the advancement of involvement. At the same time ironically, one area where there was a particular emphasis on it, poverty and disadvantage, through neighbourhood and regeneration policy, was also one where enduring Fabian traditions still impeded it. Thus anti-poverty campaigning and policy continued to be areas where such traditional exclusionary professional 'expert'-based approaches tended to operate and prevail (Beresford et al, 1999).

Workplace developments

Lastly we look at some ideas and initiatives that were primarily linked with the workplace. These were essentially ideas that were initiated by people as workers and trade unionists, although this is not to say that their attention was restricted to people in these roles. There was often also an interest in citizen and service user democracy, as well as workplace democracy and a sense that these were inter-related and indivisible.

In and against the state

This is true of our first example. *In and against the state* was an influential publication that caught a mood of its time. It was initially an illustrated pamphlet and then a paperback (London Edinburgh Weekend Return Group, 1980). The group of self-defined 'socialist economists' who wrote it, called themselves the London Edinburgh Weekend Return Group, because of the regular journeys they made to work together. The publication reflected a commitment of the time for process which reflected aims and philosophy. Thus the pamphlet was financed and produced collectively and distributed by a co-operative, the Publications

Distribution Co-op (PDC), although to reach a wider audience, the book was published by an independent leftist but commercial publisher.

Unlike the founders of the welfare state, the authors saw the state as inherently problematic, while seeing the market as even more destructive. Thus they were concerned to confront the state's role in relation to capitalism, believing that it could be repressive and was not necessarily benign. They raised the question of what the role of workers in the welfare state should be in such circumstances; how it could be progressive and avoid colluding with regressive aspects of the state. In the book they acknowledged that their focus had tended to be limited to professional state workers and that there might be different issues for manual and low paid workers, while asserting that their arguments were relevant to all workers. 'It is essential to find ways of working for change from within our jobs and our private lives; ways of developing effective, organised oppositional action which comes directly out of the everyday oppression we experience' (http://libcom.org/library/acknowledgements-preface-second-edition).

Arguing for 'a socialist vision in opposition to the capitalist state', they identified a number of strategies for state workers to build 'oppositional opportunities'. All can be seen to be concerned with workers reconceiving issues on their own, rather than the state's or other people's terms. This included:

- *challenging 'individualisation'* – by strengthening collective and class identities through doing things together
- *rejecting misleading categories* – imposed upon us and building workers' own understandings of themselves and others and developing links and alliances
- *defining our problem our way* – as a basis for change, rather than accepting the analyses imposed upon us
- *stepping outside the brief* – to see and respond to the whole problem
- *refusing official procedure* – working in more open, honest and equal ways with service users and other local people
- *rejecting managerial priorities* – stepping outside conventional hierarchical and management structures to achieve results
- *alternative forms of opposition* – for example work-ins and occupations rather than traditional strikes and working to rule (http://libcom.org/library/chapter-6-oppositional-possibilities).

As the authors observed, these principles built largely on shared understanding and empathy with service users and other local people, taking sides with them and providing them with practical help and support. They offered existing examples to support their arguments. Radical social work, which as we saw earlier in the chapter, emerged in the mid-1970s, provides a well-developed case study of such an approach and values. Its proponents sought to support service users and other local people against the disempowerment and impoverishment which they associated with the state and market (Bailey and Brake, 1975).

Lucas Aerospace

In the mid-1970s when Lucas Aerospace, a major manufacturer of military aircraft and missiles planned to close factories and lay off a fifth of its workforce, a shop stewards combined committee, representing the 13 trade unions involved, developed an 'alternative plan' for 'socially useful and environmentally desirable production'. Published in 1976, the plan gained high visibility and generated international interest and enthusiasm (Wainwright and Elliott, 1981). It was subtitled 'a positive alternative to recession and redundancy' and was based on ideas submitted by company workers. This was a real case of 'beating swords into ploughshares', with proposals for socially useful and sustainable products to manufacture in the fields of energy, medicine, transport and oceanics. The plan was not only concerned with different kinds of end products, but also with producing them in a socially desirable way. So it was also committed to 'democratic alternatives in relation to the organisation of production process' (Wainwright and Bowman, 2009). It became a rallying cry for alternative economic planning and strategies; its message communicated widely. However, the response of trade unions more generally was muted and both Lucas Aerospace and the Labour government rejected the plan and it effectively came to nothing (BBC TV, 1978; http://libcom.org/history/articles/lucas-aerospace-fight). Lucas Aerospace rejected the alternative plan's proposals as unrepresentative, unrealistic and inappropriate. In the short term Lucas Aerospace closed and demolished factories and shed thousands of jobs. While the company was dismissive of the viability and values of the plan, by August 1996, Lucas had merged with the American Varity Corporation to form LucasVarity plc, whose divisions were subsequently sold to US based companies

It is important not to overstate the significance of the alternative plan. Myths grew around it and it can be difficult to separate the reality from the hopes that came to be associated with it. However, the visionary ideas it embraced chime increasingly strongly with modern concerns about the environment and the need for a viable manufacturing base and a sustainable economy. It offers the prospect of something different to current neoliberal economics which promise more wealth to a few and the crudest kind of 'growth'. This means that its message continues to resonate with the passage of time and is reflected in proposals of the modern UK Green party (Karpf, 2012). Its focus on production to meet need rather than increasing consumption, also highlights the important if often overlooked influence of the peace and environmental movements over this period (Cahill, 1994; 2002).

Collaborative working

A key development over this period was experimentation and innovation with collaborative and cooperative working. Now, when the 'new public management' associated with neoliberalism, has increasingly become the dominant and default model of management in the public and third, as well as in the private, sector, this search for and possibility of alternatives has tended to be forgotten. Yet the problems associated with the imposition of such managerialist approaches in the public sector have increasingly been highlighted, with its undue emphasis on hierarchical control, as well as its increased bureaucracy, inefficiency and often damaging preoccupation with mechanistic organisational 'targets', rather than the well-being of its workers and end users (Locke and Spender, 2011; Simmons et al, 2009).

The late 1960s and 1970s were a time when new kinds of community and voluntary organisations began to flower, which were very different to the large Victorian charities that preceded them and which were frequently linked into the aims and values of the new social movements, influenced by leftist, feminist, LGBT and anti-racist ideals. They often had a particular commitment to be organised and work in more equal ways. There was also an impetus to create new forms of more participatory and equal governance, as traditional industries and companies began to hit the buffers in times of economic change and international recession. This resulted in experimentation with cooperative and collective working. Most visible were the big new co-ops which received government support (of which Meriden was a conspicuous example). However, three major industrial cooperatives established by the Labour government (*Scottish Daily Press*, Kirby Engineering and Triumph) all failed. The lesson learned from this seems to have been that such schemes were utopian and unworkable. In reality, they seem to have been the victims of underfunding, inexperience (both of policymakers and workforce) and having to start with failure, rather than building success. Add to this the distrust of and unease with such democratising ventures among most industrialists and politicians, and there's a clear recipe for failure (Hird, 1981). At the same time, in retrospect, it is difficult to quantify the learning gained from these ventures; the positive and longer-term outcomes for those actively involved in them, following from the new skills and understandings they gained.

Additional insights can be gained from a rare close-up exploration of a pioneering scheme for collective working in the field of social welfare. This is Alan Stanton's participatory research study following how workers in a local social services agency, Newcastle Family Service Units (which grew out of the wartime Pacifist Service Units), became a cooperative (Starkey, 2000). It shows how the aim and practice of self-management grew within the organisation's conventional hierarchy as a result of the commitment of a majority of the workers. It concluded that empowering workers was integral to an agency empowering its service users (Stanton, 1989a). Stanton makes clear that working in this different way was feasible, effective and valued by most workers. At the same time, he highlighted the big shift it demanded – with workers taking responsibility not only for the work they did, but also for running the organisation in which they worked – a big departure for most of us. Such a radical shift clearly benefits from workers themselves wanting to take this step and being supported to gain the skills and confidence to carry it through. Stanton made a further point, which highlighted additional pressures and problems then facing more collective ways of working.

> [A]pplying the experience of such [collective and collaborative] teams has been hindered by their characterisation in the 1970s as prefigurative future socialist forms. As a result, they have often been judged, less by their achievements, than against an idealised model of direct democracy. Their development in the 80s suggests a different picture. Successful collective working cannot solve, but can balance the tensions inherent in workplace democracy and in the process, offer valuable experience of the practical problems in defining and building citizenship in other forums. (Stanton, 1989b, 56)

There are many different forms of cooperative and different arrangements for their support in different countries. They include for example workers and housing cooperatives, farmers or agricultural cooperatives and credit unions. They are perhaps less unusual, even in the UK, than is generally realised. We know that they have a long history. They also have a lot more to tell us about partnership and collaborative working than more often cited, but much less democratic examples of 'employee owned businesses', like John Lewis, the chain of department stores (Cathcart, 2013). This has recently been touted as a significant model for the public sector to learn from, without apparent recognition that while its focus is upmarket, the public sector also has to take account of disadvantaged and disempowered people, frequently lacking the cash premium to pay for more expensive goods.

Beyond the fragments

While many of the ideas discussed above were associated with left of centre thinking or related to the political left, there were others that were explicitly left and socialist. Perhaps one of the most significant of these was *Beyond the fragments*, because it connected both traditional socialist concerns and the new politics of emerging social movements (Goodwin, 1980). What began as a massive national conference, drawing 1,500–2,000 people and became a book, continues to have a presence and exert an influence over both leftist politics and feminism (Cockburn, 2013; Robson, 2013; Rowbotham et al, 1979 [2013]). It sought to draw together democratic socialist and socialist feminist strands in thought and campaigning. It was concerned to critique the 'male-dominated Leninist left', unite 'the social power of the community with the industrial power of those in production, and pitch this popular power against the existing state'.

As feminists, the authors sought to challenge how revolutionary socialists organised, making the connections between the personal and the political, foregrounding personal relationships and questions of social reproduction. First written just before the advent of Thatcherism, a new edition was written 34 years later, at the height of the coalition government's neoliberal politics and social policy. It was still concerned with 'the fraught question of how to consolidate diverse upsurges of rebellion into effective, open democratic left coalitions'. What seems significant though is that such left discussions still seem separated and compartmentalised from both the struggles and the discussions of people particularly badly affected by coalition policies, such as disabled people, mental health service users, black and minority ethnic groups, homeless people and others living in poverty.

Real alternatives

All the developments discussed in this chapter either pointed to the possibility of, or developed changed relationships and structures, roles and identities for people and between people and the state. Some were directly concerned with the welfare state, others had clear implications for it. While some of these initiatives did not get past the design stage, such as the Lucas Aerospace Alternative Plan, others such as radical social work's anti-oppressive practice, or heritage railways, have become a routine part of mainstream life, touching all our lives. These initiatives have many interconnections. Interestingly Tony Benn, one of the few politicians who has come to be respected regardless of party, was almost a motif running through many of the progressive developments of the time, from Triumph motorcycles, to the Lucas Aerospace Alternative Plan, fostering new ideas and seeking to ensure them financial support. Some of the contemporary rhetoric was distant from the reality as it could be experienced on the ground (for example, Wainwright, 2000, contrasted with Beresford and Croft, 1982). In other cases, it was strongly rooted in it, particularly in the case of some welfare state professional practice and service users' day-to-day lives.

While political and ideological debates over the last 20 years have largely been restricted to the competing merits and demerits of state and market, these developments pioneered new and different approaches. This included combining voluntarism and private enterprise; paid and unpaid work (heritage railways); connecting central state and municipal socialism with community action (in services such as law centres and community work). All were concerned to encourage broad-based grassroots and worker engagement, more and less successfully. They invented new relationships between service users and providers based on increased equality and overlaps between the two. They challenged exchange relationships and conventional divisions of labour while valuing people's different skills and experience. They pointed to more equal ways of working and sustainable approaches to manufacture for socially useful and peace-based goals.

The 1970s Community Development Project, for instance, the largest UK action-research project funded by government, highlighted differences between community-based approaches to disadvantage which incorporated people and expected them to provide their own self-help solutions and models which emphasised the structural relations of disadvantage and the importance of popular struggle and political change to combat these (CDP, 1977; Loney, 1983). The latter sought to support individual, family and community agency against structural constraints, with community workers expected to 'bite the hand that fed them', by siding with local people, despite being paid by the state. Such developments offered new approaches to the division of labour and management, advancing ideas of self-management and non-hierarchical working.

Local authorities, such as the Greater London Council (GLC) under Ken Livingstone and the People's Republic of South Yorkshire (Sheffield) under David Blunkett in the 1980s, exhibited the same kind of radical municipal socialism as George Lansbury's 'Poplarism' in the 1920s. They pursued radical social policies, reducing the cost of public transport and becoming 'nuclear free zones'. This time, however, their campaigns were closely associated with the aims and values of the new social movements, including the peace, anti-nuclear, environmental, women's, gay liberation and black civil rights movements. The GLC, for example, included two of the authors of *Beyond the fragments* in key roles, one leading its 'Popular Planning Unit', which was set up to involve local workers and residents in public policy. Similarly, while the 1984–85 national miners' strike was primarily concerned with defending one of the most traditional, male-dominated industries, it generated wide support and new alliances with the social movements, as well as active roles for the many women involved, changing many lives (Sherwood, 2014; Warchus, 2014).

All this, however, can feel now like echoes from a very distant age. The big cooperatives founded in the 1970s and 1980s are now largely long gone. Most traditional 'mutuals' – home loan building societies – have either been privatised or lost their way. We have seen the co-operative movement put at unprecedented risk by the Cooperative Bank substituting free market values for socially responsible ones (Treanor, 2014). Yet this socially committed legacy lives on, with, for example:

- *social enterprises* – businesses that trade for a social or environmental purpose, whose profits are reinvested to help them do so;
- *social firms* – market-led enterprises set up specifically to create good quality jobs for people disadvantaged in the labour market (Grove et al, 1997);
- *micro employers* – service users receiving state support in the form of a 'direct payment' who employ 'personal assistants'.

Today's disabled people's and 'service user led organisations' (DPULOs and ULOs) are perhaps the latest embodiment of such principles of self-help and mutual aid. Sadly, we are also seeing neoliberal governments seeking to subvert these ideas, for example, in social services, encouraging social enterprises to undermine local authority services and reduce working conditions for staff.

There is thus an unbroken history of innovation and creativity, directly and indirectly influencing the UK's and indeed other welfare states, highlighting their potential to address diversity and enable enhanced involvement, as well as securing people's rights and needs and advancing more inclusive ideas of social citizenship. Hilary Wainwright's and Andy Bowman's observation about the Lucas Aerospace Alternative Plan could perhaps be applied more generally to many of the initiatives identified here – as the:

> classic product of the co-operative, egalitarian creativity of the late 1960s and 1970s: challenging authority and seeking individual realisation, but through a social movement… and all the more potent as a result. It came up against trade union, government and management institutions stuck in the command and control mentalities of the 1950s, and the power of the movement was destroyed by Thatcher's onslaught against the unions and radical local government in the 1980s. (Wainwright and Bowman, 2009)

Interestingly those developments that were rooted in groups of enthusiasts and the new social movements, seem to have been more successful than those more closely associated with the labour movement and the political left.

Wainwright and Bowman offer a rider, which also has wider application, commenting on such developments: 'It could be said that the creative spirit of the 1970s got separated from the social critique and organised movements in which it was initially embedded and was appropriated by the more sophisticated sections of corporate management.'

Over this period, there have been constant attempts to subvert these more liberatory impulses, as has just been touched on in relation to social enterprises. This has been a major feature of modern public policy generally and social policy specifically. It demands closer attention, otherwise we may find ourselves lost in a sea of ambiguity and rhetoric, rudderless without any star to guide us.

Liberatory rhetoric: reactionary policy

The political and ideological shift to the new right and neoliberalism that began in the mid-1970s created new complexities for social policy. While on the one hand it represented the desire to return to the pre-welfare state emphasis on the market, there was also a commitment to the rhetoric of consumer choice and involvement. We have already seen, in the last chapter, how this created confusions over one of the great policy themes of the last 30 years or so – public, patient and user involvement (PPI). While for welfare service user movements, this was primarily understood in terms of democratisation and empowerment, the managerialist consumerist model generally advanced by government was framed much more in terms of the service user as consumer and privatising and paying for services. Thus the emancipatory aspirations of people on the receiving end of welfare policy and services could be used against them. Public spending and support services were cut in the name of choice and independence as service users called for more of both. A shared language of choice, control and empowerment was used to conceal deep-seated political and policy differences. Opponents of the welfare state presented their demands in terms of overcoming its original limitations, while their underpinning ideological aim was to increase people's reliance on the market and reduce state expenditure on welfare and support for them.

Personal social services were a particular site of such developments, as we have already seen. From the mid-1970s, critics from the political right and centre argued against state services' 'institutionalising' provision, 'paternalistic' professionals and top-heavy 'bureaucracy'. Advocates of normalisation called for people to have 'circles of support' and 'citizen advocates' rather than relying on paid professionals, but while paid support jobs were cut, the infrastructure to make such alternatives widely available was never resourced. 'Red-tape' became commonly used code for attacks on state services. Instead policymakers formalised ideas of localism and 'informal' or unpaid caring, encouraging increased reliance on it. The resulting 'caring' responsibility fell particularly on women, further inhibiting their equal rights, as well as undermining the independence of older and disabled people. Pioneering developments such as 'patch-based' and community social work were increasingly tied to anti-state agendas, despite their initial innovative intentions. Instead of social services enabling people to have more say and control, they increasingly placed more responsibility on people to look after themselves (Hadley and McGrath, 1981; Beresford and Croft, 1986).

This was strongly reinforced by the community care reforms of the early 1990s. These confirmed the residual role of adult social care. While the talk was of consultation and choice, the reality was of massively increased privatisation and the imposition of charges for an increasing proportion of service users. Most recently, the direct payments developed by the disabled people's movement to enable them to live on as equal terms as possible with non-disabled people have been restructured as 'personal budgets', tied to inadequate and reducing funding and disassociated from the values of the social model of disability and the philosophy of independent living (Slasberg et al, 2013; Slasberg and Beresford, 2015). Social workers were made redundant in the name of ensuring greater choice and control and, instead, untrained staff, working to scripts, recruited to call centres; day centres were closed as segregating and stigmatising; and increasing numbers of service users were left to spend their days at home without alternatives.

Over this same period, benefits policy, perhaps the most complex and most difficult area of social policy to understand and enact, has gone through at least three phases of major change from the founding principles of the welfare state. All have been associated with an increasing political reliance on means-tested rather than universalist benefits. Under Mrs Thatcher's regime, this was mainly associated with cuts in the level of benefits and the association of increasing stigma with receiving them. Ironically, to hide the massive loss of jobs, particularly in the North and other regions through changed economic policies, numbers on sickness benefits were encouraged to increase. Under New Labour, while benefit levels were increased and the numbers eligible for financial support increased to compensate for low wages, people on benefits were subjected to increasing stigmatisation and scapegoating. Some groups, such as young people, had their access to benefits restricted.

Tony Blair set up the 'Social Exclusion Unit', drawing on progressive European terminology, ostensibly to support people's inclusion in mainstream life and challenge their marginalisation. However, 'social exclusion' was increasingly associated with failing to be in employment, signifying people's individual irresponsibility, rather than challenging the social and economic barriers they faced (Levitas, 2005). Since then, the coalition government colluded with right-wing media to attack people on benefits, not only capping the amount of benefit they may receive, regardless of their needs, but also capping the overall amount of money allocated to benefits, an unprecedented act. Disabled people and other long-term health and social care service users have been particularly badly affected by such policies. While these have been advanced using the rhetoric of 'simplifying the benefits system' and treating disabled people with equality, rather than over-protecting and patronising them, little if anything has been done to remove the barriers facing them in education, training and the labour market, where most continue to be confined to the poorest paid and lowest grade jobs, with limited career opportunities. Thus the Remploy sheltered workshops developed to provide training and employment opportunities were closed using the mainstreaming rhetoric of the disabled people's movement, with few jobs created to replace them.

Over the years, a series of words which have had positive meanings attached with them, have been degraded. For example:

- *'self-help'* has been used to mean being left unsupported, with public funding withdrawn;
- *'Big Society'*, coined by David Cameron, meaning cutting services and infrastructure and expecting people to make their own alternative arrangements, regardless of the difficulties they may already be facing;
- *'social enterprise'* becoming a fig-leaf for taking services out of local authority control, where they and their workforce were unionised and protected and instead commissioning small, insecurely funded third sector organisations to undertake key tasks. This reflects a 'core and periphery' economic model, which marginalises such provision;
- *'housing associations'* are no longer small voluntary organisations seeking to address homelessness and meet housing need, but instead becoming huge hierarchical corporations, without the formal accountability of earlier local authority housing. They increasingly provide housing for profit supposedly to fund 'social housing' increasingly in less valued areas and at market rents. These large organisations are now also extending their activities further, bidding for work they have little track record in undertaking, such as, for example, providing women's refuges, which have been forced to shut down because of a funding crisis. (Laville, 2014)

Just as the word 'community' was attached to roles and services to suggest a local and participatory orientation, so it has also come to be used to disguise provisions concerned with social control. Thus we have encountered community prison, community policeman and community treatment order – extending compulsory treatment outside psychiatric hospitals into people's own homes.

Welfare state thinking has been turned on its head in two other ways. The coalition government launched particular attacks on universalist services as wasteful, unnecessary and 'poorly targeted'. Older people were a particular candidate for such attacks, with, for example, high profile campaigning to end free travel passes for all. But at the same time, the government introduced policy measures which pointed in exactly the opposite direction. Thus its 'help to buy' scheme subsidised buyers of homes worth up to £600,000 with no restriction on income and it introduced childcare support for couples with incomes up to £300,000 (Beresford, 2013b). Indeed it sometimes seems that a different kind of welfare state has been under construction – one which supports and redistributes to the 'haves' rather than the 'have-nots'. Thus, public concerns about tax policies which allow international corporations and rich people to pay minimal tax, and planning and housing policies which are driving 'ordinary' people out of city centres and valued areas (Chakrabortty and Robinson, 2014). This trend looks set to continue under the new Conservative administration.

Second, has been the political right's creation of the concept of the 'small state' as an alternative to 'big government'. They have used this to rationalise their opposition to what they characterise as the damaging role of the 'intrusive' and 'interventionist' state in people's lives. But the reality appears to be something different. There can be no question that the policy concern has been to reduce spending and intervention on the *'supportive'* state – the local and central state which offers services, assistance, resources, learning and advice – the state as conceived by the founders of the welfare state. But there has been no reduction in the regulatory, tax raising and social control roles of the state. In this sense, we seem to have an *enlarged* state. As Tyler has said, while neoliberal ideology is 'state phobic' it seems to demand continuing repressive interventions from the state (Tyler, 2013, 6). Massive cuts in public services over the years have not been accompanied by significant cuts in taxation for most people. As local authority services have been reduced, so their direct financial demands have increased, for parking, public services, licences, searches, pest control and so on. Surveillance, data collection and exchange and the internal role of security forces, as well as the police, in response to political organising and peaceful protest have all expanded, intensified and deepened. This hardly betokens a withdrawal of 'the state', although it does highlight a very different, more repressive role for it.

Conclusion

While the last quarter of the twentieth century is most often remembered for the shift to the political right and the erosion of the welfare state, it was also a time of enormous innovation, offering the prospect of welfare for the future better equipped to advance its founding goals of achieving greater equality, involvement and empowerment. At the same time, many of these innovations were subverted by the dominant neoliberal politics, creating new ambiguities and uncertainties about the role of social policy. Nonetheless some strands of the original radical reforming impulse continued to have an impact on social policy and as we will see next, offer us visions of a new coherent 'user-led' model of welfare services and support which is inclusive, participatory and empowering.

We have seen how writers such as the London Edinburgh Weekend Return Group saw the state and state welfare as part of the capitalist system, but writing in 1979, they were already aware of the confusing situation facing them and others of having to defend a state that they did not believe in or see as 'theirs'. They therefore emphasised the crucial importance of 'fighting back oppositionally, rather than simply defending a state we know to be 'indefensible'. At the heart of this was their desire to change relationships with the state and with the services it provided, challenging identities and roles which they saw it imposing on people as citizens, service users and workers. Increasing people's involvement to increase their control was key to their approach, as it was of welfare service user movements and what this might look like for the future, first in terms of welfare policy and then services and support, is our focus in the next two chapters.

THIRTEEN

Welfare policy for the twenty-first century

The welfare state is not about dependency: it is about opportunity
(Mary O'Hara, 2014b)

Beggars do not work, it is said; but, then, what is WORK? A navvy works by swinging a pick. An accountant works by adding up figures. A beggar works by standing out of doors in all weathers and getting varicose veins, chronic bronchitis, etc. It is a trade like any other; quite useless, of course – but, then, many reputable trades are quite useless. And as a social type a beggar compares well with scores of others. He is honest compared with the sellers of most patent medicines, high-minded compared with a Sunday newspaper proprietor.
(George Orwell, 1933, 206)

Principles for welfare

The academic discipline of social policy has had a particular concern with categorising existing systems of welfare. In this chapter, the aim instead is to begin to explore what a welfare state might look like – if it both took on the ideas of its users and advocates and addressed the weaknesses identified by its critics. In earlier chapters, we explored the principles and structures of existing welfare systems, as well as exploring pioneering alternatives. In this chapter the aim is to look more closely at the latter, while offering the former as a yardstick to set them against. Here we will focus at a policy level, in the next chapter we will explore the detail of support for people's welfare and well-being.

In his influential book *The three worlds of welfare capitalism*, the Danish sociologist Gøsta Esping-Andersen identified three sub-types of welfare state models. While these classifications have come in for increasing criticism, they are still an important starting point for analysing welfare arrangements (Esping-Andersen, 1990). The three dominant types Esping-Andersen identified were:

- the universalist social democratic welfare state;
- the Christian democratic welfare state, based on the principle of subsidiarity (decentralisation) and the dominance of social insurance schemes;
- the liberal (residual and market dominated) welfare state.

While these embody fundamental differences, there are also important similarities. All have been susceptible to increasing pressures to be:

- hierarchical
- managerialist
- market-driven
- 'expert'-based.

Taken together these characteristics tend to accent inequalities, as well as differences and distinctions between welfare producers and welfare consumers. They are primarily concerned with the nature of the provider, rather than the form of provision and its relation with service users, which does not bode well for the latter.

By contrast, pulling together the principles advanced by pioneers from the 1960s onwards, from service user and workplace movements and beyond, we can see that they were more concerned with social policy that is:

- *relational* – prioritising the relationship between service users and providers, practitioners and service users, aiming for equality in such relationships and working actively to build them;
- *experientially based* – building on the lived experience of service users and the practice wisdom of workers;
- *participatory* – committed to the full, equal and effective involvement of service users, workers and other local people;
- *co-produced* – with public services delivered through an equal and reciprocal relationship between professionals, people using services, their families and neighbours (Boyle et al, 2010; Slay, 2011). Service users have an active role alongside those who have traditionally provided services, developing services and support in partnership (Needham, 2013);
- *inclusive and addressing diversity* – in all its forms, seeking to ensure effective access to make this possible (Beresford, 2013c);
- *anti-discriminatory* – countering the wide range of discriminations operating in and sometimes institutionalised in society;

- *self-managed* – working in collaborative and cooperative ways, with an emphasis on team working and shared power and responsibility, rather than on hierarchical structures;
- *mainstreaming* – with public policy geared to ensuring everyone equal access to opportunities in society, with specialist services/services for marginalised groups also consistent with this goal;
- *sustainable* – committed to radical social change in patterns of production and consumption in line with values of sustainable development and environmental justice. (Fitzpatrick and Cahill, 2002; Fitzpatrick, 2011b; Cahill, 2012)

These principles link closely with those specifically developed by service users and their movements. Of course not all of them have been present in all innovative developments. As we have seen, some of these principles have been more concerned with some developments than with others. Nor is it being suggested here that it will be easy to achieve them all. This is likely to demand commitment to different processes for welfare, as well as seeking to advance renewed goals for it. But taken together, these principles provide a road map for taking forward welfare systems capable of achieving the egalitarian, democratising and humanistic values of the post-war UK welfare state. They offer a way forward for welfare that has the potential to deal with the criticisms of the political right, as well as to address the commitments of green and left politics.

Processes for welfare production

Every welfare system and the policies and services within it are the product of a political and administrative process. While different ideologies and goals clearly exert their own influences, this process is nonetheless important in shaping what we get. It is also a process that is remarkably consistent internationally and over time. While in the UK it is one that has increasingly been shaped by market principles, much of it would still be familiar to a Henry Mayhew or Seebohm Rowntree, if like Rip Van Winkle they awoke from their sleep. It is a process that tends to be led and shaped by these key actors and elements:

- politicians and their executive;
- press and media;
- experts, administrators and managers;
- needs testing;

- regulation; and
- feedback.

Being a primary school teacher now

All it is, is targets. A lot of pressure. It's all about Ofsted (the schools regulator). You have to do certain things in certain ways that they want, so the pressure is always on. So it is less about the children and more about the targets and paper work. You are supposed to deliver perfect lessons which change all the time. It's hard to like the teaching when you are exhausted by everything else.

Rebecca Beresford
Daughter

Regulation is a more recent component, added as a simulacrum for the market – to try and regularise standards because the service user as 'public consumer' is frequently not in a position to secure such standards through customer 'voice', 'choice' and 'exit'. Such options are hardly open, for example, to most inmates of residential care, benefit claimants or people with chronic or life-limiting conditions. The consumerist model does not really fit. Regulation has been introduced to compensate, but unfortunately creates its own problems, often imposing clumsy and mechanistic bureaucratic standards, which can develop an unhelpful life of their own and which most service users have difficulty in holding to account. While provisions for public consumerist feedback have existed since the 1990s, as we have seen, they are of limited effectiveness. Taking the form of consultations, 'satisfaction surveys' and involvement in 'audit' and 'evaluation', they tend not to be valued by service users and can discourage more effective involvement. Corporate interests in welfare tend to be much more powerful than those of the individualised consumer.

The process for welfare production overall is essentially a top-down one, with the media long playing a much more significant role in in the development of welfare policy and the presentation of its recipients than most academic and policy discussions acknowledge. The unholy alliance of right-wing press and right-wing politics has long worked to undermine the UK welfare state and indeed, as we saw earlier, struggled to ensure that it was stillborn.

The progressive developments that have emerged over the last 40 or so years, point to a very different process, which would be:

- participatory, fully involving service users, workers and other local people;
- decentralised;
- anti-hierarchical;
- rights and needs-led;
- based on an inclusive reconception of universalism.

We will learn more about these when we turn to the kind of support and services envisaged for the future in the next chapter. But first we need to explore broader policy issues, beginning with the important but often overlooked issue of what is actually entailed in accessing such support.

Getting services and support

People who need help from the state or turn to it for support (or indeed who pay for their own) go through a kind of journey to secure it. This journey tends to have a beginning and an end, although it may come to a precipitate halt, without them ever reaching the destination they had hoped for, if they get lost or are judged ineligible for help. Their experience is also likely to be made more complicated because they can expect to go through a number of unconnected journeys, as they discover that they need to turn to a variety of different agencies and organisations and different policies and services to meet their (or their loved one's) needs. These ports of call are often not integrated and there may not be anyone to act as travel guide to ease people's path and keep them on track. Efforts in the past to overcome these difficulties, for example, through patch based and decentralised social services, tended to be short-lived, either because they were inadequately funded, or they were used as a smokescreen for funding cuts and shifting responsibility on to local communities (Beresford and Croft, 1986).

Working with people

About 10 years ago, while working with Connexions (and mainly giving careers advice), we were encouraged (directed) to deal with our service users in a 'client-centred', holistic way: understanding their situation and agreeing ways forward. Where appropriate we were to adopt a multiagency approach to allow for joined-up thinking, rather than just offering discrete interventions to help with the presenting issue. We were to be alert to the more vulnerable young people who could be slipping through the various nets that were in place. This philosophy had its merits. Across welfare services as a whole I guess we are still only working towards this. From experience the best outcomes from advice are when the person seeking help has an advocate, especially if they can offer a personal perspective and can support the person regularly (albeit, a friend, relative or charity). I have concerns for those on their own (for example, older people) who need to access the various welfare organisations. Services do not always have the time to act as a friend (they have their job to do). Perhaps we all have a lesson to learn from that.

Andrew Croft
My wife's cousin

Reaching the starting line

There can, however, be major obstacles in the way of people even making a start on this journey. In Chapter Six, we encountered Julian Le Grand's hypothesis that middle-class people tended to do better out of valued welfare state services than their working-class equivalents, although such services were particularly intended to challenge the disadvantage facing the latter (Le Grand, 1982). His argument was that middle-class people were better able to access and get the most help from such services – to 'work the system'. We do know that access to support and valued welfare state services has long been unequal in many ways.

Some groups are less likely to know about such services, less likely to be assertive in seeking to access them, more reluctant to seek such support (for example, older people unwilling to accept 'charity' or fearful of stigma) and less likely to identify with such support, even though they may be entitled to and benefit from it. Similarly we know that some groups face particular barriers from services in gaining their support (Beresford and Croft, 1993). Thus the inequalities facing black and minority ethnic communities accessing support and mental health service users and people with learning difficulties accessing services for physical health on equal terms have long been highlighted. Particular groups may also be reluctant to turn to services because their expectation (sometimes justified) is that they won't be welcoming, services are not sensitive to their particular (cultural) needs or may create their own additional problems. Thus service users talk of older people not picking up on help that is intended for them because they don't see themselves as 'older people', or think of increasing frailty as just part of life, rather than something that can benefit from help (Hoban et al, 2013). Some mainstream services still find it difficult to respond to the particular cultural needs of different communities – in the case of mental health services some ethnic groups tend to be conspicuously over-represented in less valued, more controlling parts of their provision.

Research on barriers in the way of people getting involved in services also offers some helpful insights here. Service users have identified five main groups of people who tend to be marginalised by or excluded from services. The first set of barriers relate to equality issues. Service users report barriers they face getting involved on the basis of gender, ethnicity, culture, belief, sexuality, age, disability and class. Older people are conspicuously under-represented. Second, they say some groups don't have an equal chance of being involved because of where they live. This includes people who are homeless, living in residential services, in prison and the penal system, travellers and gypsies. This group also includes people whose rights may be restricted. It also extends to a related group; asylum seekers and refugees – people who do not have citizenship rights and status. Communication issues also serve to exclude people. This relates to barriers on the basis both of ethnicity and impairment and includes: D/deaf people, blind people and people with visual impairments, deaf and blind people, people who do not communicate verbally and people for whom English is not their first language. An additional recent group often facing exclusions are those who are not computerate, who do not use the internet, who can now face some of the same difficulties as people who do not read or write.

Service users are also excluded because of the nature of their impairments. People with complex and multiple impairments are frequently left out. This can be because engaging with them is seen as expensive and difficult, or because of unevidenced assumptions that they are not able or interested in being involved. It can also happen where people are seen as 'awkward' or 'difficult' (for example, the growing number of people with dementia). This is a category in which people who see themselves within the range of neuro-diversity are sometimes also included. Finally, there are those seen as 'unwanted voices'. Service users frequently comment that some people and some points of view are more welcome than others – particularly those of people who agree with those in authority. Interestingly, more confident and assertive service users are often unpopular among those organising involvement activities and often dismissed as 'the usual suspects' (Beresford, 2013c).

It is for these reasons that just creating helpful services and positive support – on its own, is not enough to ensure that it is truly accessible to all – even that which takes account of issues of diversity. The lesson to be learned is that if everyone is to be at the starting point to be able to access equally what help and services are available, then some of us may need some additional initial help and support to do so. What this means is the provision of advocacy, advice and information services, which can be a key first step for equalising people's access to welfare.

It means reaching out to people and their communities rather than assuming that they can always find their own way to support, as well as providing information in truly accessible forms. We will return to this later when we look at user-led approaches to services and support. But there is a simple moral here: if welfare services are truly to reach everybody, then they need to reach *out* to people, rather than expecting these services to come to those who need them.

The service journey

Once someone embarks upon a 'service journey' there tend to be a number of stages to it, which they need to negotiate.

These stages can be different according to the service and why people come into contact with it. We should also remember that use of some services is involuntary, like the criminal justice and penal systems, and some people are not so much users of services, as having them imposed upon them, for example, where they entail restriction or removal of their rights.

The service journey includes the following stages.

Assessment

As welfare services have increasingly shifted from being universalist to residual or means-tested, so the importance of 'assessment' has grown. Assessment has always had a role to play in collective social policy, ranging from Poor Law assessments to check eligibility as a pauper, to the making of diagnoses by general practitioners. Since the 1990s, the rhetoric has been of the service user playing a more active role in assessment and this has including 'user involvement' in any assessment. In social care there has even been talk of 'self-assessment' (even though it is a legal requirement for professional assessments to take place). However, in reality, these assessment processes have become increasingly institutionalised and bureacratised. They now tend to be either form- or 'script'-based.

If service users are required to complete forms they may be many pages long. There is increasing pressure for these to be completed online, despite the large numbers of people who may need to complete these forms who aren't computerate or don't have computers, or aren't on-line at home.

The alternative to completing a form is usually to provide information by phone (which can be costly and difficult) responding to someone using a script, who is likely to be untrained and increasingly based in a call centre. The assessment process has also increasingly become a rationing process, designed to 'weed out' at the earliest possible stage people and claims not seen as eligible or qualifying. While social workers once served as advocates to help people negotiate such encounters with the service system, increasingly they are themselves only to be accessed in the same way and more and more they are expected to be part of a rationing process, rather than providing support. Because the assessment process is as much concerned with restricting as enabling access to services, it is one that readily works to discourage the less confident, less articulate and less demanding, reinforcing a vicious circle which can be expected to work against those experiencing most difficulty and most disadvantage.

Allocation

The allocation of services has more and more been framed in terms of responding to consumer choice and being 'needs-led'. More often, though, because of funding cuts, it has been budget-driven. A new vocabulary has developed for service allocation, including terms like 'care' and 'case management' and the creation of 'care packages', mirroring the language of mainstream goods and services, although professionally mediated. Access to services varies significantly according to areas and authorities, giving rise to the term 'postcode lottery' and creating problems of 'portability' – of transferring support to other areas if someone moves. Indeed, the term lottery may literally apply, with some local authorities (Westminster is a conspicuous example), for example, organising competitions which those eligible must enter if they wish, for example, to be considered for rehousing.

Service

The modern UK NHS sums up the problems facing complex welfare service systems. They are subject to many different, sometimes competing, political, ideological, professional and organisational pressures. As a result they can be highly ambiguous. It has become a truism that the NHS is deeply loved by the 'general public'. At the same time it has long been associated with examples of mistreatment, abuse and neglect, from the cases highlighted by Peter Townsend and Barbara Robb in the 1950s and 1960s through to the Bristol heart and Mid Staffs scandals of the 1990s and twenty-first century. With such large organisations – and the NHS has been identified as the largest organisation in Europe – it can be difficult for the individual to feel able to act on equal terms or exert any influence. Economies of scale readily end up resulting in standardised service and standardised treatment. Instead of services responding to the individual, the individual can feel that they are simply slotted into the service. Such a *'service-led'* system, which encourages a restricted menu of provision, is too often the experience service users' report (Beresford et al, 2011).

Review

The purpose of review has long been presented in terms of providing an opportunity to check how well services are working, whether people's situation or needs are changing – and particularly if they are increasing – and to have a regular opportunity to be in face-to-face contact with the service user, to give them a chance to speak for themselves and to make sure that they are all right. More recently, however, reviews seem to have taken on a different role. Now they tend to be a worrying and destabilising time for service users, when they can expect to be faced with the reduction or removal of benefits and/or services, in line with reducing budgets, narrowing eligibility criteria and more restrictive attitudes towards state support.

Ending

If the original aspiration of the welfare state was to ensure social security through the life course – from 'cradle to grave', increasingly the emphasis in services has been on setting time limits on support. Thus the accent is on *throughput* – getting people out of hospital as quickly as possible, short-term stay in supportive accommodation, a fixed number of talking therapy sessions, time-limited social work interventions and even limits to the duration of entitlement to welfare benefits. If the origins of this approach lie in increasingly restricted budgets, then it is presented in terms of achieving 'outcomes' of change – however feasible or not these may be. Ideas like 'recovery' and 'reablement' put the accent on transition and change – either, for example, people moving into employment – if they are of working age – or if older – into managing without continuing support. Thus accessing support no longer means that security is guaranteed and it can become as much of a struggle to retain it, as to obtain it in the first place.

The importance of the process

As can be seen, each stage of this journey can create difficulties and barriers for people, each stage can result in inequalities. Thus providing an egalitarian support system is not just a matter of offering appropriate good quality services, but also of ensuring that its *process* is consistent with its goals and that this is an accessible and participatory one. This is the only way of reducing inequalities of access to services and support. We can see this as part of the bigger picture of an alternative approach to services and support that has emerged from service users and their organisations, as well as other pioneers.

Social policies for the future

The aim of the post-war Labour government was not to create a 'state' within a 'state' – the welfare state – but to change the nature of the society that people lived in to make it a more welcoming, humane and equal place for everyone. That was why the welfare state was primarily concerned with big issues of progressive redistribution, full employment, social security, universality and housing, health and education as truly *social* services. We know that in many ways it failed in its universalist goals, basing them on a narrow, culturally-limited definition. We also know that as time went on, the welfare state came to be associated more narrowly with formal service systems, rather than the broader transformation of society. Some of these service systems, particularly for disadvantaged and marginalised groups, such as disabled and poor people, have also tended further to isolate and stigmatise them. They have come in for criticism from the political right, although the dilution of the values of the welfare state encouraged their development. As we have seen, there have been calls instead for more informal self-help and non-professional approaches to support. However, these have often been associated with the cutting of formal services and support and the placing of greater responsibility on people to 'look after themselves' without the development of any infrastructure to support this.

Alternative thinking for a future welfare state, however, draws us back to broader, more holistic and systemic approaches to ensuring that people benefit from opportunities and support. As we shall see, though, while it is not narrowly conceived in terms of 'services', it also offers models of such services profoundly different from the past.

First though, we need to look more closely at the implications of the kind of progressive developments over the last decades which we considered in the last chapter, for the broader construction of social policy. Conventional social policy textbooks often have chapters or sections taking the reader through different policy areas, such as health, social security, education and so on (for example, Castles et al, 2010; Bochel and Daley, 2014). It is helpful to consider what these might look like for the future, compared with the paths they have taken, drawing together the ideas for innovation so far set out in this book and distilling service users' and other discussions over the years.

Employment policy

Perhaps the most complex and contentious area of social policy is benefits policy. However, if there is one lesson that can be learned from the creation of the welfare state and even more so from the social policy of Mrs Thatcher, it is that this cannot be considered in isolation from *employment* policy. The two are and always have been inextricably related. Therefore it is with employment policy that we probably need to start.

There is an irony that both the post-war welfare state and its sternest critics have been primarily concerned with work – paid work. The welfare state was predicated on making possible 'full employment'. The right-wing opponents of welfare argue that it creates dependency, pulling people away from the responsibility to work, cushions them in dependence and damages wealth creation. We have already seen that we need to rethink the idea of full employment if it is to challenge historic exclusions and discriminations. But in exploring welfare for the future, it seems important to subject ideas of 'work' and 'employment' to even closer scrutiny. That means in turn that we will also need to think again about a constellation of related ideas, such as unemployment, dependence and independence (Blakemore and Warwick-Booth, 2013, 186–205).

There are, however, other lessons that need to be taken on and other questions that need to be asked: what does work mean, what is it for and whom is it for? In recent years, there has been much rethinking and change in the nature and expectations of employment. There has been a liberalisation of legislation in relation to employment. In the UK, this has meant that employment for most people has become more and more insecure. We are told that ideas such as 'jobs for life' are outmoded. There is an increased proportion of part-time and self-employment, so-called 'zero-hour contracts', which are effectively casualisation by another name, and employment generally has poorer terms and conditions for workers. Thus work as employment has changed significantly, mainly in the name of 'flexibility', for the benefit of large employers – rather than for the benefit of its workers.

It's 80 years since George Orwell dissected the purpose and value of work in his *Down and out in Paris and London*. In it he looked at the lives of Parisian 'plongeurs' or washers-up in restaurants and English 'tramps' as he sampled both (Orwell, 1933). He asked if particular jobs were actually 'necessary to civilisation' and if work was virtuous, just because it was 'hard and disagreeable'. He condemned the fetishisation of work – pointless and unnecessary work – resulting in the perpetuation of 'useless work'. At the heart of this Orwell saw a political fear of what people would do if not occupied by work and money justifying everything. What he wrote in 1933 still seems to hold today, 'money has become the grand test of virtue'. For Orwell the problem for the beggar 'which is why he or she is always despised' is that unlike the business man he has adopted a 'trade at which it is impossible to grow rich' (Orwell, 1933, 207).

Idleness, of course, was one of the five giant evils identified by Beveridge in his report. But its antithesis has subsequently been too narrowly equated with employment. We know that there are many other forms of occupation, not least childcare, unpaid caring and active involvement in your community. Beveridge saw the answer to idleness in terms of full employment, it was intended as a constructive response – that no one should be forced to be idle. But increasingly work has come to be seen by policymakers as an obligation to be fulfilled rather than as a right to be respected. Jobs become the necessary badge of conformity and those who don't have one can expect to be treated as suspect or defective. The policy emphasis now is on regulating people seen as trying to avoid work, rather than on challenging what for many is the torture of insecure, under- or unemployment.

The influence of the protestant work ethic continues to be powerful, however. I can still see myself affected by its pervasive message that it is right and good to work and wrong not to. Yet we also know that it is not as simple as that. The damage done by the banking system leading up to the 2008 recession and the disproportionate scale of bankers' bonuses since then in the UK, have made many people rethink the value and purpose of such work, since it has created so much poverty instead of wealth. Yet this has not resulted in any significant policy change. We also know that 'full employment' however defined is not readily consistent with an unfettered market. A valued role of unregulated capitalism is to reduce the amount of employment and the quality of its conditions in order to make economies, particularly 'economies of scale'. Thus there has long been an inherent contradiction between its imperatives of reducing the labour force while requiring people to work.

Orwell saw enforced idleness as the great evil of a tramp's life. At the end of his book he concluded: 'What is needed is to depauperize him, and this can only be done by finding him work – not work for the sake of working, but work of which he can enjoy the benefit.'

His answer, however: 'to make them grow their own food', hardly seems a radical solution at the end of it all (Orwell, 1933, 244–6). Since then we have gained awareness of the need for employment to be consistent with sustainability. There has been increasing recognition of the importance of the rights and needs of workers, although more and more these have been under attack. There has been the irony of 'health and safety' coming to mean a constraint on both workers and service users, when the original intent was liberatory. We have come to learn also that the achievement of equality in employment demands recognition and valuing of difference. We know that there are many barriers in the existing labour market that can exclude people from it or marginalise them in it. We also know that for some people with chronic, life limiting and other conditions or impairments, any form of 'work' as conventionally understood, on a regular basis, may be difficult or even impossible. All these complexities of work and employment must be taken into account before we can give consideration to policies for people who still either fall outside the labour market or are on its edges. And in doing so we must take into account our own knee-jerk reactions to the idea of work.

Income maintenance

For all the increasing talk in social policy of the merits of voluntarism and skills-exchange, most of us live in cash-based societies, where, whatever the prevailing balance of state and market, we need money to live. The area of social policy which addresses this is described by different headings: social security, income maintenance and, most narrowly and nowadays, often pejoratively, welfare or benefits policy. Such financial support tends to be needed through the life course at different times and for different reasons, for children, for parents, if people are incapacitated, as they grow older and of course if they lack an income from employment. Income maintenance is both a way of responding to and reducing these risks and also of redistributing income and resources. Income redistribution can take place in many ways: between generations and in families and communities; through voluntary and charitable effort; through the protection offered in the market by companies and employers and through the state (Alcock with May, 2014, 104).

Living on benefits

I don't think the experience of living on benefits has ever left me. I don't doubt out there, there's somebody who doesn't care about the sense of insecurity, failure and stigma that go with it, just like there are dishonest politicians and corrupt officials, who feel no shame. For me and others I've ever met in the same situation, this populist tabloid picture has no meaning. What it was for me was dread of official envelopes thudding through the letter box, being called for humiliating interviews and living in fear of something breaking or wearing out we couldn't afford to replace. It's one thing politicians sampling poverty for a week, another to experience it over years. Then claimants get told off for fiddling the system or well-meaning others say, of course they wouldn't do that. When benefits are low, mothers will do anything to look after their children as best they can. But when they carry out their own system of 'workfare', they get into trouble rather than command the respect they deserve. There must be respect and recognition for people who need financial help.

The author

Social policy academics talk of horizontal redistribution (across the life cycle) and vertical redistribution (from rich to poor – or indeed vice versa). All this is a complex and interactive process. Such redistribution can take place through taxation and through welfare benefits, as well as through the creation of other opportunities. Responsibilities also shift. In recent years in the UK, for example, we have increasingly seen the unloading of responsibilities from employers to the state, with, for example, poorer provisions for pensions. We have seen the state under New Labour prop up low wages through tax credits and the Coalition do the same by raising the entry level for income tax. Responsibilities for people's well-being have increasingly shifted from the private sector, to the public purse (Beresford, 2005). At the same time, the changes in demographics with fewer people of working age and many more older people are offered as an argument that 'we cannot go on as before', 'the traditional welfare state can no longer be afforded' (Alcock with May, 2014, 259–70).

Here ideological arguments seem to be conflated and confused with economic ones. Given the massively increased productivity achievable with modern technology, it is difficult to see how such old equations can be sustained. At the same time, they are a convenient and powerful rationale to adopt to justify the thrust of neoliberal social policy reforms and also to set the generations against each other. Populist anti-claimant welfare policies may serve the ideological and political purposes attached to them, but they tend to be neither effective nor to achieve their stated goals. As we have seen, they are closely associated with means-tested benefits, but these are not only costly to administer; they also tend to be associated with non-take-up by those entitled to them. Meanwhile those whom their advocates seek to discourage as 'dependent' are unlikely to be discouraged by any shame associated with them (Alcock with May, 2014, 118–19).

A modern trend in UK benefits policy, associated with policy shifts to the right, has been the desire to save money. This has been through a search for a holy grail of simplification and making its administration amenable to modern electronic technology. So far both political quests frequently seem the equivalent of the medieval alchemist's search to convert base metal to gold, resulting in the arbitrary treatment of many claimants and the creation of costly and defective IT systems that tend to cancel out any promised financial savings. Olive Stevenson was the first social work adviser to the Supplementary Benefits Commission, which was set up to provide an oversight on social security policy in 1966 by the Labour government. In her autobiography she counselled against simplifying the system, highlighting the complex nature of income maintenance policy and saying that it was not amenable to over-simplification (Stevenson, 2013).

The costs of benefits tend to be exaggerated for populist and social control purposes. Commenting on the impact of the Murdoch media empire in the wake of the phone hacking trial, the writer Nick Davies, who broke the story, wrote:

> As a single example of the distorting impact of their work, YouGov in December 2012, working for the TUC [Trades Union Congress], found that the average public perception was that 41% of the welfare budget was spent on the unemployed. The reality is 3%. And that 27% of that budget was eaten up by fraud. The reality, as far as official figures can detect, is 0.7%. (Davies, 2014, 10)

Social security policy has always been most vexed and most controversial in relation to whether people could or should be working. Such work has more often been officially seen as an obligation rather than a right – and it is a right many disabled people believe that they have been denied. Many disabled people have long felt that they have been counted out of, or marginalised in the labour market, as incapable of working. Currently a growing number feel that they are being dragooned into employment as neoliberal attitudes to welfare benefits and claimants have hardened. This political pressure for disabled people to be in employment, often couched in the disabled people's movement's own rhetoric of rights and entitlement, has resulted in some disabled people and people with long-term conditions arguing that work may not be an option for some of them because of the nature of their conditions or impairments (Crowther, 2014). We seem to have a system of income maintenance that judges people capable or incapable of work according to how well they fit its stereotypes for assessment.

Thus a tension has been articulated between two key concerns of welfare policy; *inclusion* (in the labour market and society) and *protection* (looking after those who might not be able to conform and hold a job). Certainly many disabled people are in part-time employment, but whether that is their choice, all that is available to them or encouraged by benefits policy, we can't be sure (Crowther, 2014). Others argue that whether disabled people are able to work will also depend on the nature of the work and the terms on which it is available to them. In their view, work is not an inflexible absolute, and inclusion and protection need not be mutually exclusive. In addition to challenging discrimination and other exclusionary attitudes, there are many ways in which disabled people's access to employment and careers can be better supported and encouraged. These range from improving their access to education and training, to work buddy schemes, flexitime, work shadows and replacements for periods of illness or difficulty. But service users are also saying that there may be some people who are unable to make some kind of contribution through anything that might be conceived of as 'work', temporarily or more longer term. This, however, should not be taken to mean that they make no contribution. There may be other things that they can or wish to do, which should be recognised and valued, instead of them being written off as 'dependent' and 'parasitical' (Crowther, 2014).

We need to be honest with ourselves and make clear that there is no such thing as 'scientific' or 'objective' social security policy. It all depends on what we want from it – greater social security for the overall population, or some kind of social engineering to maintain and even extend insecurities, inequalities and 'othering'. A key issue, of course, is policymakers' and people's difficulty in distinguishing between effective rather than moralistic policy and practice. Instead the benefits system, perhaps like the UK justice system, needs to start from a presumption of innocence rather than guilt. Social security, like any human system, can be abused, although the evidence has long shown this to be much less of a problem than its critics suggest. But perhaps it is the price that we have to pay to ensure justice for the majority. As we saw earlier, there seems to be much less media concern about public money lost through tax avoidance than through the benefits system – even though the sums of money involved tend to be much larger. Perhaps an underlying problem is that most of us are much more ready to focus on the perceived shortcoming of people whom we see as more like ourselves, rather than those who are rich and powerful. This would certainly help explain the success of modern UK campaigns to demonise people on benefits and the relative failure to combat high level tax avoidance and evasion.

If there are people who are not working who perhaps might, then what is needed are access and supports which will help them to, rather than a vicious benefits system, aiming to force them to. If welfare history teaches us anything, then it is that we must rethink the constellation of 'work', 'full employment', 'dependence' and indeed, as disabled people have done, 'independence'. Benefits policy needs to follow from the removal of barriers in the labour market. It needs to connect with a reconception of work in relation to diversity. What are needed are a benefits system and a labour market that are supportive of diversity. Both need to be based on a notion of work and economy that support, rather than challenge our well-being, whose primary concern indeed is enhancing, rather than undermining that well-being.

Housing

A major concern of the post-war welfare state was to decommodify housing to make possible decent housing for all. From a starting point of most people living in private rented housing, to improve health and living standards, policymakers prioritised access to good quality state rented housing. Over the years efforts were also made to improve safeguards and housing conditions for private tenants as well as provide support for people who were in inadequate housing or who were homeless. The policy direction since 1979, however, has been to *recommodify* housing, first through a drive to owner-occupation (the least flexible, most costly form of tenure) and the selling off of council housing (Somerville with Sprigings, 2005). This has had a profound and distorting effect on both the UK's and people's own personal economies (Alcock with May, 2014, 142–63; Somerville and Sprigings, 2005). At the time of writing, there are few if any legal economic activities in the UK that can generate the same high return as property and, in areas such as London and the South East, there is no way most people can earn as much by working as they can by sitting at home while the value of their home rises.

Housing policy has reinforced inequalities between groups and between regions, notably between the South East and other parts of England. UK housing, particularly in high price areas, has become a target for international investment, making the control of prices and of the housing market even more difficult for policymakers. Indeed the UK can now be seen as an extreme case study of the problematic tensions between housing as an amenity and as a commodity. As a result, the shift to owner-occupation engineered by Mrs Thatcher has been succeeded by a return to increased private renting, but now associated with serious problems of cost, insecure tenure, income segregation, the fragmentation of communities and local ties and deteriorating housing quality and increasing problems of homelessness (Blakemore and Warwick-Booth, 2013, 247–8).

At the time of writing 'owner-occupation', the fantasy based on lifelong debt encouraged by Mrs Thatcher and her fellow ideologues, has become an increasingly distant prospect for growing numbers of young people, professional as well as working-class. The changing state of the housing market has had many major unconsidered social consequences, for example, it has perpetuated young people's dependence on their parents, significantly raised the age when they can leave home, kept people in relationships they may want to end and both significantly inhibited mobility, as well as imposing it on young people unable to afford to live in their communities of origin if they wish to (Alcock with May, 2014, 142–63).

Given UK political preoccupations with housing as an ideological issue, it is interesting that so little attention seems to have been paid to advancing innovation in housing. Instead of being seen as 'machines for living' housing tends to be treated as spaces for occupation. While more has been done to address issues of energy use, little has been done on any significant scale to address some of the key issues raised for housing, either in relation to tenure or design, for example:

- how to reduce its cost to improve access for those with less money, rather than to see it as means of generating capital and income;

- how to increase the flexibility and accessibility of accommodation to meet people's different physical and social needs over the life course, as well as different cultural needs;
- how routinely to harness the latest technology for living, maintenance and accessibility, rather than just technology for easy and cheap building.

The idea of 'public housing', one of the great large-scale innovations of the post-war UK welfare state, has been displaced by a shift to segregated, so-called 'social housing'. This has increasingly come under the control of ever larger, ever more bureaucratic and unaccountable 'housing associations', whose culture and concerns, as well as role in the housing economy, have shifted massively from their original philanthropic ethos, to much more corporate structures and goals (Fearn, 2014).

Yet housing has long been in the vanguard in the development of democratising and participatory approaches to social policy and provision. The squatters', tenants' and cooperative housing movements, have all advanced these, as well as other creative approaches to housing (Ward, 1974; Bradley, 2014). Many innovative ideas have been developed since the creation of the welfare state, for example,

- low cost, self-run housing cooperatives for lesbian, gay, bisexual and trans people (as well as other groups);
- core and cluster schemes for people who need additional support;
- different, more flexible and inclusive forms of tenure;
- mainstreaming housing that is more accessible for disabled people and more readily matched to meet different/changing access needs;
- housing providing additional support for people, for example, extra care housing providing additional flexible support;
- prefabricated easy-build housing;
- self-build housing;
- housing designed to support people's social needs, challenging loneliness and isolation;
- improved housing rights;
- housing and local environments segregated from traffic, making it more child and pedestrian friendly;
- housing alternatives to nuclear family living. (Blood, 2013; Forrest, 2013; Hare, 2013)

All these have been developed, internationally, although in the UK, they have been marginal in the overall picture of housing, their progress has been slow and developments are often insecure. Such examples of innovation are both important and exciting, given that housing shapes how we live and even the quality of our lives. This makes its slow progress in the UK even more worrying and a measure of how far housing policy has drifted away from the founding concerns of the welfare state.

Education and training

Key Labour thinkers such as R.H. Tawney gave priority to education reform prior to the setting up of the welfare state (Goldman, 2013/14). However, as we saw in Chapter Six, education was perhaps the least innovative and radical policy emerging from the post-war UK settlement. It still separated people according to class and opportunity, and left the existing public school system untouched, perpetuating old divisions and inequalities. Labour governments later made efforts to challenge this with the creation of comprehensive schools and the raising of the school leaving age. However, for many young people, particularly working-class young people, schooling still meant social control and being socialised into conformity (Corrigan, 1979).

What's wrong with school

I hated school. I went to a failing inner city primary school and a mediocre but self-important girls-only comprehensive. It was the epitome of institutionalisation. It enforced obedience, stifled creativity and self-expression. You're not free to discuss and it's dictated to you what you need to learn and how. That's what I hate about school. You aren't allowed to answer back. You have to wear a uniform. When you leave school, you realise that it wasn't natural – that's not what life's like. You need to express yourself and discuss and most important, be able to engage critically and analyse what you learn and the world around you. In essence, it sets you up to fail. That wasn't how my sixth form college was – it wasn't compulsory education – there I was treated differently, my opinion mattered.

Ruth Beresford
Our youngest daughter

Yet one of the great lessons of the Second World War was the importance of education in radicalising people and creating grassroots pressure for change. The left-leaning Army Bureau of Current Affairs and Education Corps had powerful effects on troops returning home in 1945 and the voting decisions they made (Kynaston, 2008, 39; Allatt, 2014). The large-scale failure to involve people in the development of the welfare state or to educate them about it has often resulted in its isolation and public alienation from it – except where large numbers directly experience its benefits. This seems to explain the enduring popularity of the NHS (for all its problems) and the ease with which the benefits system can be attacked (despite all its strengths).

Going to new school

I'm not looking forward to going up to Year Two because that means I'll then be going into Year Three next at the new school. I don't like it. I don't want to talk about it any more.

Evie Beresford Coyte
Our granddaughter, aged six

Current debate about education reflects this. The dominant discourse focuses narrowly on 'parental choice' framed in terms of how people can get their children into the 'best schools'. This seems mainly concerned with maintaining or reinforcing 'advantage', rather than making possible greater vertical social mobility (Alcock with May, 2014, 184–201). Social mobility was greatest in the UK in the mid-1970s, the time when the welfare state reforms had achieved their greatest effect and before this started to be reversed by ideological shifts to the right (Goldthorpe, 1987; Goldthorpe and Jackson, 2007; OECD, 2010, 181–97). Education has long been seen as having a key role to play in supporting social mobility. However a continuing problem in the UK is that access to valued education remains unequal, reinforcing rather than reducing barriers in the way of upward social mobility and thus strengthening the status quo. As David Hicks states, the key 'radical critique of education is that it inevitably reproduces the social, political and economic norms of the dominant ideology' (Hicks, 2004, 137).

Likes and dislikes about school!

I like school, but I hate 'Quote of the week'. I like my teacher, but she does that 'Ones on the wall': 'Success is can, not can't' – with a picture of a can with success written on it. And in my busy book I had to write, 'Good, better, best, never let it rest, till your good is better and your better best.' I've made up rude versions.

Poppy Beresford Coyte
Our granddaughter, aged nine

Education policy nonetheless has a major role to play in advancing people's civic, ideological, political and social understanding. This would demand a different ideological approach to education policy, one which was committed to supporting our development as both citizens and human beings, helping us to understand the world in which we live, our own place in it and, to have a commitment to treating people as we would wish to be treated (Lister, 1987, 54–6). It would take us beyond conceptions of education either as a mechanism to prepare us for our allotted place in the labour market, or as a vehicle for competing in a 'meritocracy'. Instead, it could offer a counter to the dominance of increasingly narrowly based political parties and media organisations, equipping us all instead for an informed and active role in the democracies of which we are meant to be members. It could help us move towards Gramsci's idea of 'organic intellectuals', challenging dominant ideas and interests (Gramsci, 1982), with us all playing a part in forming ideology, rather than being a stage army manipulated by ideology imposed from above. Over the years since the creation of the welfare state, a growing number of ideas for improving education for children and adults have been highlighted. They offer a basis for progressive policy for both and include, for example, developments committed to:

- inclusive mainstream education for disabled people (ALLFIE, 2008; 2014);
- anti-discriminatory, anti-racist and multicultural education (Richardson and Miles, 2003);
- supporting the development of all abilities, academic, vocational, physical and social;
- pedagogic approaches such as those developed by the community educator Paulo Friere (Friere, 1972);
- the full and equal participation of school students in their education (Beresford and Croft, 1981b; Neill, 1966);
- moving to more active and participatory models of learning, helping children and adults to think critically, learning to question and not just conform;

- encouraging much greater understanding of people's rights, responsibilities and citizenship (Lister, 1987);
- Rogerian approaches which prioritise the relationship between teacher and learner and value feelings, reciprocity and understanding (Rogers, 1994, 121);
- placing more value on making and doing;
- life-long learning;
- equal opportunities for higher education and learning for everybody, including people identified as having 'learning difficulties';
- much more equal opportunities for further and higher education for people with learning difficulties;
- supporting people to understand politics better;
- involving local communities in the school;
- education on sex and sexuality based on understanding and valuing relationships and challenging discrimination;
- valuing collaborative project and group work, working outside the classroom;
- valuing all children and learners and also valuing teaching and teachers, challenging streaming, selection and segregation. (Rogers, 1994; Hicks, 2004)

Education: the great equaliser

I know still that education is the great freedom and the great equaliser. And that will always be true. There are many flaws, injustices and problems in the education system. But the fact of the matter is, that when I look in the mirror in the morning, I am amazed and grateful that I was born into this time – especially as a woman – I think it is because of my father's example, the youngest son, whose life opportunities were completely different from his brothers, because he didn't have to leave school at 14. We were just brought up to know that education was everything. We didn't realise at the time. I didn't realise I was a 'girl'. It didn't occur to me not to work, because in our house, education was seen as something amazing, bountiful and for which you had to work as well. Now whatever you may say about how under-resourced primary schools have been, I still believe primary education and in modern times, nursery education, is the most important, because if you don't get it right by the age they are seven – it's too late. Because if you lose them at the start, you never get them back. But historically primary school teachers got paid less. Why has the school teacher become the easy target for any angry parent? I hate the way education is on the political agenda. Teachers know how to educate children. Of course you need guidance and inspection, but we know how to educate children – how to set them off.

Jenny Hutchins
My sister-in-law

Planning

'Planning' has become a dirty word in social policy. Its critics have associated it with centralised control, Eastern European-style state planning and ideas such as a 'command economy'. They present it as synonymous with inefficiency, wastefulness, disempowerment and 'one size fits all' solutions. But the planning envisaged by the founders of the post-war UK welfare state arose as an alternative to market mechanisms for planning associated with economic failure, deprivation and social insecurity. Planning was an important element in their proposals. While as we have seen, it was often narrowly based, elitist and mono-cultural in nature, it nonetheless made possible major improvements in the lives of many of the population who had suffered badly under pre-war market driven conditions (Kynaston, 2008). Subsequent supporters of the welfare state sought to add grassroots involvement to strategic planning, with, as we have seen, provisions for public participation first emerging in 1960s' land-use planning legislation.

Since then, the political shift to the right in the UK has resulted in the weakening of such planning controls as well as a strong reaction against state planning, explicit in neoliberal rhetoric of the 'small state' and 'nudge' approach (Thaler and Sunstein, 2008). Without the kind of state regulation and planning advanced by the early advocates of the welfare state, planning becomes by default a process dominated by the market and the most powerful interests and institutions. Thus in the UK, while the talk since Mrs Thatcher has been of moving from 'monolithic' state provision, the reality has been one of moving towards a very small number of massive for-profit service providers, sometimes effectively operating as monopolies or in cartels, to run an increasing range of public organisations, services and utilities. This has been reflected in the development of a 'core and periphery' economic model. The core is made up of such strongly ensconced large, often multinational corporations; the periphery of insecure low-cost suppliers, smaller businesses and self-employed people.

Advocates of alternatives argue instead for a social and community planning approach which prioritises:

- people's participation;
- human-scale organisations;
- the democratic improvement of the built environment and minimal damage to the natural environment;
- integrating economic activity with social goals;
- environmental justice;
- sustainability, reducing the need for unnecessary transportation and pollution and encouraging local production;
- supporting well-being, work/life balance and mutuality;
- supporting community and family networks and social cohesion and solidarity, rather than economic segregation and isolation. (Hamdi and Goethert, 1997; Warburton, 1998; Archibugi, 2008; Schlosberg, 2007)

Culture and recreation

There tends to be little consideration of culture and recreation in conventional discussions about the welfare state. If they are discussed at all as policies, then they tend to be considered in other contexts – of the arts, entertainment, sport or public funding. Yet the significance of aesthetics has long been recognised among social reformers. They have stressed the importance of beauty for improving the lives of people facing disadvantage and impoverishment. The origins of the National Trust and garden suburbs are to be found in social reformers such as Octavia Hill and Henrietta Barnett. Nineteenth-century municipalism was strongly associated with the creation of parks, museums and public libraries for people's uplifting and betterment. Such goals and values similarly underpinned the aspirations of the welfare state's founders. This was reflected in early plans for council estates, garden suburbs and new towns.

While the welfare state was concerned with improving the conditions of 'the people' or 'the masses', as we have seen, it was, however, largely shaped initially by a narrow cultural elite. So while it was often concerned with people's moral and cultural improvement, as well as their material good, this tended to be as it was understood by their 'betters'. Thus in the early years of the welfare state, there were not only tensions between the middle and working classes – the former sometimes feeling that the gains achieved by the latter were at their expense. There were also cultural tensions between the welfare state's proponents and its intended beneficiaries. This may be an international issue in the development of welfare states. However, the cultural snobbery endemic in England can only have exaggerated the issues (Kynaston, 2008). We can also subsequently see such class tension being worked through in microcosm, in areas undergoing change and 'gentrification', where often there are major differences between the notions of 'community' of middle-class incomers and traditional working-class populations. The setting up of the Hanover Community Centre in Brighton, for instance, offers such a detailed case study, where the existing population wanted a bar, while incoming owner-occupiers were more interested in educational and 'improving' activities (Beresford and Croft, 1986, 87; Tomlinson, 1983, v, 66–8).

Snobbery and class conflict are themes that run have through UK culture and the arts over the period covered by this book. High culture and popular culture have come to be seen as very different and separate things. The tendency has been for public policy to support the former at the expense of the latter. This tradition is seen to have lingered with state funding bodies such as the Arts Council and the National Lottery, which are still associated strongly with metropolitan and high art biases. Rock and roll and television, whose histories have approximated to that of the welfare state, both offer illuminating case studies, providing insights into these issues. Pop music, with its black, Jewish and working-class roots, was devalued as lowbrow and vulgar, until eventually it became impossible to deny comparisons between the Beatles, Kinks, Bob Dylan or Bob Marley and other major figures in music through the ages (Stafford and Stafford, 2013, 82–3). The tradition established by the first General Manager of the state broadcaster, the BBC, John Reith, was a strongly paternalistic and educative one. This Reithian tradition was still heavily ensconced in the BBC in the formative years of the welfare state. This, and the misjudged association of the BBC with leftist politics, has provided fertile ground for right-wing populist discourse and developments. Spearheaded by Rupert Murdoch's media empire, the aim has been to take TV, as well as numerous high profile cultural and sports activities, out of public ownership and convert them instead into sources of private profit. However, there have also been counter-pressures underpinned by different values for arts, culture and sport, highlighting the importance, for example, of:

- challenging rather than reinforcing the commodification of art;
- supporting public art;
- supporting multicultural rather than monocultural arts and culture;
- encouraging collaborative, as well as competitive sport, supported at grassroots and not only at elite levels;
- valuing women and men equally;
- developing policy for play space and playing fields;

- challenging narrowing school curricula to encourage performing and visual arts;
- prioritising the resourcing of grassroots arts and cultural organisations and their networking;
- revaluing and resourcing disability and 'outsider' arts and cultures;
- supporting community-based arts and public involvement in art;
- resisting the narrow ownership of broadcast, electronic and print media;
- supporting more effectively, broader access to the internet, social networking and social media. (Hirschkop, 1999; Moser and McKay, 2005; Cleveland, 2008; Shape, 2012; Moran, 2013)

Health and social care

UK and indeed many other countries' health policies come in for frequent criticism for focusing upon 'illness services' and, despite the fact that we know health is determined by 'many broad factors', also being 'treatment focused', although this does not necessarily 'address the many causes of ill-health' (Blakemore et al , 2013, 225). At the same time, some commentators express caution about efforts to move beyond such narrow approaches. Thus John Hudson's observation that 'broad-based notions such as "wellbeing" or even "happiness" have become increasingly fashionable alternatives' to health and welfare in recent years and his concern that these may be used to deflect attention from big issues such as 'reducing poverty or income inequality' (Hudson, 2014, 3,11).

Tensions in health

What most concerns me, as someone working in it, is the erosion of the NHS. I started my nurse training 20 years ago. As a nurse and also as an individual who has grown up in this country, I feel proud and relieved about the existence of the NHS. It's immensely important – aiming towards a more equal society and a life where it isn't about being able to afford health and healthcare. In the five years I have been a diabetes nurse, there have been further advances in the treatment and management of diabetes. There has been expansion in medications and the technology for monitoring blood glucose. But there's a real tension between the pharmaceutical companies pushing for profit and the NHS with limited and tightening budgets. Ultimately what it means is that those who've got the money will have access to the whole range of technological developments. I remember a song we sang at primary school: 'If living were a thing that money could buy, then the rich would live and the poor would die'*. It's not an 'if' now, is it?

Catherine Beresford
Our daughter

*All My Trials, Lord

The history of the UK NHS has been one of constant reform. Yet many of the original problems remain because reform has mainly taken the form of reorganisations and restructurings. Between 1991 and 2013, there were six major reorganisations, with different structures now to be found in the four nations making up the UK. Yet fundamental problems, such as the over-dominance of medical professions (a problem undermining the NHS from its beginning), preoccupation with acute medical rather than long-term social care, lack of equity between physical and mental health, and inferior access to treatment for many groups, including disabled people, mental health service users, people with learning difficulties and members of black and minority ethnic communities, have remained unresolved (Blakemore et al, 2013, 206–26; Alcock with May, 2014, 129). The preoccupation with organisational change, managerialism and an increasing role for the private sector in the provision of services, medical insurance and capital investment, all reflect present neoliberal preoccupations.

The perfect GP

Dr Smith (real name!) was my GP when I was a young mother. He was incredibly interested and friendly. He was so kind and nice to talk to. The group practice was very responsive. They had a clinic for older people one afternoon a week and they paid for people's taxis which went round and picked them up. He did home visits. He was happy to come out to see you. I've had a lot of professional contact with GPs since as a palliative care social worker. I wish I could say that more than a minority were like him. He still stands out. For me he epitomises just how brilliant a GP can be.

Suzy Croft
My partner

Commentators also identify other problems. Determinants of health and well-being continue to be unequally distributed giving rise to health inequities and the premature onset of impairments for disadvantaged groups. This calls into question current policy assumptions that the retirement age can be extended (Coffey and Dugdill, 2013, 51, 62; Marmot, 2010). Employment is identified as a major determinant of health and well-being. While getting people into employment is prioritised as a key neoliberal social policy, poor quality, insecure employment and unemployment, all of which are associated with such policy, are more likely to promote bad than good health. 'Good work' has been linked with a number of criteria. These include stability, safety, fairness, inclusivity, opportunities for staff development, meaningfulness, support for 'work/life balance' and a measure of employee control and participation (Coffey and Dugdill, 2013, 61–2). The prevailing labour market reflects these less and less.

There is now much more talk in the UK of 'public health', but this largely seems to have been a rhetorical rather than real commitment. New Labour's policy to reduce smoking has been a rare example in the UK of adopting a social approach to tackling a large-scale health problem and has been remarkably successful. More generally the tendency has been to employ individualistic medicalised approaches, which have so far proved conspicuously unsuccessful. This has been true in relation to problems of obesity, alcohol dependence and gambling. There has been a reluctance to address class, cultural and economic issues or impose effective constraints on the industries associated with exacerbating these problems (Spicker, 2014, 112). Instead, except for Scotland, there has been a narrow focus on the individual, highlighting their deficiencies and the need for them to make changes in 'life style choices' (Alcock with May, 2014, 136). Judgements may then be applied as to whether people should receive help, since it is argued that they have brought on their own difficulties, for example, through smoking, eating and drinking behaviours.

Although the making of moral judgements in policy is particularly associated with employment and benefits policy, as we can see, moral judgements may also be applied in health policy. One of the most influential and perhaps damaging applications in health has been related to the use of non-prescription drugs. Here we can see how great the tension can be between morally based and effective or even workable policy and what happens when the two are confused. UK drug policy has been heavily influenced by US policy committed to the prohibition and criminalisation of such drug use. This is despite the long-term failure of such policy; its association with massively increased crime and violence to feed people's habits, increased morbidity and mortality and its failure as a strategy for harm minimisation (Cohen, 1993). Recent evidence shows that about a sixth of people in prison are serving sentences for drug offences and over half of prisoners report committing offences connected to their drug taking, with the need for money to buy drugs the most commonly cited factor (PFT, 2013, 7).

Why the welfare state is helpful

I think [the welfare state] is helpful because it helps children learn. Also I think that not having to pay very much for school is good because some people might not be able to go otherwise. I hope that hospitals keep on getting more advanced so that they can find cures for more things.

George Croft
My nephew by marriage, aged ten

Meanwhile in the UK and beyond, there are pressures for radical improvement in health policy, building on post-war experience and innovations, which include supporting:

- complementary treatments alongside conventional and traditional ones;
- holistic approaches to treatment and support, addressing social, psychological, spiritual and material as well as physiological issues;
- the effective unification of needs through health, social care, housing and other policy integration;
- the equalisation and integration of responses to physical and mental health;
- improved inter-disciplinary working and the challenging of professional hierarchies;
- a more publicly accountable pharmaceutical industry;
- a shift away from the narrow interpretation and dominance of the medical model and the demedicalisation of disability and learning difficulties;
- a greater emphasis on prevention rather than over-reliance on high-tech solutions;
- the challenging of ageism and other forms of discrimination;
- the valuing of palliative as well as curative care and support;
- joined-up responses to health through the life-course. (Blakemore et al, 2013; Walmsley et al, 2012; White, 2009; Rayner and Lang, 2012)

The radical social work movement, which has had a second flowering in the twenty-first century, also offers a blueprint for social care and social work reform for the future (Lavalette, 2011; Rogowski, 2013; Turbett,

2014). It has placed a particular emphasis on involving service users and carers, co-production and valuing the involvement and knowledge of practitioners. In the UK, it has been spearheaded by the Social Work Action Network (SWAN), a democratically organised national social work organisation and network. Through SWAN, radical social work has become an international movement, establishing its own journal, *Critical and Radical Social Work*, and supporting struggles in a wide range of countries as well as establishing national organisations in others, including Japan, Ireland and Greece.

Crime and criminal justice

The relationships between poverty and crime, 'the poor' and criminal law, have long been seen as significant ones. The Poor Law highlighted the relationship between the casual poor and criminality, just as social reformers sought to break the association. However, discussions about crime and criminal justice currently tend to take place separately from those about the welfare state, except where right-wing critics have sometimes sought to blame the welfare state for criminal and deviant behaviour (for example, Tanner, 1995; Bartholomew, 2004 [2013], 35). When Tony Blair, as Leader of the Labour Party, sloganised about being 'tough on crime, tough on the causes of crime' and said we 'all suffer crime and the poorest and vulnerable most of all' he seemed to be re-establishing this link (British Political Speech, 1995). Yet this did not seem to be carried through effectively in his or subsequent social policies.

Statistics for the UK prison population for the twenty-first century make disturbing reading and strongly reinforce associations with welfare issues. For example, data accumulated by the Prison Reform Trust reveals that:

- in 2013 there were more than 83,000 people in prison in England and Wales; the numbers more than doubled between 1993 and 2012;
- there is no consistent correlation between prison numbers and levels of crime;
- in 2009 more than 200,000 children had a parent in prison, twice the number for the same year affected by divorce in the family;
- the proportion of the sentenced prison population serving a life or indeterminate sentence for public protection (IPP) increased from 9 per cent in 1993 to 19 per cent in 2012;
- 47 per cent of adults are reconvicted within one year of being released. (PFT, 2013 p 1)

There are strong associations with social deprivation and disadvantage:

- 47 per cent of prisoners say they have no qualifications; this compares to 15 per cent of the working-age general population in the UK;
- 15 per cent of newly sentenced prisoners reported being homeless before custody; 9 per cent were sleeping rough. (p 8)

The data also suggests that prison serves as a place of last resort for people who may be failed by other services as well as reflecting broader discriminations and exclusions in our society. Thus:

- 25 per cent of children in the youth justice system have identified special educational needs, 46 per cent are rated as underachieving at school and 29 per cent have difficulties with literacy and numeracy;
- 49 per cent of women prisoners in a Ministry of Justice study were assessed as suffering from anxiety and depression, compared with 19 per cent of the female UK population;
- 46 per cent of women in prison have been identified as having suffered a history of domestic abuse;
- 53 per cent of women in prison reported having experienced emotional, physical or sexual abuse as a child, compared to 27 per cent of men;
- more than 17,240 children were estimated to be separated from their mother in 2010 by imprisonment;
- currently 15 per cent of women in prison, 617, are foreign nationals, some of whom are known to have been coerced or trafficked into offending;
- out of the British national prison population, 10 per cent are black and 6 per cent are Asian, compared with the 2.8 per cent of the general population;
- there is now greater disproportionality in the number of black people in prisons in the UK than in the United States;
- as at 8 October 2012, there were 557 immigration detainees held in prison. (pp 4–5)

There is also an over-representation of older, disabled people and mental health service users in the prison system. As institutional settings for such service users have declined in mainstream social policy, so prison seems to have come to serve as an alternative for growing numbers of people. It also seems to serve as a default social care system as this has become increasingly residualised. Thus:

- people aged 60 and over are now the fastest growing age group in the prison system; the number aged 60 and over rose by 103 per cent between 2002 and 2011;
- an estimate of 36 per cent of prisoners interviewed in a Ministry of Justice study were considered to have an impairment when survey answers about disability and health, including mental health, were screened;
- 20–30 per cent of all offenders have learning disabilities or difficulties that interfere with their ability to cope with the criminal justice system;
- 49 per cent of women and 23 per cent of male prisoners in a Ministry of Justice study were assessed as suffering from anxiety and depression; this can be compared with 16 per cent of the general UK population (12 per cent of men and 19 per cent of women);
- levels of drug use are high among offenders, with the highest levels of use found among the most prolific offenders; 64 per cent of prisoners reported having used drugs in the four weeks before custody. (pp 5–6)

A range of additional problems have also emerged:

- the increasing psychiatrisation of crime, associating crime with 'mental disorder' without independent evidence, further stigmatising mental health service users;
- cuts in the legal aid system;
- the criminalisation of drug dependence;
- the disproportionately damaging effects on poor people of fining policy as a source of income generation, for example, in parking policy.

At the same time, while the prison system has in many ways continued to dominate the criminal justice system, other positive developments have taken place since the creation of the welfare state, which offer hope for future policy and practice. These include:

- the development of the probation service from the 1940s, offering advocacy, support and effective community-based alternatives to prison (see www.probationassociation.co.uk/about-us/history-of-probation) (sadly overshadowed by more recent privatisation);
- the ending of corporal and capital punishment, regardless of populist appeals for their reinstatement;

- improved recognition of and response to previously ignored or marginalised offences, including rape (including within marriage), domestic violence, child sexual abuse and historic abuse, hate crime, for example in relation to disabled people and lesbian, gay, bi-sexual and transgendered people;
- the development of court diversion schemes, for example, for offenders with mental health problems (Parsonage, 2009);
- the greater use of more effective community sentences (PFT, 2013, 11);
- policy which supports parenting rather than weakening and undermining it;
- the emergence of prisoner/user-led organisations advancing user involvement, peer support schemes and alternative approaches to criminal justice (see www.uservoice.org/our-work/library/publications/) (PFT, 2013, 13);
- increased emphasis on education, training, mentoring policy and practice for offenders.

Conclusion

In this chapter we identified a series of emerging principles for future welfare. While much of the recent history of the welfare state has been concerned with seeking to roll it back or write its epitaph, these principles highlight its future potential rather than its need for replacement. At their heart, however, lies a concern with a changed relationship between people and services, support and service users. This is neither the paternalistic relationship intuitively adopted by the welfare state's original proponents, nor the consumerist relationship argued for since by its right-wing critics. We have seen that both have profound limitations. Instead it is a more equal, more collaborative, participatory and active relationship. It is also a relationship that starts from recognition that merely providing services and support is not enough. Instead there has to be acknowledgement of the need for a process which makes for equal understanding of and access to services and support.

This exploration of policy also offers a reminder of the importance of the inter-relation of economic and social policy and the need to rethink both, as well as to rethink the nature and purpose of paid work. This was at the heart of early welfare state thinking, but the political shift to the right since its founding has led to a narrow and regressive preoccupation with free market economics, regardless of their damaging effects on an ever-growing proportion of the population.

Furthermore as we explore each of the key policies first embraced by the post-war welfare state, we can see both their weaknesses and limitations as first implemented and then as deviated from subsequently. But we can also see the innovations and improvements that offer hope for the future. In the next chapter we move from policy to practice and provision. We will look in more detail at the forms that future support may take, building on the principles, ideas, initiatives and innovation that have developed since the founding of the welfare state.

FOURTEEN

Supporting each other in the future

One thing is certain – service users have asserted themselves. They have made it known that they are, like Eliot's Magi, 'no longer at ease here, in the old dispensation', where they were expected to take what was offered. Concepts of citizenship and rights have replaced old ideas of benevolence and good intentions.

(Foreword, *A challenge to change: Practical experiences of building user led services*, Beresford and Harding, 1993)

Patient-controlled services: a real alternative to the institutions that destroy the confident independence of so many.

(Judi Chamberlin, 1988)

Social policy has to be directed not only to maximising GNP [gross national product] but to securing the wellbeing of individuals in a secure society.

(A.H. Halsey, sociologist, *Guardian* obituary, 17 October 2014)

Rethinking public services

When we look at public services in the UK, despite the massive technological and other changes that have taken place in modern times, it is difficult to see any matching pattern of improvement over the years. If anything, essential services, such as street cleaning, road repairs and rubbish collection, seem to have deteriorated in quality, with less well maintained roads and pavements, fewer collections and more demands made on householders. Utilities are still subject to failure and breakdown and massively increased in cost. Public transport, such as local bus, coach and train services, while sometimes more truly public services in the sense of being more accessible to disabled people, are much reduced in scale, reach and flexibility. They are generally much more expensive than their European counterparts, particularly rail, in spite of continuing large-scale public subsidy. These shortcomings continue despite massive improvements in transport reliability, efficiency, speed and environmental impact. In rural areas, for example, many older people are under enormous pressure to drive, despite increasing frailty, for rear of having their mobility and lives drastically restricted.

The one service where people can point to dramatic improvements (despite all its other organisational and funding difficulties) is the National Health Service. Here radically improved treatments, interventions, drugs and procedures, have played a revolutionary part in improving all our lives, particularly those of people with chronic conditions, reducing mortality and morbidity rates, as well as making possible survival from previously life-threatening and life-limiting illnesses and conditions. Sadly these improvements largely seem to be confined to physical healthcare. Mental health services still seem to be grossly underfunded and tied to outmoded over-medicalised thinking. The only other example of general improvement that this author has been able to think of has been public transport in London, which has been subject to more regulation and restrictions in the public interest than elsewhere (Smithers, 2014). While expensive, it now offers both an improved and more accessible service.

Beyond these two examples, whatever the scientific and technological advances made in the 70 years since the creation of the welfare state, the increasingly market-led ideological, political and organisational drivers that have shaped policy, do not seem to have kept pace. Significantly, we seem to take this lack of progress over such a long period for granted, as we step over broken pavements, in poorly lit, sometimes unsafe streets and drive on potholed urban roads. Instead, technological advances seem to have been used primarily to make cost savings for service providers (in both the public and private sectors rather than to improve the experience of people as citizens and service users.

My friend Chris

I got to know Chris through the survivors' movement. He had big ups and downs. On this occasion he was very down, something that hadn't happened for a while. First he was admitted to a psychiatric ward in the local general hospital. That was ok. Then he was transferred to the psychiatric hospital – a big Victorian institution, still in operation today. It had long echoey corridors. Chris didn't take his radio with him. He was frightened it would be stolen. He said that on this occasion, things weren't too bad. Nothing nasty happened to him. He didn't see any physical or verbal violence. The food was poor and he noticed less time with the nurses and psychiatrists than before. Always more cuts. He was 'specialed' –

people followed him round to check he was ok, but as he said, 'Were they worried about me or watching their backs?' And when they said 'You'll be ok', was this just what they said to everyone? It always felt like being in hospital was another trial that Chris had to deal with rather than something that was helpful for him. Why couldn't it be the other way round and then perhaps, just perhaps, later he wouldn't have killed himself.

The author

Social care policy epitomises this problem. It has been at the vanguard of ideological and political reform from the time of Mrs Thatcher. It has served as a laboratory for cutting-edge neoliberal ideological policy change. Yet when its service users are asked what they think of it, many repeatedly report reduced access to support, and less and poorer quality support (Beresford et al, 2005; Branfield et al, 2006; Beresford and Hasler, 2009; Beresford, 2010b; Beresford and Andrews, 2012). This is a reminder that whatever the intentions and rhetoric of policymakers, the defining issue for policy is what it is actually like on the receiving end – how it is experienced. This is as true for neoliberal as for socialist policy. In this book we have already encountered many first-hand accounts of both failing to match their stated intentions. We have also seen that until welfare service users themselves began to organise, relatively little attention was paid to their accounts of their experience of policy 'on the receiving end'.

Social care, with its early interest in setting 'standards' and 'targets', offers important insights with much wider application for public services. 'Outcome' measures as a key way of defining and measuring quality gained prominence in social care in the 1990s. What was intended to distinguish such outcome measures was that they would assess not what services or organisations did, but what they actually *achieved* (Netten et al, 2010). This tended to be framed in terms of improvements to people's 'quality of life' or 'wellbeing'. Shaping Our Lives, which subsequently became a national user-led organisation and network, saw this as an important development. But it also noted that discussions about outcomes were mainly professionally-led, embodying essentially bureaucratic processes and standards. Between 1996 and 1998 it carried out its own research projects to explore service users' views about 'outcomes'. Shaping Our Lives concluded that it was 'essential that users' views were primary in this process and that evaluation included the subjective perspectives of individual users' (Shaping Our Lives National User Network et al, 2003, 3). This led it to challenge the emphasis on outcomes and to conclude that the process people went though was crucial and inseparable.

> Outcomes and process: the process of getting a service and the way in which it is delivered can have a major impact on a user's experience of a service. These experiences include problems such as poor access to services, delays in service provision, poor treatment from service providers, lack of consultation or consultation which is ignored or not acted upon. Such experiences have an impact on the outcome of the service and are not detached from the outcome in users' perceptions. This view is contrary to the prevailing view among academics and professionals, who have focused primarily on outcomes in terms of the end result of a service (Shaping Our Lives National User Network et al, 2003).

This emphasis on starting with and being guided by people's own direct experience of services and support, is what distinguishes the user-led approaches that offer a transformative model for the future. It stands in sharp contrast to traditional policymakers' models of starting with their own ideology, ideas and assumptions. Policy follows from what works for people on the receiving end, rather than vice versa. Instead of people having to fit into a service-led system – the model that has predominated from the Poor Law, through the post-war welfare state, to neoliberal welfare ideology – services and support follow from the experience, views, ideas and preferences of service users themselves.

This approach has been pioneered by service users and their allies through the whole process of providing services and support. For them, what is most important is the service and support people actually receive on the ground. As far as they are concerned, all follows from this. Such a user-led approach is based on and committed to service users' involvement and control (Carr, 2004). Ensuring such involvement provides a basis for long-term change. As Enid Levin, a committed ally, wrote in an early guide: 'The service user movement emphasises the importance of models of participation that are based on human rights, equalities, inclusion and the social model of disability' (Levin, 2004, 9).

First, service users began to explore and articulate their personal experience, then they shared it with each other to develop collective accounts and understandings. Next they sought to influence those who worked with them. This has extended to all aspects of the provision that affects their lives, including:

- occupational and professional education and training;
- public service practice;
- new forms of collective services and individual support/assistance;
- new organisational forms.

We will now look at each of these.

Transforming occupational and professional education and training

There was early recognition among the mental health service users/survivors and disabled people's movements, that how the people who worked with them were socialised into their roles was critical to how they understood and behaved towards them. Thus an early priority for these movements was to transform such education and training so that it was much more in tune with what worked with and was helpful for service users. Traditional approaches to professional education could actually have the opposite effect, emphasising the distance between service users and providers; alienating the one from the other. Survivors and disabled people soon put an emphasis on their involvement in such professional education. From the late 1980s, there were initiatives to develop 'service user trainers' and training for 'user trainers' so that people as service users could inject their direct experience of public services, their 'experiential knowledge' into professional training. As Enid Levin wrote:

> Training for service user and carer trainers is high on the agenda of their organisations. Different types and levels of training should be offered. There is scope for service user and carer organisations to develop their own training and support systems, and for national bodies to develop accredited training leading to qualifications. (Levin, 2004, 2)

Service user pioneers gained training skills and developed courses (Perry, 2005). Disabled People's organisations such as the Derbyshire Coalition for Inclusive Living developed roles and courses to help service users deal with services on more equal terms as well as to help service workers work with them more equally (http://www.dcil.org.uk/about/). As well as service users and their organisations working to make an impact on professional training from the outside, such training itself began to change because of the pressure it came under from service users. The major breakthrough took place in social work.

303

When degree level qualification for social workers was introduced in England in 2003, it became a requirement for there to be service user and carer involvement in all aspects and all stages of qualifying courses. Not only this, but funding from central government was made available to all training providers to support such involvement and to make its implementation a practical possibility (Levin, 2004).

Thus user involvement in professional education and learning progressed from being an add-on offered by service users, to an integrated and essential part of qualifying courses. Since then, requirements for user involvement in professional education has extended to psychiatry, medicine and the wide range of health related professions regulated by the Health and Care Professions Council (Fadden et al, 2005). A government response to a consultation in 2014 reported the strong support for such involvement in social work and for retaining central funding from educators, service users and students (DH, 2014). Service users and their organisations are now involved in all aspects of professional education and training. This includes involvement in recruitment, in shaping the curriculum, providing training, provision of course work and learning materials, as well as evaluating and assessing students (Beresford, 1994; Branfield, 2007; 2009; Branfield et al, 2007).

Such involvement, of course, can have its limitations. We know from the evidence that its implementation can be patchy and that as well as agencies which are innovative and committed, there are others where it is implemented with less enthusiasm (Branfield, 2009). It can also be co-opted to serve existing professional agendas, rather than to challenge them. Service users on benefits can also be excluded by unsympathetic benefits policy and practice which inappropriately treat their efforts to get involved as evidence that they can and should be in employment (Turner and Beresford, 2005b; CSCI, 2007).

Such involvement, however, can also be seen to have had a revolutionary impact on professional education, not least because increasingly training courses are only approved and revalidated if it is properly adopted. Service users have long emphasised that such involvement has the potential to change the culture of professional practice and public services, making it much more user centred. Service users talk about it being the best way of getting better workers. This way, would-be practitioners can meet service users on equal terms, get a better understanding of them, find out how practice is actually experienced and what works and doesn't work. It makes it possible to develop more equal relationships between service users and providers, because service users are involved in valued roles as educators. Perhaps for the first time, would-be professionals see them on equal terms, being helped *by them*, rather than always seeing them in times of crisis and difficulty, when *they* need help (Tew et al, 2004; Wykurz and Kelly, 2002).

Social work elitism: a continuing issue

My postgraduate career began by my studying for a two-year diploma in social and administrative studies at Oxford University's Department of Social Administration in 1968. It ran alongside the social work course and we joined the social work students in some of their professional activities. One of these was a visit to Pressed Steel Fisher, part of the car making conglomerate at Cowley, now largely gone. It was at a time typified by industrial unrest and the continuing decline of the British car industry. We saw the production line and what stays in my memory were the women who worked the machines for making seat covers. This involved stretching forward and then pulling back and this was endlessly repeated. It looked grim in a noisy, pressured environment. This was far from the breezy atmosphere of *Made in Dagenham*. But what I remember most was having lunch. We ate in a management restaurant. This was clearly separate from the workers' canteen. I wondered what kind of thinking meant that trainee social workers were associated with management rather than workforce, when it was much more likely that they would be working with people from the latter. The talk then was of Oxford social work students being the social service department directors of the future – a similar philosophy to that underpinning the *Frontline* scheme set up in 2014 to recruit a new 'elite' to social work and social work management, reflecting the same 'them and us' assumptions.

The author

Public service practice

Ultimately most social policy boils down to interactions between service providers and service users or recipients. This can range from the unequal, intimidating, often brutal relationships associated with the Poor Law, to helping relationships linked with professions such as nursing and palliative care social work. Contact may be superficial or intimate, fleeting or longstanding. It may relate to mundane, day-to-day issues such as getting planning permission, or attending a school open day, to more complex and difficult matters, such as making a claim for benefits, or undergoing a medical intervention. There are the same pressures in social policy, as with all goods and services, to use modern technology to replace human contact and involvement, thereby reducing labour costs, often the largest element in expenditure. This has led to increasing reliance on online communication and in health and social care, to the development of 'telecare'. This is meant to provide remote support to older and disabled people, although there are also concerns about it increasing surveillance and control (Francis and Holmes, 2010). Neither of these two developments has been initiated or particularly welcomed by service users. Many, especially those most likely to need on-going support from social policy, see direct human contact as a positive rather than a negative factor. The nature of relationships is thus a key but often overlooked issue in social policy, especially as it can involve both support and control and the two have sometimes become blurred.

Good welfare?

It's about relationships – good relationships. You have to have people – a lot of people – well trained, not necessarily highly qualified – you need some of them, too, of course. You most need people who are prepared to spend time building up relationships, building up trust, getting to know people, not being judgemental, treating people with equality. That is what works, basically.

Suzy Croft
My partner

There have tended to be a limited range of relationships in public service. There has been the traditional paternalistic/'doing good' model from charity: the public service approach of the post-war welfare state and, more recently, the exchange relationship of the market which has been grafted on to it. But another model has also begun to emerge from service users and their organisations. This has been determinedly based on values of equality, shared experience and understanding. It has found some of its most advanced expressions in health and social care, but it also connects with social policy provision much more generally. This provides a model for future occupational and professional practice. It challenges deference, condescension and inequality in professional relationships. Traditionally such public service practice has been shaped by service providers and professionals, but more recently service users and their organisations have influenced it. They place an emphasis on what service users want from such practice.

Research now provides us with a clear picture of what people seem to value from their contact with public services, particularly from helping services. They highlight a range of qualities and skills that they associate with good practice and good practitioners. This holds across a range of services and of service users. Repeatedly people highlight the importance of practice that offers respect, credibility, empathy, a commitment to confidentiality and privacy, reliability and continuity, as well as practical skills and a sense of judgement about 'risk' (Harding and Beresford, 1996, 24; Beresford et al, 2011, 225–8). They place an emphasis on communication skills and 'listening' to what people say. Service users repeatedly highlight a range of human qualities which they value. These include:

- warmth
- empathy
- respect
- listening
- treating people with equality
- reliability
- being non-judgemental. (Beresford et al, 2007)

People often talk about these as personal characteristics or human qualities. They can also be seen as hard-earned skills, gained through careful training. They also emphasise the importance of the *relationship* between the service worker and service user if public services and support are to be helpful and successful. A study of the views of young people about their experience of educational social work highlighted this broader issue. It concluded that: 'The most important finding… was the central importance of their relationship with their educational social worker and the associated practical help and guidance, which was so highly valued' (Pritchard et al, 1998, 930).

Social work practitioners have paid particular attention to this relationship, arguing for practice which is both relationship-based and which supports rather than undermines people's relationships (for example, Featherstone et al, 2014). This contrasts strongly with the emphasis in neoliberal social policy on technical and organisational issues, as though the experience of services and support could be reduced to a series of bureaucratic or mechanical transactions. This trend with user-controlled support towards more humanistic provision is at some odds with prevailing approaches to services. Here reliance on regulation and guidance based on bureaucratic standards seems to have the effect of depersonalising relationships between service users and workers, making them risk averse and restricted (Andrews, 2014a; 2014b). While such a shift to practice which prioritises the human relationship is clearly important for health and welfare practice, which may have an intimate impact on people's lives, it is also likely to be helpful for all public policy practice, if it is to work in an egalitarian, inclusive and accessible way.

Self-defined needs

At the heart of practice is assessment. Traditionally in social policy, people go to services, see practitioners and these offer them what they are used to providing or what they think people need. We know that this doesn't work well. But equally just being told that you can make choices and have what you want doesn't necessarily mean much if you have low expectations, little idea or information about what might be possible and have spent years in disempowering and institutionalising situations. People need first to be in a position to make meaningful choices.

Rights and the meeting and safeguarding of people's civil and human rights need to be central in a reformed approach to social policy. As we have seen, services have traditionally been based on ideas of 'need'. This approach has been problematic because generally it has rested on the definitions and judgements of professionals and their organisations. It has emphasised people's deficiencies, rather than their capacities and in order to qualify for support, people have had to demonstrate these deficiencies. As Judi Chamberlin said many years back now, 'The definition of need would come from the client' (Chamberlin, 1988, 18). It is important to move to a model based on self-definition of needs where, with appropriate advocacy, information and support, service users are able to identify what support they would want to do the things they would like to do. A key part of practice is making it possible for people to define their own needs rather than have them defined for them. Practitioners can help service users work out what they want, although outside and independent advice and advocacy is also likely to be helpful. Instead of being a bureaucratic process, assessment can take the form of a conversation and be the way in which service user and practitioner make contact, get to know each other and begin building their relationship,

Person-centred practice

There is increasing interest in 'personalised' or 'person-centred practice' in public services. This is seen as an approach that puts the service user first, is strongly value based and where the relationship between service user and worker is of central importance (Beresford et al, 2011,

39–63). A number of characteristics are associated with good quality relationships (Beresford et al, 2011, 240 and following). These include:

- *continuity* – so that people are able to get to know particular workers when necessary, rather than these constantly changing;
- *accessible and inclusive communication* – with all service users, regardless of the language they use or if they communicate differently;
- *user involvement* – seeing the service user as a *co-producer* of practice, shaping it through their engagement and interactions, rather than practice being something solely determined by the service worker;
- *reciprocity* – so that the service user is not left to feel either like a passive participant, or totally responsible for their own well-being;
- *emotional attachment* – not behaving mechanically or impersonally, instead, finding the right balance, maintaining professionalism, having an awareness of appropriate boundaries, but being sensitive, flexible and enabling. Service users in helping settings sometimes talk about practitioners as 'more like a friend', by which they mean they display the characteristics which they associate with a trusted friend;
- *shared experience* – encouraging the recruitment of practitioners who may have better understanding of service users' situation because of their own lived experience, as, for example, a service user or a disabled person. Where once such experience might have been seen as disqualifying someone from such a career, it is now increasingly coming to be valued and seen as a positive factor;
- *collating the learning from individual practice* – to inform and guide broader practice and policy.

Practice now becomes a process of co-production with the worker taking their cue from the ideas and comments of the service user, rather than themselves taking the lead. The worker can offer information and suggestions for people to bounce their own ideas off, but crucially by being relationship-based, practice can now become a two-way street, rather than a journey directed by the practitioner.

Such an approach may always have been the basis for good practice in public policy, but it, and the elements associated with it, are now being advanced systematically by service users and their supporters as the route to achieving it. These features all highlight overlaps and interaction between service workers and service users. Some more consumerist approaches to experiencing practice have also been developed in recent years, such as the 'mystery shopper', service sampling and managers spending time on 'the shop floor'. However, these are not based on the same commitment to equalising relationships between service users and providers.

> ### When my mother died
>
> My mother and I had a very difficult relationship. Shortly after she was admitted to hospital, she was moved to the local hospice and died there after two weeks. She really liked being in the hospice. They were non-judgemental. They gave no impression of thinking we or she were good or bad; behaving well or badly. They enabled me and my partner Suzy to say what we felt properly and to think about and work through our often strong feelings. They enabled my mother as far as she could and wanted to, to do the same. On the last night she could speak, she spoke a lot to a nurse about her feelings of regret and the nurse wrote it down for us. The hospice offered us opportunities to come to some resolutions about our relationships and what had happened. Staff gave all of us a sense of respect and of our own value. We could also see this happening with other people they were working with. All members of staff seemed to share this positive culture and attitude. We weren't just appendages to my mother, nor she to us. There was no taking sides. They involved everyone including our then young children. They could move freely about the hospice, play with the cat, with no sense of 'children should be seen and not heard'. Conditions at the hospice were good. No sense of being a second class citizen. It was clean, bright, friendly, attractive, *human*. You had the sense my mother was getting the best treatment available. There was continuity. After she died there were opportunities, which we took, to see the counsellor and a card on the first anniversary offering a chance for more contact. They were culturally and ethnically sensitive. The hospice had Christian origins, but knowing my mother was Jewish, they removed the cross where she was lying when we visited her after she died. The hospice was everything you'd hope for from a social service.
>
> *The author*

The 'gap-mending' approach

This interest in challenging divisions between service users and practitioners, recipients and providers, has found expression in a new idea which has come to be called the 'gap-mending' approach. This grew out of a European project, PowerUs, focusing on social work education and has extended its focus to professional education and practice (www.powerus.se). Starting with a concern that care practitioners and service users were often separated by differences in class, status and experience, which professional training could reinforce, the aim has been to bridge the gaps through enabling them to be involved in learning together. This has taken the form both of service users being actively involved in professional education and training, as described earlier and in developing courses for both service users and trainee professionals to learn and gain qualifications together. Both have helped build mutual trust, develop shared understandings and provided a basis for better training and practice. They have challenged the 'them and us' distinction which has historically marred social policy.

New forms of collective services and peer support/ assistance

A further expression of such a gap-mending approach is where the 'gap' between service users and providers is blurred and overcome by people with experience as service users themselves providing support. Such user-controlled support has developed in two directions; the provision of collective services and of individual arrangements for support.

User-controlled services

At the heart of a radically altered approach to providing support for people for the future are self-run or user-controlled services. They are key to transforming policy and practice and the lives of service users. There is now a long track record of people pioneering their own user-controlled services. The famous American mental health service user/survivor, Judi Chamberlin, was writing about 'patient controlled services' in her groundbreaking book, *On our own*, in 1977 (Chamberlin, 1988). This can be seen as part of a broader development of user-controlled services developed by service users and disabled people. This has a history of about 30 years' innovation. These services include safe and crisis houses, drop-in and day-centres, help lines, information, advice, advocacy, peer support, counselling and personal assistance schemes, residential, housing and employment projects, voluntary work, training schemes, environmental and gardening projects.

Such services are based on a series of principles, which we have already encountered earlier in the book. These include:

- prioritising self-advocacy
- being rights based
- building on social models and the philosophy of independent living
- self-management and self-support

- commitment to anti-oppressive practice
- supporting race equality and cultural diversity
- minimising compulsion – breaking the 'mad/bad' link
- prioritising participation
- equalising power relations. (Beresford, 2010c, 62–80)

In the mental health field, user-controlled services have tended to break out of the narrow medicalised, psychiatric approach to responding to mental health problems, instead framing support in broader social terms that addresses the wider problems and barriers that service users highlight. They have been organised as cooperatives, social enterprise schemes and charitable organisations. They can be, as Judi Chamberlin highlighted, a network of provision and support, flexible so that people can move within it as they need more or less or different kinds of support (Chamberlin, 1988, 18). Such services have been run and managed by service users and had service user workers. They offer a model for transforming traditional services (Beresford and Harding, 1993; Morris, 1994). We have reliable evidence about such user-controlled services. The ground-breaking user-controlled research project, *Creating independent futures*, provides some of the most detailed findings about such user-controlled services. It explored the views of all stakeholders involved with such services, from the service user trustees responsible for their governance and the user practitioners providing them, to, crucially, the service users who accessed and used them. The results were overwhelmingly positive, in contrast to many people's experience of traditional mainstream services. Service users valued such user-controlled services, felt that they were more supportive and sensitive than other traditional arrangements and highlighted their benefits. Such services were particularly popular among service users and improved their quality of life. This has important economic and social benefits for the service user, their family and the local community (Barnes et al, 2000a; 2000b; 2001; Barnes and Mercer, 2006). This is an international development, finding expression in both western industrialised nations and the South/developing world. Tina Coldham, a longstanding survivor activist, has offered a helpful explanation for the wide appeal of user-controlled services.

> To some, user-led services might seem like the lunatics running the asylum. However, mad people are moved to provide user-led provision for their peers for very good reasons. Firstly, we can have enormous insight into our distress and develop incredible empathy towards others as

a result of this. Secondly, because we are grounded in our experiences, users can be very objective and committed to making what matters work. More so, we harbour a deeper understanding of what matters and therefore are driven by a passion for getting it right, particularly when we feel others miss the point. User involvement is a means to an end; that end is people being able to get on with their lives mentally well. However, involvement often becomes a whole industry with a purpose of its own, and doesn't actually impact upon people's lives as the end product. Users and survivors are brave to challenge the vast mental health system from within. Some of us are running alternatives to this as a way of challenging the status quo in a positive manner that can have real impact upon people's lives. We can be 'madly' creative and innovative in developing solutions to our problems, and in doing so, inspire others, and develop user leadership. I was once told 'If you want commitment, get people who have been committed!' What more can I say? (Quoted in Beresford, 2010c, 87)

The natural home for user-controlled services has been user-controlled organisations or ULOs (user-led organisations) as they are also known. Such services have developed alongside campaigning, as part of ULOs' activities and it is questionable whether they are likely to work effectively in any other organisational setting. The *Creating independent futures* project reported that 'The interviewees were adamant that user led organisations were far more responsive to their individual needs both in terms of what was on offer and how it was offered. The level of peer support that individuals received was a key consideration' (Barnes et al, 2001, 5).

Yet a longstanding problem, certainly in the UK, but also beyond, has been the failure of governments to support either user-led organisations or user-controlled services to play their much valued part in social policy. Such services remain marginal in public policy, despite all the rhetoric about ending the 'monopoly' of state provision (Woodin, 2006). This is not for want of service users trying. Service users and their organisations have worked hard to expand the kind of non-medicalised provision that they have shown a particular capacity to provide successfully. However, they have continued to face big barriers. As Colin Barnes of the Centre for Disability Studies at Leeds University has said of the pioneering developments by disabled people:

> In spite of entrenched opposition from established service providers, services such as Disability Information and Advice Lines (DIAL), peer counselling and support facilities, integrated accessible housing schemes for disabled and non-disabled people, direct payment schemes for personal assistance and technical aids and equipment, were all pioneered and provided by grassroots CIL type groups during the 1970s and 80s. (Quoted in Beresford, 2010c, 89)

User-controlled services still face the same barriers that Judi Chamberlin identified more than 30 years ago. To overcome these, a strategic approach to supporting the development of user-controlled and self-run services is key for the future. This will need the allocation of specific (secure) funding to kickstart such provision. Such services also offer important employment, training and career opportunities for mental health service users/survivors and other groups of service users. More support and evaluation will be needed to maximise these opportunities and to enhance skill development and career opportunities for service users. They offer a ground-breaking and unique way in which 'the helped' can be helpers and the helping helped.

Peer support

There are many approaches to peer support. These can be more and less formal. Service users/survivors have long highlighted the value they get from the support that they can offer each other because of the shared understandings and experience that they have which provides a key basis for trust-building and mutuality. Some service users develop 'mentoring' relationships with others which provide guidance and support. Others have formed counselling relationships with each other based on friendship and shared experience. For example, a long-term mental health service user described to me an arrangement that he and two other survivors had used over several years. Initially it was a support group where they would meet, and then became a virtual support group. They would begin by taking turns talking about their situation without interruption for about five minutes, only occasionally giving feedback to each other. People were listened to and found it really helpful to talk about what was happening to them (Beresford, 2010c, 91).

It is also worth quoting Anne Wilson (the pseudonym formerly used by mental health service user/survivor, Kathy Boxall) at length about the positives she has gained from 'co-counselling'.

I was a mental health service user and was well and truly caught up in the psychiatric system. I met someone who was involved in co-counselling and was really interested in what she told me. When I told the mental health professionals working with me that I wanted to try co-counselling, all of them advised against it because they said people like me (with 'schizophrenia') 'needed trained mental health professionals, not amateurs'.

Doing co-counselling 'fundamentals' training has to be the best thing I have ever done in my life. Co-counsellors work in pairs and half way through, 'client' and 'counsellor' swap places so you each spend an equal amount of time as both client and counsellor. It is therefore a relationship of equals and there is no possibility of an 'expert' or 'professional' telling you what is 'wrong with you', as when it is your turn to be the client, you are in charge. This was a revelation, but nothing like as much of a revelation as the most important thing for me about co-counselling which was hearing other people talk about their experiences and concerns when they were the client and I was the counsellor. What I realised was that a lot of the 'symptoms' and strange perceptions I experienced (which psychiatrists had attributed to 'schizophrenia' in my case) were in fact quite common experiences – I realised this because I co-counselled with many, many people who during the course of their co-counselling sessions spoke about being in stressful situations and experiencing some of what I experienced, maybe in not such an extreme way or over such extended periods, but nevertheless very similar experiences to my own. I can't tell you what they said as the content of co-counselling sessions is strictly confidential, and confidentiality is something which co-counsellors take very seriously. Through co-counselling therefore I came to see myself as a 'normal' person. This was a fantastic achievement given all the negative and damning roles I'd been assigned by the psychiatrists; roles which I had also deeply internalised. And I also made many friends.

Being involved in CCI (Co-Counselling International, www.co-counselling.org.uk) has also enabled me to develop friendship networks locally, nationally and internationally. (Quoted in Beresford, 2010c, 92–4)

315

There is a constant pressure from the existing service system to subvert innovative approaches such as peer support. While it has increasingly adopted the rhetoric of 'peer support', often this reflects no more than the rebranding of conventional divisions of labour and status differences within dominant psychiatric ideology (Faulkner and Kalathil, 2012; Fabris, 2013). That's why it is important to be clear about peer support's intended nature and purpose and to keep it truly user led. As the survivor Anne Beales has said:

> At its heart, peer support exists to benefit the individuals who engage with it, through building mutually beneficial relationships based on shared experience, trust and empathy. Evidence shows that these relationships provide people with self-help strategies that professionals may not be able to offer or even know about. Peer support is by its very nature a community activity, and so it helps people break out of social exclusion. Peer support also ticks the 'co-production' box as it cannot be done to or for us, and it begins to address our own agenda around what we (service users/survivors) mean by wellbeing. Whilst we can't avoid the fact that any potential cuts will have a devastating impact on frontline services for people with mental health issues the service user movement should also recognise the opportunity to mobilise and promote the value of service user involvement as critical as well as cost-effective, because it *works*. (Quoted in Beresford, 2010c, 103)

Personal assistance schemes

The main way in which the disabled people's movement has advanced the idea of 'independent living' based on a social model of disability, has been through the introduction of 'self-run personal assistance' schemes, funded by 'direct payments' or 'personal budgets'. What these mean, essentially, is that the individual service user, if entitled, receives an allocation of state funding directly themselves, with which they are then able to purchase the 'package of support' which *they* want, to meet their support needs as they define them and over which they can have control. Disabled people have often used this money to employ 'personal assistants' (whom they hire and fire) to meet their support requirements. So far, such direct payments schemes, which have subsequently been extended by legislation to become a mandatory option for a wider range of service users, have represented the strongest expression of individualised 'user-controlled' support for health and social care service users (Campbell, 1993). They transform the relationship between service user and worker. Instead of being an 'over and under' relationship, there is the potential for equality, with the personal assistant working to the wishes of the service user and also receiving training in line with their preferences and requirements.

They can provide wonderful opportunities for service users to get the kind of socially-based support that the traditional service system has so often failed to provide. They make it possible for service users to reassess their support needs in non-medicalised terms and secure the kind of assistance which they find helpful. This includes personal assistance, out of hours help, help with day-to-day tasks (such as cooking, going out and shopping), counselling, advice and 'talking therapies'. Some service users are also combining parts of their budgets to buy things together such as training and recreational opportunities.

The evidence from direct payments schemes for disabled people also highlights that the health of people receiving such schemes tends to improve and that they gain transferable skills which help them return to employment if they so wish. Mental health service users/survivors receiving them report fewer in-patient hospital stays and the possibility of avoiding crises through having support in advance of their situation worsening. The transformative effects such schemes can have for people are summed up by Andy Smith, a mental health service user and strong advocate of direct payments:

> In many respects people like me are the most persuasive argument in favour of self-directed support. Having used the funds to liberate myself and gain control and independence, the logical next step was to get myself educated to a level that would permit me to attempt to similarly improve the lives of other service users. Since my involvement with SDS [self-directed support] both my leisure and career options have multiplied. If it worked for me, it might work for you. (Quoted in Beresford, 2010c, 98)

New organisational forms

User-controlled services and support have largely been linked with the self-run organisations controlled by disabled people and other service users. Such ULOs are generally very different in form, aims and culture from the organisations in which traditional services tend to be located. They are typically small, local organisations. However, most services still tend to be located in large, bureaucratic, more centralised organisations and agencies, such as local government and health authorities and commercial corporations. ULOs come much closer to small progressive voluntary organisations. What is most important and distinctive about them, however, is that they are controlled by the people for whom they are intended. Thus, these are the organisations *of*, rather than *for*, which the disabled people's movement pioneered, where the aim is for governance to be under the control of service users themselves and service users are also more likely to work in them, shape their culture and share experience and understanding with their own 'service users'.

Humanising services and support

All these developments have led to the creation of new roles and relationships, to all of which service users themselves have a particular contribution to make. With the advent of self-run services and individual support, the whole gamut of approaches to self-management, mutual aid and self-support, drawing on complementary, holistic and traditional health and care approaches, can be mobilised by service users to help each other. These can now take a much more humanistic, reciprocal, egalitarian and flexible form. Critics of formal, professionalised support services, including the normalisation movement, however, have long argued instead for people to look after each other on the basis of informal relationships, voluntarism, neighbourliness and a sense of social responsibility. They make the case that none of us wants to rely on or be restricted to 'professional' relationships. They talk of 'circles of support', 'citizen advocates' and the involvement of people with 'valorised social roles'. However, experience suggests that this does not provide an adequate or reliable support system for everyone needing it. The same problems seem to apply as operate with other ideas which try and shift responsibility to people's unpaid, informal efforts to provide mutual support, from the 'Big Society', to reliance on 'informal care' and voluntary action.

It's good, it's fun!

[There are] good things at school like on a Tuesday we have PE – they hired this total sports coaching thing till the end of this year – like a member of staff – not a teacher – comes and teaches us for about an hour, hour and a half, with proper equipment, like with proper professionals. They do it really well, like activities you've never done before, that are challenging. You warm up and stretch properly, you sit down and he tells you about what you are doing and

> he explains it very well and you do different activities, like football, tag rugby, running with a ball, athletics. On Fridays, Leeds United Academy coaches came in for a few weeks and they taught us about football, everyone, easy first then harder. Two coaches came in, split the class at random – it's boys and girls. One team does activities like passing the ball, dribbling with cones and passing, and team two plays mini matches and then swop and talk about what we've done in the day. And there's man of the match or girl of the match and then they come again the next week. It's fun.
>
> *Mattie Hatton*
> *Grandson, aged ten*

This is perhaps hardly surprising in an advanced western industrial society that is primarily based on a wage earning economy, where increasingly people are also expected to work longer hours for more years of their life and women as well as men are expected to be in employment, even during their child-bearing years. The constant current highlighting of older people's loneliness and isolation and pleas for the rest of us to strike up conversations with them and visit, highlight the inanity of such aspirations. We can see instead the social, cultural and economic factors that both exacerbate such isolation and also make it unlikely that it can be overcome by simplistic appeals to altruistic or patronising interventions.

Given these realities, few of us can expect that a sustainable system of health and welfare can really rely on our unpaid efforts as friends and neighbours, however much such images from a rose-tinted past or colonialistic images of different more traditional cultures are highlighted by politicians and policymakers. Before his death in 2011, Wolf Wolfensberger, founder of normalisation and 'social role valorization', became increasingly critical of the 'functionality of service systems'. Instead he argued for 'the need to emphasise personal relationships between valued and devalued people' (Social Role Valorization, 2011). This is exactly what the pioneers of user-controlled services and support have both argued for and been doing. However, what they have sought to do is to transform and equalise those relationships, locate them within sustainable *formal* provision, replacing previous consumerist and paternalistic models and challenge the division of people into 'valued' and 'devalued' people. This provides a much more realistic, egalitarian and user-led model for social policy services and support, which builds on the reality of a wage-based economy, while seeking to transform the nature of its relationships.

We can identify at least four historical relationships between us as human beings and non-kinship-based support. These are the spiritual/ moral relationship linked with church-based welfare, the paternalistic relationship with secular charity, the exchange relationship with the market and the unequal relationship between the citizen and the state. User-controlled provision offers the possibility of another, based on equal, mutual structured relationships with each other.

All these expressions of user-controlled support challenge distinctions and divisions that have developed between those reliant on welfare support and those not. They emphasise the importance of people being able to be part of the mainstream, rather than being treated separately and differently. They highlight the overlaps between formal and informal support and between service users and providers. This is exemplified by direct payments schemes, which have been particularly helpful in enabling disabled people and other service users to think creatively about how they might enhance their well-being, live their lives on more equal terms with non-disabled people and also maximise their life chances. Examples range from disabled people spending their money on gaining new skills or doing new things and a person living with Alzheimer's subscribing to satellite television to support their concentration, to people with learning difficulties going to a gym or paying for transport, and a mental health service user having someone they trust to stay with them overnight to avoid the onset of a crisis (Lewis, 2005). Similarly survivor research has shown how mental health service users may benefit much more from human contact, physical exercise, developing hobbies and interests and strategies for gaining peace of mind and being able to think positively, than from medication and medicalised notions of 'treatment' (Faulkner and Layzell, 2000).

The issue is not just that some of us may need formal support all our lives or that others of us may need it at particular times in our lives. The reality seems to be that *more and more of us* are likely to need such support. It is becoming an increasingly unremarkable aspect of our lives and societies, although this does not as yet seem to have been widely recognised or understood by politicians and policymakers. Who 'we' are is changing.

The changing welfare demographics

It's not just that a new approach to practice, provision and support has emerged which is avowedly more humanistic, democratic and egalitarian. The need for such support in society is significantly increasing. These issues were highlighted in 2012, by the London

Olympic and Paralympic Games. At the time, it was almost as if some UK politicians and media wanted us to believe there were two disabled populations, one competitive and contributing, the other deviant and dependent and needing to be controlled by benefit reform. Policymakers often still treat disabled people as a marginal group with low priority. But the reality is that this is a group massively increasing in both size and significance. Can we really assume that policy and attitudes will be able to stay the same if that is the case? H.G. Wells the science fiction writer first made the point just over a hundred years ago, in his novel *The country of the blind* (Wells, 1911). A non-disabled traveller chancing upon a country of sightless people, assumed that in such a land, the 'one-eyed man' would be king. Instead, he discovered that it was he who was disadvantaged and so that he was not blinded by its inhabitants to make him 'normal', he had to flee!

We only have to do the maths to see how radically the demographics are changing in the UK and indeed other societies. There are already over ten million people with a long-term illness, impairment or disability in Great Britain (DWP and ODI, 2014). The population is projected to rise most quickly for the oldest age groups and it is in these groups that disabled people are most concentrated. The number of people aged 85 and over is projected to more than double over the next 25 years reaching 3.5 million (ONS, 2011). This is associated with increasing physical and mental frailty. Current estimates are for massively increased numbers and proportions of people living with dementia. Figures are already being offered that one in six of us will live to be a hundred (www.learningdisabilities.org.uk).

The political focus on disability has been on older people because of policymakers' preoccupations with the 'burden' of care, but the numbers and proportion of disabled people are increasing all-round, for all ages. This is the result of many factors. More pre-term babies are being born and surviving with major and multiple impairments. People born with impairments are living much longer and those with inherited impairments are more often living to have children who may themselves have impairments. Conditions previously identified as terminal, notably, but not only cancer, are now increasingly being reframed as long-term conditions and those experiencing them increasingly being recognised as 'survivors', although often living with impairments (Maddams et al, 2008). The mental health charity, MIND, already says that one in four of us will experience mental health problems in our lifetime. These problems are now being identified at an increasing rate, among children, adolescents and adults, with rises expected in depression and anxiety-related conditions, linked with an increasingly stressed, insecure and fragmented society. Almost a million of us are diagnosed as having a learning difficulty and this is predicted to increase significantly. Major increases are also predicted in so-called 'life-style disorders', such as type 2 diabetes associated with obesity, as well as with increasing problems of long-term alcohol and drug dependence. No less important are significantly increasing, previously unsurvivable life-changing traumas from proliferating wars, terrorist attacks, road traffic and other accidents.

While it might be possible for governments to tinker round the edges of these figures by extending draconian assessments for disability benefits, or cutting back, as now, on support for children identified as having 'special needs', we can expect the UK soon to have at least a massive minority of disabled people and possibly even a majority. The fact that UK cities such as Leicester may soon no longer have one predominant ethnic group, while California already has an ethnic majority, is already giving rise to major rethinking on issues of race. We may soon have to start doing the same about disability.

It is difficult to imagine that we will still be able to think of social care, benefits and other services as low priority policies and ignore their funding needs, as this recognition takes root. Politicians and media will find it much more difficult to stigmatise and ignore disabled people as they gain increasing political potential. The political realisation may begin to dawn that disabled people seem so numerous not because more and more people are dishonestly claiming the identity, but rather because who 'we' are as a society is changing rapidly, fundamentally and perhaps permanently. Disability policy may at last get up to speed. The fact that we have recently had two prime ministers with disabled children is perhaps a portent of this change. Soon it may also have to be reflected in as high profile and as positive a way in our politics, as it already has had to be in elite world sport.

Childcare: case study of the importance of ensuring support

Already there is strong evidence that failing to invest publicly in support services has its own serious costs. Childcare is a significant example of this. Over half of all families with children – over four million – use formal childcare every year. Successive governments have paid lip service to its value to children, families, society and the economy. Yet, since 2009, prices have gone up by 27 per cent while wages have remained the same, making childcare ever more unaffordable for parents. Costs even for a small family can exceed mortgage repayments. This puts enormous pressure on families' budgets. There are also serious and ongoing gaps in provision across the country for working parents, school-aged children, disabled children, those living in rural areas and two-year-olds who qualify for free early education (Rutter and Stocker, 2014, 3). As the 2014 childcare costs survey reported:

> Childcare is something that affects most of us, as parents, as grandparents, as practitioners and as tax payers...the current childcare system is not working for anyone. Children are losing out on vital early education and families remain trapped in poverty because they cannot make work pay. Childcare providers struggle with debts. Women fail to return to the labour market after they have children and the economy loses their skills and their taxes. The state faces greater welfare bills and high administrative costs for delivering a complex support system. (Rutter and Stocker, 2014, 1–3)

It is not only good affordable childcare that brings important social as well as personal gains, however. For example, we know that good housing and good healthcare improve the health of the nation. Good education – and not only for those who can afford to pay for it – can help maximise people's talents and abilities, as well as build a diverse and highly skilled workforce. An effective social security system can help tide people over difficult personal and economic times, as well as maintaining an active and healthier older population. These were the abiding lessons of the post-war welfare state. Dedicated support services for particular groups, such as disabled people, mental health service users, people with long-term conditions and people with learning difficulties, all have a particular role to play in maximising their life chances and in enabling them to contribute to society in whatever ways they wish and are able. This can include accessing them to mainstream education and employment, being active in their communities, forming relationships and bringing up families. We know from the research that good support, such as that which many disabled people have accessed through direct payments, can help make all these opportunities more achievable and also result in wider health benefits (Prime Minister's Strategy Unit, 2005). This has always been the message of the social model of disability: that providing support does not signal people's deficits, but rather enables them to live independently – that is to say, have 'the same choice, control and freedom as any other citizen – at home, at work, and as members of the community' (Zarb, 2003).

The economics of social policy

A key emphasis of social policy textbooks is that social policy is closely related to economic structure and policy. They tend to examine different economic structures: agrarian, feudal, capitalist, post-industrial and globalised; and different policies and theories: laissez-faire, Marxist, Keynesian, monetarist, 'supply-side' and so on (Alcock with May, 2014, 241). A second stress of social policy textbooks is on how welfare is to be paid for (Alcock with May, 2014, 259–70). A key standard text, which has run to several editions, originating with the London School of Economics, the academic founding home of UK social policy, is even called *Paying for welfare* (Glennerster, 2014). Indeed, it is difficult to think of any other policy area where there is so much concern with the issue of how it is paid for. It certainly doesn't seem to apply to war/defence, penal or banking policy! This seems to reflect the acceptance by social policy as a discipline of neoliberal conventional wisdoms about the economics of welfare. The modern tendency, certainly since the coming to power of Mrs Thatcher, has been to present welfare services in a negative light and as a drain on the economy. They are seen to encourage dependence, to privilege inefficient state intervention and to discourage wealth creation. 'Welfare *reform*' is therefore framed in terms of getting people *off* benefits and reducing expenditure. Human welfare has increasingly been framed as an individual responsibility. So we are encouraged, for example, to *invest* in our children's education, our personal pensions, health and social care – through private sectors whose expansion has been encouraged by neoliberal social policy. On the other hand public expenditure on such services, is presented as a *cost* rather than 'investment'. Accordingly it has been dramatically cut by UK governments since 2010, on the grounds of 'economy' and to reduce the 'public deficit'.

Enabling creativity

Since leaving home I've had little experience of the welfare state. Out of luck, more than anything, I went straight from education into work and I'm not even currently registered with a doctor. In spite of this I am more than happy to pay taxes that contribute to something that should ensure everyone in our society receives their basic needs.

I've never received JSA [Jobseeker's Allowance], however, knowing that it is there along with the NHS gives me a safety net that means I don't have to be constantly saving money in case of emergency. It allows people to be entrepreneurial and take chances, knowing that if a venture fails or a move doesn't work, they will have something to fall back onto.

From people I know who have been on JSA, the accusations of 'Benefits Britain' is media hype and for the majority of people being on JSA is not a desirable choice, it is something they'd like to change. One thing I have learnt from these people's experiences is how impersonal and statistics-driven the job centre is. They don't look to help people into work in a way that will benefit people in the long term, but look more to pushing people into any work as quickly as possible. I have known several people pursuing creative careers who are progressing well and earning money, but not yet enough to fully come off Jobseeker's Allowance, that have had benefits suspended for going on tour for example and had to give up to apply for minimum wage jobs unrelated to any aspiration or skill set of theirs. Though I can see why this is necessary and the government can't support people on JSA for years while they try and achieve their dream job, along with cuts to Arts funds and grants this is damaging to creative industries. Evidence of that now is perhaps that the majority of emerging musicians are all from wealthy backgrounds.

Edd Croft
Nephew by marriage

Acceptance of welfare/social policy spending as a 'cost' is also common among its supporters, as well as its critics. Like their Fabian forefathers and mothers before them, however, they argue that this is a worthwhile cost, sometimes suggesting that the money could be found from other sources (for example, defence) or by giving social policy greater political priority. However, service users and their organisations point to a much more radical reappraisal of the role and purpose of social policy, as well as its relationship with the economy.

The conventional academic argument is essentially that social policy follows economic policy – 'the economic context ... is important in determining the scale and scope of welfare services' (Alcock with May, 2014, 259). Essentially 'you must cut your coat according to your cloth'. Yet the discussion here, not least the ideas advanced and developed by service user movements, may lead us to a very different set of conclusions. Crucially they suggest that:

1. The present economic base for social policy is not sustainable long term.
2. Social policy interventions can helpfully be interpreted as positive investments rather than negative costs.

3. User-controlled services are both most consistent with such a public
   investment approach and most valued by service users.

1. The present economic base for social policy is not sustainable long term

The founders of the welfare state, such as the leftist thinkers who
helped inspire and influence it, were preoccupied, by the individual
as *worker*. Thus, their concern with 'full employment'. Its right-wing
critics, as advocates of the market, have mainly been concerned with
the individual as *consumer*. We have moved from a society concerned
with (full) employment to one based on increasing consumption. Both
goals, however, have been reliant on economic growth, understood in
terms of increased production in order for it to work. In our modern
world the evidence is increasingly that this is an unsustainable approach
for the future because of its destructive effects on the environment
and the biosphere, using up finite resources and perpetuating conflict,
both domestically and internationally (Klein, 2014).

2. Social policy interventions can helpfully be interpreted as positive investments rather than negative costs

Gerry Zarb the disabled activist and theoretician has set out the gains
from supporting independent living for disabled people. As he has said,
discussion has been restricted by the tendency of existing approaches
to expenditure on supporting disabled people to be seriously limited:
'by the narrow focus on individual investment decisions (as typified,
for example, by the process of assessment for social care) … and a very
narrow focus on the costs to public finances. This … rules out any
meaningful discussion of overall costs and benefits.'

By increasing disabled people's participation in social and economic
life, it would be possible to reduce their reliance on and the associated
costs of family carers, social security and segregated services. It would
require the removal of barriers to education, transport and employment,
but this would bring its own longer term economic and social benefits.
It would also offer broader benefits, associated with a civilised society,
helping ensure social justice and full civil and human rights for all its
citizens (Zarb, 2003). We can see how this model can similarly apply
for many other groups too and support their development, health and
capacity to contribute.

3. User-controlled services are both most consistent with such a public investment approach and most valued by service users

User-controlled services have both been inspired by the goals of ensuring service users choice, control and freedom and also most valued by service users for making this possible. If traditional residential and institutional services, which they have challenged, have encouraged segregation, stigma and dependence, these have been inspired by social models, a commitment to independent living and to supporting to live on as equal terms as possible alongside any other citizen (Zarb, 2003; Zarb and Nadash, 1994).

Economic policy for social well-being

All of this points to both the possibility of and the need for a different relationship between economic and social policy. Instead of thinking of economic policy shaping social policy, we should perhaps be thinking of economic policy aimed at achieving social policy goals. This would reconnect us with the original meaning of the 'welfare state'. This was not narrowly concerned with *state* welfare, as its subsequent right-wing critics have insisted. Instead it was committed to a society concerned fundamentally with advancing its citizens' welfare and well-being. There can be no question but that this was the primary purpose of the post-war welfare state. Thus the emphasis on addressing people's social citizenship rights (Marshall, 1950). Where it fell short was in engaging its citizens on an equal basis in this project and in appreciating and valuing their diversity and responding to it with equality. Here we can see a past tension between the individual as worker *and* citizen, just as now one has developed between us as consumers and citizens. Neither approach adequately responds to people's right to *equal citizenship*. A primary concern with people's well-being, however, offers the prospect of an economy that does not have to be based on 'growth'. It would take account of changing demographics and our increasing requirements for support during the life course. Supporting, maintaining and improving people's well-being would thus become the central aim of economic activity, by:

- prioritising the creation of valued employment to support people's well-being;
- developing learning and skills to support such a workforce;
- encouraging research, development and innovation to achieve these objectives.

Such a needs-based and person-centred economy would value us equally and be concerned with our well-being whatever our role: worker, service user or simply citizen. Of course, directing economic policy and priorities to improving human welfare and well-being now seems almost counterintuitive. We have long been encouraged instead to accept policy based on *undermining* our well-being – increasing inequality, reducing social and economic security, commodifying needs to be met by mass production, expanding low grade employment in 'service' industries and the creating of luxury goods and services to satisfy the demands of resulting elites. In essence, the model seems to be that 'we' will improve our well-being by clambering up the food chain and pushing those below us further down. It is, of course, an illusion. It is perhaps time instead to transform the way the economy is conceived and discussed (Massey and Rustin, 2013; Seymour, 2014; Chang, 2004a; 2004b). Already radically different ways of thinking about the economy are emerging, such as feminist perspectives on political ecology. These explore the impact of changing environments on people's lives and livelihoods and place unequal power relations on the basis of sex, age, class, education, political representation and so on, at the centre of the debate (Abeysekera, undated; Robbins, 2012).

According to Marx, the relations of production shape our relations with each other more generally. Having an economy ultimately geared to the advancement of our well-being offers the long-term possibility of relationships of production that may not alienate us either from our labour or from each other, since the primary purpose of production will be to take care of each other. The principles of the original welfare state with their shift away from exchange and charitable relationships and attempt to control the accumulation of capital and respond to need, held just such a promise, if they had not first been diluted and then reversed. It is difficult to see why an economy based on supporting the well-being of members of society is likely to be any less workable and effective than one geared to the accumulation of capital or human destruction. We should remind ourselves that the 'economic recoveries' of both the UK and Nazi Germany in the 1930s rested on massive rearmament to fight the cataclysmic Second World War. We would perhaps all do well to pause and wonder if this seems a sustainable or sensible model for the future!

This also matches the reality of modern production. Capitalist concerns to cut production costs while requiring everyone to be employed, are increasingly at odds with each other (Harvey, 2014). As automation and other technical development continues at an exponential rate, production is likely to provide less and less employment. This is unlikely to be a problem for those denied the requirement to spend long hours carrying out endless, repetitive, pointless tasks. But it will be a problem for any society or economy that has not developed alternatives. Looking after each other will always be labour intensive. It also provides some of the most creative, meaningful and interesting opportunities for work, whether we are talking about work in education, health, support, housing, administration, research or management. Current demographic changes enhance opportunities for such positive employment, revalued, rather than, as now, devalued (Dorling, 2012).

As Gerry Zarb has suggested, an economy geared to independent living or well-being would demand a different kind of accountancy for calculating economic success (Zarb, 2003). But we already have evidence to help us do this. Social care in the UK, for example, has long been devalued, with most workers paid around the minimum wage, receiving little training or support. This has also resulted in an over-reliance on migrant workers (Christensen and Guldvick, 2014). Social care is treated by policymakers as a low priority, for which adequate investment is not politically feasible. We should again remind ourselves this is the policy on which millions of older and disabled people are reliant and which any of us might need to turn to one day. Yet an independent analysis of the economic value of the adult social care sector in England showed:

- its direct economic value in 2011/12 was more than £20 billion;
- its indirect effects are estimated to add a further £16 billion of GVA (gross value added) to the English economy and support a further one million full time equivalent (FTE) jobs;
- it employs 1.5 million workers and produces around £13,250 of GVA per worker;
- it contributes 1.8 per cent of all GVA in England and provides jobs for 6.4 per cent of the total workforce in England. (ICF GHK, 2013)

Similar calculations could be made for other public services in the UK and other countries: health, education, welfare benefits, housing and so on, demonstrating their contribution to the existing economy, as well as to our well-being. They can be seen to create wealth, jobs, skills, opportunities and also overseas markets and investment. Yet these social policies have been increasingly presented as inefficient, their funding cut and their workers attacked as a net drain rather than benefit to the economy and society (*Daily Mail* endlessly).

Such a switch in economic priorities would also benefit from careful re-examination of what is meant by 'well-being' and 'welfare'. Such terms have long been appropriated by professional 'experts' and this trend has continued to the present. However, work has also begun to develop to enable people with experiential knowledge, for example, older people, to say what such terms mean for them. Significantly they frame them in terms of connectedness, health, occupation and activity. They also emphasis the importance of approaches to supporting their well-being that are based on their participation, rather than having things done to or for them (Hoban et al, 2013). This, as we have seen, has been the distinguishing feature of user-controlled services and support.

Conclusion

In modern social policy, which has typically been developed top-down, least attention seems to be paid to the actual services, practice and support that service users receive. Yet these probably have the greatest impact on their experience. Such provision may also bear little relation to the values and ideology originally informing policy. This can be lost in transmission. Service users and their organisations, not surprisingly, pay much more attention to their own experience. The user-controlled provision which they have pioneered reflects this and represents a sea-change from much that has come before. They have prioritised lived experience, user involvement, equal relationships, the philosophy of independent living and a commitment to inclusion and supporting people to be part of mainstream life. They have sought to break down barriers between service users and providers and emphasise the overlaps between us. They have developed new approaches to support based on participatory practice, user involvement in training, self-run collective services and peer support. These offer a practical alternative to vague pleas to humanise support by people looking after each other informally, which take no account of social and economic realities.

The user-controlled support developed by service users and their organisations provides a starting point for transforming social policy. Instead of conceiving of it as a drain on wealth, perpetuating divisions and dependence, we can see it as a wealth creator, maximising people's well-being and their capacity to contribute as citizens, service users and providers. Instead of social policy that at best often only serves to reduce the damage and inequalities created by economic policies and structures, this provides a vision of economic policy guided by a primary commitment to maximising human well-being. This is much more likely to be sustainable than continuing to rely on economics based on growth through increasing production and consumption. How we may achieve such policy transformation, we examine in the next chapter where we will explore making change in social policy.

FIFTEEN

Changing welfare

Any change must come from the bottom up.
(Tony Benn, quoted in Dore, 2003)

If there is hope it lies in the proles.
(George Orwell, *Nineteen Eighty-Four*)

The philosophers have only interpreted the world ...The
point, however, is to change it.
(Karl Marx)

The creation of the welfare state represents one of the most radical changes that have taken place in recent UK society. As we documented in the first three chapters of this book, it took enormous pressures and seismic shifts in politics, ideology, economics and international relations for it to happen. If the aim is to return to a similar commitment to improving people's well-being, then a massive process of change will again be needed. This time, there aren't the same spurs for action. There has been no successful ending of a global conflict, even if economic uncertainty and division are increasing.

Calls for reform, proposals for change, tend to be weakest when it comes to spelling out how they are to be achieved. Often this issue is left unstated and unexplored as though the mere strength of the argument and the evidence offered will create its own force for change. Sadly such hopes almost invariably seem to be disappointed. The sense that 'something must be done' about horrors reported, injustices highlighted and appalling policy identified, ignores the real world of power, politics and policy. We know from the world of international 'realpolitik' that the most terrible conflicts tend to continue until one side wins or resources are exhausted. Yet when it comes to domestic policy, a sense lingers that somehow morality or ethics will triumph. Sadly, as the coiner of the term, 'realpolitik', himself said, more often it seems that 'the law of power governs the world of states just as the law of gravity governs the physical world' (von Rochau. 1853). Again sadly, it seems that texts highlighting the evils of inequality or the cruelty of austerity, ultimately are likely to make little difference (for example, Wilkinson and Pickett, 2009; Dorling, 2014; Atkinson, 2015).

Social policy as both activity and discipline has its own unhelpful history here as regards change. As set out in Chapter Eight, the dominant and persistent Fabian model for reform – for making change – was based on:

- a notion of 'scientific' analysis;
- the production of evidence to inform and influence public policy;
- the key role of the 'expert' in this social policy process.

This model has tended to ignore issues of power, because it has rested on the unstated power of its proponents – socially and politically privileged people, from the Webbs, to Peter Townsend and Julian Le Grand. The process has centred on self-defined 'experts' producing 'evidence' to 'educate the public' to achieve reform. There is no clearly worked out process or explanation of how or why this would work. As we have seen, this top-down elitist approach to social policy, with its cult of the expert, has dominated UK social policy thinking and practice for many years (Kynaston, 2008, 35–6). It came under attack in the 1970s from the emergent disabled people's movement (UPIAS, 1976). They criticised it for taking control from and excluding disabled people and instead advancing such 'experts' own failed prescriptions for change. The scale of its failure became clear with the advent of Thatcherism.

Essential, but not understood

To me, the welfare state is essential though vastly underestimated. If it was not for the welfare state, I would not have been able to train as a social worker. Tax credits were granted to me for childcare. I also relied on child benefit to help with caring for my own children. As a social worker, I see how the welfare state and Children Act can provide housing and benefits to vulnerable people. However, my view is that the welfare state is being dismantled with close support if not prompting from the media. The effect of this can be clearly seen in social work. More referrals relating to financial hardship, domestic violence, alcohol misuse and neglect. There is now a sense of hopelessness with social workers that there are no services to refer people to, yet no money to take children into care. This has created a system of constant struggle, stress and blaming. Many newly qualified social workers now seem to also have the jaded view of benefit claimants which does nothing to help the vulnerable people with whom they work. I feel depressed about the welfare state, as it is essential, yet disappearing.

Esther Beresford
Our daughter

Imposed from above and lacking broad-based support, Fabian policies were swiftly trumped by Mrs Thatcher's right-wing populism. This appealed to people's narrow self-interest and offered them short-term gains. Thus the policy of selling off council houses cheap to their tenants and discounted utility share offers promising a quick return.

This is not to say that Fabians or Fabianism can be seen as monolithic or unchanging. The Fabians of the 1940s and 1960s were very different to their twenty-first century successors. Fabian moves to welfare pluralism in the 1980s in the face of Thatcherism, highlighted its preparedness to shift its own position in the political spectrum (Beresford and Croft, 1984). The Fabian Society was a key influence in the political shift of New Labour to the right (*Guardian*, 2001). The London School of Economics, as we have seen, was the birthplace of Fabianism, but in the twenty-first century has been associated with academics such as Sir Julian Le Grand (Richard Titmuss Professor of Social Policy, knighted by the Coalition government), who have advanced neoliberal policies of privatising health services and education and acted as advisers to neoliberal governments. Ironically, the Fabian tradition has culminated in a kind of quasi-neoliberalism of its own. Where Fabianism has remained unchanging has been in its tradition of advancing narrowly-based 'expert' prescriptions for policy. While Fabian approaches to social policy have generally failed to carry the popular appeal of right-wing ones, they have nonetheless frequently succeeded in marginalising more critical approaches, which have shown greater promise of advancing service user and public involvement and the democratisation of social policy and provision.

If there is one lesson that UK social policy has offered us, it is that if change is not imposed by the powerful, then to stick, it has to be widely owned and supported by the majority of people – however much they might seem signed up to the status quo. Progressive change will not come through the process of top-down 'public education' as understood by the Fabians or the notion of 'consumer' as sovereign promised by the market, but reduced in reality, to examples such as multinational crisp companies offering people the opportunity to 'vote now' for their favourite new flavour (Bamford, 2014). Social policy academics continue to offer powerful evidence to show that welfare does not divide us crudely into a 'them and us': 'strivers' who pay for it and 'skivers' who 'scrounge' from it. And still their messages seem to carry little force or conviction with a 'public' bombarded by powerful political and media messages to the contrary (see, for example, Hills, 2014).

Theoretical approaches to change

Change is a key sociological concept. Sociologists have identified many forms of change, including behavioural, organisational, social, economic, cultural, ideological and political change (Haralambos and Holborn, 2008). As we have seen, there has been a tendency in modern public policy to focus narrowly on organisational change. This reflects the impact of modern managerialism. Yet the factors affecting social policy and the needs it must meet are much broader, including political, social, economic, cultural and demographic factors. Some theoreticians have also explored the interrelations between assumptions about human motivation and the provision of welfare. Julian le Grand, for example, highlighted the shift from ideas based on individual altruism underpinning the creation of the welfare state, to beliefs based on people's innate selfishness, guiding the advocates of market-led welfare (Le Grand, 1997). Unfortunately in developing such ideas, little attention has actually been paid to the views and ideas of people on the receiving end and the actual experience and impact of different welfare regimes on them.

Processes of change themselves change too. Thus, as we shall see, social networking and social media are becoming important in highlighting issues, mobilising people for change and as part of processes for change. In recent years, with the advent of a 'celebrity culture' we have seen the introduction of 'celebrities' into the business of public policy change. For example, the celebrity chef, Jamie Oliver, has been involved in high profile schemes to improve school meals which have gained a serious response from government. The death of Jade Goody, the reality TV star, from cervical cancer, became a rallying call for young women to be screened for early symptoms. While there may be resistance to taking such developments seriously because of a sense that they trivialise or cloud conventional policy processes, it would be a serious mistake to ignore them as unimportant.

Models of change

Change takes place at different levels and in different ways. In the contentious field of child protection, for example, an unhelpful cycle of change can be identified – as followed the appalling death of Victoria Climbié:

> a hopeless process of child care tragedy, scandal, inquiry, findings, brief media interest and ad hoc political response. There is now a rare chance to take stock and rebuild ... The trawl for solutions now needs to go beyond the traditional calls for restructuring, more training and new organisations. These haven't worked before. There is no reason to imagine they will work in the future. (Beresford, 2003c)

As the Baby Peter and Daniel Pelka cases have sadly demonstrated since then, there has yet to be any serious reassessment of policy change in this field at least. Despite the fact that child protection is a multi-agency issue which also tends to involve schools, police and health, the prevailing process seems to be one of a short-lived media 'moral panic', usually particularly focused on social work, the allocation of blame – generally restricted to the least powerful practitioners, and an opportunity for ideologically based interventions which rarely help to avoid yet another tragedy (Jones, 2014).

A number of different approaches to conceptualising change have been developed, which offer helpful insights. The first of these draws a distinction between 'top-down' and 'bottom-up' approaches. A top-down approach is characterised as imposing change from above on those who must work with it, while bottom-up change is presented as coming from 'the grassroots', originating from and being owned by the people on the ground, who will have to work with it. While the reality is likely to be more complex, with a blurring of boundaries between the two and the two perhaps operating in parallel, this typology is helpful because it draws our attention to the origin of pressure for change and the possible implications that this may have.

A related distinction that is drawn is between *externally imposed* and *internally adopted* change. In social policy, the former has been associated with frequent reorganisations and restructurings which may lead to little or no perceived improvements by staff or service users. The latter is linked with changes in how people work and what support they offer and service users receive. It can be internally initiated or externally supported and can result in a changed experience for service users.

Much of the innovation at micro and larger level that was discussed in Chapter Twelve can be seen as following from such internally adopted change. Externally imposed change often results in confusion and anxiety for service users and practitioners (Beresford et al, 2011, 363).

A textbook on changing practice in health and social care identified two expressions of change. It made the point that practice had both changed as a result of broader policy change and that it was possible for practitioners, with service users and supported by managers themselves to change it. Its authors argued that 'practitioners are not passive puppets' (Davies et al, 2000, 1). This is a view that is shared here, while acknowledging the importance of addressing broader structural issues too.

Watzlewick and others have drawn another helpful distinction between two forms of change. They identified *first order change* as incremental change within a system, while *second order change* was seen as radical, changing the system itself and thus meaning 'change of change', that is to say, change that is fundamental in nature and implications (Watzlewick et al, 1974, 11). In an influential UK report on changing public services, the Audit Commission not only explored methods for bringing about change, but also key actors who would need to be engaged, including politicians and senior managers, if such change were to be achieved (Audit Commission, 2001).

While, as we have seen, there has been a tendency for policymakers and services to focus on organisational change, service users, their organisations and movements have had much broader concerns, working for liberatory change. Like academic commentators such as Le Grand, they make connections between individual understandings and psychology and broader policy. However, these are of a different nature and for a different purpose. Here what has developed is a concern with personal empowerment through collective action, as a basis for making broader social and political change (Arches and Fleming, 2006). Change in services and support is considered within this context, as part of a broader agenda for overcoming oppression and discrimination and achieving people's human and civil rights (Oliver, 1996 and 2009).

Change thus raises issues about *power*, the location and distribution of power and the relative power of different stakeholders in the process of change. This will be particularly apparent where change is imposed from the top-down or externally. The experience of change for people in control of such change, is likely to be very different to that of people who are at the mercy of it. Where people have significant experiences of disempowerment, or of practice that is designed to blame, interpret and accuse (Fleming et al, 1983, 17) and have little understanding of their own capacity to exert power, even where there is a desire to increase their say and control, it may be difficult for them to make much use of such opportunities for empowering change. It can be difficult for many of us actually to see ourselves as change makers.

Our relation with change

For most of us, then, change can be something that is more likely to happen to us, rather than something that we make happen. Not surprisingly, therefore, people often find change threatening and difficult. This can be true at every level, from the micro to the macro. Our relation with change is likely to shape our views about it. Different stakeholders involved tend to have different attitudes towards it. Service users, for example, who have lived in an institution or been disempowered in other ways, may be fearful of change, even though they might welcome its hoped-for outcomes. People may have many reasons for resisting change, depending on their understanding of its consequences.

> Change does not automatically lead to improvement. And what represents improvement to one person or group may be seen as a loss or cost to others. Those who doubt that improvement will result from the proposal or those who see undesirable consequences often challenge proposals of improvement. We should remember that 'quality is in the eye of the beholder'. (Martin, 2003, 111)

The social work management consultant Gerry Smale summed up a key issue: 'The consequences of change are quite different for those who feel in charge, with "their hands on the rug", from those "standing on the rug" as it is whipped away from under them' (Smale, 1998, 316).

Smale argued that: 'no one person or group can expect to be in control of all the many factors that will affect change' (Smale, 1998, 321). However, the role of key individuals, particularly managers, is often emphasised by those working in and those writing about change in public service organisations. Martin, for example, says: 'The complexity of change in these closely interlinked services can be both confusing and frightening for service users, but local leaders can recognise the problems that service users might face during periods of change and can provide guidance to help people to find a pathway through the apparent chaos' (Martin, 2003, 104).

We need to consider change at personal, organisational, policy and structural levels. The preoccupation with *organisational* change in public policy has often been to the exclusion of consideration of its other domains – reflecting the expanded interest in and influence of managerialism under neoliberal ideology. Nonetheless, the frequently problematic nature of the organisational base of much social policy provision, its over-large, complex, impersonal and bureaucratic nature, emphasises the continuing importance of addressing change in relation to it. Some commentators, such as McMillan, use 'complexity' theories to describe change within organisations as a more organic experience that is unpredictable and hard to control and that defies linear theories or approaches. She describes the approach of many traditional change theorists (for example, Walsham, 1993) in these terms:

> Their idea of change is a controlled move from one stable state to another. There may be difficulties and short periods of uncertainly as the change takes place, but handled properly, that is all. It is a view which tends to consider the world as essentially stable and orderly and change as a disruptive and temporary aberration in the scheme of things…There is an assumption that the direction the change has to take is clear and that by using specific and appropriate skills the required destination will be reached. This is a view of change that assumes that the future is predictable and that the organisation has enough information about itself and its environment to make predictable and effective plans. (McMillan, 2004, 63)

She clarifies the differences of a complexity approach:

> Every organisation is unique with its own culture, its own environment and its own complex web of living individuals. Thus each organisation has its own unique set of initial conditions. Thus it is not possible to transfer a set of organisation initiatives and successful models from one organisation to another and expect similar results. The differences in initial conditions are likely to lead to widely different outcomes. (McMillan, 2004, 87)

The culture – or more accurately – cultures, of organisations can be one of the most significant barriers to change. This is often due to views and practice becoming entrenched over time.

> Culture is a strong force and can be a major impediment to change. It is a system of beliefs and way in which people confer meaning on what they do, which suggests that it is not something that can be easily changed. Beliefs and values just aren't like that ... When they do change, the process is more likely to be a gradual, bit by bit affair than a sudden wholesale conversion to a completely new set of beliefs ...Organisational cultures can take a generation or more to build up. It is therefore likely that they will also take an appreciable time to change. (Martin, 2003, 158)

There is some irony in the fact that while in social policy practice there has long been a preoccupation with organisational change, focusing narrowly on restructuring and reordering organisations, this has rarely challenged the increasingly uniform, hierarchical and monolithic nature of organisations, where pressures have increasingly been towards them growing larger, linked with 'new public management' thinking (Ferlie et al, 1996). Yet the lesson from history seems to be that real innovation and change seem to demand and follow from a different kind of organisational base. We saw in Chapter Twelve that some of the most innovative developments from the 1970s onwards were associated with new kinds of organisations, from collectives to cooperatives, community-based and user-led organisations. While we might hope for or expect more diversity in organisational form, yet these different pioneering organisational approaches have rarely been looked at, nor the humanistic nature and scale of user-led organisations drawn on by mainstream organisations and services. Key breakthroughs in technology, production and services repeatedly make the point though, that innovative organisation fosters innovation.

We can see this in the Second World War when the most advanced, adaptable and innovative allied aircraft, the Mosquito, was built using sustainable and underused materials, drawing on readily available traditional skills, with production decentralised and devolved into small local workshops and sometimes people's homes (Bishop, 1995; Copping, 2013; www.youtube.com/watch?v=c7cVvYdLeek). A similar picture to such 'mosquito economics' emerges at the heart of modern innovation, notably computer technology. Apple and Microsoft may have become conventional global corporate giants, but they owe their origins to people such as Steve Wozniak, Steve Jobs, Bill Gates and Paul Owen testing out their ideas and prototypes in bedrooms and college computer rooms and starting small companies with friends (Wikipedia, ndc). Here we can see the same blend of enthusiasm, commitment and skill that was associated with the development of heritage railways and the modern canal movement. Here initially at least we see the importance of different organisational structures, values and goals being developed to support new ideas and innovations.

Involving staff and service users in change

Existing experience has indicated that attempts to bring about major change in embedded cultural beliefs and established institutional practices face almost insurmountable obstacles without the support of face-to-face staff. This must be taken account of in any attempt to transform policy, practice or provision. Research has shown how resettlement from the old 'mental handicap hospitals', for example, was systematically impeded and even sabotaged by staff who felt alienated, rejected and abandoned by the policy (Collins, 1992; 1993; Fitzgerald, 1998). More recent research into the modernisation of day services for people with learning difficulties (Dowson, 1998) and into obstacles in the way of direct payments (Henderson and Bewley, 2000) has produced similar findings.

McMillan suggests that the involvement and empowerment of workers can lead to change within an organisation, but cautions that this may be resisted by some.

> A complexity approach would suggest that encouraging and empowering people to make small changes in their own spheres of influence and activity can be a highly effective way of transforming an organisation. However, it is worth bearing in mind that, while some people welcome empowering processes, others do not. They find the old controlling order familiar and in an odd way comfortable. Often they are afraid of change. (McMillan, 2004, 86)

We also know that face-to-face practitioners in social services have long experienced low morale (Balloch and McLean, 1999; Lymbery, 2001; Postle, 2001), resulting in poor recruitment and retention rates, which have had knock-on effects for the people with whom they work and their own ability to consider and implement change and innovation. The sheer scale and regularity of change has tested the capacity of staff for further adaptation.

Change can be especially difficult for service users, particularly when they have been subjected to institutionalising and disempowering regimes. Even the most positive changes can be threatening and difficult to deal with and adjust to. Therefore trust between service users and managers becomes particularly important.

This brings us back to issues of power and participation in relation to change. The political sociologist Steven Lukes developed the idea of three dimensions of power. The third dimension refers to the social construction of practices, ideologies and institutions that secure people's consent to or at least acceptance of domination (Lukes, 2004). The community and developmental educationalist John Gaventa drew on this to support approaches to social change rooted in the perspectives of marginalised communities. Instead of looking for the sources and the solutions of social problems in the theories and ideas of social science and social policy experts, he validated the narratives of the oppressed populations involved. In Gaventa's theory, such methodological subjectivity makes it possible for the framing of a social problem and its solution, to arise from within the group. This both has an empowering effect on the group and provides a basis for it to take collective action to challenge dominant discourses and develop alternatives (Gaventa, 1982).

An empowering approach to change

This parallels the approach to social policy adopted by welfare service user movements and articulated by the disabled people's movement. As we saw earlier, this has often been based on the organising concept of *empowerment*, pioneered by the black civil rights movement. This draws a distinction between two related aspects of empowerment – personal and political empowerment. It acknowledges the importance of both personal and political change and their inter-relation. Thus service users highlight:

- *personal empowerment* – meaning the need for change within us if we are to be actively and meaningfully involved in making change. Otherwise we may only serve as a stage army. Such personal empowerment is likely to include gaining confidence, knowledge and skills; and
- *political empowerment* – which is understood as the need for making change at wider structural and political levels.

This model emphasises the need to address both of these elements of empowerment if people are to be truly rather than tokenistically involved in making change (Beresford and Croft, 1995). Disabled people and service users have generally seen developing their self-organisation through their own 'user-led organisations' (ULOs) as the major method of doing this. Such organisations can support people's personal empowerment as a first step to them becoming actively collectively involved to achieve change. This can be gained through the greater strength that comes from developing collective ideas and agendas and working together to achieve them in their own organisational space (Campbell and Oliver, 1996).

Enabling everyone's involvement

Earlier in this chapter, we commented that if change is be achieved and to be durable, rather than merely imposed, then it needs to be owned by people. This is key for progressive social policy change. However, it is one thing to talk about enabling people to be part of change. It is another to make it possible for their involvement to be real. It is also yet another for such involvement to be truly inclusive and address diversity in all its forms. The evidence has long been that there are class, gender, ethnic, age and other biases in who is actually likely to get involved. In the UK, historically, initiatives first for public participation and then for 'public, patient and user involvement' (PPI) have typically been by white middle-aged middle-class men (Beresford and Croft, 1982; Beresford and Croft, 1993). Evidence from service users and service user movements repeatedly highlights that people primarily want to be involved in order to bring about change (Beresford, 2013c). They talk about 'making a difference', 'telling it like it is' and improving things for people like them. Two elements make it more possible for people to get involved. These are *support* and *access*. *Support* includes support for:

- *people's personal development* – building their confidence, assertiveness, expectations and self esteem
- *practical skill development* – to support the kind of skills that getting involved tends to require as well as giving people greater confidence to do things in their own ways
- *practical support* – to be able to take part, including costs for travel, activities, subsistence, and payment where necessary
- *support to get together* – meeting places and funding for people's self-organisation. (Croft and Beresford, 1993)

This takes account of people's need for personal empowerment to build their capacity, as well as supporting the ULOs that are valued as the key route to achieving it.

Access means that there are ways into organisations and decision-making structures, so that people are able to engage with and have a real say in them. There need to be opportunities for people to get involved, particularly ongoing ones, which encourage and facilitate their active engagement. Experience suggests that both support and access are needed if involvement is to be broad-based. Frequently, however, they are not in place. Without access – if doors remain closed – then all people can do is knock harder, whatever their personal abilities and experience. But without support, only the most confident and determined are likely to get involved.

The development of provisions for public, patient and user involvement in the UK and other countries has highlighted that some groups face particular and additional exclusions. They have sometimes been called 'seldom-heard' voices, although service users also talk of them as 'seldom-listened to' voices! The *Developing Diversity* research project sought to find out more about such exclusions and how they might be overcome. This suggested that it was often the most oppressed and disadvantaged groups which tended to be excluded from arrangements and opportunities for participation. Thus, instead of compensating for prevailing barriers and exclusions, arrangements for involvement can actually often mirror and reinforce them. There seem to be five main reasons why people are denied equal opportunities to get involved (Beresford, 2013c). These relate to:

1. Equality issues
Service users report the barriers which they face in trying to get involved, on the basis of gender, ethnicity, culture, belief, sexuality, age, disability and class. Older people are conspicuously under-represented.

2. Where people live
This includes people who are:

- homeless
- living in residential services
- in prison and the penal system
- travellers and gypsies.

This group also includes people whose rights may be restricted. It also extends to a related group: asylum seekers and refugees; people who do not have citizenship rights and status.

3. Communication issues
This relates to barriers on the basis both of ethnicity and impairment and includes:

- deaf people
- blind people and people with visual impairments
- deaf and blind people
- people who do not communicate verbally
- people for whom English is not their first language.

An additional recent group often facing exclusions are those who are not computerate, who do not use the internet, who can now face some of the same difficulties as people who do not read or write.

4. The nature of impairments
People with complex and multiple impairments are frequently left out. This can be because their involvement is seen as expensive and difficult, or because of unevidenced assumptions that they are not able or interested in being involved. It can also happen where people are seen as 'awkward' or 'difficult' (for example, people with dementia). It is a category in which people who see themselves within the range of neuro-diversity are sometimes included.

5. Unwanted voices
Service users frequently comment that some points of view are more welcome than others – particularly those of people who agree with what's on offer. More confident and assertive service users are often unpopular among those organising involvement activities and often dismissed as 'the usual suspects'. To ensure diversity these more experienced and determined voices, which agencies may not want to hear, need to be included as a key part of the overall picture.

The project also highlighted that people are not only discouraged from getting involved if they don't relate to the idea. They will also ignore such opportunities if:

- they cannot see any change as a result of their involvement;
- they feel that decisions have already been taken on which their opinion is being sought;
- they feel that they are just 'ticking the box';
- their access requirements are not met.

In other words, people have to see a point in getting involved. They have to feel that it has the potential to make worthwhile change. Much of the apparatus that has developed in the name of consumerist involvement does not really make this possible. Enabling people's participation is a slow, developmental process, requiring the building of confidence, trust and familiarity. This is not the way that mainstream politics or ideology tends to work. Predominantly they are hierarchical, top-down and instrumental in nature and in democracies like the UK have only ever really engaged a small unrepresentative minority of people (Beresford, 2013c).

Towards inclusive participation for change

We know that there are many barriers to people's involvement, but the *Developing Diversity* project also shows how these can be overcome. Some of the key lessons to learn include:

Offering different routes to involvement

This can be achieved by offering innovative approaches to involving people which can work for the widest range and move beyond traditional reliance on meetings and surveys, written and verbal skills. Service users prioritise developing a variety of methods of involvement that can work for different people and are based on different forms of communication. They highlight the helpfulness of meetings and activities that are organised by service users themselves and/or are for service users only, offering them safe opportunities to develop their ideas and agendas. Where meetings are still used, there are many ways in which these can be made more attractive, accessible and inclusive. Service users participating in the project placed an emphasis on involvement:

- making it possible for people to have a good time and ensuring that they enjoy themselves;
- providing good, free food and refreshments which are culturally appropriate;
- offering a warm, safe and supportive environment;
- where people can gain knowledge, awareness and understanding.

They identified a wide range of ways of doing this, for example, through providing entertainment (particularly by service users), supportive activities, informal and appropriate venues and encouraging networking.

Outreach and development work

People in the project emphasised the importance of *reaching out* to involve people, especially those identified as 'hard to reach', rather than expecting them to come to you. In this way people who were isolated or weren't 'joiners' were more likely to be engaged, although service users do not feel that this currently happens enough. Suggestions for outreach work included:

- reaching out directly to people – checking out their views and what works best for them;
- reaching out to their communities – for example, local black and minority ethnic communities, travellers' communities, people in residential services;
- reaching out to 'community leaders' – who command trust and can support service users to engage – but not stopping with them.

Advocacy

Advocacy is a key but under-developed component for supporting people's participation. It is especially important for people who are disempowered and isolated and this is true of many of those excluded by existing arrangements for participation. Six forms of advocacy are identified all of which help people speak and act for themselves. They are:

- legal advocacy
- professional advocacy
- lay or citizen advocacy
- peer advocacy
- self-advocacy
- collective advocacy.

Service users stress the importance of advocacy and also the essentials of advocacy if it is to make a difference and enable everyone to be at the starting line for getting involved, becoming empowered and making a difference. They also make clear that it is generally in short supply and not given enough priority by policymakers and services.

Supporting sustainable involvement

Key to enabling *everyone* to get involved is providing on-going opportunities for people to get involved which make it possible to build trust and relationships with them. Such an infrastructural, rather than ad hoc, one-off approach to involvement, makes for sustainable arrangements which are likely to attract people who haven't got involved before, as well as retaining others. This makes it possible to build up interest, experience and expertise. It addresses the constant need to balance the mixture of new people and old hands, new participants from 'seldom heard' groups as well as more established activists. As we heard earlier, the latter, with their track record of successful involvement, are often devalued as 'the usual suspects'.

Involvement from outside

Getting involved in formal structures and arrangements, whether as part of arrangements for representative or participatory democracy, is not the only way of participating for change. Pressure group politics, single issue campaigning and other forms of collective action all have long histories. Historically, however, in countries such as the UK, these have often been narrowly based and very limited in who they actually engage. As we saw earlier, movements such as the disabled people movement were initially highly suspicious of the parliamentary route to change, even if such attitudes seemed to alter over time

Many people under neoliberal regimes such as that of the UK have become increasingly wary of getting involved with statutory and service structures and organisations, as little often seems to come of it (Beresford, 2012). This has been exacerbated by government policies determinedly committed to cuts in services and major welfare reform policies. These seem to have taken little notice of what disabled people and other service users say. Service users' organisations have also become more insecure and over-stretched as funding for them has been cut.

This shift in focus has had at least three expressions. First, welfare service users seem increasingly to try to get involved to make change beyond formal arrangements for user involvement, in more oppositional and conflict-based approaches, explicitly challenging government policy. This takes the form of campaigning for and taking direct action to achieve change. Second, welfare service users have been developing new collective forms of involvement which are more accessible to them and take account of their impairments and the barriers that they may face. Many new campaigning and mutual aid groups have emerged.

They are both working together to campaign with people with shared experience and also linking up with allied groups and causes.

Third, new forms of service user campaigning and protest have become increasingly based on social media and social networking technologies. These also enable people to get involved in 'virtual' ways which can overcome many of the traditional barriers relating to mobility, 'access' and inclusion facing disabled and chronically ill people and other service users. Traditionally, people were expected to find their way to join participatory initiatives, rather than, as it were, participation coming to them. Service users are thus blogging, vlogging, podcasting, tweeting and creating their own Facebook and other groups. They are impacting on mainstream media, as well as policymakers and the political process, influencing wider discussion and public consciousness (Beresford, 2012; 2013c).

Alliances for change: a case study

We can also see change as something we can all work for together in our different roles and identities, starting with the valuing of the experiential knowledge and ideas of groups facing oppression and discrimination. This is exemplified by the recent emergence of 'mad studies'. Its coming of age was signalled most clearly by the publication in 2013 of the Canadian text, *Mad matters* (Le Francois, Menzies and Reaume, 2013). Since then other key books have also been published (Burstow et al, 2014; Burstow, 2015). Canada particularly has been taking forward discussion and action on what it has unambiguously called 'mad studies' and now the idea has reached the UK and is developing as an international movement (Spandler et al, 2015). Psychiatry continues to be committed to a narrow 'disease' based model of understanding (Lieberman, 2015). However, this growing cannon of work may make it possible to move beyond psychiatry's dominance and the current alliance between psychiatry and neoliberalism and at last find a more helpful way forward out of distress, madness, mental health problems.

What is particularly valuable about *Mad matters* and subsequent texts and why they offer promise internationally, is that they highlight ways of melding insight and understanding with making change. Here is 'praxis' and 'conscientisation' as the radical social reformer Paulo Friere would understand and argue for them (Friere, 1972). The struggle of mental health service users/survivors against the damaging effects of psychiatry has often seemed a lonely and difficult one. But this movement and the books associated with it, demonstrate that people with direct experience, supportive professionals, academics, educators and researchers can together take forward mad studies and mad action. In *Mad matters*, for example, no one speaks for others, but instead offers their own different contributions and understandings, from their experience and from working together. And here we can see the value, the strength and the possibilities of such alliances.

Survivors have made it clear that they do not want yet another dominating explanation or set of ideas imposed on them or risk imposing them on themselves (Beresford et al, 2009; 2015). At the same time, as we have seen, they value more social approaches to their situation and experience. Books such as *Mad matters* take us further forward on this search, by bringing so many strands of critique from non-medicalised perspectives together. In doing so they help reclaim the important but devalued idea of madness, exploring the history, culture and language of madness and mad people. This movement highlights the diversity of mad experience and understandings, the damaging effects of psychiatry, the ambiguity of its reformism and the emergence of survivor research and academic engagement. Here also is a real prospect of a positive alternative to the ambiguity of 'recovery' as a driver both for survivors' struggles and public policy.

Humanising and democratising change

Any individual movement or political party committed to renewing the welfare state is likely to need to grow broader and public support and involvement for it. This increasingly appears necessary both to ensure that such change is achievable and takes the form that people want. We can see how insubstantial anything else is likely to be by how rapidly the large-scale welfare state reforms of New Labour were halted. Their renewed emphasis on challenging child poverty and fiscal reform through tax credits were subsequently rapidly reversed by the Coalition and Conservative governments. However, if getting involved in such change is to be attractive to people, then it will need to be a humanistic process. This draws us back to the second wave feminist slogan of the 1960s, 'the personal is political'. This is mainly taken to mean that politics needs to be clearly concerned with the personal matters that affect us and these need to be seen as political. Thus politics needs to be concerned with issues such as sex, abortion, childcare and the division of labour. As Carol Hanisch, a prominent figure in the Women's Liberation Movement, wrote, 'personal problems are political problems. There are no personal solutions at this time. There is only collective action for a collective solution' (Hanisch, 1969). But there was also another sense in which this slogan was being used – to highlight the need for politics to be personalised and humanised. Thus Hanisch emphasised the importance of consciousness-raising groups and of women discussing their issues among themselves.

This is a long way away from many people's understandings and experience of conventional politics and the political process as anti-personal, instrumental, alienated and confusing. This suggests that if we want to achieve broad-based change, then not only must ways be found to make such popular involvement possible, but also the processes of change themselves will need to change and become much more accessible and acceptable to many more of us.

Welfare state innovations such as the National Health Service were revolutionary in both their conception and impact. But the welfare state, as we have seen, was an incomplete revolution and one that has been followed by counter-revolution. A return to a society that seeks to prioritise the well-being of its people represents a revolutionary change but it demands a different kind of revolution. We have come to distrust old assumptions that revolutions transform everything and realise that they often leave existing social relations unchanged and merely substitute one powerful group for another. What's needed instead, as feminists and welfare service users have argued, is a revolution that starts from within. A revolution in how we look after each other will need to be a humanistic, rather than instrumental one, based on a process of change that is itself *person-centred* – just as any future system of welfare or well-being will need to be. Service users, disabled people, their organisations, movements and related campaigns, provide a basis for making this kind of change: placing an emphasis on connecting the personal and the structural, building alliances, working in new inclusive and humanistic ways. They also highlight the importance of such change seeking to engage and connect with the ordinary people whose lives it is meant to improve. If we are really committed to giving new priority to looking after each other, then this must be the road to take.

Conclusion

We have seen strong ideologically based forces come together over the last 40 years to attack and undermine the post-war welfare state. These have included a new establishment of the rich and powerful (Owen, 2014) as well as an influential mass media bent to the will of a narrowing number of right-wing international proprietors. While there has been increasing talk of public involvement and participatory democracy, structures of representative democracy, both local and in

Westminster, have been compromised and public engagement with them has diminished.

Significantly, the users of the welfare state, through their movements and organisations have emerged as a significant voice, both to challenge the old welfare state and also subsequent neoliberal plans for it. They have offered new visions of how we might advance our well-being and look after each other better in more participatory, equal and inclusive ways. They have developed new forms of support and service as well as user-led organisations which have hosted these. They have pointed to what a new society committed to its inhabitants' well-being might look like and prefiguring ways of achieving it.

At the same time, these movement, organisations and ideas remain in many ways vulnerable and marginal, just like the groups that have pioneered them. We can also see that the welfare state has been increasingly marginalised, as well as hollowed out by cuts, privatisation, reduced public expectations and its association with stigma. There has already been much crying wolf about the welfare state: that it is in crisis, outmoded or even unnecessary. But even if announcements of its death have been premature, there can be little question that the principles associated with it, particularly associated with its most important embodiment, the National Health Service, are now at unprecedented risk. It is these principles – of progressive redistribution, social citizenship, well-being, equality and support for marginalised people – which it now seems important to uphold, rather than to see lost by default.

The future: a different way forward?

> [The phone hacking] trial came to embody the peculiar
> values of this particular century – its materialism and the
> inequality that goes with it, the dominance of corporation
> over state.
>
> (Nick Davies, *Guardian*, 2014)

> Poor dear Leslie – he has given his life for all of us – God
> grant that in the years to come, we may be worthy of his
> sacrifice – and may you all be given strength to bear your
> loss.
>
> (Letter to the family of Able Seaman Leslie Norris
> from his schoolteacher following his death in action,
> 29 September 1944)

> Are you going to have greed for money or power ousting
> decency from the world as they have in the past, or are you
> going to make the world a different place?
>
> (*A Diary for Timothy*, Jennings, 1945)

The radical restructuring of UK social policy has made an impact on
almost all of us. For some its effects have been extreme. Welfare reform
has been associated with an upsurge in suicide (Blackburn, 2013). It
has forced people to leave neighbourhoods in which they have lived
for years, losing friends, networks and support services (BBC News,
2014). It has been linked with 'hate crime' against disabled people
stigmatised by high profile government and media 'anti-scrounger'
campaigns (Walker, 2012). Between 2010 and 2014, the number of
prescriptions for anti-depressants increased by 25% (O'Hara, 2014b).
Yet it is difficult, amid all these difficulties, not to detect some degree
of complacency in social policy academic writings. These have shown
a reluctance to take on the bold new ideas and arguments developed
by welfare user movements. A strong sense of Fabian 'business as usual'
lingers. For example, in 2014, in the latest edition of what's described
as a 'best-selling social policy textbook', the academic Professor Paul
Spicker concludes that: 'People who are poor, disabled, mentally ill

or unemployed cannot be expected to overcome the problems they face simply because they have more effective control over services' (Spicker, 2014, 351)

He goes on to make the much wider point:

> It is important, too, not to overestimate the potential effects of this kind of procedure. Dwyer (2004, 59–60) lists some of the chief objections to user-based approaches. There are conflicts of interest between users of different types; users are often in competition for scarce resources with others; user groups can lose touch with their grass roots; and the process as a whole can contribute to the exclusion of marginal groups. (Spicker, 2014, 351)

There are doubtless elements of truth in each of his points. But it is difficult to see on what evidence his objections to 'user-based approaches' are based. In his compendious index, amid all the mentions of Abel-Smith, Townsend, Titmuss, Le Grand and himself, there is only one mention of anyone associated with the movements of disabled people and welfare service users, Mike Oliver. Yet it has been service users and their campaigns which have spearheaded high profile opposition to such welfare reform, even if conventional commentators have subsequently confirmed their claims and offered them their legitimation (Beresford, 2012). They have also pioneered effective, much valued systems of user-led support (Barnes and Mercer, 2006). It is as if the international disabled people's, psychiatric system survivors' and other welfare service user movements had never existed. It is as if disability studies and mad studies still had to be invented. It is as if the social model of disability, the philosophy of independent living, user-led services and user-led organisations were all unknown and hadn't been shown to have revolutionary implications for service users, social policy and society.

Meanwhile, as the left-wing commentator Owen Jones has suggested, the neoliberal project actually seems to have created a new reverse welfare state for the rich and powerful (Jones, 2014). It has resulted in a massive redistribution of wealth and opportunity from poor and ordinary people, to very large commercial organisations and a growing class of super rich. Cuts in public service, as well as their privatisation and outsourcing, the private finance initiative, increasingly regressive taxation practices and the scaling back of provisions for social security, have all transferred public money from public welfare to private corporate profit, in the process undermining civil liberties, human rights and democracy (Mendoza, 2015; Toynbee and Walker, 2015).

The need to renew social policy

If there is one thing I have learned from the history explored in this book, it is that, whatever our ideological position, new approaches will be needed for sustainable social policy. Related to this has been the stress on participation across all ideological positions, even if this has sometimes seemed at best rhetorical and at worst disingenuous. It is the new social movements, including notably welfare service user movements, that offer both some of the most cogent insights and prefigurative examples for social policy to build on here. Neither as a discipline nor an activity, however, has social policy developed a strong track record of engaging and involving its subjects effectively. If there is to be a counter to increasing international moves to neoliberal social policy, then this will have to change.

We should remember that even if the post-war welfare state was implemented top-down, the massive pressure for it came from the *bottom up*. The strong sense of a demand for change communicated itself to the 'activators': the powerful progressives, who shaped the welfare state. It gave them a mandate, both psychologically and electorally (Kynaston, 2008). So while the detail of the welfare state remained with them, we cannot see its creation as unrelated to what people wanted. This is in sharp contrast to much of the damage that has since been done to it.

As was noted at the beginning of the book, much has already been lost without recognition of the fact. This is a measure of the shortness of political and collective memory. Universal funeral and maternity grants are now long gone and so is the severe disability allowance. Patients are now unlikely to be given time in convalescence homes to help them recover fully, as in the past. Grants for moving or setting up home were first whittled down to loans under the 'social fund' and now are no longer available from central funding. We have seen the ending of undergraduate and postgraduate student grants which offered opportunities for higher education for all. The wonderful role of the 'home help' is now unknown to many. First established to help new mothers bringing up their babies, the role was then developed for older and disabled people. Home helps cleaned and shopped, chatted and generally helped people maintain their independence. It was a 'proper job', with decent terms and conditions, based on an ongoing relationship, instead of reducing domiciliary care as now, to a procession of strangers passing through people's homes, on minimum wage and below, and 'zero hours' contracts.

Experiencing the welfare state

My personal experience of the welfare state was when I graduated from a good university with a good degree in engineering and then spent the next six months applying for jobs in the field without getting a single interview. That time spent unemployed and attending the job centre weekly was eye opening in seeing how the state begrudgingly and impersonally offers support to people.

When I was unable to attend a weekly meeting in order to go to my graduation ceremony, my adviser casually suggested I book it as holiday on the absence form (while leaving a comment that it was my graduation) which was the wrong procedure and caused me to be sanctioned and lose all JSA [Jobseeker's Allowance] payments for a month.

Having then got a job in my degree field in the first interview I had, I have paid back the amount I claimed over my period unemployed many, many times, yet the entire time over that period, I and other peers in my situation were encouraged to go after minimum wage, unskilled jobs, which would then increase the pressure on an already saturated sector of the job market.

I think a tax-funded welfare state is part of the price of living in a civilised country, so in the same way we pay for roads we won't drive on and street lights we won't walk under, paying for a welfare state ensures at least a basic level of quality of life and options for people we won't ever be familiar with, but would wish they would receive if we did know them. For the future, I think it is important that the welfare state is capable of treating the individual in the same manner we would hope someone such as a nephew or neighbour would be treated – by offering them sensible and suitable options relevant to their circumstances, and supporting them in their aspirations.

Frank Croft
Nephew by marriage

At the same time, new technology, bioethics, developments like 'assisted dying' are all raising new issues for social policy. They raise complex philosophical, moral, ethical and practical problems as well as creating new challenges for accountability and inclusion. We are likely to need a reinvigorated, more democratic social policy to address them effectively. What has become increasingly apparent, writing this book, has been the continuing poverty of much of social policy academic literature. Seventy years ago a major – if not the major – limitation of the welfare state was its failure to involve the people with whom it was concerned and whose lives it sought to improve. This still seems to be true of much social policy writing. As we have repeatedly seen, there is a reluctance to explore issues of participation and democratisation seriously. Mainstream social policy is still frequently social administrative in its nature, charting policy developments and legislation, framing them in its own 'expert' theorising, offering its own recipes for solution. Perhaps this is why some of the most helpful literature that I have found has come from historians, social historians, geographers, cultural commentators, feminist and other thinkers and activists concerned with difference.

A new paradigm

There has been an essential consistency in social policy since its emergence in the nineteenth century as a specific policy area and discipline. This has been true of both left and right-wing social policies. This is reflected in the irony that the LSE, the birthplace of Fabianism, has more recently become a key source of analysis and advice for neoliberal social policymakers. All such social policy has claimed to be scientific and to be based on evidence, which is established by its own band of 'experts'. One of the paradoxes of the post-war welfare state is that while in many ways it was rooted in the old top-down approach to social policy, it can also actually be seen as a fundamental break with the past, because the real pressure for its implementation did come from the bottom up. The same cannot be said of any earlier or subsequent social policies, from the Poor Law to twenty-first century coalition and Conservative welfare reform, all of which have had their origins in dominant politics and ideology.

The American philosopher of science, Thomas S. Kuhn, introduced the idea of 'paradigm shift', arguing that scientific understanding and ideas do not progress solely in a linear and continuous way but also undergo periodic 'paradigm shifts' (Kuhn, 1970). Hidden assumptions, beliefs, habits of mind and action, influence how we see and do things. We can see from the failure of the prevailing social policy paradigm to offer an effective challenge to neoliberal social policy the need for such a paradigm shift. What is needed, as we have seen, is not to another theory or model, but a wholly different approach to social policy, based on different knowledges, ways of understanding and on a different process.

This book has been concerned with exploring and taking forward just such a paradigm shift – one based on participatory social policy. This represents a fundamental break with traditional social policy thinking, since it is no longer concerned with 'experts' developing their different policy ideas and proposals. There have been nods in the direction of involving individuals and sometimes groups in the social policy process. But this book has highlighted both the need for and possibility of social policy in which we as service users, workers and other citizens have a real say and involvement at an analytic, structural and socio-political level. It highlights the need to focus on more than just the struggle of individual service users to exercise their individual welfare rights, suggesting that if we do so, these struggles are much more likely to be successful. Such a methodology isn't just concerned with a different approach to the process and structures of social policy. It offers the basis for the development of different kinds of analysis and different theory.

This is concerned with supporting the democratisation of social policy by giving priority to people's own lived experience of social policy and their central involvement in producing it. Kuhn argued that rival paradigms are incommensurable – that is, it is not possible to understand one paradigm through the conceptual framework and terminology of another rival paradigm. This helps us to understand both why the exponents of traditional social policy haven't valued the participatory social policy advanced by service users and their organisations and the resulting limitations of their critiques. As Kuhn says, 'the transfer of allegiance from one paradigm to another is a conversion experience that cannot be forced' (Kuhn, 1970, 198–204). This is the kind of epiphany that millions of disabled people and other service users have undergone, as they have come together, organised, shared their experience and developed their own ideas and alternatives – as we have seen in this book.

Revaluing our welfare

As human beings we are heir to many personal troubles in our life: illness, impairment, distress, loneliness, the loss of loved ones, broken hopes and relationships. We may also face many other social problems: of poverty and want; of prejudice and discrimination. These may be magnified by our place in society and the nature of society. The evidence has long highlighted that the two are inter-related; that our personal problems may be magnified by social situation and turned into social problems. The more disadvantaged we are in society, the greater our personal troubles are likely to be – and also the greater the difficulty we will face in dealing with them. The welfare state was created to address all of these inter-related issues.

Is this what we expected?

There seems no doubt that those of us who have jobs, comfortable homes and eat well have an obligation to help the unemployed, the homeless and the hungry. The setting up of food banks by churches and other organisations, both religious and secular, is to be applauded and the volunteers who work in them sincerely thanked for expressing their humanity in such a practical way. And yet… perhaps we need to consider why setting them up has been so necessary. How have we arrived at this dire state of affairs? Is this the UK we expected in the twenty-first century? Does the existence of food banks encourage government in a laissez-faire policy? Has the welfare state failed in its duty? Should we put pressure on government to provide what is necessary?

Rosita Rosenberg
Second cousin

Reflecting on myself

My father died when I was four, so I was brought up by my mother. The key influences in my childhood came from my Jewish working-class background, not the upper-class wealth and opportunities that had existed in my father's family.

Looking back I have a sense of pride in what it has been possible for me to achieve in my mother's parents' adopted country. They came to Britain at the turn of the twentieth century in the wake of one of the appalling anti-Jewish pogroms then taking place in Poland. They came as immigrants and 'asylum seekers', with nothing. My grandmother never learned to speak English. My mother left school at 14. Yet here am I, someone brought up in a lone parent family, who got a grant to go to Oxford University, who was promoted to Professor working at Brunel University London and who was awarded an OBE for my work, which I received from the Queen. If they had lived long enough to witness this, it would have been a fairy story for my mother and my grandparents, Barnet and Dora.

I am proud of what I have achieved. But don't think any of this would have been possible or happened without the British welfare state and the values associated with its foundation: universalism, redistribution, social mobility, social justice and increased equality. More to the point, increasingly I wonder if any of this would be possible if I were to be starting again *now*. And sadly I think the answer is probably no. This is an indictment of the direction our society has taken. It is also a strong recommendation for the welfare state and its founding values, which increasingly demonstrate their timeless and undeniable worth. Of course they were not perfect and pioneers since then have addressed key omissions of participation, inclusion and diversity, only to see these compromised by right-wing attacks on welfare.

Writing this book has been a journey in itself, drawing me back to past experiences, looking at old photographs, old interviews, old publications, sometimes for the first time in many years. Also coming across documents and finding out things for the first time, like my entry in the admissions book for my primary school, Wix's Lane, Battersea, and the thoughtful Ministry of Education report on the infant school the year that I left (HM Inspectors, 1956)! It has also reminded me of much less helpful experiences: of being bullied at primary school and fearing going back on Mondays; of the hopeless local environmental health services which left us in a damp, half-finished flat after they required work to be 'done by default' because of the landlord's neglect and the builders botching it and stealing from us. Then, the sad death of my father-in-law because he dreaded having to go back into the local psychiatric hospital, with the renewed onset of depression and how awful it was to live on benefits, learning to dread the thump of the post each morning in case it brought new problems.

Of course, extreme critics of the welfare state could say that these were exactly the kind of problems that they predicted of it; that it would encourage and support 'aliens' and upset the applecart, provide poor quality services and encourage dependence. But that is only half the story. It ignores the achievements. It forgets that services in the private sector, like Southern Cross and Winterbourne View, have shown themselves well able to match the worst that the state has ever provided.

I was one of the generation fortunate enough to miss the Second World War and 'national service' conscription and to be young in the bright, brave, radical, silly and successful 1960s. Ever since then, however, the theme has been cuts and retreat. Cuts in state spending, cuts in public services, a constant mantra that there is less public money. This is regardless of however rich we are told the UK may be, however well the economy is meant to be doing, and the fact that most of us seem to be paying more not less in taxes. The trend in the half-century since the 1960s has been of cuts in mainstream public services and of a flight of money from the public to the private sphere – both in terms of a flight to the market and to increase individual wealth. We should remember what the American economist JK Galbraith had to say about this. He famously suggested that there was an inverse correlation between the growth of private wealth and the public good, with private opulence leading to public squalor (Galbraith, 1958, 203).

I rarely look on my experience of mental distress, or even my 12 years in the psychiatric system, as entirely negative. To do so would be to deny the support which I gained from skilled and kind workers, alongside the many unnecessary difficulties I also experienced. But most important, if this hadn't happened, I would never have become involved in service user organisations or movements. I would never have come to know the strength that comes from working out who you are and being able to be yourself with others with shared understanding and experience. I wouldn't wish it on anyone to have to learn this vital lesson from such harsh experience. But it opened my eyes to the importance of people developing their own viewpoints and knowledges together and how important this is for truly effective social policy. The social policy academic John Hills has challenged one 'them and us' of social policy: the neoliberal argument that some benefit at the expense of the rest of us, but unfortunately another 'them and us' still seems to predominate – which results in one, more privileged, group offering its prescriptions for another, marginalised and devalued, group. How else can we explain the routine exclusions that books like Spicker's seems to rest on?

My biography is an unusual one. I have often found it difficult to think of two parents so far removed from each other as mine. My mother was the daughter of immigrant Jews who had fled murder and rape in Eastern Europe. They lived in Russian-occupied Poland and my grandfather served in the Imperial Russian Army as a conscript (see photograph) and worked all his life as a tailor. My father, on the other hand came from an aristocratic family and was much older than my mother. My mother would never tell us how they met. I think having this strange mixture of parents is one reason why I have always found the snobbery, class consciousness and discrimination that have long characterised England, particularly obnoxious. Their influence can be seen as a powerful thread running through the history of the welfare state and its antecedents and sadly still seems powerful today. In the past the talk was of 'outcasts' and the 'residuum'; now it is of 'skivers', 'scroungers' and 'Benefits Street'. When I look at the photographs in this book and some of the extremes of inequality they highlight from the past, it increasingly feels to me that we are coming full circle, with poverty, social division and inequality on the rise again.

All our children

Nursery class

I like school. I like to write my name.

Martha Hatton
Granddaughter, aged three

I worry for our children and grandchildren. What futures will they have? Where will they live? Will they be able to get jobs? When I speak to other people, I hear the same worries about their offspring. They are unlikely to have the same inheritance as our parents and grandparents hoped for, for us. I also hear facile policymakers telling us how we must maximise our networks, build 'social capital', help each other, when they have put more and more barriers in the way of people ever being able to do this. Of course we will all do our best – as individuals – as 'the bank of Mum and Dad', helping pay off our children's university debts, having them stay with us at home much longer, as grandparent childminders and so on. Some social policymakers have tried determinedly to divide the generations, just as they have sought to turn those in work against those on benefits, apparently unaware of the enormous overlaps there are between the two. In fact inter-generational solidarity seems to be growing – as a matter of necessity. But such individualised helping is unlikely to be enough. This was the lesson of the first half of the twentieth century and why it was so important that people's difficulties and struggles were translated into the *collective* efforts of the post-war welfare state.

Seeking the views of members of my extended family about the welfare state has been a small research project in its own right. But now reflecting on them – drawing as they do on the experiences of people aged from three to 90 – I am struck by how complex, but also positive a picture is revealed. There seem to be some significant themes here: fear of loss of the welfare state, a sense that it is being restructured in unhelpful ways, but also how important and essential it still is. Not all of us understand it in the same way and some of us may understand it less than others, particularly those who are very young. However, there seems so much shared thinking among people of all ages, with very different lives, experience and aspirations. I don't see divisions between the generations here, with the young thinking the old are freeloading at their expense, as some commentators are anxious to tell us. Of course this is just one family, but it challenges many political stereotypes about the welfare state and instead suggests a very broad commitment to it.

The welfare state truly is something that affects almost all of us – everyone as far as this family is concerned. I am not suggesting that we are in any way typical. We know that there are some standpoints which are nothing but hostile to ideas of welfare and the welfare state. But it is clear to me from pulling all these comments together, that public debate has been ill-served by the crudity of political and media judgements and agendas about welfare. All opinion formers owe us more than this. Most of all they owe us opportunities to have an equal part in debates and discussions about something so precious as our well-being and that of future generations. Such pleas, of course, are likely to cut little ice, but their importance is the reminder they offer that there's one issue about welfare where there does seem to be some serious consensus among the powerful, wherever they place themselves on the ideological map. That is to involve us, mostly if at all, only as a stage army to buttress their own particular arguments and ideas. If there is one theme emerging for me from this book, then it has been the primary failing of much social policy, including the creation of the welfare state and its successors, to do much more than this. It is also this which it is most important to challenge, as welfare service user movements have inspired us to do.

From baby Timothy to baby Isobel

At the time of writing, it is 70 years since the birth of baby Timothy who featured in Humphrey Jennings' wartime documentary, *A Diary for Timothy*. It would have been impossible to guess then where Timothy and rest of us would be all these years later.* The 'iron curtain' dividing Europe has come and gone. The UK has been divested of its empire. This is not the world imagined by post-war futurologists, of flying cars, mechanical robots, the end of office blocks, endless recreation for all and international peace afforded by the new United Nations. Instead our lives have been transformed by mobile phones, personal computers and jet travel, the rise of religious fundamentalism, the free movement of money and ever-tightening controls on population through globalisation, endless conflict and genocide.

As I write this, our youngest granddaughter, Isobel, is just a year old. She is our twenty-first century 'Timothy'. She was born on 11 June 2014. On that day, there were 'insurgent' attacks on Mosul in Iraq, pro-Russian conflict in Ukraine, continued fighting with al-Qaeda in

Yemen and a formal European Commission investigation announced into the tax arrangements of three global companies. Representatives of over 100 countries had come together at a global summit in London to End Sexual Violence in Conflict. Just as we couldn't know what was to come in 1945, so now we can't imagine the future for baby Isobel, Most important, we shouldn't take anything for granted about the future – even with the election of a Conservative government in 2015 committed to welfare and public service cuts on an unprecedented scale. We shouldn't assume that neoliberalism is here for keeps and that there is no alternative. We mustn't allow our fears to become self-fulfilling prophesies that immobilise us. We owe our children and grandchildren much more than that. We must pass the baton on to the new generations and support them as our parents and grandparents supported us. To paraphrase the narrator in Jennings' documentary:

> Well dear Isobel…up to now we've done the talking…What are you going to say about it and what are you going to do?... [A]nother war and then more unemployment. Will it be like that again?...Or are you going to make the world a different place – you and the other babies? (Jennings, 1945)

In 1945, as a contemporary review of *A Diary for Timothy* said, the documentary maker pinned their hope 'for a better world in the ideals of a new generation' (*Popular Photography*, 1946, 90). This time, more than ever, we must also accept *our* responsibility.

Note

* In a documentary on Humphrey Jennings made for Channel 4 television by Kevin MacDonald in 2000, it was revealed that the baby who was the subject of the film (Timothy James Jenkins, the son of a British soldier, born 3 September 1944) later moved to Brighton in the 1960s and became a mod before settling down to become a teacher. He died in November 2000 (https://en.wikipedia.org/wiki/A_Diary_for_Timothy). As Kevin Jackson, biographer of Humphrey Jennings later wrote of Timothy and his career as a comprehensive school teacher, 'not such a bad choice for anyone who, instead of lusting for money and power, wants to work towards making the world a better place' (Jackson, 2004, 305).

APPENDIX ONE

The family

First-hand ideas and experience about social policy play an important part in this book. In the spirit of a participatory approach highlighting 'user involvement', I wanted to give equal priority to experiential accounts alongside conventional 'expert' knowledge. Thus within these pages you will find much that originates with welfare service users and their organisations, as well as policy theoreticians and service providers. This includes comments of my own, but I wanted to open this up more broadly and decided also to seek the views of members of my extended family about the welfare state. In some cases, material that has been included already existed and I have signalled its source. In most others I specifically sought people's views. I tried to do this in a way which would have as little influence as possible on what people had to say. I have included at the end of this Appendix written guidance which I gave to family members which reflects what I said to everyone. There are contributions from people of every age here. I tried to set logical limits to whom I asked, because otherwise it began to feel that 'family' could extend to many hundreds if not thousands of people! Apologies to anyone close who feels left out. I am pleased to say that everyone I asked was kind enough to offer a contribution, so here is one survey that can claim a 100 per cent response rate.

Peter Beresford
The author, born 1 May 1945

Educated Wix's Lane Primary School Battersea, Emanuel School, Wandsworth, University College, Oxford, BA Hons, Middlesex University, PhD

Emeritus Professor of Social Policy, Brunel University, long-term user of mental health services, Co-Chair of Shaping Our Lives, the disabled people's and service users' organisation and network

Maureen Beresford,
Born 24 May 1942

My sister, educated Wix's Lane Primary School and Clapham County Grammar School, Clapham, lived her adult life in New York

Worked as a secretary/personal assistant

Died 2000

The Honourable Mrs William Beresford

Née Ida Kaufman (also known as Kaye)

Born 23 May 1909

My mother, born of immigrant Jewish parents, East End, London, first cousin of Sally Gould, left school aged 14

Milliner in East End sweat shops until her marriage

Met my father in 1934

Died 1990, Trinity Hospice, Clapham

(Tape recorded interviews 1989★)

The Honourable William Arthur de la Poer Horsley Beresford,

Born 9 August 1878

My father, youngest son of William Robert John Horsley-Beresford, third Baron Decies

'Of independent means', soldier, rancher, hotelier

He killed himself 11 July 1949

Joan Croft

Née Norris

Born 25 June 1924

Mother of Suzy Croft

Retired primary school teacher and housewife

(24 May 2014★)

John Croft PhD

Father of Suzy Croft

Born 27 November 1925

Principal, Norwich City College, 1967–83, ordained 1974

He killed himself 25 September 1985

Suzy Croft

Born 27 December 1952

Partner of and collaborator of Peter Beresford, numerous primary and secondary schools, Durham University, BA Hons, CQSW, Goldsmiths College London

Worked as a qualified face-to-face social worker for 25 years, Senior Social Worker, St John's Hospice, London

Catherine Jenny Beresford

Born 12 August 1976

Oldest daughter of Suzy Croft and Peter Beresford, mother of Poppy, Evie and Elsie with her partner Matt Coyte

Senior Diabetes Specialist Nurse, Band Seven, National Health Service, BNurs (Hons), MSc

(4 October 2014★)

Poppy Beresford Coyte

Born 26 September 2005

Oldest daughter of Catherine Beresford

Primary school student

(28 July 2014★)

Evie Beresford Coyte

Born 3 November 2007

Second daughter of Catherine Beresford

Primary school student

(28 July 2014★)

Elsie Leah Beresford Coyte

Born 3 May 2013

Third daughter of Catherine Beresford

Attends childminder

(11 April 2015)

Esther Beresford

Born 13 February 1979

Second daughter of Suzy Croft and Peter Beresford

Married to Tom Hatton, children Charlie, Mattie and Martha

Team Leader, child protection services, qualified social worker
(7 September 2014★)

Charlie Hatton
Born 24 February 2002
Oldest child of Esther Beresford
Primary school student
(10 August 2013★)

Mattie Hatton
Born 22 March 2004
Second child of Esther Beresford
Primary school student
(12 August 2014★)

Martha Hatton
Born 13 February 2011
Third child of Esther Beresford
Goes to nursery class
(2 October 2014★)

Rebecca Beresford
Born 16 May 1983
Third daughter of Suzy Croft and Peter Beresford
Mother of Isobel with partner Phil Crilly, a technical support engineer
and step-mother to Abigail, Adam and Ryan
Primary school teacher
(26 May 2014★)

Isobel Hannah Marie Crilly
Born 11 June 2014
Daughter of Rebecca Beresford

Ruth Emily Beresford
Born 26 February 1992
Youngest daughter of Suzy Croft and Peter Beresford

Just completed her MA in social research

Currently working as a paid intern for the Sheffield Students' Union, before undertaking a PhD at Sheffield University

(15 June 2014★)

Doreen Croft
Née Marshall

Born 30 November 1929

Married to Tom, older brother of John Croft

Doreen retired as a night-sister midwife in 1990 with the closure of the Oakham Hospital Maternity Unit

Died 6 December 2013

Baroness Catherine Decies
Born c1844

Third Baroness Decies and Dowager Baroness, my paternal grandmother

Died 1941

(Quotation taken from Decies, 1902)

Jenny Louise Hutchins
Née Croft

Born 9 April 1954

Younger sister of Suzy Croft

Primary school teacher, currently teaching in Qatar

(12 August 2014★)

Toby Hutchins
Born 4 October 1985

First son of Jenny Croft and nephew of Suzy Croft

Advertising executive for an independent media company

(9 October 2014★)

Freddie Hutchins
Born 9 March 1987

Second son of Jenny Croft and nephew of Suzy Croft

Professional actor

(7 September 2014★)

Harry Hutchins
Born 23 December 1991

Third son of Jenny Croft and nephew of Suzy Croft

Part-time care worker, looking for full-time work

(9 October 2014★)

Charlie (David John Hugh) Croft
Born 11 June 1961

Younger brother of Suzy Croft, father of Frank, Edd, George and Hannah

Local government officer

(15 September 2014★)

Frank Croft
Born 10 November 1989

Oldest son of Charlie Croft and Christine Croft and nephew of Suzy Croft

Manufacturing engineer

(6 October 2014★)

Edd Croft
Born 30 July 1991

Second son of Charlie Croft and nephew of Suzy Croft

Lighting engineer/designer and boy band member

(16 October 2014★)

George Croft
Born 11 September 2004

Son of Charlie and Katie Croft and half-brother of Frank and Edd

Primary school student

(28 September 2014★)

Hannah Croft
Born 12 May 2006

Daughter of Charlie and Katie Croft and half-sister of Frank and Edd

Primary school student

(28 September 2014★)

Robert Croft
Born 30 December 1953

Cousin of Suzy Croft

Civil servant

(23 September 2014★)

Andrew Croft
Born 26 April 1956

Cousin of Suzy Croft

A retired careers adviser (13–21 age range), first employed by the local authority in teenage services until transferred to Connexions and then in 2008 returned to the county council

(28 September 2014★)

Ida Kaufman

See The Honourable Mrs William Beresford

Dora Kaufman
My grandmother

Became visually impaired 1947, never learned to speak, read or write in English, spoke Yiddish, worked for her brother, the tailor when she was young before she got married

Died 1952, aged 69

Barnet Kaufman
My grandfather

A tailor all his working life, specialised in silk facings for dinner jackets, working for some of the big companies, including Aquascutum

Kaufman means shopkeeper, he was known in the family as 'Banish'

Died 1955, aged 73

Leslie Norris

Born 28 January 1923

Able Seaman AL Norris, Royal Navy, HMS Liddlesdale, aged 21, C/JX 347565

Joan Croft's brother, Suzy Croft's uncle

Died of wounds 29 September 1944

Rosita Rosenberg

Née Gould

Born 2 September 1933

Younger daughter of Lou (Lewis) and Sally Gould; Barnet was Sally's father's brother

Retired Executive Director Union of Liberal and Progressive Synagogues

(8 October 2014★)

Note

★ The date when the account was provided or obtained.

Sample letter/email

peter.beresford@brunel.ac.uk

Dear

I am currently completing a book about the welfare state. It looks at its past present and possible futures. I don't take a simple view of it being a good or a bad thing, but I do think we as a society need to do better at looking after each other.

The book is an academic one in the sense of being based on evidence and research. But I am also keen to include first-hand voices of experience, including people's perspectives identified from research, but I wanted to go beyond this.

I thought it would be helpful to include brief boxed comments from members of the family – what little I have and Suzy's, so I have been contacting people to ask for such comments. These could be anything from 50 to a couple of hundred words. I am writing to ask you if you would kindly contribute. I have already got most people but want to include all perspectives, so it will range from Joan at 90 to the small children of those closest to me.

Please could you send me something. I am asking people to offer a short thing which may be about their views, some experience, ideas, whatever, relating to what we understand as the welfare state. It could be positive, negative, or neither, historic, or about the future or speculative. What matters is that it is what you think.

Please could you do this – and hopefully soon. Just get in touch if you want any more guidance. With all best regards,

Peter

Research projects and related publications

Below are listed some of the key research projects which I have carried out and been involved in during my working life. Most have involved collaborations and partnerships; my work has particularly developed in partnership with Suzy Croft. These research projects have both informed and shaped the arguments and views I have offered in this book. Most are specific research projects, although some represent more general focuses in research work that I have carried out. I have also provided key references linked with these studies. Looking back on the projects I have undertaken what strikes me is how many of them have been empirical projects, developing new findings about their subject area, rather than relying on existing information, ideas and assumptions.

Vagrancy and single homelessness

An action research study of the perpetuation of a social problem through its categorisation and treatment

Beresford, P, 1975, Problems of homelessness, *Social Services Quarterly*, Winter 1974–75, 263–4

Beresford, P, 1975, Reception centres: An index of social service inadequacy, *British Journal of Social Work* 5, 2, 175–92

Beresford, P, 1979, The public presentation of vagrancy, in T Cook (ed) *Vagrancy: Some new perspectives*, pp 141–65, London: Academic Press

Public participation in land-use planning

Community-based study, surveying local people's views of public participation in planning and their community: a community-based empirical study

Beresford, P, Croft, S, 1982, *A say in the future: Planning, participation and meeting social need*, Second edition with a new introduction, London: Battersea Community Action

Beresford, P, Croft, S, 1980, Public participation and local politics, *Town And Country Planning* 49, 11 (December), 412–14

Children in care in North Battersea

Exploring the experience of families and children in care in North Battersea: an empirical community-based study

Beresford, P, Kemmis, J, Tunstill, J, 1987, *In care in North Battersea*, Guildford: University of Surrey

Patch-based social services

Exploring local people's views of a new initiative in social services and its broader political and social relations: a community-based empirical study

Beresford, P, Croft, S, 1984, Patch and participation: The case for citizen research, research monograph, *Social Work Today*, 17 September, 18–24

Beresford, P, Croft, S, 1984, *Patch in perspective: Decentralising and democratising social services*, London: Battersea Community Action

Beresford, P, Croft, S, 1986, *Whose welfare: Private care or public services?*, Brighton: Lewis Cohen Urban Studies Centre at University of Brighton

Beresford, P, Croft, S, 1986, Patching up service delivery: Decentralisation and its implications for planning and participation, *Planning* 674, 27 (June), 8–9

Service user and citizen involvement

The development of policy and practice for user and public involvement in social and other services: an empirical study

Beresford, P, Croft, S, 1990, *From paternalism to participation: Involving people in social services*, London: Joseph Rowntree Foundation and Open Services Project, with a foreword by Sir Roy Griffiths and Lady Wagner

Beresford P, Croft, S, 1993, *Citizen involvement: A practical guide for change*, Basingstoke: Macmillan

Beresford, P, Croft, S, 1993, *Getting involved: A practical manual*, London: Joseph Rowntree Foundation and Open Services Project

Involving poor people in poverty analysis and research

Lister, R, Beresford, P, 1991, *Working together against poverty: Involving poor people in action against poverty*, London: Open Services Project/ Department of Applied Social Studies, University of Bradford

Beresford, P, Croft, S, 1996, Reply to: A response to Beresford and Croft, 'It's our problem too', by Peter Golding, *Critical Social Policy* 16, 48 (3 August), 109–15

Beresford, P, Green, D, Lister, R, Woodard, K, 1999, *Poverty first hand*, London: Child Poverty Action Group

Beresford, P, Lister, R, 2000, Where are 'the poor' in the future of poverty research?, in J Bradshaw, J Sainsbury (eds) *Researching poverty*, pp 284–304, Aldershot: University of York/Joseph Rowntree Foundation, Ashgate

Beresford, P, Hoban, M, 2005, *Effective participation in anti-poverty and regeneration work and research*, August, York: Joseph Rowntree Foundation

The citizens' commission on the future of the welfare state

A service user-led project exploring the proposals and experience of welfare state service users

Beresford, P, Turner, M, 1997, *It's our welfare: Report of the citizens' commission on the future of the welfare state*, London: National Institute for Social Work

Beresford, P, 1997, The citizens' commission: A starting point for a local authority welfare strategy, Anti-Poverty Matters, *Journal of the Local Government Anti-Poverty Unit*, Local Government Management Board 14, Autumn, 16–17

Leonard Cheshire empowerment project

A national research project led by disabled people examining an initiative established with the stated aim of 'empowering' disabled people in the organisation: an empirical study

Beresford, P, Branfield, F, Wade, H, 2000, *Involvement, empowerment and independence: From learning to changing, mid-term report of the evaluation of the Leonard Cheshire Disabled People's Forum*, Middlesex: Centre for Citizen Participation, Brunel University

Beresford, P, Branfield, F, 2001, *Involvement, empowerment and independence: From learning to changing, final report to Leonard Cheshire of the evaluation of the Leonard Cheshire Disabled People's Forum*, Middlesex: Centre for Citizen Participation, Brunel University

Researching with disabled people

Sutherland, A, Beresford, P, Shamash, M, 2004, *Consultation with disabled people for the disability rights commission*, London: Edward Lear Foundation

Sutherland, A, Beresford, P, Shamash, M, 2006, *Getting back to normal: An assessment of the direct payments service in Poole*, Poole: Poole Rights On Disability

Service user networking and knowledge

A user-controlled research project

Branfield, F, Beresford, P, with Andrews, EJ, Chambers, P, Staddon, P, Wise, G, Williams-Findlay, B, 2006, *Making user involvement work: Supporting service user networking and knowledge*, York: Joseph Rowntree Foundation, York Publishing Services

Beresford, P, Branfield, F, 2006, Developing inclusive partnerships: User defined outcomes, networking and knowledge – a casestudy, *Health and Social Care in the Community* 14, 5, 436–44

Advancing user involvement in and user-controlled research

Turner, M, Beresford, P, 2005, *User controlled research: Its meanings and potential*, Final report, Shaping Our Lives and the Centre for Citizen Participation, Brunel University, Eastleigh: National Institute for Health Research (NIHR) INVOLVE

Sweeney, A, Beresford, P, Faulkner, A, Nettle, M, Rose, D (eds), 2009, *This is survivor research*, Ross-on-Wye: PCSS Books

Beresford, P, Nicholls, V, Turner, M, 2009, *Examples of user controlled research*, Report of a Project Commissioned by NIHR INVOLVE, London: Shaping Our Lives

Beresford, P, Carr, S (eds), 2012, *Service users, social care and user involvement*, Research Highlights Series, London: Jessica Kingsley Publishers

Beresford, P, Croft, S, 2012, *User controlled research: Scoping review*, London: NHS National Institute for Health Research (NIHR) School for Social Care Research, London School of Economics, sscr.nihr. ac.uk/PDF/SSCR-Scoping-Review_5_web.pdf

Palliative care

Participatory research projects exploring the views of people with life limiting conditions and facing bereavement

Beresford, P, Adshead, L, Croft, S, 2007, *Palliative care, social work and service users: Making life possible*, London: Jessica Kingsley

Beresford, P, Croft, S, Adshead, L, 2008, 'We don't see her as a social worker': A service user case study of the importance of the social worker's relationship and humanity , *British Journal of Social Work* 38, 7, 1388–407

Cotterell, P, Beresford, P, Harlow, G, Morris, C, Sargeant, A, Sitzia, J, Staley, K, Hanley, B, 2008, The impact of involvement on palliative care service users, London: Macmillan Cancer Care

Person-centred support: The standards we expect

Defining and developing person-centred support

The standards we expect: A collaborative research and development project

Glynn, M, Beresford, P, Bewley, C, Branfield, F, Butt, J, Croft, S, Dattani Pitt, K, Fleming, J, Flynn, R, Patmore, C, Postle, K, Turner, M, 2008, *Person-centred Support: What service users and practitioners say*, Illustrated summary, York: Joseph Rowntree Foundation, York Publishing Services

Beresford, P, Fleming, J, Glynn, M, Bewley, C, Croft, S, Branfield, F, Postle, K, 2011, Supporting people: Towards a person-centred approach, Bristol: Policy Press, www.jrf.org.uk/sites/files/jrf/social-care-personal-support-summary.pdf

Involving older people

Participatory research projects with older people

Carter, T, Beresford, P, 2000, *Age and change: Models of involvement for older people,* York: Joseph Rowntree Foundation, York Publishing Services

Hoban, M, James, V, Pattrick, K, Beresford, P, Fleming, J, 2011, *Voices on wellbeing: A report of research with older people*, November, Cardiff: Shaping Our Age, WRVS,

Hoban, M, James, V, Beresford, P, Fleming, J, 2013, *Shaping our age – involving older age: The route to twenty-first century well-being. Final Report*, Cardiff: Royal Voluntary Service, www.royalvoluntaryservice. org.uk/our-impact/involving-older-people

Beyond the usual suspects

A user-controlled research and development project

Beresford, P, 2013, *Beyond the usual suspects: Towards inclusive User Involvement – research report*, London: Shaping Our Lives

Beresford, P, 2013, *Beyond the Usual Suspects: Towards inclusive User Involvement – practical guide*, London: Shaping Our Lives.

Beresford, P, 2013, *Beyond the Usual Suspects: Towards inclusive User Involvement – findings*, London: Shaping Our Lives

Towards a social model of madness and distress

Survivor-controlled research exploring mental health service users' understandings of mental distress

Beresford, P, Nettle, M, Perring, R, 2009, *Towards a social model of madness and distress?: Exploring what service users say*, 22 November, York: Joseph Rowntree Foundation, York Publishing Services

Beresford, P, 2009, Thinking about mental health: Towards a social model, in J Reynolds, R Muston, T Heller, J Leach, M McCormick, J Wallcraft, M Walsh (eds) *Mental health still matters*, pp 53–7, Basingstoke: Palgrave

Beresford, P, Nettle, M, Perring, R, Wallcraft, J, 2015, *From mental illness to a social model of madness and distress, Report of a Second Stage Project*, London: Shaping Our Lives and National Survivor User Network (NSUN)

Developing service user knowledge

Beresford, P, 2000, Service users' knowledges and social work theory: Conflict or collaboration, *British Journal of Social Work* 30, 4, 489–504

Beresford, P, 2003, *It's our lives: A short theory of knowledge, distance and experience*, London: Citizen Press in association with Shaping Our Lives, www.shapingourlives.org.uk/documents/ItsOurLives.pdf

Beresford, P, 2007, The role of service user research in generating knowledge-based health and social care: From conflict to contribution, *Evidence and Policy* 3, 4, 329–41

Beresford, P, 2013, Experiential knowledge and the reconception of madness, in S Coles, S Keenan, B Diamond (eds) *Madness contested: Power and practice*, pp 181–96, Ross-on-Wye: PCCS publishing

Beresford, P, Boxall, K, 2013, Where do service users' knowledges sit in relation to professional and academic understandings of knowledge?, in P Staddon (ed) *Mental health service users in research*, pp 69–86, Bristol: Policy Press

Russo, J, Beresford, P, 2015, Between exclusion and colonisation: Seeking a place for mad people's knowledge in academia, *Disability and Society* 30, 1 (2 January), 153–7, DOI: 10.1080/09687599.2014.957925

First-hand experience

Reporting experiential knowledge linked to the development of service user narratives and experience

Beresford, P, Croft, S, 1988, Being on the receiving end: Lessons for community development and user involvement, *Community Development Journal* 23, 4 (October), 273–9

Beresford, P, Croft, S, 1988, Full house: A first-hand account of overcrowding and its implications for social services practice and policy, *Community Care*, 26 May, 23–4

Beresford, P, 1991, Against enormous odds: Being involved as a service user, in C Thompson (ed) *Changing the balance*, pp 12–13, London: National Council for Voluntary Organisations

Beresford, P, 2010, *A straight talking guide to being a mental health service user*, Ross-on-Wye: PCCS Books

References

Abeysekera, S, undated, Shifting feminisms: From inter-sectionality to political ecology, *Isis International*, http://isiswomen.org/index.php?option=com_content&view=article&id=911

Adams, S, Phillips, D, 2013, *An ex-ante analysis of the effects of the UK Government's welfare reforms on labour supply in Wales*, London: Institute for Fiscal Studies

Addison, P, 1975, *The road to 1945*, London: Jonathan Cape

Adie, K, 2013, *Fighting on the home front: The legacy of women of World War One*, London: Hodder and Stoughton

Alcock, P, 1996, *Social policy in Britain: Themes and issues*, Basingstoke: Macmillan

Alcock, P, 1997, *Understanding poverty* (2nd edn), Basingstoke: Macmillan

Alcock, P, 2006, *Poverty in Britain* (3rd edn), Basingstoke: Palgrave Macmillan

Alcock, P, 2008, *Social policy in Britain* (3rd edn), Basingstoke: Palgrave/Macmillan

Alcock, P, 2012a, The subject of social policy, in P Alcock, M May, S Wright (eds) *The student's companion to social policy* (4th edn), pp 5–11, London: Wiley-Blackwell

Alcock, P, 2012b, Poverty and social exclusion, in P Alcock, M May, S Wright (eds) *The student's companion to social policy* (4th edn), pp 180–6, London: Wiley-Blackwell

Alcock, P with May, M, 2014, *Social policy in Britain* (4th edn), Basingstoke: Palgrave Macmillan

Alcock, P, May, M, Wright, S (eds), 2012, *The student's companion to social policy* (4th edn), London: Wiley-Blackwell

Alford, J, 2009, *Engaging public sector clients: From service delivery to co-production*, Basingstoke: Palgrave Macmillan

Allatt, P, 2014, Lating impact of armed forces education, Letter to the Editor, *Guardian*, 21 June, p 33

ALLFIE (Alliance for Inclusive Education), 2008, Creating a movement: The struggle for inclusive education in the UK 1990–2006, London: co-published by Stefan Szczelkun's RuB label and The Alliance for Inclusive Education, www.allfie.org.uk/docs/DVD%20flyer.pdf

ALLFIE, 2014, How was school?: Disabled people's experience of school over the last century, website with teaching resources, London: The Alliance for Inclusive Education, http://howwasschool.org.uk

Andrews, ND, 2014a, Who's helping who? Challenging professional boundaries..., Blog, 28 May, Co-production Wales, http://allinthistogetherwales.wordpress.com/2014/05/28/whos-helping-who-challenging-professional-boundaries/

Andrews, ND, 2014b, *Simple, but not simplistic: Developing evidence enriched practice*, Interim report for phase 1, May, Swansea: All Wales Social Care Collaboration and the Joseph Rowntree Foundation

Annetts, J, Law, A, McNeish, W, Mooney, G, 2009, *Understanding social welfare movements*, in association with the Social Policy Association, Bristol: Policy Press

Anstruther, I, 1984, *The scandal of the Andover workhouse*, Gloucester: Alan Sutton

APPGHR (All Party Parliamentary Group on Heritage Railways), 2013, *The social and economic value of heritage railways*, July, London: All Party Parliamentary Group on Heritage Railways

Arches, J, Fleming, J, 2006, Young people and social action: Youth participation in the UK and USA, *New Directions for Youth Development* 111, Fall, 81–91

Archibugi, F, 2008, *Planning theory: From the political debate to the methodological reconstruction*, Milan: Springer

Army Council, 1921, *General annual report of the British army 1912–1919*, Parliamentary Paper 1921, XX, Cmd 1193, Part IV pp 62–72, London: HMSO

Ashcroft, J, 2012, Forty years of UK trade, 1979–2010, April, Economics discussion paper, Manchester, *Saturday Economist*, pro.manchester, www.johnashcroft.co.uk/wp-content/uploads/2012/06/Discussion-Paper-Forty-Years-of-UK-Trade.pdf

Aspers, P, 2011, *Markets*, Cambridge: Polity Press

Aspis, S, 1997, Self-advocacy for people with learning difficulties: does it have a future?, *Disability and Society* 12, 4, 647–54

Atkinson, AB, 1989, *Poverty and social security*, London: Harvester Wheatsheaf

Atkinson, AB, 2015, *Inequality: What can be done?*, London: Harvard University Press

Atkinson, D, Williams, F (eds), 1990, *Know me as I am: An anthology of prose, poetry and art by people with learning difficulties*, London: Hodder Stoughton

Audit Commission, 2001, *Change here!: Managing change in local services*, 11 July, London: Audit Commission

Badcock, C, 2008, *Eugenics*, London: London School of Economics and Political Science

Bailey, R, Brake, M (eds), 1975, *Radical social work*, London: Edward Arnold

Baldock, J, 2012, Social policy, social welfare and the welfare state, in J Baldock, L Mitton, N Manning, S Vickerstaff (eds) *Social policy* (4th edn), pp 7–26, Oxford: Oxford University Press

Baldock, J, Mitton, L, Manning, N, Vickerstaff, S (eds), 2012, *Social policy* (4th edn), Oxford: Oxford University Press

Baldwin, C, 2013, *Narrative social work: Theory and application*, Bristol: Policy Press

Balloch, S, McLean, J (eds), 1999, *Social services: Working under pressure*, Bristol, The Policy Press

Bamford, D, 2014, Walkers crisps reveal winner of Do Us All A Flavour Campaign, *The Grocer*, 21 October, accessed 7 September 2015, www.thegrocer.co.uk/buying-and-supplying/marketing/walkers-crisps-reveals-winner-of-do-us-a-flavour-campaign/372753.article

Banham, M, Hillier, B (eds), 1976, *A tonic to the nation: The festival of Britain 1951*, London: Thames and Hudson

Barnes, C, 1991a, *Disabled people in Britain and discrimination: A case for anti-discrimination legislation*, in association with the British Council of Organisations of Disabled People, London: Hurst and Company

Barnes, C, 1991b, Discrimination: Disabled people and the media, *Contact* 70, Winter, 45–8, http://disability-studies.leeds.ac.uk/files/library/Barnes-Media.pdf

Barnes, C, 1996, Foreword, in, J Campbell, M Oliver (eds) *Disability politics: Understanding our past, changing our future*, pp ix–xii, London: Routledge

Barnes, C, 1997, A legacy of oppression: a history of disability in Western culture, in L Barton and M Oliver (eds), *Disability studies: Past, present and future*, pp 3-24, Leeds: Disability Press

Barnes, C, Mercer, G (eds), 1997, *Doing disability research*, Leeds: Disability Press, University of Leeds

Barnes, C, Mercer, G, 2006, *Independent futures: Creating user-led disability services in a disabling society*, Bristol: Policy Press in association with the British Association of Social Workers

Barnes, C, Mercer, G, Shakespeare, T, 1999, *Exploring disability: A sociological introduction*, Cambridge: Polity Press

Barnes, C, Mercer, G, Morgan, H, 2000a, *Creating independent futures: An evaluation of services led by disabled people*, Stage one report, Leeds: Disability Press

Barnes, C, Mercer, G, Morgan, H, 2000b, *Creating independent futures: An evaluation of services led by disabled people*, Stage two report, Leeds: Disability Press

Barnes, C, Mercer, G, Morgan, H, 2001, *Creating independent futures: An evaluation of services led by disabled people*, Stage three report, Leeds: Disability Press

Barnes, C, Oliver, M, Barton, L (eds), 2002, *Disability studies today*, Cambridge: Polity Press

Barnes, M, 2012, Welfare users and social policy, in P Alcock, M May, S Wright (eds) *The student's companion to social policy* (4th edn), pp 278–83, London: Wiley-Blackwell

Barnes, M, Cotterell, P (eds), 2012, *Critical perspectives on user involvement*, Bristol: Policy Press

Barnes, M, Shardlow, P, 1996, Effective consumers and active citizens: Strategies for users' influence on service and beyond, *Research, Policy and Planning* 14, 1, 3–38

Barnes, M, Harrison, S, Mort, M, Shardlow, P, 1999, *Unequal partners: User groups and community care*, Bristol: The Policy Press

Barnett, C, 1996, *The audit of war: The illusion and reality of Britain as a great nation*, London, Pan

Barnett, C, 2002, *The collapse of British power*, London: Pan

Barnett, J, Hammond, S, 1999, Representing charity in disability promotions, *Community and Applied Social Psychology* 9, 14 (July/August), 309–14

Barron, D, 1996, *A price to be born: My childhood and life in a mental institution*, Harrogate: Mencap Northern Division

Bartholomew, J, 2004, *The welfare state we're in*, London: Biteback Publishing, 2nd edn, 2013

Barts Health NHS Trust, 2015, Our history, www.bartshealth.nhs.uk/our-hospitals/mile-end-hospital/our-history/

BBC News UK, 2010, New bank bail-out risk, New Economics Foundation warns, Business, BBC TV, 4 October, www.bbc.co.uk/news/business-11462440

BBC News UK, 2012, Timeline: Winterbourne View abuse scandal, BBC TV, 10 December, www.bbc.co.uk/news/uk-england-bristol-20078999

BBC News UK, 2014, Housing benefits: Changes 'see 6% of tenants move', BBC TV, 28 March, www.bbc.co.uk/news/uk-26770727

BBC TV, 1978, Doesn't anybody want to know? The story of the Lucas aerospace shop stewards alternative corporate plan, Milton Keynes: Open University/BBC TV, www.youtube.com/watch?v=0pgQqfpub-c

BBC TV, 1983, *Triumph Motorcycles Meriden: Their fight for survival*, introduced by Valerie Singleton, The Money Programme, London: BBC TV, www.youtube.com/watch?v=y4rNAa3oOrM

BCODP (British Council of Organisations of Disabled People), 1997, *The Disabled People's Movement: The way forward. Book Four: A resource pack for local groups of disabled people*, Derbyshire, British Council of Organisations of Disabled People, http://disability-studies.leeds. ac.uk/files/library/BCODP-workbook4.pdf

Beerbohm, M, 1914, *Mr Sidney Webb on his birthday, 1914*, Cartoon, WA1945.14 (in the Hart-Davies catalogue, No 1747), Oxford: Ashmolean Museum

Bellis, M, 2015, Microsoft: History of a computing giant, About.com, http://inventors.about.com/od/CorporateProfiles/p/Microsoft-History.htm

Bendit, P and Bendit, L, 1946, *Living together again*, London: Gramol

Benn, M, 2014, Telling a different kind of truth about reformer Richard Titmuss – with the odd bombshell, Review, *Guardian*, 8 November, p 6, www.theguardian.com/books/2014/nov/07/father-and-daughter-ann-oakley-richard-titmuss-review-memoir

Bentley, JA, 1933, *The submerged tenth: The story of a down and out*, London: Constable

Beresford, P, 1969, The relieving officer: Poor law personified, *New Society*, 6 November, 721–3

Beresford, P, 1975a, Reception centres: An index of social service inadequacy, *British Journal of Social Work* 5, 2, 175–92

Beresford, P, 1975b, The demise of the lodging house and hostel, *Contemporary Review* 227, 1316, 137–40

Beresford, P, 1979, The public presentation of vagrancy, in T Cook (ed) *Vagrancy: Some new perspectives*, pp 141–65, London: Academic Press

Beresford, P, 1994, Changing the culture: involving service users in social work education, *Central Council of Education and Training in Social Work (CCETSW) Paper* 32, 2, London: CCETSW

Beresford, P, 2001, Cheshire: The biography of Leonard Cheshire, VC, OM, *Review, Disability and Society* 16, 3, 456–7

Beresford, P, 2002, Participation and social policy: transformation, liberation or regulation, in R Sykes, C Bochel and N Ellison (eds), *Social Policy Review 14*, pp 265–90, Bristol: Policy Press

Beresford, P, 2003a, User involvement in research: exploring the challenges, *Nursing Times Research* 8, 1, 36–46

Beresford, P, 2003b, *It's our lives: A short theory of knowledge, distance and experience*, London: Citizen Press in association with Shaping Our Lives

Beresford, P, 2003c, Listen and learn: rebuilding child protection policy following the report of the inquiry into the murder of Victoria Climbié, Perspectives Column, *Community Care*, 30 January–6 February, p 18

Beresford, P, 2005, Redistributing profit and loss: rhe new economics of the market and social welfare, *Critical Social Policy* 25, 4 (November), 464–82

Beresford, P, 2007, User involvement, research and health inequalities: developing new directions, *Health and Social Care in the Community* 15, 4, 306–12

Beresford, P, 2009, Control, in J Wallcraft, B Schrank, M Amering (eds) *Handbook of service user involvement in mental health research*, World Psychiatric Association, pp 181–98, Chichester: Wiley-Blackwell

Beresford, P, 2010a, Service users and social policy: developing different discussions, challenging dominant discourses, in I Greener, C Holden, M Kilkey (eds) *Social policy review 22: Analysis and debate in social policy, 2010*, pp 227–52, Bristol: Policy Press in association with Social Policy Association

Beresford, P, 2010b, *Funding social care: What service users say*, Viewpoint, York: Joseph Rowntree Foundation

Beresford, P, 2010c, *A straight talking guide to being a mental health service user*, Ross-on-Wye: PCCS Books

Beresford, P, 2012, From 'vulnerable' to vanguard: challenging the coalition, in S Davison, J Rutherford (eds) *Welfare reform: The dread of things to come*, Soundings On, pp 66–77, London: Lawrence Wishart

Beresford, P, 2013a, Francis report: Creating patient power is the only way forward, *Guardian Professional*, 19 February, www.guardian.co.uk/healthcare-network/2013/feb/19/francis-report-patient-power.

Beresford, P, 2013b, Those already in need will be hardest hit by increasing means testing, *Guardian*, Social Care Network, 18 June, www.guardian.co.uk/social-care-network/2013/jun/18/those-in-need-hit-by-means-testing

Beresford, P, 2013c, *Beyond the usual suspects: Towards inclusive user involvement*, Research report, London: Shaping Our Lives

Beresford, P, 2014, Remembering Mr Benn, Readers' letters, *The Classic Motorcycle*, August, p 19

Beresford, P, Andrews, E, 2012, Caring for our future: what service users say, *Joseph Rowntree Foundation (JRF) Programme Paper, Paying for long-term care*, York: JRF

Beresford, P, Campbell, P, 2004, Participation and protest: mental health service users/survivors, in MJ Todd, G Taylor (eds) *Democracy and participation: Popular protest and new social movements*, pp 326–42, London: Merlin Press

Beresford, P, Croft, S, 1978, *A say in the future: Planning, participation and meeting social need*, London: Battersea Community Action

Beresford, P, Croft, S, 1981a, Intermediate treatment, special education and the personalisation of urban problems, in W Swann (ed) *The practice of special education*, pp 187–207, Oxford: Basil Blackwell/Open University Press

Beresford, P, Croft, S, 1981b, *No more kidding: Young people, participation and power*, London: Battersea Community Action

Beresford, P, Croft, S, 1982, *A say in the future: Planning, participation and meeting social need* (2nd edn with a new introduction), London: Battersea Community Action

Beresford, P, Croft, S, 1984, Welfare pluralism: the new face of Fabianism, *Critical Social Policy*, 9 (Spring), 19–39

Beresford, P, Croft, S, 1986, *Whose welfare?: Private care or public services*, Brighton: Lewis Cohen Urban Studies Centre

Beresford, P, Croft, S, 1993, *Citizen involvement: A practical guide for change*, Basingstoke: Macmillan

Beresford, P, Croft, S, 1995, Whose empowerment? Equalising the competing discourses in community care, in R Jacks (ed) *Empowerment In community care*, pp 59–73, London: Chapman and Hall

Beresford, P, Croft, S, 2004, Service users and practitioners reunited: The key component for social work reform, *The future of social work: Special Issue, British Journal of Social Work* 34 (January), 53–68

Beresford, P, Croft, S, 2012, *User controlled research: Scoping review*, London: NHS National Institute for Health Research (NIHR) School for Social Care Research, London School of Economics, sscr.nihr.ac.uk/PDF/SSCR-Scoping-Review_5_web.pdf

Beresford, P, Harding, T (eds), 1993, A challenge to change: practical experiences of building user-led services, London: National Institute for Social Work

Beresford, P, Hasler, F, 2009, Transforming social care: transforming the future together, London: Brunel University, Centre for Citizen Participation

Beresford, P, Wilson, A, 2002, Genes spell danger: Mental health service users/survivors, bioethics and control, *Disability and Society* 17, 5, 541–53

Beresford, P, Green, D, Lister, R, Woodard, K, 1999, *Poverty first hand*, London: Child Poverty Action Group

Beresford, P, Shamash, O, Forrest, V, Turner, M, Branfield, F, 2005, *Developing social care: Service users' vision for adult support*, Report of a consultation on the future of adult social care, Adult services report 07, London: Social Care Institute for Excellence (SCIE) in association with Shaping Our Lives

Beresford, P, Adshead, L, Croft, S, 2007, *Palliative care, social work and service users: Making life possible*, London: Jessica Kingsley

Beresford, P, Nettle, M, Perring, R, 2009, *Towards a social model of madness and distress?: Exploring what service users say*, 22 November, York, Joseph Rowntree Foundation

Beresford, P, Fleming, J, Glynn, M, Bewley, C, Croft, S, Branfield, F, Postle, K, 2011, *Supporting people: Towards a person-centred approach*, Bristol: Policy Press

Beresford, P, Perring, R, Nettle, M, Wallcraft, J, 2015, *From mental illness to a social model of madness and distress*, London: Shaping Our Lives and National Survivor User Network

Bersani, H, 1998, From social clubs to social movement: landmarks in the development of the international self-advocacy movement, in L Ward (ed) *Innovations in advocacy and empowerment for people with intellectual disabilities*, Chorley: Lisieux Hall Publications

Beveridge, W, 1942, *The Beveridge report: Report of the Inter-Departmental Committee on Social Insurance and Allied Services*, London: HMSO

Bishop, E, 1995, *The wooden wonder* (3rd edn), Shrewsbury: Airlife Publishing Ltd

Blackburn, W, 2013, Suicide and the unspoken side of welfare 'reform', Comment is Free, *Guardian*, 31 May, www.theguardian.com/commentisfree/2013/may/31/suicide-welfare-reform-cuts

Blackhurst, C, 1996, Thatcher directed arms crusade, *Guardian*, 16 February, www.independent.co.uk/news/thatcher-directed-arms-crusade-1319226.html

Blakemore, K, Warwick-Booth, L, 2013, *Social policy: An introduction* (4th edn), Maidenhead: Open University Press

Blakemore, K, Warwick-Booth, L, Warwick-Giles, L, 2013, Are professionals good for you?: The example of health policy and health professionals, in K Blakemore, L Warwick-Booth (eds) *Social policy: An introduction* (4th edn), pp 206–26, Maidenhead: Open University Press

Blood, I, 2013, *A better life: Valuing our later years*, York: Joseph Rowntree Foundation, www.jrf.org.uk/publications/better-life-valuing-our-later-years

Bochel, H, 2012, The Conservative tradition, in P Alcock, M May, S Wright (eds) *The student's companion to social policy* (4th edn), pp 64–9, London: Wiley-Blackwell

Bochel, H, Daley, G (eds), 2014, *Social policy* (3rd edn), London: Routledge

Boffey, D, 2014, The care workers left behind as private equity targets the NHS, *Observer*, 10 August, www.theguardian.com/society/2014/aug/09/care-workers-private-equity-targets-the-nhs

Booth, C, 2001, B351 [Notebooks], London: London School of Economics and Political Science, http://booth.lse.ac.uk/notebooks/b351/jpg/39.html

Booth, W, 1890, *In darkest England and the way out*, London: Salvation Army

Booth, W, Booth, T, 1998, *Advocacy for parents with learning difficulties: Developing advocacy support*, Brighton: Pavilion Publishing

Borkman, T, 1976, Experiential knowledge: a new concept for the analysis of self-help groups, *Social Services Review*, 50, 445–56

Borsay, A, 2002, History, power and identity, in C Barnes, M Oliver, L Barton (eds) *Disability studies today*, pp 98–119, Cambridge: Polity

Borsay, A, 2005, *Disability and social policy in Britain since 1750*, Basingstoke: Palgrave Macmillan

Bosanquet, N, Townsend, P, 1980, *Labour and equality*, London: Heinemann Educational Books

Boseley, S, 2013, Britain told social inequality has created 'public health timebomb', *Guardian*, 30 October, www.theguardian.com/society/2013/oct/30/britain-inequality-public-health-timebomb-marmot

Boston Consulting Group, 1975, *Strategy alternatives for the British motorcycle industry: A report prepared for the Secretary of State for Industry*, 30 July, London: Her Majesty's Stationery Office, www.gov.uk/government/uploads/system/uploads/attachment_data/file/235319/0532.pdf

Bourdieu, P, 1999, *Acts of resistance: Against the tyranny of the market*, New York: The New Press

Boyle, A, 1955, *No passing glory: The full and authentic biography of Group Captain Cheshire VC, DSO, DFC*, London: Collins

Boyle, D, Coote, A, Sherwood, C, Slay, J, 2010, *Right here, right now: taking co-production into the mainstream*, Discussion paper, London: National Economic Foundation (NEF) in association with NESTA and The Lab

Braddon, R, 1956, *Cheshire VC: A story of war and peace*, London: The Companion Book Club

Bradley, Q, 2014, *The tenants' movement: Resident involvement, community action and the contentious policy of housing*, London: Routledge

Branfield, F, 2007, *User involvement in social work education: Report of regional consultations with service users to develop a strategy to support the participation of service users in social work education*, London: Shaping our Lives

Branfield, F, 2009, *Developing user involvement in social work education*, Workforce development report 29, London: Social Care Institute for Excellence (SCIE)

Branfield, F, Beresford, P, Danagher, N, Webb, R, 2005, *Independence, wellbeing and choice: A response to the Green Paper on adult social care, Report of a consultation with service users*, London: National Centre for Independent Living and Shaping Our Lives

Branfield, F, Beresford, P with Andrews, EJ, Chambers, P, Staddon, P, Wise, G, Williams-Findlay, B, 2006, *Making user involvement work: Supporting service user networking and knowledge*, York: Joseph Rowntree Foundation, York Publishing Services

Branfield, F, Beresford, P, Levin, E, 2007, *Common aims: A strategy to support service user involvement in social work education*, Position paper 7, London: Social Care Institute for Excellence (SCIE)

Bremner, RH, 1965, 'An iron scepter twined with roses': The Octavia Hill system of housing management, *Social Service Review* 39, 2 (June), 222–31

Briant, E, Watson, N, Philo, G, Inclusion London, 2012, *Bad news for disabled people: How the newspapers are reporting disability*, Strathclyde Centre for Disability Research and Glasgow Media Unit, in association with Inclusion London, Glasgow: University of Glasgow

British Political Speech, 1995, Tony Blair (Labour), Leader's speech, Brighton, Speech Archive, www.britishpoliticalspeech.org/speech-archive.htm?speech=201

British Academy, 2008, Britain in the 50s: Consensus or conflict?, http://www.britac.ac.uk/perspectives/0802britainin50s-1.cfm

British Psychological Society, 2015, Special Issue: 'Recovery'?, *Clinical Psychology Forum*, 268, April, Division of Clinical Psychology, www.bps.org.uk/system/files/Public%20files/recovery.pdf

Bullock, A, 2002, *Ernest Bevin*, London: Politico's Publishing

Burdett, E, 2014, Eugenics, in C Cameron (ed) *Disability studies: A student's guide*, pp 53–6, London: Sage

Burnett, J, 1986, *A social history of housing 1815–1985,* London: Methuen

Burstow, B, 2015, *Psychiatry and the business of madness: An ethical and epistemological accounting*, Basingstoke: Palgrave Macmillan

Burstow, B, LeFrancois, BA, Diamond, S (eds), 2014, *Psychiatry disrupted: Theorising resistance and crafting the (r)evolution*, Ithaca, NY: McGill-Queen's University Press

Buruma, I, 2013, *Year Zero: A history of 1945*, London: Atlantic Books

Butler, I, Drakeford, M, 2001, Which Blair project?: Communitarianism, social authoritarianism and social work, *Journal of Social Work* 1, 1, 7–19

Butler, P, 2013, Poverty rose by 900,000 in the coalition's first year, Society, *Guardian*, 13 June, www.theguardian.com/society/2013/jun/13/1million-more-people-poverty-coalition-first-year

Cahill, M, 1994, *The new social policy*, Oxford: Blackwell

Cahill, M, 2002, *The environment and social policy*, London: Routledge

Cahill, M, 2012, Green perspectives, in P Alcock, M May, S Wright (eds) *The student's companion to social policy* (4th edn), pp 90–5, London: Wiley-Blackwell

Calder, A, 1971, *The People's War: Britain 1939–45*, London: Jonathan Cape

Campbell, J, 1993, Personal assistance schemes under the control of disabled people: a practical guide, in P Beresford, T Harding (eds) *A challenge to change: Practical experiences of building user-led services*, pp 52–8, London: National Institute for Social Work

Campbell, J, Oliver, M, 1996, *Disability politics: Understanding our past, changing our future*, London: Routledge

Campbell, P, 1999, The service user/survivor movement, in C Newnes, G Holmes, C Dunn (eds) *This is madness: A critical look at psychiatry and the future of mental health services*, pp 195–209, Ross-on-Wye: PCCS Books

Campbell, P, 2005, From Little Acorns: the mental health service user movement, in A Bell, P Lindley (eds) *Beyond the water towers: The unfinished revolution in mental health services, 1985–2005*, pp 73–82, London: Centre for Mental Health, www.centreformentalhealth.org.uk/pdfs/Beyond_the_water_towers.pdf

Campbell, P, 2009, The service user/survivor movement, in J Reynolds, R Muston, T Heller, J Leach, M McCormick, J Wallcraft, M Walsh (eds) *Mental health still matters*, pp 46–52, Basingstoke: Palgrave

Cardus, S (ed), 1989, *Back street Brighton*, Brighton: Queens Park Books

Carr, S, 2004, Has service user participation made a difference to social care services?, *Position Paper* 3, March, London: Social Care Institute for Excellence (SCIE)

Carter, T, Beresford, P, 2000, *Age and change: Models of involvement for older people*, York: York Publishing

Casey, L, 2012, *Listening to troubled families: A report by Louise Casey CB, Department for Communities and Local Government*, July, London: Department for Communities and Local Government

Castles, FG, Leibfried, S, Lewis, J, Obinger, H, Pierson, C (eds), 2010, *The Oxford handbook of the welfare state*, Oxford Handbooks in Politics and International Relations, Oxford: Oxford University Press

Cathcart, A, 2013, The John Lewis model reveals the tensions and paradoxes at the heart of workplace democracy, *Democratic Audit UK*, 30 July, www.democraticaudit.com/?p=1166

CDP (Community Development Project), 1977, *Gilding the ghetto: The state and the poverty experiments*, London: Community Development Project Inter-project Editorial Team

Centre for Independent Living, 1982, Independent living: the right to choose, in, M Eisenberg, C Griggins, R Duval (eds) *Disabled people as second class citizens*, pp 247–60, New York: Springer Publishing Company

Chakrabortty, A, 2014, The nightmare of renting started in Westminster, *Guardian*, 26 August, p 26, www.theguardian.com/commentisfree/2014/aug/25/nightmare-renting-westminster-human-kennels-housing-policy

Chakrabortty, A, Robinson-Tillett, S, 2014, The remaking of Woodberry Down, Special Report, G2, *Guardian*, 19 May 2014, pp 6–12

Chamberlin, J, 1988, *On our own: Patient-controlled alternatives to the mental health system*, Front Cover, London: MIND

Chang, H-J, 2004a, *Economics: A user's guide*, London: Pelican

Chang, H-J, 2004b, How an economic fairy-tale led Britain to stagnation, *Guardian*, 20 October, p 27

Charlton, JI, 1998, *Nothing about us without us: Disability, oppression and empowerment*, Oakland, CA: University of California Press

Cheshire, L, 1943, *Bomber pilot*, London: Hutchinson

Cheshire, L, 1961, *The face of victory*, London: Hutchinson

Cheshire, L, 1981, *The hidden world*, London: William Collins

Cheshire, L, 1985, *The light of many suns: The meaning of the bomb*, London: Methuen

Chester, L, 1993, Obituary: T Dan Smith, People, *Independent*, 28 July, www.independent.co.uk/news/people/obituary-t-dan-smith-1487528.html

Chesworth, S, 2014, *File on 4: Abused not heard*, Victims of sexual abuse at Knowl View School in Rochdale tell their side of the story, BBC Radio 4, reporter Jane Deith, www.bbc.co.uk/programmes/b04grs67; Programme Transcript: http://news.bbc.co.uk/1/shared/bsp/hi/pdfs/16_09_14_fo4_abusedbutnotheard.pdf

Christensen, K, Guldvik, I, 2014, *Migrant care workers: Searching for new horizons*, Farnham: Ashgate

Churchill, WS, 2011, *All will be well: Good advice from Winston Churchill*, London: Ebury Publishing

Clarke, J, 2012, Managing and delivering welfare, in P Alcock, M May, S Wright (eds) *The student's companion to social policy* (4th edn), pp 265–70, London: Wiley-Blackwell

Cleveland, W, 2008, *Art and upheaval: Artists on the world's frontlines*, Oakland, CA: New Village Press

Close, M, 2011, *Timeline history of the disabled people's movement*, October, Lancashire: Disability Equality North West, equality.org.uk/uploads/files/fb979acea0dfe4ec8163fc610ffcf305.pdf

Coates, K, Silburn, R, 1967, *St Ann's: Poverty, deprivation and morale in a Nottingham community*, Nottingham: Spokesman Books

Coates, K, Silburn, R, 1970, *Poverty: The forgotten Englishmen*, London: Penguin

Cockburn, C, 2013, 'Beyond the fragments': I'm a socialist feminist. Can I be a radical feminist too?, *50:50: inclusive democracy* blog, *Open Democracy*, 26 October, www.opendemocracy.net/5050/cynthia-cockburn/"beyond-fragments"-i'm-socialist-feminist-can-i-be-radical-feminist-too

Coffey, M, Dugdill, L, 2013, Health and well-being, in P Dwyer, S Shaw (eds) *An introduction to social policy*, London: Sage

Cohen, AM, Stavri, PZ, Hersh, WR, 2004, A categorisation and analysis of the criticism of evidence-based medicine, *International Journal of Medical Informatics* 73, 35–43

Cohen, P, 1993, *Rethinking drug control policy: Historical perspectives and conceptual tools*, Paper presented at the United Nations Research Institute for Social Development (UNRISD) Geneva, 7–8 July, Palais des Nations, Symposium: The crisis of social development in 1990s, www.cedro-uva.org/lib/cohen.rethinking.html

Cohen, S, 1972, *Folk devils and moral panics*, London: MacGibbon and Kee

Cohen, S, Humphries, B, Mynott, E, 2002, *From immigration controls to welfare controls*, London: Routledge

Coleridge, P, 1993, *Disability, liberation and development*, Oxford: Oxfam in association with Action on Disability and Development

Collins, J, 1992, *When the eagles fly*, London, Values Into Action

Collins, J, 1993, *The resettlement game*, London, Values Into Action

Collins, P, 2013, Who benefits?: First principles of a welfare state, *Prospect*, June, pp 28–32

Copping, J, 2013, Is the Mosquito the greatest warplane of all?, *Telegraph*, 21 July, www.telegraph.co.uk/history/world-war-two/10192280/Is-the-Mosquito-the-greatest-warplane-of-all.html

Corker, M, 1998, *Deaf and disabled, or deafness disabled?*, Buckingham: Open University Press

Corrigan, P, 1979, *Schooling the Smash Street Kids*, Basingstoke: Macmillan

Corrigan, P, Leonard, P, 1978, *Social work practice under capitalism: A Marxist approach*, Basingstoke: Macmillan

Cotterell, P, Morris, C, The capacity, impact and challenge of service users' experiential knowledge, in M Barnes and P Cotterell (eds), *Critical perspectives on user involvement*, pp 57-69, Bristol, Policy Press

Cotterell, P, Harlow, G, Morris, C, Beresford, P, Hanley, B, Sargeant, A, Sitzia, J, Staley, K, 2011, Service user involvement in cancer care: the impact on service users, *Health Expectations* 14, 2, 159–69

Cowdrill, DA, 2009, *The Conservative Party and Thatcherism, 1970–1979: A grass-roots perspective*, Thesis submitted for the degree of Master of Philosophy, Department of Medieval and Modern History, Birmingham: Birmingham University

Cozens, A, 2013, Can social care shed its poor law roots?, *Local Government Chronicle*, 22 July, www.lgcplus.com/briefings/can-care-shed-its-poor-law-roots/5060490.article

Crenshaw, KW, 1991, Mapping the margins: intersectionality, identity politics, and violence against women of color, *Stanford Law Review* 43, 6, 1241–99

Croft, S, Beresford, P, 1993, *Getting involved: A practical manual*, London: Open Services Project

Crowther, N, 2014, We need to talk about the elephant (trap) in the room, *Making Rights Make Sense* blog, posted June 2, see also accompanying comments, http://makingrightsmakesense.wordpress.com/2014/06/02/we-need-to-talk-about-the-elephant-trap-in-the-room/

CSCI (Commission for Social Care Inspection), 2007, *Benefit barriers to involvement: Finding solutions*, London: Commission for Social Care Inspection

Cunningham, J, Cunningham, S, 2012, *Sociology and social work*, Exeter: Learning Matters.

Daily Beast, 2013, Murdoch's News of the World editors admit to phone-hacking, 30 October, www.thedailybeast.com/articles/2013/10/30/murdoch-s-news-of-the-world-editors-admit-to-phone-hacking.html

Daily Star, 2012, Jimmy Savile brother sacked for groping patient, *Daily Star*, 15 October, www.dailystar.co.uk/news/latest-news/277112/Jimmy-Savile-brother-sacked-for-groping-patient

Damer, S, Hague, C, 1971, Public participation in planning: A review, *The Town Planning Review* 42, 3 (July), 217–32, http://isites.harvard.edu/fs/docs/icb.topic793411.files/Wk%202_Sept%2010th/Damer%20_%20Hague_1971_Public%20Participation%20Review.pdf

Darke, R, Darke, J, 1979, *Who needs housing?*, Basingstoke: Macmillan

Davies, C, 2014, Support for death penalty in UK falls, survey finds, *Guardian*, 12 August, www.theguardian.com/world/2014/aug/12/less-half-britons-support-reintroduction-death-penalty-survey

Davies, C, Finlay, L, Bullman, A (eds), 2000, *Changing practice in health and social care*, London: Sage in association with the Open University

Davies, K, 1993, On the movement, in J Swain, V Finklestein, S French, M Oliver (eds) *Disabling barriers: Enabling environments*, London: Sage and Open University Press

Davies, N, 2014, Trial over: but a toxic cocktail of power remains, *Guardian*, 26 June, pp 1, 8–10

Dawkins, R, 1976, *The selfish gene*, New York: Oxford University Press

De Jong, G, 1983, Defining and implementing the independent living concept, in N Crewe, I Zola (eds) *Independent living for physically disabled people*, London: Jossey-Bass

De La Bedoyere, G, 2011, *The home front*, Shire Living Histories, Oxford: Shire Publications

Decies, Lady C, 1902, *Journal of a tour to B Columbia and Vancouver*, annotated by author, typewritten copy of *Journal Through Canada Stopping Calgary and Vancouver, 1902*, Unpublished

Delderfield, RE, 1958a, *The dreaming suburb: Book 1 (1919–1940) of The Avenue*, London: Hodder and Stoughton

Delderfield, RE, 1958b, *The Avenue goes to war: Book 2 (1940–1947) of The Avenue*, London: Hodder and Stoughton

DeMarasse, R, 2014, Circles of support, *Circles Network*, www.circlesnetwork.org.uk/index.asp?slevel=0z114z115&parent_id=115

DH (Department of Health), 2014, *Reforming the Education Support Grant: The government response to the consultation*, SER/WSD/WD/3500, May, Leeds: Social Care Workforce, DH, www.gov.uk/government/uploads/system/uploads/attachment_data/file/310546/ESG_response.pdf

Docherty, D, Hughes, R, Phillips, P, Corbett, D, Regan, B, Barber, A, Adams, M, Boxall, K, Kaplan, I, Izzidien, S, 2010, This is what we think, in L Davis (ed) *The disability studies reader* (3rd edn), pp 432–40, New York: Routledge

Dolan, A, Bentley, P, 2013, Vile product of Welfare UK: man who bred 17 babies by five women to milk benefits system is guilty of killing six of them, *Daily Mail*, 24 May, p 1, www.dailymail.co.uk/news/article-2303120/Mick-Philpott-vile-product-Welfare-UK-Derby-man-bred-17-babies-milk-benefits-GUILTY-killing-six.html

Dore, R, 2003, Tony Benn at the arts club, Blog, *National Union of Journalists (NUJ) Brighton and Sussex Branch*, 6 August, http://nujbrighton.blogspot.co.uk/2003/08/tony-benn-at-arts-club.html

Dorling, D, 2012, The future is caring, Comment is Free, *Guardian*, 2 October, p 30, www.theguardian.com/commentisfree/2012/oct/01/population-future-caring-ageing-good-news

Dorling, D, 2013, *Unequal health: The scandal of our times*, Bristol: Policy Press

Dorling, D, 2014, *Inequality and the 1%*, London: Verso

Dorling, D, Thomas, B, 2011, *Bankrupt Britain: An atlas of social change*, Bristol: Policy Press

Dowson, S, 1990, *Keeping it safe: Self-advocacy by people with learning difficulties and the professional response*, London: Values Into Action

Dowson, S, 1998, *Certainties without centres*, London, Values Into Action

Doyal, L, Gough, I, 1991, *A theory of human need*, Basingstoke: Macmillan

Doyle, P, 2012, *First World War Britain*, Shire Living Histories, Oxford: Shire Publications

Drake, R F, 1996, A critique of the role of the traditional charities, in L Barton (ed) *Disability and society: Emerging issues and insights*, pp 147–56, London: Longman

Duffy, S, 2014, *Counting the cuts: What the Government doesn't want the public to know*, London: Centre for Welfare Reform on behalf of the Campaign for a Fair Society

Dunn, S, 2009, Six scandals from the darkest days of an already murky industry, *Observer*, 21 June, www.theguardian.com/money/2009/jun/21/financial-advisers-scandals

Dustin, D, 2007, *The Mcdonaldization of social work*, Farnham: Ashgate

DWP (Department for Work and Pensions), ODI (Office for Disability Issues), 2014, *Disability facts and figures*, Gov.UK, http://odi.dwp.gov.uk/disability-statistics-and-research/disability-facts-and-figures.php

Dwyer, P, 2004, *Understanding social citizenship*, Bristol: Policy Press

Eaton, G, 2013, How public spending rose under Thatcher, *The Staggers* blog, *New Statesman*, 8 April, www.newstatesman.com/politics/2013/04/how-public-spending-rose-under-thatcher

EB, 1995, London East End, www.ibiblio.org/yiddish/Places/London/london.htm

Eden Camp, 2013, Museum of the Second World War, information provided with exhibits, www.edencamp.co.uk, Malton: North Yorkshire

Ellison, N, 2012, Neo-liberalism, in P Alcock, M May, S Wright (eds) *The student's companion to social policy* (4th edn), pp 57–63, London: Wiley-Blackwell

Emerson, E, 1992, What is normalisation?, in H Brown, H Smith (eds) *Normalisation: A reader for the nineties*, London: Tavistock

Emmerson, C, 2015, *Public finances: The consolidation so far and a dicey decade ahead*, London: Institute for Fiscal Studies

Esping-Andersen, G, 1990, *The three worlds of welfare capitalism*, Princeton, NJ: Princeton University Press

Fabris, E, 2013, Mad success: what could go wrong when psychiatry employs us as 'peers'?:, in BA Le Francois, R Menzies, G Reaume, G (eds) *Mad matters: A critical reader in Canadian mad studies*, pp 130–9, Toronto, Canada: Canadian Scholars Press

Fadden, G, Shooter, M, Holsgrove, G, 2005, Involving carers and service users in the training of psychiatrists, *Psychiatric Bulletin* 29, 270–4, http://pb.rcpsych.org/content/29/7/270.full

Farnsworth, K, 2013, Bringing corporate welfare in, *Journal of Social Policy* 42, January, 1–22

Faulkner, A, 2010, *Changing our worlds: Examples of user controlled research in action*, Eastleigh: National Institute for Health Research (NIHR) INVOLVE

Faulkner, A, Kalathil, J, 2012, *The freedom to be, the chance to dream: Preserving user-led peer support in mental health*, London: Together, www.together-uk.org/wp-content/uploads/2012/09/The-Freedom-to-be-The-Chance-to-dream-Full-Report1.pdf

Faulkner, A, Layzell, S, 2000, *Strategies for living: A report of user-led research into people's strategies for living with mental distress*, London: The Mental Health Foundation

Fearn, H, 2014, Notting Hill housing chief: 'The ends justify the means', Interview, Society, *Guardian*, 23 April, www.theguardian.com/society/2014/apr/23/social-housing-notting-hill-kate-davies-private-sector

Featherstone, B, White, S, Morris, K, 2014, *Re-imagining child protection: Towards humane social work with families*, Bristol: Policy Press

Ferlie, E, Ashburner, L, Fitzgerald, L, Pettigrew, A, 1996, *New public management in action*, Oxford: Oxford University Press

Ferry, K, 2010, *Holiday camps*, Shire Library, Botley: Shire Publications

Field, F, 2013, Here's my answer: parties are promising the wrong things on public spending and benefits, *Prospect*, June, pp 32–3

Finkelstein, V, 1980, *Attitudes and disabled people: Issues for discussion*, New York: World Rehabilitation Fund

Finkelstein, V, 2009, The 'social model of disability' and the disability movement, in, M Oliver (ed) *Understanding disability: From theory to practice* (2nd edn), pp 142–52, Basingstoke: Palgrave Macmillan

Finn, D, 2008, *The British welfare market: Lessons from contracting out welfare to work programmes in Australia and the Netherlands*, November, York: Joseph Rowntree Foundation

Fischer, DH, 1996, *The great wave: Price revolutions and the rhythm of history*, Oxford: Oxford University Press

Fitzgerald, J, 1998, *Time for freedom*, London: Values Into Action

Fitzpatrick, T, 2011a, *Welfare theory: An introduction to the theoretical debates in social policy* (2nd edn), Basingstoke: Palgrave Macmillan

Fitzpatrick, T (ed), 2011b, *Understanding the environment and social policy*, Bristol: Policy Press

Fitzpatrick, T, Cahill, M (eds), 2002, *Greening the welfare state*, Basingstoke: Palgrave Macmillan

Fleming, J, Harrison, M, Perry, A, Purdy, D, Ward, D, 1983, Action speaks louder than words, *Youth and Policy* 2, 3 (Winter 1983/4), 16–19

Fletcher, G, 1966, *Down among the meths men*, London: Hutchinsons

Foord, M, Palmer, J, Simpson, D, 1998, *Bricks without mortar: 30 years of single homelessness*, London: Crisis

Forrest, V, 2013, *Preparing to grow old together: How can housing co-operatives best support their older residents*, York: Joseph Rowntree Foundation, www.jrf.org.uk/publications/preparing-grow-old-together

Fotopoulos, T, 2001, Globalization, the reformist Left and the anti-globalization 'movement', *Democracy and Nature: The International Journal of Inclusive Democracy* 7, 2 (July), www.inclusivedemocracy.org/dn/vol7/takis_globalisation.htm

Foucault, M, 2001, *Madness and civilization: A history of insanity in the age of reason*, London: Routledge

Francis, J, Holmes, P, 2010, *Report 30: Ethical issues in the use of telecare*, London: Social Care Institute for Excellence (SCIE)

Francis, R, 2013, *Report of the Mid Staffordshire NHS Foundation Trust public inquiry*, Three Volumes and Executive Summary, 6 February, London: The Stationery Office

Fraser, D, 2010, *The evolution of the British welfare state* (4th edn), Basingstoke: Palgrave

Freedland, J, 2012, Eugenics: the skeleton that rattles loudest in the left's closet, Comment is Free, *Guardian*, 17 February, www.theguardian.com/commentisfree/2012/feb/17/eugenics-skeleton-rattles-loudest-closet-left

French, P, 2013, The complete Humphrey Jennings. Volume Three: A diary for Timothy, Review, Film, *Guardian*, www.theguardian.com/film/2013/jul/28/complete-humphrey-jennings-volume-three#start-of-comments

Fricker, M, 2007, *Epistemic injustice: Power and the ethics of knowing*, Oxford: Oxford University Press

Fried, A, Ellman, R (eds), 1969, *Charles Booth's London*, London: Hutchinson

Friere, P, 1972, *Pegagogy of the oppressed*, London: Penguin

Fryer, P, 1984, *Staying power: The history of black people in Britain*, London: Pluto Press

Fulcher, G, 1996, Beyond normalisation but not Utopia, in L Barton (ed) *Disability and society: Emerging issues and insights*, pp 167–90, London: Longman

Galbraith, JK, 1958, *The affluent society*, Chicago, IL: Houghton Mifflin Harcourt

Gallagher, HG, 1990, *By trust betrayed: Patients, physicians and the license to kill in Nazi Germany*, New York: Henry Holt and Company

Garabedian, F, 2014, Independent living, in C Cameron (ed) *Disability studies: A student's guide*, pp 81–4, London: Sage

Gardiner, J, 2004, *The Thirties: An intimate history*, London: Harper Press

Gaventa, J, 1982, *Power and powerlessness: Quiescence and rebellion in an Appalachian valley*, Chicago, IL: University of Illinois Press

George, V, Wilding, P, 1976, *Ideology and social welfare*, London: Routledge and Kegan Paul

Gibbons, T, undated, 'Max Beerbohm and the shape of things to come, http://library.brown.edu/cds/mjp/pdf/GibbonsBeerbohm.pdf

Giddens, A, 1991, *The consequences of modernity*, Cambridge: Polity Press

Giddens, A, 1998, *The Third Way: The renewal of social democracy*, Cambridge, Polity Press

Gilbert, BB, 1970, *British social policy 1914–1939*, London: Batsford

Gilmour, I, 1992, *Dancing with dogma: Britain under Thatcherism*, London: Simon and Schuster

Ginsburg, N, 1979, *Class, capital and social policy*, Basingstoke: Macmillan

Girl A, 2013, *Girl A, my story: The truth about the Rochdale sex ring by the victim who stopped them*, London: Ebury Press

Gladstone, D, 2008, History and social policy, in P Alcock, M May and K Rowlingson (eds), *The student's companion to social policy* (3rd edn), pp 19-25, Oxford, Blackwell Publishing.

Glasby, J, Beresford, P, 2006, Who knows best? Evidence-based practice and the service user contribution, commentary and issues, *Critical Social Policy* 26, 1, 268–84

Glendenning, F, 1999, The institutional abuse of old people in residential settings: An overview, in N Stanley, J Manthorpe, B Penhale (eds) *Institutional abuse: Perspectives across the life course*, pp 175–88, London: Routledge

Glendinning, M, Muthesius, S, 1994, *Tower block: Modern public housing in England, Scotland, Wales, and Northern Ireland*, New Haven, CT: Yale University Press

Glennerster, H, 2012, Crisis, retrenchment, and the impact of neo-liberalism (1976–1997), in P Alcock, M May, S Wright (eds) *The student's companion to social policy* (4th edn), pp 130–4, London: Wiley-Blackwell

Glennerster, H, 2014, *Paying for welfare: Towards 2000* (3rd edn), London: Routledge

GMCDP (Greater Manchester Coalition of Disabled People), 2010, A brief history of disabled people's self-organisation, November, Manchester: Greater Manchester Coalition of Disabled People, http://gmcdp.com/wp-content/uploads/2011/11/Booklet-A-Brief-History-of-Disabled-Peoples-Self-Organisation.pdf

Goffman, E, 1961, *Asylums: Essays on the social situation of mental patients and other inmates*, New York: Doubleday

Golding, P, Middleton, S, 1982, *Images of welfare: Press and public attitudes to poverty*, Oxford: Martin Robertson

Goldman, L, 2013/14, Tawney's century: RH Tawney and the origins of capitalism in Tudor and Stuart England, *The Oxford Historian*, Issue X1, pp 46–50

Goldthorpe, D, 1987, *Social mobility and class structure in modern Britain*, Oxford: Clarendon Press

Goldthorpe, J, Jackson, M, 2007, Intergenerational class mobility in contemporary Britain: Political concerns and empirical findings, *British Journal of Sociology* 58, 4, 525–46

Goldthorpe, JH, Lockwood, D, Bechhofer, F, Platt, J, 1969, *The affluent worker in the class structure*, Cambridge: Cambridge University Press

Goodley, D, 2000, *Self-advocacy in the lives of people with learning difficulties*, Buckingham: Open University Press

Goodley, D, 2013, Dis/entangling critical disability studies, *Disability and Society* 28, 5, 631–44

Goodley, D, Ramcharan, P, 2010, Advocacy, campaigning and people with learning difficulties, in G Grant, R Ramcharan, M Flynn, M Richardson (eds) *Learning disability: A life cycle approach*, pp 87–100, Maidenhead: Open University Press

Goodwin, C, 1980, Beyond the fragments, *International Socialism* 2, 9 (Summer), Marxists internet archive, www.marxists.org/history/etol/newspape/isj2/1980/no2-009/goodwin.html

Gostin, LO, 2010, *From a civil libertarian to a sanitarian: 'A life of learning'*, Presidential Address for the Faculty Convocation, Georgetown University Law Center, Washington, October, Washington DC: Georgetown University Law Center

Gough, I, 1979, *The political economy of the welfare state*, Basingstoke: Macmillan

Gould, D, 2012, *Service users' experiences of recovery under the 2008 Care Programme Approach: A research study: executive summary*, London, National Survivor User Network and Mental Health Foundation

Gramsci, A, 1982, *Selections from the prison books*, London: Lawrence and Wishart

Grant, C (ed), 1992, Built to last? Reflections on British housing policy, *ROOF Magazine*, p 214

Graves, R, 1960, *Goodbye to all that*, Harmondsworth, Penguin

Gray, AM, 1982, Inequalities in health – the Black report: A summary and comment, *International Journal of Health Services* 12, 3, 349–80

Gray, F, 1931, *The tramp: His meaning and being*, London: Dent

Gregg, V, with Stroud, R, 2011, *Rifleman: A front-line life from Alamein and Dresden to the fall of the Berlin Wall*, London: Bloomsbury

Griffin, I, 2013, Triumph Motorcycles annual sales hit 50,000 milestone, 12 December, *Leicester Mercury*, www.leicestermercury.co.uk/Triumph-annual-sales-hit-50-000-milestone/story-20312484-detail/story.html

Grove, B, Harding, A, Freudenberg, M, O'Flynn, D, 1997, *Social firms: New directions in the employment, rehabilitation and integration of people with mental health problems*, London: Pavilion

Guardian, 2001, Thinktanks: The Fabian Society, 13 August, www.theguardian.com/politics/2001/aug/13/thinktanks.uk

Guardian, 2012, Jimmy Savile's Broadmoor role came with a bedroom and keys, 12 October, www.theguardian.com/media/2012/oct/12/jimmy-savile-broadmoor-volunteer-role

Guardian, 2013, Margaret Thatcher: The lady and the land she leaves behind, Editorial, 8 April, www.theguardian.com/commentisfree/2013/apr/08/margaret-thatcher-editorial

Guardian, 2014, Guardian View on the Rotherham child abuse scandal: No excuse, Leader, 27 August, www.theguardian.com/commentisfree/2014/aug/27/guardian-view-rotherham-child-abuse-scandal

Guido Fawkes, 2013, Welfare state was evil Philpott's accomplice, Blog, http://order-order.com/2013/04/03/welfare-state-was-evil-philpotts-accomplice/#/VJQxAD9lb4_QlA

HM Inspectors, 1956, *Report on Wix County Primary School (Infants), Battersea, London: Inspected 4th, 5th and 6th December, 1956*, Ministry of Education, London: Her Majesty's Stationery Office

Habermas, J, 1991, *The structural transformation of the public sphere: An Inquiry into a category of bourgeois society*, Studies in contemporary German social thought, Cambridge, MA: Massachussetts Institute of Technology (MIT) Press

Hadley, R, Hatch, S, 1981, *Social welfare and the failure of the state*, London: Allen and Unwin

Hadley, R, McGrath, M, 1981, *Going local: Neighbourhood social services*, London: Bedford Square Press/NCVO

Hahn, H, 1986, Public support for rehabilitation programmes: the analysis of US disability policy, *Disability, Handicap and Society* 1, 2, 121–38

Hamdi, N, Goethert, R, 1997, *Action planning for cities*, London: John Wiley

Hammersley, M, 2000, *Partisanship and bias in social research*, Buckingham: Open University Press

Hanisch, C, 1969, The personal is political, *Essay*, www.carolhanisch.org/CHwritings/PIP.html

Haralambos, M, Holborn, M (eds), 2008, *Sociology: Themes and perspectives* (7th rev edn), London: Collins Educational

Harding, T, Beresford, P (eds), 1996, *The standards we expect: What service users and carers want from social services workers*, London: National Institute for Social Work

Hardy, D, 1999, *Tomorrow and tomorrow: The TCPA's first hundred years and the next...*, Commemorative Booklet, London: Town and Country Planning Association (TCPA)

Hare, P, 2013, All in it together: widening our choices for our old age, Blog, Joseph Rowntree Foundation, 16 January, www.jrf.org.uk/blog/2013/01/all-in-it-together

Harper, DJ, Speed, E, 2012, Uncovering recovery: the resistible rise of recovery and resilience, *Studies in Social Justice*, 6, 1, 9–25

Harris, B, 2004, *The origins of the British welfare state: Society, state and social welfare in England and Wales, 1800–1945*, Basingstoke: Palgrave

Harris, B, 2012, Nineteenth century beginnings, in P Alcock, M May, S Wright (eds) *The student's companion to social policy* (4th edn), pp 111–16, London: Wiley-Blackwell

Harvey, D, 2005, *A short history of neoliberalism*, Oxford: Oxford University Press

Harvey, D, 2014, *Seventeen contradictions and the end of capitalism*, London: Profile Books

Hemmings, S (ed), 1982, *Girls are powerful: Young women's writings from Spare Rib*, London: Sheba Feminist Press

Henderson, E, Bewley, C, 2000, *Too little, too slowly*, London: Values Into Action

Hennessy, P, 1992, *Never again: Britain 1945–51*, London: Jonathan Cape

Herbert, AP, 1919, *The secret battle*, London: Methuen

Hevey; D, 1992, *The creatures time forgot: Photography and disability imagery*, London: Routledge

Hicks, D, 2004, Radical education, in S Ward (ed) *Education studies: A student's guide*, pp 134–48, London: Routledge

Hills, J, 2012, Re-reviews: The political economy of the welfare state, Ian Gough, *Social Policy and Administration* 46, 5 (October), 1–6

Hills, J, 2014, *Good times, bad times: The welfare myth of them and us*, Bristol: Policy Press

Hird, C, 1981, The crippled giants, *New Internationalist Magazine* 106 (December), http://newint.org/features/1981/12/01/giants/

Hirschkop, K, 1999, *Mikhail Bakhtin: An Aesthetic for democracy*, New York: Oxford University Press

Historic England, 2015, Disability since 1945, https://historicengland.org.uk/research/inclusive-heritage/disability-history/1945-to-the-present-day/

Hoban, M, James, V, Beresford, P, Fleming, J, 2013, *Involving older age: The route to twenty-first century wellbeing. Shaping our age*, Final report, June, Cardiff: Royal Voluntary Society

Hoggett, P, Bishop, J, 1986, *Organising around enthusiasms: Patterns of mutual aid in leisure*, London: Comedia

Holden, C, 2008, International trade and welfare, in N Yeates (ed) *Understanding global social policy*, pp 101–21, Bristol: The Policy Press

Hood, C, 1991, A public management for all seasons, *Public Administration* 69, 1 (Spring), 3–19

Hopkins, G, 2007, What have we learned? Child death scandals since 1944, *Community Care*, 10 January, www.communitycare. co.uk/2007/01/10/what-have-we-learned-child-death-scandals-since-1944/

Hopkinson, T (ed), 1970, *Picture Post 1938–50*, Harmondsworth: Penguin

Hopwood, B, 1981, *Whatever happened to the British motorcycle industry?*, Yeovil: Foulis

Hudson, J, 2014, Welfare, in P Dwyer, S Shaw (eds) *An introduction to social policy*, pp 3–13, London: Sage

Hughes, R, 1991, *The shock of the new: Art and the century of change*, London: Thames and Hudson

Hunt, P (ed), 1966a, Introduction, *Stigma: The experience of disability*, London: Geoffrey Chapman, http://disability-studies.leeds.ac.uk/library/author/hunt.paul

Hunt, P, 1966b, A critical condition, in T Shakespeare (ed) *The disability reader*, pp 7–19, London and New York: Cassell

Hunt, P, 1972a, Letter, *Guardian*, 20 September, http://disability-studies.leeds.ac.uk/files/library/Hunt-Hunt-1.pdf

Hunt, P, 1972b, Parasite people, *Cheshire Smile*, 18, 3 (Autumn), 15

Hunt, P, 1981, Settling accounts with the parasite people: A critique of 'A life apart' by EJ Miller and GV Gwynne, *Disability Challenge* 1, 37–50

Hylton, S, 2010, *Careless talk: The hidden history of the home front 1939–45*, Stroud: The History Press

ICF GHK,2013, *The economic value of the adult social care sector in England*, Final report, 27 February, London: Skills for Care

INVOLVE, 2007, *What's it all about? Public information pack, 1: How to get actively involved in NHS, public health and social care research*, Eastleigh: National Institute for Health Research (NIHR) INVOLVE

Jackson, K, 2004, *Humphrey Jennings: The definitive biography of one of Britain's most important film-makers*, London: Picador

Jay, A, 2014, *Independent inquiry into child sexual exploitation in Rotherham, 1997–2014*, 21 August, Rotherham: Rotherham Metropolitan Borough Council

Jennings, H (director), 1945, *A diary for Timothy*, Documentary film, London: Crown Film Unit

Jennings, M (ed),1982, *Humphrey Jennings: Film-maker, painter, poet*, London: British Film Institute

Johnson, C, 1991, *The economy under Mrs Thatcher, 1979–1990*, London: Penguin

Johnson, J, Rolph S, Smith, R, 2010, *'The last refuge' revisited: Continuity and change in residential care for older people*, Basingstoke: Palgrave Macmillan

Jones, C, Murie, A, 2006, *The right to buy: Analysis and evaluation of a housing policy*, Oxford: Blackwell

Jones, O, 2014, It's socialism for the rich and capitalism for the rest of us in Britain, *Guardian*, 29 August, www.theguardian.com/books/2014/aug/29/socialism-for-the-rich

Jones, R, 2014, *The story of Baby P: Setting the record straight*, Bristol: Policy Press

Jones, S, 2010, Daily Mail and Sun pay out to hunger striker, *Guardian*, 29 July, www.theguardian.com/media/2010/jul/29/daily-mail-sun-parameswaran-subramanyam

Jordan, T, Lent, A (eds), 1999, *Storming the millennium: The new politics of change*, London: Lawrence and Wishart

Karpf, A, 2012, Green jobs: a utopia we nearly had, *Guardian*, 31 January, www.theguardian.com/commentisfree/2012/jan/31/jobs-growth-workers-vision

Keating, P (ed), 1976, *'Into unknown England', 1866–1913: Selections from the social explorers*, London: Fontana/Collins

Kerr, A, Shakespeare, T, 2002, *Genetics politics: From eugenics to genome*, Cheltenham: New Clarion Press

Klein, N, 2014, *This changes everything: Capitalism versus the climate*, London: Allen Lane

Koerner, S, 2013, *The strange death of the British motorcycle industry*, Lancaster: Crucible Books

Kramer, RM, 1981, *Voluntary agencies in the welfare state*, Berkeley, CA and London: University of California Press

Kuhn, TS, 1970, *The structure of scientific revolution* (2nd edn), Chicago, IL: University of Chicago Press

Kynaston, D, 2008, *Austerity Britain 1945–51*, London: Bloomsbury

Kynaston, D, 2010, *Family Britain 1951–57*, London: Bloomsbury

Kynaston, D, 2014, *Modernity Britain: A shake of the dice, 1959–1962*, London: Bloomsbury

Land, H, 2012, Altruism, reciprocity, and obligation, in P Alcock, M May, S Wright (eds) *The student's companion to social policy* (4th edn), pp 48–54, London: Wiley-Blackwell

Lavalette, M (ed), 2011, *Radical social work today: Social work at the crossroads*, Bristol: Policy Press

Laville, S, 2014, Women's refuges forced to shut down by funding crisis, *Guardian*, 4 August, pp 1–2

Lawrence, F, 2013, *Not on the label: What really goes into the food on your plate*, London: Penguin

Laybourn, K, 1999, *Modern Britain since 1906: A reader*, London: Tauris

Le Francois, BA, Menzies, R, Reaume, G (eds), 2013, *Mad matters: A critical reader in Canadian mad studies*, Toronto: Canadian Scholars Press

Le Grand, J, 1982, *The strategy of equality: Redistribution and the social services*, London: George Allen and Unwin

Le Grand, J, 1997, Knights, knaves or pawns? Human behaviour and social policy, *Journal of Social Policy* 26, 2, 149–69

Leavitt, D, 2007, *The man who knew too much: Alan Turing and the invention of the computer*, London: Phoenix

Lent, A, 2002, *British social movements since 1945: Sex, colour, peace and power*, Basingstoke: Macmillan/Palgrave

Levin, E, 2004, *Involving service users and carers in social work education*, Social Care Institute for Excellence (SCIE) Guide 4, March, London: SCIE

Levitas, R, 2005, *The inclusive society?: Social exclusion and New Labour (2nd edn)*, Basingstoke: Palgrave Macmillan

Lewis, S, 2005, *Direct payments: Answering frequently asked questions*, Adult Services Guide, 10, London: Social Care Institute for Excellence (SCIE)

Library of Congress, 2010, *Library collaborates with Chicago History Museum to preserve radio icon Studs Terkel's historic recordings*, 14 May, Washington: Library of Congress, www.loc.gov/today/pr/2010/10-115.html

Lieberman, JA, 2015, *Shrinks: The untold story of psychiatry*, London: Weidenfeld and Nicolson

Liegghio, M, 2013, A denial of being: psychiatrization as epistemic violence, in BA Le Francois, R Menzies, G Reaume (eds) *Mad matters: A critical reader in Canadian mad studies*, pp 122–9, Toronto: Canada: Canadian Scholars Press

Lister, I, 1987, Global and international approaches to political education, in C Harber (ed) *Political education in Britain*, Lewes: Falmer Press

Lister, R, 2003, *Citizenship: Feminist perspectives* (2nd edn), Basingstoke: Palgrave/Macmillan

Loach, K, 2013, *The spirit of '45*, film, London: Dogwoof

Locke, RR, Spender, JC, 2011, *Confronting managerialism: How the business elite and their schools threw our lives out of balance*, London: Zed Books

London Cycling Campaign, 2013, Van Gogh walk in Lambeth is a fabulous people-friendly street but highlights need for more Dutch-style residential zones, Blog, 6 June, http://lcc.org.uk/articles/van-gogh-walk-in-lambeth-is-a-fabulous-people-friendly-street-but-highlights-need-for-more-dutch-style-residential-zones

London Edinburgh Weekend Return Group, 1980, *In and against the state*, London: Pluto Books, http://libcom.org/library/preface-first-edition

Loney, M, 1983, *Community against government: The British community development project 1968–78: A study of government incompetence*, London: Heinemann

Longmate, N, 1974, *The workhouse*, London: Maurice Temple-Smith

Longmate, N, 2011, *The real Dad's Army: The story of the home guard*, Stroud: Amberley Publishing

Lowe, K, 2013, *Savage continent: Europe in the aftermath of World War Two*, London: Penguin

Lowe, R, 1993, *The welfare state in Britain since 1945*, London: Macmillan

Lowe, R, 2004, Modernizing Britain's welfare state: The influence of affluence, in L Black, H Pemberton (eds) *An affluent society? Britain's post-war 'Golden Age' revisited*, Farnham: Ashgate

Lowe, R, 2005, *The welfare state in Britain since 1945* (3rd edn), Basingstoke: Palgrave

Lukes, S, 2004, *Power: A radical view* (2nd edn), Basingstoke: Palgrave Macmillan

Lymbery, M, 2001, Social work at the crossroads, *British Journal of Social Work*, 31, 3, 369–84

MACE (Media Archive for Central England), 2012, *Bits stuck anywhere: The decline of BSA and the Birmingham motorcycle industry*, Lincoln: MACE, Lincoln University, http://vimeo.com/47240533

McClenaghan, P (ed), 2009, *Spirit of '68: Beyond the barricades*, Londonderry: Guildhall Press

MacInnes, T, Aldridge, H, Bushe, S, Kenway, P, Tinson, A, 2013, *Monitoring poverty and social exclusion*, London: New Policy Institute, in association with Joseph Rowntree Foundation

McKenzie, L, 2015a, *Getting by: Estates, class and culture in austerity Britain*, Bristol: Policy Press

McKenzie, L, 2015b, The estate we're in: How working class people became the 'problem', Society, *Guardian*, 21 January, p 34, www.theguardian.com/society/2015/jan/21/estate-working-class-problem-st-anns-nottingham

McMillan, E, 2004, *Complexity, organisations and change: an essential introduction*, London: Routledge

Maddams, J, Moller, C, Devane, C, 2008, *Cancer prevalence in the UK*, London: Thames Cancer Registry and Macmillan Cancer Support, http://www.thames-cancer-reg.org.uk/news/uk_prevalence_14072008.pdf

Maddox, B, 2013, Wishful thinking on welfare, Foreword, *Prospect*, June, p 3

MailOnline, 2012, Jimmy Savile's older brother sacked from hospital after being accused of raping psychiatric patient, MailOnline, 14 October, www.dailymail.co.uk/news/article-2217561/Jimmy-Saviles-older-brother-sacked-hospital-accused-raping-psychiatric-patient.html

Malcolmson, R, Malcolmson, P, 2013, *Women at the ready: The remarkable story of the Women's Voluntary Services on the home front*, London: Little, Brown and Company

Marcus, S, 2005, Queer theory for everyone: A review essay, *Signs: Journal of women in culture and society* 31, 1 (Autumn), 191–218, www.jstor.org/stable/10.1086/432743

Marmot, M, Wilkinson, RG (eds), 2006, *Social determinants of health* (2nd edn), Oxford: Oxford University Press

Marmot, M, Allen, J, Goldblatt, P, Boyce, T, McNeish, D, Grady, M, Geddes, I, 2010, *Fair society, healthy lives*, The Marmot Review, London: The Marmot Review

Marr, A, 2009, *A history of modern Britain*, London: Pan Macmillan

Marshall, H, 1971, *Twilight London: A study in degradation*, London: Vision

Marshall, TH, 1950, *Citizenship and social class and other essays*, Cambridge: Cambridge University Press

Martin, V, 2003, *Leading change in health and social care*, London: Routledge

Marwick, A, 1976, *The home front*, London: Thames and Hudson

Massey, D, Rustin, M, 2013, Whose economy? Reframing the debate, in S Hall, D Massey, M Rustin (eds) *After neoliberalism?: The Kilburn Manifesto*, Soundings, www.lwbooks.co.uk/journals/soundings/pdfs/s57_Massey_Rustin.pdf

Mathieu, P, Parks, S, Rousculp, T (eds), 2012, *Circulating communities: The tactics and strategies of community publishing*, Lanham, MD: Lexington Books

Matthew, S, 2011, *The West End front: The wartime secrets of London's grand hotels*, London: Faber and Faber

May, T, 1999, *The Victorian workhouse*, Princes Risborough: Shire Publications

Mayes, I, 2013, Ray Gosling Obituary, *Guardian*, 20 November, www.theguardian.com/uk-news/2013/nov/20/ray-gosling

Mayhew, H, 1950, *London's underworld*, edited by Peter Quennell, London: Spring Books

Mayhew, H, 2009, *London labour and the London poor: A cyclopaedia of the conditions and earnings of those that will work, those that cannot work and those that will not work, Vol 1* (in four volumes), New York: Cosimo Books

Mayhew, H, 2010, *London labour and the London poor*, edited by Douglas-Fairhurst, Oxford: Oxford University Press

Means, R, Richards, S, Smith, R, 2008, *Community care: Policy and practice*, Basingstoke: Palgrave/Macmillan

Mearns, A, 1883, *The bitter cry of outcast London: An enquiry into the condition of the abject poor*, London: London Congregational Union

Mearns, G, 2011, 'Long trudges through Whitechapel': The East End of Beatrice Webb's and Clara Collet's social investigations, *19: Interdisciplinary Studies in the Long Nineteenth Century*, 13, London: Birkbeck University of London, www.19.bbk.ac.uk/index.php/19/article/view/634/746

Meek, J, 2014a, *Private island: Why Britain now belongs to someone else*, London: Verso

Meek, J, 2014b, Sale of the century: The privatisation scam, *Guardian*, 23 August, www.theguardian.com/politics/2014/aug/22/sale-of-century-privatisation-scam

Mendoza, K-A, 2015, *Austerity: The demolition of the welfare state and the rise of the zombie economy*, Oxford: New Internationalist Publications

Mercer, G, 2002, Emancipatory disability research, in C Barnes, M Oliver, L Barton (eds) *Disability Studies Today*, pp 228–49, Cambridge: Polity

MHF (Mental Health Foundation), 2015, Rights, dementia and the social model of disability: a new direction for policy and practice?, *Draft policy discussion paper*, London: Mental Health Foundation

MHHC (Mental Health Commission of Canada), 2009, *Towards recovery and well-being: A framework for a mental health strategy for Canada*, Calgary, MHHC

Miliband, R, 1954, The politics of Robert Owen, *Journal of the History of Ideas* 15, 2 (April), 233–45

Miller, EJ, Gwynne, GV, 1972, *A life apart*, London: Tavistock Publications and Lippincott

Mills, CW, 1959, *The sociological imagination*, Oxford: Oxford University Press

Milton, D, 2014, Autistic expertise: a critical reflection on the production of knowledge in autism studies, *Autism* 18, 7, 794–802

Milton, D, Bracher, M, 2013, Autistics speak but are they heard?, *Medical Sociology Online* 7, 2, 61–9

Milton, D, Moon, L, 2012, The normalisation agenda and the psycho-emotional disablement of autistic people, *Autonomy, the Critical Journal of Interdisciplinary Autism Studies*, 1, 1, 11 October, www.larry-arnold.net/Autonomy/index.php/autonomy/article/view/AR3/21

Minns, R, 1999, *Bombers and mash: The domestic front 1939–45*, London: Virago

Mitton, L, 2012, The history and development of social policy, in J Baldock, L Mitton, N Manning, S Vickerstaff (eds) *Social policy* (4th edn), pp 27–51, Oxford: Oxford University Press

Moran, J, 2013, *Armchair nation: An intimate history of Britain in front of the TV*, London: Profile Books

Morley, D, Worpole, K (eds), 2009, *The republic of letters: Working class writing and local publishing*, Philadelphia, PA and Syracuse, NY: New City Community Press/Syracuse University Press

Morris, J, 1993, *Independent lives? Community care and disabled people*, Basingstoke: Macmillan

Morris, J, 1994, Transferring features of user-controlled services to other social services organisations, *Social Care Summary* 2, October, York: Joseph Rowntree Foundation, www.jrf.org.uk/sites/files/jrf/sc2.pdf

Morris, J, 1996, *Encounters with strangers: Feminism and disability*, London: Women's Press

Morris, R, 2000, *Cheshire: The biography of Leonard Cheshire, VC, OM*, London: Viking

Morrow, M, 2013, Recovery: progressive paradigm or neoliberal smokescreen, in *Mad matters: A critical reader in Canadian mad studies*, pp 323–33, Toronto, Canadian Scholars Press

Moser, P, McKay, G (eds), 2005, *Community music: A handbook*, Lyme Regis: Russell House Publishing

Mowat, C, 1961, *The Charity Organisation Society, 1869–1913: Its ideas and works*, London: Taylor and Francis

Munro, E, 2011, *Munro review of child protection: Final report – a child centred system*, Independent Report, June, London: Department for Education

Murie, A, 1989, Housing and the environment, in D Kavanagh, A Seldon (eds) *The Thatcher effect*, pp 213–25, Oxford: The Clarendon Press

Murray, A, 2002, *Off the rails: The crisis on Britain's railways*, London: Verso

Murray, C, 1996, *Charles Murray and the underclass: The developing debate*, The IEA Health and Welfare Unit in association with the Sunday Times, *Choices In Welfare* 33, London: Institute of Economic Affairs

Narey, M, 2014, *Making the education of social workers consistently effective, January*, London: Department for Education, www.gov.uk/government/publications/making-the-education-of-social-workers-consistently-effective

Needham, C, 2013, *Co-production in social care: What is it and how to do it*, Adults' Services, Social Care Institute for Excellence (SCIE) Guide 51, London: SCIE

Neill, AS, 1966, *Summerhill: A radical approach to education*, London: Gollancz

Nelson, J, 1978, *No more walls*, London: Bonfire Press

Netten, A, Beadle-Brown, J, Trukeschitz, B, Towers, M-A, Welch, E, Forder, J, Smith, J, Alden, E, 2010, Measuring the outcomes of care homes: Final report, *Personal Social Services Research Unit (PSSRU) Discussion Paper* 2696/2, Kent: PSSRU, www.pssru.ac.uk/archive/pdf/dp2696_2.pdf

Newton, C, 2002, *My Grandmother Rachel: The story of Windsor's Jewish community, 1940–1950*, Bakewell: Country Books

Nicholson, V, 2012, *Millions like us: Women's lives during the second world war*, London: Penguin

O'Hara, M, 2014a, Mental health and race: the blight of dual discrimination, *Guardian*, 26 March, www.theguardian.com/society/2014/mar/26/black-minority-ethnic-mental-health-dual-discrimination

O'Hara, M, 2014b, *Austerity bites: A journey to the sharp end of cuts in the UK*, Bristol: Policy Press

Oakeshott, M, 1962, *Rationalism in politics, and other essays*, London: Methuen

Oakley, A, 1979, *Becoming a mother*, Oxford: Martin Robertson

Oakley, A, 2014, *Father and daughter: Patriarchy, gender and social science*, Bristol: Policy Press

ODI (Office for Disability Issues), 2008, *The Independent Living Strategy: A cross government strategy about independent living for disabled people*, London: ODI

OECD (Organisation for Economic Cooperation and Development), 2010, *Going for growth: Economic policy reforms*, Paris: OECD

Oliver, M, 1983, *Social work and disabled people*, Basingstoke: Macmillan

Oliver, M, 1990, *The politics of disablement*, Basingstoke: Macmillan and St Martin's Press

Oliver, M, 1992, Review of *Raising voices: Social services departments and people with disabilities* by N Connelly, *Critical Social Policy* 33, Winter, 115–16

Oliver, M, 1996, *Understanding disability: From theory to practice*, Basingstoke: Macmillan

Oliver, M, 2004, The social model in action: if I had a hammer?, in C Barnes, G Mercer (eds) *Implementing the social model of disability: Theory and research*, pp 18–31, Leeds: Disability Press

Oliver, M, 2009, *Understanding disability: From theory to practice* (2nd edn), Basingstoke: Palgrave Macmillan

Oliver, M, Barnes, C, 1998, *Disabled people and social policy: From exclusion to inclusion*, London: Longman

Oliver, M, Barnes, C, 2012, *The new politics of disablement*, Basingstoke: Palgrave Macmillan

Oliver, M, Zarb, G, 1989, The politics of disability: a new approach, *Disability, Handicap and Society* 4, 3, 221–39

ONS (Office for National Statistics), 2011, Frequently asked questions, 2010-based national population projections, www.ons.gov.uk/ons/dcp171776_240644.pdf

Orwell, G, 1933, *Down and out in Paris and London*, London: Victor Gollancz

Orwell, G, 1937, *The road to Wigan Pier*, London: Victor Gollancz

Overy, R, 2009, *The morbid age: Britain between the wars*, London: Allen Lane/Penguin

Overy, R, 2010, *The twilight years: The paradox of Britain between the wars*, London: Penguin

Page, RM, 2012, The post-war welfare state, in P Alcock, M May, S Wright (eds) *The student's companion to social policy* (4th edn), pp 124–29, London: Wiley-Blackwell

Parker, J, 2011, *The golden age of the canals*, television programme, London: White Light in association with the BBC

Parker, T, 1963, *The unknown citizen*, London: Hutchinson

Parker, T, 1965, *The plough boy*, London: Hutchinson

Parker, T, 1997, *Studs Terkel, a life in words*, London: Harper Collins

Parker, T with Allerton, R, 1962, *The courage of his convictions*, London: Hutchinson

Parsonage, M, 2009, *Diversion: A better way for criminal justice and mental health*, London: Sainsbury Centre for Mental Health

Parton, N, 2004, From Maria Colwell to Victoria Climbie: Reflections on a generation of public inquiries into child abuse, Plenary paper for the BASPCAN conference, July 2003, *Child Abuse Review* 13, 2, 80–94, www.gptsw.net/papers/clwlclmbi.pdf

Pascall, G, 2012, Health and health policy, in J Baldock, L Mitton, N Manning, S Vickerstaff (eds) *Social policy* (4th edn), pp 260–84, Oxford: Oxford University Press

Pearce, R, 2012, *1930s Britain*, Oxford: Shire Publications

Pearson, C, 2012, Independent living, in N Watson, A Roulstone, C Thomas (eds) *Routledge handbook of disability studies*, pp 240–52, London: Routledge

Peck, J, Phillips, R, 2008, *Focus group politics and the death of the citizen in the late twentieth century*, Part Two, Chapter Five, Citizen Renaissance, ebook, www.citizenrenaissance.com/the-book/

Pendle, G, 1952, *Uruguay: South America's first welfare state*, London: Royal Institute of International Affairs

Penketh, L, 2006, Racism and social policy, in M Lavalette, A Pratt (eds) *Social policy: Theories, concepts and issues* (3rd edn) , pp 87–104, London: Sage

PEP (Political and Economic Planning), 1961, *Family needs and the social services*, London: PEP, George Allen and Unwin.

Perkin, J, 2002, Sewing machines: liberation or drudgery for women?, *History Today* 52, 12 (December), www.historytoday.com/joan-perkin/sewing-machines-liberation-or-drudgery-women

Perry, N (ed), 2005, *Getting the right trainers: Enabling service users to train social work students and practitioners about the realities of family poverty in the UK*, London: ATD Fourth World

Petersen, W, 1999, *Malthus* (2nd edn), London: Heinemann

Pettit, M, Corbett, GH, Kohli, M, Bagnell, K, 2013, *Home children bundle: The Golden Bridge/The Little Immigrants/Mary Janeway/Nation Builders/Whatever Happened to Mary Janeway?*, December, www.dundurn.com/books/home_children_bundle

PFT (Prison Reform Trust), 2013, Prison: the facts, *Bromley Briefings*, Summer, London: Prison Reform Trust, www.prisonreformtrust.org.uk/Portals/0/Documents/Prisonthefacts.pdf

Piachaud, D, 1981, Peter Townsend and the Holy Grail, *New Society*, 10 September, p 421

Pickett, KE, Wilkinson, RG (eds), 2009, *Health and inequality: Major themes in health and social welfare*, Four volumes, London: Routledge

Pierson, C, 2006, *Beyond the welfare state: The new political economy of welfare* (3rd edn), Cambridge: Polity Press

Pierson, C, Castles, FG (eds), 2006, *The welfare state reader* (2nd edn), Cambridge: Polity Press

Pollard, N, Smart, P, 2012, Making writing accessible to all: the Federation of Worker Writers and Community Publishers and TheFED, in P Mathieu, S Parks, T Rousculp (eds) *Circulating communities: The tactics and strategies of community publishing*, pp 21–35, Lanham, MD: Lexington Books

Popular Photography, 1946, Diary for Timothy, *Popular Photography*, April, pp 90–4, https://books.google.co.uk/books?id=wWMzAQ AAMAAJ&pg=PA94&dq=Diary+for+Timothy+popular+photogr aphy&hl=en&sa=X&ved=0CCAQ6AEwAGoVChMI3a-quIbnxw IVbJrbCh14rQ9T#v=onepage&q=Diary%20for%20Timothy%20 popular%20photography&f=false

Porter, RA, 1987, *A social history of madness: Stories of the insane*, London: Weidenfeld and Nicolson

Porter, R, 2001, *The Enlightenment* (2nd edn), Studies in European history, Basingstoke: Palgrave

Postle, K, 2001, 'The social work side is disappearing: it started with us being called care managers', *Practice*, 13, 1, 13-26

Pratten, CF, 1987, Mrs Thatcher's economic legacy, in K Minogue, M Biddiss (eds) *Thatcherism: Personality and politics*, pp 72–94, Basingstoke: Macmillan

Prideaux, S, 2006, New Labour, old functionalism, Paper presented at Annual Conference, Canadian Political Science Association, 1–3 June, Canada, York University, www.cpsa-acsp.ca/papers-2006/ Prideaux.pdf

Priestley, M, 1997, Whose research? A personal audit, in C Barnes, G Mercer (eds) *Doing disability research*, pp 88–107, Leeds: Disability Press

Priestley, M, 1999, *Disability politics and community care*, London: Jessica Kingsley

Priestley, M, 2012, Disability, in P Alcock, M May, S Wright (eds) *The student's companion to social policy* (4th edn), pp 405–11, London: Wiley-Blackwell

Prime Minister's Strategy Unit, 2005, *Improving the life chances of disabled people*, London: Cabinet Office

Pritchard, C, Cotton, A, Bowen, D, Williams, R, 1998, Young people's views on educational social work, *British Journal of Social Work* 28, 915–38

Purvis, J (ed), 1995, *Women's history: Britain 1850–1945*, London: UCL Press

Ramesh, R, 2013, Atos apologises to long-term sick wrongly assessed as fit for work, *Guardian*, 17 April, www.theguardian.com/society/2013/apr/17/atos-apologises-long-term-sick

Ramon, S, Williams, JE (eds), 2005, *Mental health at the crossroads: The promise of the psychosocial approach*, Farnham: Ashgate

Rayner, G, Lang, T, 2012, *Ecological public health: Reshaping the conditions of good health*, Abingdon: Earthscan/Routledge

Rees, R, 2001, *Poverty and public health 1815–1949*, London: Heinemann

Remarque, EM, 1929, *All quiet on the Western Front* (translation by AW Wheen), London and New York: Little, Brown and Company

Ribton-Turner, CJ, 1889, *A History Of Vagrants And Vagrancy and beggars and begging*, London: Chapman and Hall.

Richards, H, 2005, The 'uneventful life' that embraced philosophy and science as well as penal reform and fridges, *Times Higher Education Supplement*, 9 September, www.utilitarianism.com/jeremy-bentham/life.html

Richardson, R, Miles, B, 2003, *Equality stories: Recognition, respect and raising achievement*, Stoke-on-Trent: Trentham Books

Ritzer, G, 2008, *The McDonaldization of society*, Los Angeles, CA: Pine Forest Press

Robb, B, 1967, *Sans everything: A case to answer*, Edinburgh: Nelson

Robbins, P, 2012, *Political ecology: A critical introduction* (2nd edn), Oxford: Blackwell

Robertson, G, 2008, We should say sorry too, Comment is Free, *Guardian*, 13 February, www.theguardian.com/commentisfree/2008/feb/14/australia

Robinson, J, 2015, *Family way: Illegitimacy between the great war and the swinging sixties*, London: Viking

Robson, A, 2013, *Beyond the fragments* is more than history, *Red Pepper* blog, 21 April, www.redpepper.org.uk/beyond-the-fragments-is-more-than-history/

Rock, P, MacIntosh, M (eds), 1974, *Deviance and social control*, Explorations in Social Policy, London: Tavistock Publications

Rogers, C, 1994, *Freedom to learn: for the 80s* (3rd edn), Columbus, OH: Charles Merrill

Rogowski, S, 2013, *Critical social work with children and families: Theory, context and practice*, Bristol: Policy Press

Rolt, LTC, 1944, *Narrow boat*, London: Eyre Methuen

Rolt, LTC, 1950, *The inland waterways of England*, London: George Allen and Unwin

Rosamund, J, 2009, *Save the Triumph Bonneville: The inside story of the Meriden Workers' Co-operative*, Dorchester: Veloce

Rose, D, 2009, Collaboration, in J Wallcraft, B Schrank, M Amering (eds) *Handbook of service user involvement in mental health research*, pp 169–79, Chichester: Wiley-Blackwell

Rose, D, Wykes, T, Leese, M, Bindman, J, Fleischmann, P, 2003, Patients' perspectives on electroconvulsive therapy: systematic review, *British Medical Journal* 326, 1363–6

Rose, D, Wykes, T, Bindman, J, Fleischmann, P, 2005, Information, consent and perceived coercion: consumers' views on ECT, *British Journal of Psychiatry* 186, 54–9

Rose, D, Wykes, T, Farrier, D, Dolan, A-M, Sporle, T, Bogner, D, 2008, What do clients think of cognitive remediation therapy? A consumer-led investigation of satisfaction and side effects, *American Journal of Psychiatric Rehabilitation* 11, 2, 181–204

Rose, D, Sweeney, A, Leese, M, Clement, S, Burns, T, Catty, J, Wykes, T, 2009, Developing a user-generated measure of continuity of care: Brief report, *Acta Psychiatrica Scandinavica* 119, 320–4

Rowbotham, S, 1997, *A century of women*, London: Viking

Rowbotham, S, Segal, L, Wainwright, H, 1979, *Beyond the fragments: Feminism and the making of socialism*, London: Merlin Press (new edn, 2013)

Rowntree, BS, 1901, *Poverty: A study of town life*, London: Macmillan

Rowntree, BS, Lavers, GR, 1951, *English life and leisure: A social study*, London: Longman, Green and Co

Rummery, K, 2002, *Disability, citizenship and community care: A case for welfare rights?*, Farnham: Ashgate

Russo, J, 2015, In dialogue with conventional narrative research in psychiatry and mental health, *Philosophy, Psychiatry and Psychology* 22, 1

Rutter, J, Stocker, K, 2014, *Childcare costs survey 2014*, London: Family and Childcare Trust

Sandford, J, 1971, *Down and out in Britain*, London: Peter Owen

Sandford, J, 1976a, *Cathy come home*, London: Marion Boyars

Sandford, J, 1976b, *Edna, the inebriate woman*, London: Marion Boyars

Sanjek, R, 2009, *Gray panthers*, Philadelphia, PA: University of Pennsylvania Press

Sansom, C, 2013, *Dominion*, London: Pan

Savage, M, 2005, Working-class identities in the 1960s: revisiting the affluent workers study, *Sociology* 39, 5, 929–46

Saville, J, 1957, The welfare state: an historical approach, *The New Reasoner* 3, Winter 1957–58, 5–25, www.marxists.org/archive/saville/1957/xx/welfare.htm

Schlosberg, D, 2007, *Defining environmental justice: Theories, movements, and nature*, Oxford: Oxford University Press

Schwarz, B, 1993, History on the move: reflections on history workshop, *Radical History Review* 57, 203–20

Sebestyen, V, 2014, *The making of the modern world*, Basingstoke: Macmillan

Sedgwick, P, 1982, *Psycho politics*, London: Pluto Press

Seebohm Report, 1968, *Report of the committee on local authority and allied personal social services*, Cmnd No 3703, London: HMSO

Sen, A, 1983, Poor, relatively speaking, *Oxford Economic Papers* 35, 1 (July), 153–69

Seymour, R, 2014, *Against austerity: How we can fix the crisis they made*, London: Pluto Press

Shakespeare, T, 1993, Disabled people's self-organisation: a new social movement?, *Disability, Handicap and Society* 8, 3, 249–64

Shakespeare, T, 2006, *Disability rights and wrongs*, London: Routledge

Shape, 2012, *Disability arts: A brief history*, www.shapearts.org.uk/Pages/FAQs/Category/disability-arts-chronology

Shaping Our Lives National User Network, Black User Group (West London), Ethnic Disabled Group Emerged (Manchester), Footprints and Waltham Forest Black Mental Health Service User Group (North London), and Service Users' Action Forum (Wakefield), 2003, *Shaping our lives – from outset to outcome: What people think of the social care services they use*, York: Joseph Rowntree Foundation

Shera, W, Wells, LM (eds), 1999, *Empowerment practice in social work: Developing richer conceptual foundations*, Toronto: Canadian Scholars' Press

Sherwood, H, 2014, The women of the miners' strike: 'We caused a lot of havoc', *Guardian*, Women, 7 April, www.theguardian.com/lifeandstyle/2014/apr/07/women-miners-strike-1984-wives-picket-lines

Shragge, E, 1984, *Pensions policy in Britain: A socialist analysis*, London: Routledge and Kegan Paul

Shulman, M, 1973, *The least worst television in the world*, London: Barrier and Jenkins

Simmons, R, Powell, M, Greener, I (eds), 2009, *The consumer in public services: Choice, values and difference*, Bristol: Policy Press

Simpkin, M, 1979, *Trapped within welfare*, Basingstoke: Macmillan

Skeffington, A, 1969, *People and planning: Report of the Committee on Public Participation in Planning* ('Skeffington Report'), London: HMSO

Skidelsky, R, 2010, *Keynes: A very short introduction*, Oxford: Oxford University Press

Slasberg, C, Beresford, P, 2015, Building on the original strengths of direct payments to create a better future for social care, *Disability and Society* 30, 3, 305–9, www.tandfonline.com/doi/full/10.1080/0968 7599.2015.1007672#abstract

Slasberg, C, Beresford, P, Schofield, P, 2013, The increasing evidence of how self-directed support is failing to deliver personal budgets and personalisation, *Research Policy and Planning* 30, 2, 91–105, http://ssrg. org.uk/wp-content/uploads/2012/01/SLASBERG-et-al-7Jan14.pdf

Slay, J, 2011, *In this together: Building knowledge about co-production*, London: New Economics Foundation

Smale, G, 1998, *Managing change through innovation*, London: National Institute for Social Work

Smith, A, 2009, *The wealth of nations*, Blacksburg, VA: Thrifty Books

Smith, GD, Bartley, M, Blane, D, 1990, The Black Report on socioeconomic inequalities in health 10 years on, *British Medical Journal* 301, 173–7

Smithers, R, 2014, Bus deregulation outside London a failure – report, *Guardian*, p 9, 26 August

Social Role Valorization, 2011, *Announcing death of Dr Wolf Wolfensberger*, www.socialrolevalorization.com/training/trainers/ wolfensberger/index.html

Somerville, P, with Sprigings, N (eds), 2005, *Housing and social policy*, London: Routledge

Sommerlad, N, 2013, Great Tory housing shame: Third of ex-council homes now owned by rich landlords, *Daily Mirror*, 6 March

Soothill, K (ed), 1999, *Criminal conversations: An anthology of the work of Tony Parker*, London: Routledge

Soothill, K, 2001, Opening doors and windows for Tony Parker, in R Tarling (ed), Papers from the British Society of Criminology Conference, Leicester, July 2000, *The British Criminology Conference, Selected proceedings* 4, http://britsoccrim.org/new/volume4/002.pdf

Spandler, H, Anderson, J, Sapey, B (eds), 2015, *Madness, distress and the politics of disablement*, Bristol: Policy Press

Spicker, P, 2011, *How social security works: An introduction to benefits in Britain*, Bristol: Policy Press

Spicker, P, 2014, *Social policy: Theory and practice* (3rd edn), Bristol: Policy Press

Spufford, A, 2014, 'Scrooge would have been admired': The original response to Dickens' character, in discussion with Neil Brand, BBC Radio 4, 16 January, www.bbc.co.uk/programmes/p02fc02g

Squires, R, 2008, *Britain's restored canals*, London: Landmark Publishing

Stafford, D, Stafford, C, 2013, *Cupid stunts: The life and radio times of Kenny Everett*, London: Omnibus Press

Stanley, N, Manthorpe, J, Penhale, B (eds), 1999, *Institutional abuse: Perspectives across the life course*, London: Routledge

Stanton, A, 1989a, *Invitation to self management*, Ruislip: Dab Hand Press

Stanton, A, 1989b, Citizens of workplace democracies, *Critical Social Policy* 9, 26 (September), 56–65

Starkey, P, 2000, *Families and social workers: The work of Family Service Units 1940–1985*, Liverpool: Liverpool University Press

Stedman Jones, G, 1971, *Outcast London: A study in the relationship between classes in Victorian society*, Oxford: Clarendon Press

Stedman Jones, G, 1984, *Outcast London: A study in the relationship between classes in Victorian society*, with a new Preface, Aylesbury: Peregrine Books

Stedman Jones, G, 2013, *Outcast London: A study in the relationship between classes in Victorian society* (2nd revised edn), with a new Preface, London: Verso Books

Stevenson, O, 2013, *Reflections on a life in social work: A personal and professional memoir*, Buckingham: Hinton House

Stone, E, Priestley, M, 1996, Parasites, pawns, and partners: Disability research and the role of non-disabled researchers, *British Journal of Sociology* 47, 4, 699–716

Survivors History Group, 2012, Survivors History Group takes a critical look at historians, in M Barnes, P Cotterell (eds) *Critical perspectives on user involvement*, pp 7–18, Bristol: Policy Press

Sutcliffe-Braithwaite, F, 2012, Neo-liberalism and morality in the making of Thatcherite social policy, *The Historical Journal* 55, 02 (June), 497–520

Sutcliffe-Braithwaite, F, 2013, Margaret Thatcher, individualism and the welfare state, *History and Policy*, 15 April, www.historyandpolicy. org/opinion-articles/articles/margaret-thatcher-individualism-and-the-welfare-state

Sutherland, AT, 1981, *Disabled we stand*, London: Human Horizons Series, Souvenir Press

SWAN (Social Work Action Network) (eds), 2014, *In defence of social work: Why Michael Gove is wrong*, London: A Social Work Action Network Pamphlet

Sweeney, A, Beresford, P, Faulkner, A, Nettle, M, Rose, D (eds), 2009, *This is survivor research*, Ross-on-Wye: PCSS Books

Sweet, M, 2011, *The West End Front: The wartime secrets of London's grand hotels*, London, Faber and Faber

Tanner, MD, 1995, Relationship between welfare state and crime, testimony, Subcommittee on Youth Violence Committee on the Judiciary United States Senate, 7 June, Washington, DC: Cato Institute, www.cato.org/publications/congressional-testimony/relationship-between-welfare-state-crime-0

Taylor, I, Walton, P, Young, J, 1973, *The new criminology: For a social theory of deviance*, London: Routledge

Taylor, L, 1970, Review of *Becoming deviant* by David Matza, *British Journal of Criminology* 10, 3 (July), 288–91

Taylor, MW, 2007, *The philosophy of Herbert Spencer*, London: Continuum

Taylor-Gooby, M, 1981, The state, class, ideology and social policy, *Journal of Social Policy* 10, 4, 433–51

Taylor-Gooby, P, 1985, *Public opinion, ideology and state welfare*, London: Routledge and Kegan Paul

Taylor-Gooby, P, 2012, Equality, rights and social justice, in P Alcock, M May, S Wright (eds) *The student's companion to social policy* (4th edn), pp 26–39, London: Wiley-Blackwell

Telegraph, 2013, Timeline: How G4S's bungled Olympics security contract unfolded, Finance, *Telegraph*, 21 May, www.telegraph.co.uk/finance/newsbysector/supportservices/10070425/Timeline-how-G4Ss-bungled-Olympics-security-contract-unfolded.html

Terkel, S, 1966, *Division street: America*, New York: Pantheon Books

Terkel, S, 1970, *Hard times: An oral history of the great depression*, New York: Pantheon Books

Terkel, S, 1974, *Working: People talk about what they do all day and what they feel about what they do*, New York: Pantheon Books

Terkel, S, 1984, *The good war: An oral history of World War II*, New York: New Press

Terkel, S, 1992, *Race: What blacks and whites think and feel about the great American obsession*, New York: New Press

Terkel, S, 1995, *Coming of age: The story of our century by those who've lived it*, New York: New Press

Terkel, S, 2001, *Will the circle be unbroken? Reflections on death, rebirth, and hunger for a faith*, New York: Ballantine Books

Tew, J, 2011, *Social approaches to mental distress*, Basingstoke: Palgrave Macmillan

Tew, J, Gell, C, Foster, S, 2004, *Learning from experience: Involving service users and carers in mental health education and training*, Nottingham: Mental Health in Higher Education, National Institute for Mental Health in England (West Midlands), Trent Workforce Development Confederation

Thaler, R, Sunstein, CR, 2008, *Nudge: Improving decisions about health, wealth, and happiness*, New Haven, CT: Yale University Press

Thane, P, 1996, *The foundations of the welfare state* (2nd edn), London: Longman

The Times, 2014, Beveridge's bequest, Leader, 12 August, p 28

Thomas, C, 2007, *Sociologies of disability and illness: Contested ideas in disability studies and medical sociology*, Basingstoke: Palgrave Macmillan

Tilley, S, 2004, *The history of self-advocacy for people with learning difficulties: International comparisons*, Report on the conference held on 6–7 May, at the Open University, Milton Keynes, Open University, www2. open.ac.uk/hsc/ldsite/pdfs/tilleyconfrep04.pdf

Timmins, N, 2001, *The five giants: A biography of the welfare state* (revised edn), London: HarperCollins

Titmuss, RM, 1950, *Problems of social policy*, London: HMSO

Titmuss, RM, 1970, *The gift relationship*, London: George Allen and Unwin

Tomlinson, A, 1983, The illusion of community: cultural values and the meaning of leisure in a gentrifying neighbourhood, in A Tomlinson (ed) *Leisure and popular cultural forms*, pp 66–8, Brighton: Chelsea School of Human Movement

Tonkin, B, 2010, The good life of a gentle anarchist, *Independent*, 19 February, www.independent.co.uk/arts-entertainment/books/features/boyd-tonkin-the-good-life-of-a-gentle-anarchist-1903818.html

Touraine, A, 1981, *The voice and the eye: An analysis of social movements*, Cambridge, Cambridge University Press.

Townsend, P, 1962, *The last refuge: A survey of residential institutions and homes for the aged in England and Wales*, London: Routledge and Kegan Paul

Townsend, P, 1979, *Poverty in the United Kingdom: A survey of household resources and standards of living*, Harmondsworth: Penguin

Townsend, P, Bosanquet, N, 1972, *Labour and inequality*, London: Fabian Society

Townsend, P, Davidson, N, 1982, *Inequalities in health: The Black report*, Harmondsworth: Penguin

Townsley, R, Ward, L, Abbott, O, Williams, V, 2009, *The implementation of policies supporting independent living for disabled people in Europe: Synthesis report*, Utrecht: Academic Network of European Disability Experts

Toynbee, P, Walker, D, 2010, *The verdict: Did Labour change Britain?*, London: Granta Books

Toynbee, P, Walker, D, 2015, *Cameron's coup: How the Tories took Britain to the brink*, London: Guardian Faber Publishing

Travis, A, 2012, Margaret Thatcher's role in plan to dismantle welfare state revealed, *Guardian*, 28 December, www.theguardian.com/politics/2012/dec/28/margaret-thatcher-role-plan-to-dismantle-welfare-state-revealed

Treanor, J, 2014, Co-operative group turmoil takes toll on sector, *Guardian*, 23 June, p 20

Turbett, C, 2014, *Doing radical social work*, Basingstoke: Palgrave Macmillan

Turner, M, Beresford, P, 2005a, *User controlled research: Its meanings and potential*, Final report, Shaping Our Lives and the Centre for Citizen Participation, Brunel University, Eastleigh: National Institute for Health Research (NIHR) INVOLVE

Turner, M, Beresford, P, 2005b, *Contributing on equal terms: Getting involved and the benefit system*, London: Shaping our Lives

Tyler, I, 2013, *Revolting subjects: Social abjection and resistance in neoliberal Britain*, London: Zed Books

UPIAS (Union of the Physically Impaired Against Segregation)/Disability Alliance, 1976, *Fundamental principles of disability: Being a summary of the discussion held on 22nd November, 1975 and containing commentaries from each organization,* London: The Union of the Physically Impaired Against Segregation and the Disability Alliance

Veit-Wilson, J, 1986, Paradigms of poverty: A rehabilitation of BS Rowntree, *Journal of Social Policy* 15, 1, 69–99

Von Rochau, AL, 1853, *Grundsätze der Realpolitik: Ausgewendet auf die staatlichen Zustände Deutschlands*, Stuttgart: K Gopel

Wainwright, H, 2000, The good old days: Hilary Wainwright remembers the thrills and the challenges of working at County Hall in the 80s, *Guardian*, 6 April, www.theguardian.com/politics/2000/apr/06/londonmayor.uk

Wainwright, H, Elliott, D, 1981, *The Lucas Plan: A new trade unionism in the making*, London: Alison and Busby

Walker, A, 2009, Professor Peter Townsend: Campaigner for social justice who co-founded the Child Poverty Action Group, Obituaries, *Independent,* 13 June, p 42

Walker, P, 2012, Benefit cuts are fuelling abuse of disabled people, say charities, Society, *Guardian*, 5 February, www.theguardian.com/society/2012/feb/05/benefit-cuts-fuelling-abuse-disabled-people

Wallcraft, J, 2001, *Turning towards recovery? A study of personal narratives of mental health crisis and breakdown*, PhD thesis, London: South Bank University

Wallcraft, J, 2007, User-led research to develop an evidence base for alternative approaches, in P Stastny, P Lehmann (eds) *Alternatives beyond psychiatry*, Berlin: Peter Lehmann Publishing

Wallcraft, J, Read, J, Sweeney, A, 2003, *On our own terms: Users and survivors of mental health services working together for support and change*, London: Sainsbury Centre for Mental Health

Waller, M, 2012, *A family in wartime: How the Second World War shaped the lives of a generation*, London: Conway in association with the Imperial War Museum

Wallich-Clifford, A, 1974, *No fixed abode*, Basingstoke: Macmillan

Wallich-Clifford, A, 1976, *Caring on skid row*, Dublin: Veritas Publications

Walmsley, J, Davies, C, Hales, M, Flux, R (eds), 2012, *Better health in harder times: Active citizens and innovation on the frontline*, Bristol: Policy Press

Walsham, G, 1992, Management science and organisational change: a framework for analysis, *Omega: International Journal of Management Science*, 20, 1, 1–9

Walton-Lewsey, EW, 1963, *Diamonds in the dust*, London: London Embankment Mission

Wanless, P, 2013, Jimmy Savile scandal: one year on, we must focus on preventing child abuse, Comment is Free, *Guardian*, 2 October, www.theguardian.com/commentisfree/2013/oct/02/jimmy-savile-one-year-prevent-child-abuse

Warburton, D (ed), 1998, *Community and sustainable development: Participation in the future*, London: Earthscan

Warchus, M, 2014, *Pride*, feature film, London: BBC Films and others

Ward, C, 1974, *Tenants take over*, London: Architectural Press

Ward, C, 1978, *The child in the city*, London: Pantheon Books

Ward, C, 1988, *The child in the country*, London: Robert Hale and Bedford Square Press

Ward, C, 1996, Obituaries: Tony Parker, People, *Independent*, 11 October, www.independent.co.uk/news/people/obituaries-tony-parker-1357790.html

Warner, J, 1998, Learning to sell the family silver, *Independent*, 13 June www.independent.co.uk/news/business/learning-to-sell-the-family-silver-1164661.html

Watzlewick, P, Weakland, J, Fisch, R, 1974, *Change: Principles of problem formation and problem resolution*, New York: WW Norton and Co

Webb, B, 1888, Pages from a work-girl's diary, *Nineteenth Century*, 24 (September), 301–14

Weicht, P, 2011, Review of *Residential care transformed: Revisiting 'The Last Refuge'* by Julia Johnson, Sheena Rolph and Randall Smith (2010), *International Journal of Ageing and Later Life* 6, 1, V–VIII

Wells, HG, 1911, *The country of the blind and other stories*, London: Thomas Nelson and Sons

Wells, M, 2002, The hundred greatest Britons: Lots of pop, not much circumstance, *Guardian*, 22 August, p 3

Welshman, J, 2007, Knights, knaves, pawns and queens: attitudes to behaviour in postwar Britain, *Journal of Epidemology and Community Health* 61, 2, 95–7

Welshman, J, 2012, Troubled families: the lessons of history, 1880–1912, Paper based on a presentation at a History and Policy seminar for the Department for Education on 24 November 2011, *History and Policy*, www.historyandpolicy.org/papers/policy-paper-136.html

Welshman, J, 2013, *Underclass: A history of the excluded since 1880* (2nd edn), London: Bloomsbury

Wheeler, B, Shaw, M, Mitchell, R, Dorling, D, 2005, *Life in Britain: Using millennial census data to understand poverty, inequality and place*, Bristol: Policy Press

White, K, 2009, *An introduction to the sociology of health and illness* (2nd edn), London and New York: Sage

White, S, 2010, Colin Ward: Pioneer of mutualism, *Next left, A Fabian Society* blog, 14 February, www.nextleft.org/2010/02/colin-ward-pioneer-of-mutualism.html

Whiteside, N, 2012, The liberal era and the growth of state welfare, in P Alcock, M May, S Wright (eds) *The student's companion to social policy* (4th edn), pp 117–23, London: Wiley-Blackwell

Widgery, D, 1979, *Health in danger: Crisis in the National Health Service*, Basingstoke: Macmillan

Wikipedia, ndb, Cones hotline, http://en.wikipedia.org/wiki/Cones_Hotline

Wikipedia, ndc, Steve Wozniak, http://en.wikipedia.org/wiki/Steve_Wozniak

Wikipedia, ndd, Tony Parker (author), https://en.wikipedia.org/wiki/Tony_Parker_(author)

Wilcox, P, 1977, *Between hell and Charing Cross*, London: George Allen and Unwin

Wilkinson, RG (ed), 1986, *Class and health: Research and longitudinal data*, for the Economic and Social Research Council (ESRC), London: Tavistock

Wilkinson, RG, Pickett, KE, 2009, *The spirit level: Why more equal societies almost always do better*, London: Allen Lane

Willetts, D, 2011, *The pinch: How the baby boomers took their children's future – and why they should give it back*, London: Atlantic Books

Williams, F, 1989, *Social policy: A critical introduction, issues of race, gender and class*, Cambridge: Polity Press

Williams, P, Shoultz, B, 1982, *We can speak for ourselves*, London: Souvenir Press

Williams, Z, 2014, Alternative parenting show: a really noticeable atmosphere of togetherness, *Guardian*, 19 September, www.theguardian.com/lifeandstyle/2014/sep/19/alternative-parenting-show-london-family-fertility

Willis, P, 1977, *Learning to labour: How working-class kids get working-class jobs*, Farnborough: Saxon House

Wilson, A, Beresford, P, 2000, 'Anti-oppressive practice': Emancipation or appropriation?, *British Journal of Social Work* 30, 553–73

Wilson, S, 1991, *British motorcycles since 1950: Volume 5, Triumph: The company*, Somerset: Patrick Stephens Limited

Winter, NC, 2014, Tony Benn (1925–2014), Obituary, *The Classic Motorcycle*, June, p 11

Wintour, P, 2014, Forget Labour's old ideas, Blair tells party, *Guardian*, 22 July, 2

Wise, S, 2009, *The blackest streets: The life and death of a Victorian slum*, London: Vintage Books

Witcher, S, 2013, *Inclusive equality: A vision for social justice*, Bristol: Policy Press

Wohl, A, 1984, *Endangered lives: Public health in Victorian Britain*, London: Methuen

Wolfensberger, W, 1983, Social role valorisation: a proposed new term for the principle of normalization, *Mental Retardation* 26, 6, 234–9

Wolmar, C, 2005, *On the wrong line: How ideology and incompetence wrecked Britain's railways*, London: Aurum Press

Woodin, S, 2006, *Mapping user-led organisations: User-led services and centres for independent/integrated/inclusive living: A literature review prepared for the Department of Health*, Supplementary report 1, Leeds: University of Leeds, http://disability-studies.leeds.ac.uk/files/library/woodin-v2-user-led-CIL-Literature-Review-3.pdf

Woodward, K, 2006, Feminist critiques of social policy, in M Lavalette, A Pratt (eds) *Social policy: Theories, concepts and issues* (3rd edn), London: Sage, 66–86

Worpole, K, 2010, Colin Ward obituary, Society, *Guardian*, 22 February, www.theguardian.com/society/2010/feb/22/colin-ward-obituary

Wyatt, RJ, 2000, *Octavia Hill and the Crown Estate: A continuing legacy?*, London: The Crown Estate

Wykurz, G, Kelly, D, 2002, Developing the role of patients as teachers: Literature review, *British Medical Journal* 325, 818–21

Yeates, N, Holden, C (eds), 2009, *The global social policy reader*, Bristol: The Policy Press

Zarb, G, 2003, *The economics of independent living*, Farsta, Sweden: Independent Living Institute, www.independentliving.org/docs6/zarb2003.html

Zarb, G, Nadash, P, 1994, *Cashing in on independence: Comparing the costs and benefits of cash and services*, Derby: British Council of Organisations of Disabled People (BCODP)/Policy Studies Institute (PSI)

Zenderland, L, 1998, *Measuring minds: Henry Herbert Goddard and the origins of American intelligence testing*, Cambridge: Cambridge University Press

Zweiniger-Bargielowska, I, 2002, *Austerity in Britain: Rationing, controls and consumption, 1939–1955*, Oxford: Oxford University Press

Index